Contents

Preface

The first edition of this anthology, published in 1981, provided a reader for students, to go along with my *Seven Theories of Human Nature* (first edition 1974, second edition 1987), though it was also usable independently. Even before the production of the third, enlarged edition (*Ten Theories of Human Nature*, with chapters on Confucianism and Hinduism by David Haberman, 1998), there were suggestions for a revised edition of the anthology, but the publication of *Ten Theories* provided the final spur.

In this second edition of the reader, I have chosen substantial selections to represent, inter alia, the theories discussed in the book—Judaism and Christianity as presented in the Bible; Hinduism, Confucianism, Plato, Kant, Marx, Freud, and Sartre; Skinnerian behaviorism; and Konrad Lorenz's ethological approach. This should make the reader especially useful to those instructors who are also making some use of *Ten Theories of Human Nature*. But that is surely not a necessary condition of usefulness. Students or general readers who do not read that book can still read part or all of this anthology—with benefit, I trust. As well as the ten "theories" mentioned above, I have provided some representation of thought about human nature in the Islamic tradition, by seventeenth- and eighteenth-century philosophers (Descartes, Hobbes, Hume, Rousseau), by recent thinkers concerned especially with issues of gender and race, and by sociobiologists or evolutionary psychologists. This interdisciplinary reader should therefore be a helpful resource for anyone interested in learning about a wide variety of views about human nature from ancient times, and many cultures, to the present day.

In preparing this revised edition, I have included more substantial selections from the Hindu and Confucian traditions than in the first edition. In the case of Plato, I have taken more from *The Republic* and nothing from other dialogues. Christianity is here better represented by including the main arguments of St. Paul's Letter to the Romans. I have made what I hope is an intelligible selection from two of Kant's late works, on anthropology and on religion. I have taken the opportunity to select what now seem to me rather more readable, student-friendly extracts from the writings of Marx, Sartre, Skinner, and Lorenz.

Comparison with the earlier edition of the reader will reveal that the more technically difficult philosophers, such as Aristotle, Aquinas, Spinoza, Davidson, and Habermas, have disappeared. It is difficult indeed to understand much of such thinkers on brief acquaintance. Contemporary professional philosophers do not appear in this new edition (although I am supposed to be one of them!). But there already are plenty of anthologies in the philosophy of mind and in cognitive science—and there was no hope of my being able to cover these areas properly here. My concluding selections are from would-be scientific thinkers who strive to apply evolutionary biology to describe and explain human nature. I am aware that there is vastly more work in this fast-moving field than could be represented here. (I have not divided the selections into different categories, as I did in the first edition.)

Feminist issues are raised in the extracts from Rousseau, Mill, and Holmstrom, and racial issues in that by Bracken. But there is an enormous literature in these areas too, including plenty of anthologies, and though it seemed important to show how these issues connect with theories of human nature, there was room for only a few selections. (I have indicated some connections in the introductions to Hume and Kant, Wilson and Rose.)

I am grateful for helpful suggestions from Louise Antony, Celeste Friend, David Haberman, and Louis Pojman, and from Robert Miller of Oxford University Press.

L. S.

The Hebrew Bible
(the Old Testament)

The Jews were, and remain, "the people of the Book." What Christians call the Old Testament consists of histories of the Jewish people, their laws, psalms, and wisdom literature, and the "prophetic" writings from later periods. This disparate collection of literature was seen as a revelation of the Word of God. The monotheism of the ancient Hebrews is awesome in its concentration on the supreme majesty and power of the Creator and Judge of the universe (like that of Islam, another book-centered monotheistic religion that grew from the same historical root).

In the famous creation story of *Genesis* chapters 1 to 3, we are presented with an account of the origin of the whole universe and the place of human beings within it. Two different stories can be distinguished in the text—1:1–2:3 and 2:4–25—which differ on certain points. Scholars have concluded that the book of Genesis as it has come down to us must have been put together by unknown ancient editors using at least two sources.

Man is said to be "formed of dust from the ground" (2:7), which suggests a materialist rather than a dualist view of human beings (the latter is more a Greek conception than a Hebrew one—see the introduction to Plato below). Yet man is made "in the image of God," and is given a special authority over the rest of creation (1:27–28). In the story of the Fall of humanity in Chapter 3, Adam and Eve disobey God's prohibition by eating the fruit of the tree of knowledge of good and evil (3:16–17). This is the end of primeval innocence; it involves the attainment of knowledge, self-awareness, and shame, and condemnation to the pain, toil, and mortality of human existence. (There are interesting comments on the Fall by the Islamic philosopher Mutahhari, and by Kant and Lorenz, in the selections below.)

The relation of women to men in the Hebrew scheme of creation is somewhat ambiguous from the start. One story represents the whole human race as created together (1:27), the other tells of Eve being made second, out of one of Adam's ribs (2:21–23). The former suggests equality, the latter suggests a dependence of woman on man.

A later stage of Jewish thought is represented here by the classic poetry of *Psalms* 8 and 90. The emphasis is on the everlasting power of God and, in contrast, the mortality and sinfulness of humanity. The longing for God to forgive, and to intervene to redeem his people from their plight, is expressed throughout the history of the Jews. There is no suggestion of human immortality here; but redemption from sin remains a hope.

Genesis 1–3

The Creation of the Universe

1 In the beginning God created the heavens and the earth. [2]The earth was a vast waste, darkness covered the deep, and the spirit of God hovered over the surface of the water. [3]God said, "Let there be light," and there was light; [4]and God saw the light was good, and he separated light from darkness. [5]He called the light day, and the darkness night. So evening came, and morning came; it was the first day.

[6]God said, "Let there be a vault between the waters, to separate water from water." [7]So God made the vault, and separated the water under the vault from the water above it, and so it was; [8]and God called the vault the heavens. Evening came, and morning came, the second day.

[9]God said, "Let the water under the heavens be gathered into one place,

Revised English Bible © Oxford University Press and Cambridge University Press 1989.

so that dry land may appear"; and so it was. ¹⁰God called the dry land earth, and the gathering of the water he called sea; and God saw that it was good. ¹¹Then God said, "Let the earth produce growing things; let there be on the earth plants that bear seed, and trees bearing fruit each with its own kind of seed." So it was; ¹²the earth produced growing things: plants bearing their own kind of seed and trees bearing fruit, each with its own kind of seed; and God saw that it was good. ¹³Evening came, and morning came, the third day.

¹⁴God said, "Let there be lights in the vault of the heavens to separate day from night, and let them serve as signs both for festivals and for seasons and years. ¹⁵Let them also shine in the heavens to give light on earth." So it was; ¹⁶God made two great lights, the greater to govern the day and the lesser to govern the night; he also made the stars. ¹⁷God put these lights in the vault of the heavens to give light on earth, ¹⁸to govern day and night, and to separate light from darkness; and God saw that it was good. ¹⁹Evening came, and morning came, the fourth day.

²⁰God said, "Let the water teem with living creatures, and let birds fly above the earth across the vault of the heavens." ²¹God then created the great sea-beasts and all living creatures that move and swarm in the water, according to their various kinds, and every kind of bird; and God saw that it was good. ²²He blessed them and said, "Be fruitful and increase; fill the water of the sea, and let the birds increase on the land." ²³Evening came, and morning came, the fifth day.

²⁴God said, "Let the earth bring forth living creatures, according to their various kinds: cattle, creeping things, and wild animals, all according to their various kinds." So it was; ²⁵God made wild animals, cattle, and every creeping thing, all according to their various kinds; and he saw that it was good. ²⁶Then God said, "Let us make human beings in our image, after our likeness, to have dominion over the fish in the sea, the birds of the air, the cattle, all wild animals on land, and everything that creeps on the earth."

> ²⁷God created human beings in his own
>   image;
> in the image of God he created them;
> male and female he created them.

²⁸God blessed them and said to them, "Be fruitful and increase, fill the earth and subdue it, have dominion over the fish in the sea, the birds of the air, and every living thing that moves on the earth." ²⁹God also said,

"Throughout the earth I give you all plants that bear seed, and every tree that bears fruit with seed: they shall be yours for food. ³⁰All green plants I give for food to the wild animals, to all the birds of the air, and to everything that creeps on the earth, every living creature." So it was; ³¹and God saw all that he had made, and it was very good. Evening came, and morning came, the sixth day.

2 Thus the heavens and the earth and everything in them were completed. ²On the sixth day God brought to an end all the work he had been doing; on the seventh day, having finished all his work, ³God blessed the day and made it holy, because it was the day he finished all his work of creation.

Adam and Eve

⁴THIS is the story of the heavens and the earth after their creation.

When the LORD God made the earth and the heavens, ⁵there was neither shrub nor plant growing on the earth, because the LORD God had sent no rain; nor was there anyone to till the ground. ⁶Moisture used to well up out of the earth and water all the surface of the ground.

⁷The LORD God formed a human being from the dust of the ground and breathed into his nostrils the breath of life, so that he became a living creature. ⁸The LORD God planted a garden in Eden away to the east, and in it he put the man he had formed. ⁹The LORD God made trees grow up from the ground, every kind of tree pleasing to the eye and good for food; and in the middle of the garden he set the tree of life and the tree of the knowledge of good and evil.

¹⁰There was a river flowing from Eden to water the garden, and from there it branched into four streams. ¹¹The name of the first is Pishon; it is the river which skirts the whole land of Havilah, where gold is found. ¹²The gold of that land is good; gum resin and cornelians are also to be found there. ¹³The name of the second river is Gihon; this is the one which skirts the whole land of Cush. ¹⁴The name of the third is Tigris; this is the river which flows east of Asshur. The fourth river is the Euphrates.

¹⁵The LORD God took the man and put him in the garden of Eden to till it and look after it. ¹⁶ "You may eat from any tree in the garden" he told the man, ¹⁷"except from the tree of the knowledge of good and evil; the day you eat from that, you are surely doomed to die." ¹⁸Then the LORD God said, "It is not good for the man to be alone; I shall make a partner

suited to him." ¹⁹So from the earth he formed all the wild animals and all the birds of the air, and brought them to the man to see what he would call them; whatever the man called each living creature, that would be its name. ²⁰The man gave names to all cattle, to the birds of the air, and to every wild animal; but for the man himself no suitable partner was found. ²¹The Lord God then put the man into a deep sleep and, while he slept, he took one of the man's ribs and closed up the flesh over the place. ²²The rib he had taken out of the man the Lord God built up into a woman, and he brought her to the man. ²³The man said:

> "This one at last
> is bone from my bones,
> flesh from my flesh!
> She shall be called woman,
> for from man was she taken."

²⁴That is why a man leaves his father and mother and attaches himself to his wife, and the two become one. ²⁵Both were naked, the man and his wife, but they had no feeling of shame.

3 THE serpent, which was the most cunning of all the creatures the Lord God had made, asked the woman, "Is it true that God has forbidden you to eat from any tree in the garden?" ²She replied, "We may eat the fruit of any tree in the garden, ³except for the tree in the middle of the garden. God has forbidden us to eat the fruit of that tree or even to touch it; if we do, we shall die." ⁴"Of course you will not die," said the serpent; ⁵"for God knows that, as soon as you eat it, your eyes will be opened and you will be like God himself, knowing both good and evil." ⁶The woman looked at the tree: the fruit would be good to eat; it was pleasing to the eye and desirable for the knowledge it could give. So she took some and ate it; she also gave some to her husband, and he ate it. ⁷Then the eyes of both of them were opened, and they knew that they were naked; so they stitched fig-leaves together and made themselves loincloths.

⁸The man and his wife heard the sound of the Lord God walking about in the garden at the time of the evening breeze, and they hid from him among the trees. ⁹The Lord God called to the man, "Where are you?" ¹⁰He replied. "I heard the sound of you in the garden and I was afraid because I was naked, so I hid." ¹¹God said, "Who told you that you were naked? Have you eaten from the tree which I forbade you to eat from?" ¹²The man replied. "It was the woman you gave to be with me who gave

me fruit from the tree, and I ate it." ^{13}The LORD God said to the woman, "What have you done?" The woman answered. "It was the serpent who deceived me into eating it." ^{14}Then the LORD God said to the serpent:
   'Because you have done this you are cursed alone of all cattle and the creatures of the wild.

> "On your belly you will crawl,
> and dust you will eat
> all the days of your life.
> ^{15}I shall put enmity between you and the woman,
> between your brood and hers.
> They will strike at your head,
> and you will strike at their heel."

^{16}To the woman he said:

> "I shall give you great labour in childbearing;
> with labour you will bear children.
> You will desire your husband,
> but he will be your master."

^{17}And to the man he said: "Because you have listened to your wife and have eaten from the tree which I forbade you,

> on your account the earth will be cursed.
> You will get your food from it only by labour
> all the days of your life;
> ^{18}it will yield thorns and thistles for you.
> You will eat of the produce of the field,
> ^{19}and only by the sweat of your brow will you win your bread
> until you return to the earth;
> for from it you were taken.
> Dust you are, to dust you will return."

^{20}The man named his wife Eve because she was the mother of all living beings. ^{21}The LORD God made coverings from skins for the man and his wife and clothed them. ^{22}But he said, "The man has become like one of us, knowing good and evil; what if he now reaches out and takes fruit from the tree of life also, and eats it and lives for ever?" ^{23}So the LORD God banished him from the garden of Eden to till the ground from which he had been taken. ²⁴When he drove him out, God settled him to the east of the garden of Eden, and he stationed the cherubim and a sword whirling and flashing to guard the way to the tree of life.

Psalms

Psalm 8

¹Lord our sovereign,
how glorious is your name throughout the world!
Your majesty is praised as high as the heavens,
²from the mouths of babes and infants at the breast.
You have established a bulwark against your adversaries
to restrain the enemy and the avenger.

³When I look up at your heavens, the work of your fingers,
at the moon and the stars you have set in place,
⁴what is a frail mortal, that you should be mindful of him,
a human being, that you should take notice of him?

⁵Yet you have made him little less than a god
crowning his head with glory and honour.
⁶You make him master over all that you have made,
putting everything in subjection under his feet:
⁷all sheep and oxen, all the wild beasts,
⁸the birds in the air, the fish in the sea,
and everything that moves along ocean paths.

⁹Lord our sovereign,
how glorious is your name throughout the world!

Psalm 90

¹Lord, you have been our refuge
throughout all generations.
²Before the mountains were brought forth

or the earth and the world were born,
from age to age you are God.

[3]You turn mortals back to dust,
saying, "Turn back, you children of mortals,"
[4]for in your sight a thousand years
are as the passing of one day
or as a watch in the night.
[5]You cut them off;
they are asleep in death.
They are like grass which shoots up;
[6]though in the morning it flourishes and shoots up,
by evening it droops and withers.
[7]We are brought to an end by your anger,
terrified by your wrath.
[8]You set out our iniquities before you,
our secret sins in the light of your presence.
[9]All our days pass under your wrath;
our years die away like a murmur.
[10]Seventy years is the span of our life,
eighty if our strength holds;
at their best they are but toil and sorrow,
for they pass quickly and we vanish.
[11]Who feels the power of your anger,
who feels your wrath like those who fear you?
[12]So make us know how few are our days,
that our minds may learn wisdom.

[13]LORD, how long?
Turn and show compassion to your servants.
[14]Satisfy us at daybreak with your love,
that we may sing for joy and be glad all our days.
[15]Grant us days of gladness for the days you have humbled us,
for the years when we have known misfortune.
[16]May your saving acts appear to your servants,
and your glory to their children.
[17]May the favour of the Lord our God be on us.
Establish for us all that we do,
establish it firmly.

Hinduism

The Upanishads, esoteric teachings passed on by ancient masters of meditation, are classic writings of Indian civilization, dating from about 800 B.C.E. onward. Like the Hebrew Bible, they do not have a single author, but are a compilation of very ancient teachings. They are among the sacred scriptures of the Hindu religion, but they also introduce some concepts shared by later religious developments such as Buddhism and Jainism. These concepts include the cycle of rebirth and reincarnation, the law of karma (reward or punishment for one's past life), and ascetic techniques to achieve liberation from the cycle of rebirth.

The oldest and longest of these texts is the *Brihad Aranyaka Upanishad* ("the Great and Secret Teachings of the Forest"). The short extract here is the creation story from Chapter 1, section 4, which makes an interesting comparison with the Hebrew story from *Genesis* above. The term *brahman* means "ultimate reality" or "the ground of all existence"—in some respects like the Judaic-Christian concept of God, but rather more impersonal in nature. The term *atman* means "the ultimate or essential self," "the inner core or ground of one's being"—in some ways like Christian or Greek concepts of the soul, but again, more impersonal and less individualized—the atman is thought to be somehow connected to all other beings.

The second extract is from the *Katha Upanishad,* chapters 1 to 3. It begins in the form of a dialogue between a character called Naciketas, who seeks spiritual enlightenment, and a voice called Death, who delivers increasingly long answers (after some initial reluctance). In this passage, Death recommends that Naciketas find wisdom in the knowledge of his true self, the atman. In Chapter 2, liberation is to be achieved by esoteric knowledge or contemplation, in which one can reach not only the atman within oneself, but also brahman, the supreme reality or spirit of the universe. (Compare the image of the cave in Plato's *Republic,* below. The image of the chariot and horses, representing the diverse elements in human nature in Chapter 3 of the *Katha Upanishad,* also recurs in Plato's *Phaedrus.*)

Brihad Aranyaka Upanishad

In the beginning this world was just a single body (*ātman*) shaped like a man. He looked around and saw nothing but himself. The first thing he said was, "Here I am!" and from that the name "I" came into being. Therefore, even today when you call someone, he first says, "It's I," and then states whatever other name he may have. That first being received the name "man" (*puruṣa*), because ahead (*pūrva*) of all this he burnt up (*uṣ*) all evils. When someone knows this, he burns up anyone who may try to get ahead of him.

²That first being became afraid; therefore, one becomes afraid when one is alone. Then he thought to himself: "Of what should I be afraid, when there is no one but me?" So his fear left him, for what was he going to be afraid of? One is, after all, afraid of another.

³He found no pleasure at all; so one finds no pleasure when one is alone. He wanted to have a companion. Now he was as large as a man and a woman in close embrace. So he split (*pat*) his body into two, giving rise to husband (*pati*) and wife (*patnī*). Surely this is why Yājñavalkya used to say: "The two of us are like two halves of a block." The space here, therefore, is completely filled by the woman.

He copulated with her, and from their union human beings were born. ⁴She then thought to herself: "After begetting me from his own body (*ātman*), how could he copulate with me? I know—I'll hide myself." So

Upanishads, translated by Patrick Olivelle © Oxford University Press 1996.

she became a cow. But he became a bull and copulated with her. From their union cattle were born. Then she became a mare, and he a stallion; she became a female donkey, and he, a male donkey. And again he copulated with her, and from their union one-hoofed animals were born. Then she became a female goat, and he, a male goat; she became a ewe, and he, a ram. And again he copulated with her, and from their union goats and sheep were born. In this way he created every male and female pair that exists, down to the very ants.

⁵It then occurred to him: "I alone am the creation, for I created all this." From this "creation" came into being. Anyone who knows this prospers in this creation of his.

⁶Then he churned like this and, using his hands, produced fire from his mouth as from a vagina. As a result the inner sides of both these—the hands and the mouth—are without hair, for the inside of the vagina is without hair. "Sacrifice to this god. Sacrifice to that god"—people do say these things, but in reality each of these gods is his own creation, for he himself is all these gods. From his semen, then, he created all that is moist here, which is really Soma. Food and eater—that is the extent of this whole world. Food is simply Soma, and the eater is fire.

This is *brahman's* super-creation. It is a super-creation because he created the gods, who are superior to him, and, being a mortal himself, he created the immortals. Anyone who knows this stands within this super-creation of his.

⁷At that time this world was without real distinctions; it was distinguished simply in terms of name and visible appearance—"He is so and so by name and has this sort of an appearance." So even today this world is distinguished simply in terms of name and visible appearance, as when we say, "He is so and so by name and has this sort of an appearance."

Penetrating this body up to the very nailtips, he remains there like a razor within a case or a termite within a termite-hill. People do not see him, for he is incomplete as he comes to be called breath when he is breathing, speech when he is speaking, sight when he is seeing, hearing when he is hearing, and mind when he is thinking. These are only the names of his various activities. A man who considers him to be any one of these does not understand him, for he is incomplete within any one of these. One should consider them as simply his self (*ātman*), for in it all these become one. This same self (*ātman*) is the trail to this entire world, for by following it one comes to know this entire world, just as by following their tracks one finds [the cattle]. Whoever knows this finds fame and glory.

⁸This innermost thing, this self (*ātman*)—it is dearer than a son, it is dearer than wealth, it is dearer than everything else. If a man claims that

something other than his self is dear to him, and someone were to tell him that he will lose what he holds dear, that is liable to happen. So a man should regard only his self as dear to him. When a man regards only his self as dear to him, what he holds dear will never perish.

⁹Now, the question is raised: "Since people think that they will become the Whole by knowing *brahman,* what did *brahman* know that enabled it to become the Whole?"

¹⁰In the beginning this world was only *brahman,* and it knew only itself (*ātman*), thinking: "I am *brahman.*" As a result, it became the Whole. Among the gods, likewise, whosoever realized this, only they became the Whole. It was the same also among the seers and among humans. Upon seeing this very point, the seer Vāmadeva proclaimed: "I was Manu, and I was the sun." This is true even now. If a man knows "I am *brahman*" in this way, he becomes this whole world. Not even the gods are able to prevent it, for he becomes their very self (*ātman*). So when a man venerates another deity, thinking, "He is one, and I am another," he does not understand. As livestock is for men, so is he for the gods. As having a lot of livestock is useful to a man, so each man proves useful to the gods. The loss of even a single head of livestock is painful; how much more if many are lost. The gods, therefore, are not pleased at the prospect of men coming to understand this.

¹¹In the beginning this world was only *brahman,* only one. Because it was only one, *brahman* had not fully developed. It then created the ruling power, a form superior to and surpassing itself, that is, the ruling powers among the gods—Indra, Varuṇa, Soma, Rudra, Parjanya, Yama, Mṛtyu, and Īśāna. Hence there is nothing higher than the ruling power. Accordingly, at a royal anointing a Brahmin pays homage to a Kṣatriya by prostrating himself. He extends this honour only to the ruling power. Now, the priestly power (*brahman*) is the womb of the ruling power. Therefore, even if a king should rise to the summit of power, it is to the priestly power that he returns in the end as to his own womb. So, one who hurts the latter harms his own womb and becomes so much the worse for harming someone better than him.

¹²*Brahman* still did not become fully developed. So it created the Vaiśya class, that is, the types of gods who are listed in groups—Vasus, Rudras, Ādityas, All-gods, and Maruts.

¹³It still did not become fully developed. So it created the Śūdra class, that is, Pūṣan. Now, Pūṣan is this very earth, for it nourishes this whole world, it nourishes all that exists.

¹⁴It still did not become fully developed. So it created the Law (*dharma*), a form superior to and surpassing itself. And the Law is here the ruling power standing above the ruling power. Hence there is nothing higher than the Law. Therefore, a weaker man makes demands of a stronger man by appealing to the Law, just as one does by appealing to a king. Now, the Law is nothing but the truth. Therefore, when a man speaks the truth, people say that he speaks the Law; and when a man speaks the Law, people say that he speaks the truth. They are really the same thing.

¹⁵So there came to be the priestly power, the ruling power, the Vaiśya class, and the Śūdra class. Among the gods the priestly power (*brahman*) came into being only in the form of fire, and among humans as a Brahmin; it further became a Kṣatriya in the form of a Kṣatriya, a Vaiśya in the form of a Vaiśya, and a Śūdra in the form of a Śūdra. In the fire, therefore, people seek to find a world for themselves among the gods, and in the Brahmin a world among humans, for *brahman* came into being in these two forms.

If someone were to depart from this world without perceiving his own world, it will be of no use to him as it remains unknown to him, just like the Veda that is not recited or a rite that is left undone. If a man who does not know this performs even a grand and holy rite, it is sure to fade away after his death. It is his self (*ātman*) alone that a man should venerate as his world. And if someone venerates his self alone as his world, that rite of his will never fade away, because from his very self he will produce whatever he desires.

¹⁶Now, this self (*ātman*) is a world for all beings. So, when he makes offerings and sacrifices, he becomes thereby a world for the gods. When he recites the Vedas, he becomes thereby a world for the seers. When he offers libations to his ancestors and seeks to father offspring, he becomes thereby a world for his ancestors. When he provides food and shelter to human beings, he becomes thereby a world for human beings. When he procures fodder and water for livestock, he becomes thereby a world for livestock. When creatures, from wild animals and birds down to the very ants, find shelter in his houses, he becomes thereby a world for them. Just as a man desires the well-being of his own world, so all beings desire the well-being of anyone who knows this. All this is known and has been thoroughly examined.

¹⁷In the beginning this world was only the self (*ātman*), only one. He had this desire: "I wish I had a wife so I could father offspring. I wish I had wealth so I could perform rites." That is the full extent of desire; one does

not get anything more, even if one desires it. So even today when one is single, one has the desire: "I wish I had a wife so I could father offspring. I wish I had wealth so I could perform rites." As long as someone has not obtained either of these, he considers himself to be utterly incomplete. Now, this is his completeness—his mind is himself (*ātman*); his speech is his wife; his breath is his offspring; his sight is his human wealth, for people find wealth with their sight, while his hearing is his divine wealth, for people hear about it with their hearing; and his body (*ātman*) is his rites, for one performs rites with one's body. This is the five-fold sacrifice—the sacrificial animal is fivefold, the human being is fivefold, and this whole world, whatever there is, is fivefold. Anyone who knows this obtains this whole world.

Katha Upanishad

Chapter 1

NACIKETAS.   [20]There is this doubt about a man who is dead.
                        "He exists," say some; others, "He exists not."
                        I want to know this, so please teach me.
                              This is the third of my three wishes.

DEATH.   [21]As to this even the gods of old had doubts,
                        for it's hard to understand, it's a subtle doctrine.
                  Make, Naciketas, another wish.
                        Do not press me! Release me from this.

NACIKETAS.   [22]As to this, we're told, even the gods had doubts;
                        and you say, O Death, it's hard to understand.
                  But another like you I can't find to explain it;
                        and there's no other wish that is equal to it.

DEATH.   [23]Choose sons and grandsons who'd live a hundred years!
                  Plenty of livestock and elephants, horses and gold!
                  Choose as your domain a wide expanse of earth!
                  And you yourself live as many autumns as you wish!

²⁴And if you would think this is an equal wish—
You may choose wealth together with a long life;
Achieve prominence, Naciketas, in this wide world;
And I will make you enjoy your desires at will.

²⁵You may ask freely for all those desires,
    hard to obtain in this mortal world;
Look at these lovely girls, with chariots and lutes,
    girls of this sort are unobtainable by men—
I'll give them to you; you'll have them wait on you;
    but about death don't ask me, Naciketas.

NACIKETAS.   ²⁶Since the passing days of a mortal, O Death,
    sap here the energy of all the senses;
And even a full life is but a trifle;
    so keep your horses, your songs and dances!

²⁷With wealth you cannot make a man content;
Will we get to keep wealth, when we have seen you?
And we get to live only as long as you will allow!
So, this alone is the wish that I'd like to choose:

²⁸What mortal man with insight,
    who has met those that do not die or grow old,
    himself growing old in this wretched and lowly place,
    looking at its beauties, its pleasures and joys,
        would delight in a long life?

²⁹The point on which they have great doubts—
    what happens at that great transit—
    tell me that, O Death!
This is my wish, probing the mystery deep.
Naciketas wishes for nothing
    other than that.

Chapter 2

DEATH.   ¹The good is one thing, the gratifying is quite another;
    their goals are different, both bind a man.
Good things await him who picks the good;
    by choosing the gratifying, one misses one's goal.

²Both the good and the gratifying
  present themselves to a man;
The wise assess them, note their difference;
  and choose the good over the gratifying;
But the fool chooses the gratifying
  rather than what is beneficial.

³You have looked at and rejected, Naciketas,
  things people desire, lovely and lovely to look at;
This disk of gold, where many a man founders,
  you have not accepted as a thing of wealth.

⁴Far apart and widely different are these two:
  ignorance and what's known as knowledge.
I take Naciketas as one yearning for knowledge;
  the many desires do not confound you.

⁵Wallowing in ignorance, but calling themselves wise,
  thinking themselves learned, the fools go around,
    staggering about like a group of blind men,
    led by a man who is himself blind.

⁶This transit lies hidden from a careless fool,
  who is deluded by the delusion of wealth.
Thinking "This is the world; there is no other,"
  he falls into my power again and again.

⁷Many do not get to hear of that transit;
  and even when they hear,
    many don't comprehend it.
Rare is the man who teaches it,
  lucky is the man who grasps it;
Rare is the man who knows it,
  lucky is the man who's taught it.

⁸Though one may think a lot, it is difficult to grasp,
  when it is taught by an inferior man.
Yet one cannot gain access to it,
  unless someone else teaches it.
For it is smaller than the size of an atom,
  a thing beyond the realm of reason.

⁹One can't grasp this notion by argumentation;
  Yet it's easy to grasp when taught by another.

You're truly steadfast, dear boy,
   you have grasped it!
Would that we have, Naciketas,
   one like you to question us!

[10]What you call a treasure, I know to be transient;
   for by fleeting things one cannot gain the perennial.
Therefore I have built the fire-altar of Naciketas,
   and by fleeting things I have gained the eternal.

[11]Satisfying desires is the foundation of the world;
Uninterrupted rites bring ultimate security;
Great and widespread praise is the foundation—
   These you have seen, wise Naciketas,
   And having seen, firmly rejected.

[12]The primeval one who is hard to perceive,
   wrapped in mystery, hidden in the cave,
   residing within th'impenetrable depth—
Regarding him as god, an insight
   gained by inner contemplation,
   both sorrow and joy the wise abandon.

[13]When a mortal has heard it, understood it;
   when he has drawn it out,
   and grasped this subtle point of doctrine
He rejoices, for he has found
   something in which he could rejoice.
To him I consider my house
   to be open Naciketas.

NACIKETAS. [14]Tell me what you see as—
   Different from the right doctrine and from the wrong;
   Different from what's done here and what's left undone;
   Different from what has been and what's yet to be.'

DEATH? [15]The word that all the Vedas disclose;
   The word that all austerities proclaim;
   Seeking which people live student lives;
   That word now I will tell you in brief—
     It is oṃ!

[16]For this alone is the syllable that's *brahman!*
For this alone is the syllable that's supreme!

When, indeed, one knows this syllable,
   he obtains his every wish.

[17]This is the support that's best!
  This is the support supreme!
  And when one knows this support,
   he rejoices in *brahman*'s world.

DEATH.   [18]The wise one—
    he is not born, he does not die;
    he has not come from anywhere;
    he has not become anyone.
  He is unborn and eternal, primeval and everlasting.
  And he is not killed, when the body is killed.

[The dialogue between Naciketas and Death ends here.]

[19]If the killer thinks that he kills;
  If the killed thinks that he is killed;
  Both of them fail to understand.
   He neither kills, nor is he killed.

[20]Finer than the finest, larger than the largest,
   is the self (*ātman*) that lies here hidden
    in the heart of a living being.
  Without desires and free from sorrow,
   a man perceives by the creator's grace
    the grandeur of the self.

[21]Sitting down, he roams afar.
  Lying down, he goes everywhere.
  The god ceaselessly exulting—
   Who, besides me, is able to know?

[22]When he perceives this immense, all-pervading self,
  as bodiless within bodies,
  as stable within unstable beings—
   A wise man ceases to grieve.

[23]This self cannot be grasped,
   by teachings or by intelligence,
   or even by great learning.
  Only the man he chooses can grasp him,
   whose body this self chooses as his own.

²⁴Not a man who has not quit his evil ways;
　　Nor a man who is not calm or composed;
　　Nor even a man who is without a tranquil mind;
　　　　Could ever secure it by his mere wit.

²⁵For whom the Brahmin and the Kṣatriya
　　are both like a dish of boiled rice;
　　and death is like the sprinkled sauce;
　　　　Who truly knows where he is?

Chapter 3

　　Knowers of *brahman,* men with five fires,
　　　　and with the three fire-altars of Naciketas,
　　They call these two "Shadow" and "Light,"
　　　　the two who have entered—
　　　　　　the one into the cave of the heart,
　　　　　　the other into the highest region beyond,
　　　　both drinking the truth
　　　　　　in the world of rites rightly performed.

²May we master the fire-altar of Naciketas,
　　a dike
　　　　for those who have sacrificed;
　　the imperishable, the highest *brahman,*
　　the farther shore
　　　　for those who wish to cross the danger.

³Know the self as a rider in a chariot,
　　and the body, as simply the chariot.
　　Know the intellect as the charioteer,
　　　　and the mind, as simply the reins.

⁴The senses, they say, are the horses,
　　and sense objects are the paths around them;
　　He who is linked to the body (*ātman*), senses, and mind,
　　　　the wise proclaim as the one who enjoys.

⁵When a man lacks understanding,
　　and his mind is never controlled;
　　His senses do not obey him,
　　　　as bad horses, a charioteer.

⁶But when a man has understanding,
    and his mind is ever controlled;
His senses do obey him,
    as good horses, a charioteer.

⁷When a man lacks understanding,
    is unmindful and always impure;
He does not reach that final step,
    but gets on the round of rebirth.

⁸But when a man has understanding,
    is mindful and always pure;
He does reach that final step,
    from which he is not reborn again.

⁹When a man's mind is his reins,
    intellect, his charioteer;
He reaches the end of the road,
    that highest step of Viṣṇu.

¹⁰Higher than the senses are their objects;
Higher than sense objects is the mind;
Higher than the mind is the intellect;
Higher than the intellect is the immense self;

¹¹Higher than the immense self is the unmanifest;
Higher than the unmanifest is the person;
Higher than the person there's nothing at all.
That is the goal, that's the highest state.

¹²Hidden in all the beings,
    this self is not visibly displayed.
Yet, people of keen vision see him,
    with eminent and sharp minds.

¹³A wise man should curb his speech and mind,
    control them within th'intelligent self;
He should control intelligence within the immense self,
    and the latter, within the tranquil self.

¹⁴Arise! Awake! Pay attention,
    when you've obtained your wishes!
A razor's sharp edge is hard to cross—
    that, poets say, is the difficulty of the path.

[15]It has no sound or touch,
   no appearance, taste, or smell;
It is without beginning or end,
   undecaying and eternal;
When a man perceives it,
   fixed and beyond the immense,
He is freed from the jaws of death.

[16]The wise man who hears or tells
the tale of Naciketas,
an ancient tale told by Death,
will rejoice in *brahman*'s world.

[17]If a man, pure and devout, proclaims this great secret
in a gathering of Brahmins,
or during a meal for the dead,
it will lead him to eternal life!

Confucianism

Ancient Chinese thought seems to have been more human centered and less obviously religious than that of the Middle East or India. The wisdom of Confucius (551–479 B.C.E.), as recorded or interpreted in the *Analects*, consists mostly of practical precepts about human relations, ethics, and politics, with only a little about underlying human nature, or about the metaphysical background mysteriously called "Heaven."

An interesting debate about human nature subsequently arose in the Confucian tradition, between Mencius or Meng K'e (371–289 B.C.E.), and Hsun-tzu (298–238 B.C.E.). It is often said in crude summary that the former asserted the natural goodness of human beings, whereas the latter said that human nature is inherently evil. But a careful reading of the selections from these two philosophers may suggest that there is actually much more agreement between them than these simple slogans suggest.

The first extract, from *Mencius* (Chapter 6, Part A of the translation noted below) begins with sections of dialogue in which (in a Chinese style of arguing) Mencius uses somewhat distant analogies to oppose the suggestion (made by someone called Kao Tzu) that human nature is neither good nor bad. Mencius certainly asserts our intrinsic goodness, but he is very much concerned with the conditions that will allow it to develop and flourish. Like

Plato in the *Republic* (see below) he emphasizes how important it is for us to be guided by the most important element in our human nature—the thinking organ, which he calls "the heart" (which is presumably what Plato calls "reason").

The second extract—from the writings of Hsun-tzu—argues more straightforwardly. Hsun-tzu emphasizes the need for education, culture, moral training—what he calls "ritual principles"—to restrain our selfish tendencies, which he labels "evil." Human goodness is for him the result of conscious efforts, not natural inclination. The debate about the role of nature and nurture is continued in the seventeenth and eighteenth centuries by Hobbes, Rousseau, and Kant, and in the psychology of our own day (see the selections from Skinner, Lorenz, Wilson, Rose et al., and Ridley below).

Mencius, "Human Nature Is Good"

1. Kao Tzu said, "Human nature is like the *ch'i* willow. Dutifulness is like cups and bowls. To make morality out of human nature is like making cups and bowls out of the willow."

"Can you," said Mencius, "make cups and bowls by following the nature of the willow? Or must you mutilate the willow before you can make it into cups and bowls? If you have to mutilate the willow to make it into cups and bowls, must you, then, also mutilate a man to make him moral? Surely it will be these words of yours men in the world will follow in bringing disaster upon morality."

2. Kao Tzu said, "Human nature is like whirling water. Give it an outlet in the east and it will flow east; give it an outlet in the west and it will flow west. Human nature does not show any preference for either good or bad just as water does not show any preference for either east or west."

"It certainly is the case," said Mencius, "that water does not show any preference for either east or west, but does it show the same indifference to high and low? Human nature is good just as water seeks low ground. There is no man who is not good; there is no water that does not flow downwards.

Mencius, translated by D. C. Lau, © Penguin Classics 1970.

"Now in the case of water, by splashing it one can make it shoot up higher than one's forehead, and by forcing it one can make it stay on a hill. How can that be the nature of water? It is the circumstances being what they are. That man can be made bad shows that his nature is no different from that of water in this respect."

• • •

6. Kung-tu Tzu said, "Kao Tzu said, 'There is neither good nor bad in human nature,' but others say, 'Human nature can become good or it can become bad, and that is why with the rise of King Wen and King Wu, the people were given to goodness, while with the rise of King Yu and King Li, they were given to cruelty.' Then there are others who say, 'There are those who are good by nature, and there are those who are bad by nature. For this reason, Hsiang could have Yao as prince, and Shun could have the Blind Man as father, and Ch'i, Viscount of Wei and Prince Pi Kan could have Tchou as nephew as well as sovereign.' Now you say human nature is good. Does this mean that all the others are mistaken?

"As far as what is genuinely in him is concerned, a man is capable of becoming good," said Mencius. "That is what I mean by good. As for his becoming bad, that is not the fault of his native endowment. The heart of compassion is possessed by all men alike; likewise the heart of shame, the heart of respect, and the heart of right and wrong. The heart of compassion pertains to benevolence, the heart of shame to dutifulness, the heart of respect to the observance of the rites, and the heart of right and wrong to wisdom. Benevolence, dutifulness, observance of the rites, and wisdom are not welded on to me from the outside; they are in me originally. Only this has never dawned on me. That is why it is said, 'Seek and you will find it; let go and you will lose it.' There are cases where one man is twice, five times or countless times better than another man, but this is only because there are people who fail to make the best of their native endowment. The *Book of Odes* says,

> Heaven produces the teeming masses,
> And where there is a thing there is a norm.
> If the people held on to their constant nature,
> They would be drawn to superior virtue.[4]

Confucius commented, 'The author of this poem must have had knowledge of the Way.' Thus where there is a thing there is a norm, and because the people hold on to their constant nature they are drawn to superior virtue."

7. Mencius said, "In good years the young men are mostly lazy, while in bad years they are mostly violent. Heaven has not sent down men whose endowment differs so greatly. The difference is due to what ensnares their hearts. Take the barley for example. Sow the seeds and cover them with soil. The place is the same and the time of sowing is also the same. The plants shoot up and by the summer solstice they all ripen. If there is any unevenness, it is because the soil varies in richness and there is no uniformity in the fall of rain and dew and the amount of human effort devoted to tending it. Now things of the same kind are all alike. Why should we have doubts when it comes to man? The sage and I are of the same kind. Thus Lung Tzu said, 'When someone makes a shoe for a foot he has not seen, I am sure he will not produce a basket.' All shoes are alike because all feet are alike. All palates show the same preferences in taste. Yi Ya was simply the man first to discover what would be pleasing to my palate. Were the nature of taste to vary from man to man in the same way as horses and hounds differ from me in kind, then how does it come about that all palates in the world follow the preferences of Yi Ya? The fact that in taste the whole world looks to Yi Ya shows that all palates are alike. It is the same also with the ear. The whole world looks to Shih K'uang, and this shows that all ears are alike. It is the same also with the eye. The whole world appreciates the good looks of Tzu-tu; whoever does not is blind. Hence it is said: all palates have the same preference in taste; all ears in sound; all eyes in beauty. Should hearts prove to be an exception by possessing nothing in common? What is common to all hearts? Reason and rightness. The sage is simply the man first to discover this common element in my heart. Thus reason and rightness please my heart in the same way as meat pleases my palate."

• • •

11. Mencius said, "Benevolence is the heart of man, and rightness his road. Sad it is indeed when a man gives up the right road instead of following it and allows his heart to stray without enough sense to go after it. When his chickens and dogs stray, he has sense enough to go after them, but not when his heart strays. The sole concern of learning is to go after this strayed heart. That is all."

12. Mencius said, "Now if one's third finger is bent and cannot stretch straight, though this neither causes any pain nor impairs the use of the hand, one would think nothing of the distance between Ch'in and Ch'u if

someone able to straighten it could be found. This is because one's finger
is inferior to other people's. When one's finger is inferior to other people's, one has sense enough to resent it, but not when one's heart is inferior. This is known as failure to see that one thing is the same in kind as
another."

13. Mencius said, "Even with a *t'ung* or a *tzu* tree one or two spans
thick, anyone wishing to keep it alive will know how it should be tended,
yet when it comes to one's own person, one does not know how to tend it.
Surely one does not love one's person any less than the *t'ung* or the *tzu*.
This is unthinking to the highest degree."

14. Mencius said, "A man loves all parts of his person without discrimination. As he loves them all without discrimination, he nurtures
them all without discrimination. If there is not one foot or one inch of his
skin that he does not love, then there is not one foot or one inch that he
does not nurture. Is there any other way of telling whether what a man
does is good or bad than by the choice he makes? The parts of the person
differ in value and importance. Never harm the parts of greater importance for the sake of those of smaller importance, or the more valuable
for the sake of the less valuable. He who nurtures the parts of smaller
importance is a small man; he who nurtures the parts of greater importance is a great man. Now consider a gardener. If he tends the common
trees while neglecting the valuable ones, then he is a bad gardener. A man
who takes care of one finger to the detriment of his shoulder and back
without realizing his mistake is a muddled man. A man who cares only
about food and drink is despised by others because he takes care of the
parts of smaller importance to the detriment of the parts of greater importance. If a man who cares about food and drink can do so without neglecting any other part of his person, then his mouth and belly are much more
than just a foot or an inch of his skin."

15. Kung-tu Tzu asked, "Though equally human, why are some men
greater than others?"

"He who is guided by the interests of the parts of his person that are of
greater importance is a great man; he who is guided by the interests of the
parts of his person that are of smaller importance is a small man."

"Though equally human, why are some men guided one way and others guided another way?"

"The organs of hearing and sight are unable to think and can be misled
by external things. When one thing acts on another, all it does is to attract
it. The organ of the heart can think. But it will find the answer only if it
does think; otherwise, it will not find the answer. This is what Heaven has

given me. If one makes one's stand on what is of greater importance in the first instance, what is of smaller importance cannot displace it. In this way, one cannot but be a great man."

16. Mencius said, "There are honours bestowed by Heaven, and there are honours bestowed by man. Benevolence, dutifulness, conscientiousness, truthfulness to one's word, unflagging delight in what is good,— these are honours bestowed by Heaven. The position of a Ducal Minister, a Minister, or a Counsellor is an honour bestowed by man. Men of antiquity bent their efforts towards acquiring honours bestowed by Heaven, and honours bestowed by man followed as a matter of course. Men of today bend their efforts towards acquiring honours bestowed by Heaven in order to win honours bestowed by man, and once the latter is won they discard the former. Such men are deluded to the extreme, and in the end are sure only to perish."

17. Mencius said, "All men share the same desire to be exalted. But as a matter of fact, every man has in him that which is exalted. The fact simply never dawned on him. What man exalts is not truly exalted. Those Chao Meng exalts, Chao Meng can also humble. The *Book of Odes* says,

> Having filled us with drink,
> Having filled us with virtue, . . .

The point is that, being filled with moral virtue, one does not envy other people's enjoyment of fine food and, enjoying a fine and extensive reputation, one does not envy other people's fineries."

Hsun-tzu, "Human Nature Is Evil"

Man's nature is evil; goodness is the result of conscious activity. The nature of man is such that he is born with a fondness for profit. If he indulges this fondness, it will lead him into wrangling and strife, and all sense of courtesy and humility will disappear. He is born with feelings of envy and hate, and if he indulges these, they will lead him into violence

From Basic Writings of Mo Tzu, Hsun Tzu and Han Fei Tzu, trans. Burton Watson, © 1967 Columbia University Press. Reprinted with the permission of the publisher.

and crime, and all sense of loyalty and good faith will disappear. Man is born with the desires of the eyes and ears, with a fondness for beautiful sights and sounds. If he indulges these, they will lead him into license and wantonness, and all ritual principles and correct forms will be lost. Hence, any man who follows his nature and indulges his emotions will inevitably become involved in wrangling and strife, will violate the forms and rules of society, and will end as a criminal. Therefore, man must first be transformed by the instructions of a teacher and guided by ritual principles, and only then will he be able to observe the dictates of courtesy and humility, obey the forms and rules of society, and achieve order. It is obvious from this, then, that man's nature is evil, and that his goodness is the result of conscious activity.

A warped piece of wood must wait until it has been laid against the straightening board, steamed, and forced into shape before it can become straight; a piece of blunt metal must wait until it has been whetted on a grindstone before it can become sharp. Similarly, since man's nature is evil, it must wait for the instructions of a teacher before it can become upright, and for the guidance of ritual principles before it can become orderly. If men have no teachers to instruct them, they will be inclined towards evil and not upright; and if they have no ritual principles to guide them, they will be perverse and violent and lack order. In ancient times the sage kings realized that man's nature is evil, and that therefore he inclines toward evil and violence and is not upright or orderly. Accordingly they created ritual principles and laid down certain regulations in order to reform man's emotional nature and make it upright, in order to train and transform it and guide it in the proper channels. In this way they caused all men to become orderly and to conform to the Way. Hence, today any man who takes to heart the instructions of his teacher, applies himself to his studies, and abides by ritual principles may become a gentleman, but anyone who gives free rein to his emotional nature, is content to indulge his passions, and disregards ritual principles becomes a petty man. It is obvious from this, therefore, that man's nature is evil, and that his goodness is the result of conscious activity.

Mencius states that man is capable of learning because his nature is good, but I say that this is wrong. It indicates that he has not really understood man's nature nor distinguished properly between the basic nature and conscious activity. The nature is that which is given by Heaven; you cannot learn it, you cannot acquire it by effort. Ritual principles, on the other hand, are created by sages; you can learn to apply them, you can work to bring them to completion. That part of man which cannot be learned or acquired by effort is called the nature; that part of him which can be acquired by learning and brought to completion by effort is called conscious activity. This is the difference between nature and conscious activity.

It is a part of man's nature that his eyes can see and his ears can hear. But the faculty of clear sight can never exist separately from the eye, nor can the faculty of keen hearing exist separately from the ear. It is obvious, then, that you cannot acquire clear sight and keen hearing by study. Mencius states that man's nature is good, and that all evil arises because he loses his original nature. Such a view, I believe, is erroneous. It is the way with man's nature that as soon as he is born he begins to depart from his original naïveté and simplicity, and therefore he must inevitably lose what Mencius regards as his original nature. It is obvious from this, then, that the nature of man is evil.

Those who maintain that the nature is good praise and approve whatever has not departed from the original simplicity and naïveté of the child. That is, they consider that beauty belongs to the original simplicity and naïveté and goodness to the original mind in the same way that clear sight is inseparable from the eye and keen hearing from the ear. Hence, they maintain that [the nature possesses goodness] in the same way that the eye possesses clear vision or the ear keenness of hearing. Now it is the nature of man that when he is hungry he will desire satisfaction, when he is cold he will desire warmth, and when he is weary he will desire rest. This is his emotional nature. And yet a man, although he is hungry, will not dare to be the first to eat if he is in the presence of his elders, because he knows that he should yield to them, and although he is weary, he will not dare to demand rest because he knows that he should relieve others of the burden of labor. For a son to yield to his father or a younger brother to yield to his elder brother, for a son to relieve his father of work or a younger brother to relieve his elder brother—acts such as these are all contrary to man's nature and run counter to his emotions. And yet they represent the way of filial piety and the proper forms enjoined by ritual principles. Hence, if men follow their emotional nature, there will be no courtesy or humility; courtesy and humility in fact run counter to man's emotional nature. From this it is obvious, then, that man's nature is evil, and that his goodness is the result of conscious activity.

Someone may ask: if man's nature is evil, then where do ritual principles come from? I would reply: all ritual principles are produced by the conscious activity of the sages; essentially they are not products of man's nature. A potter molds clay and makes a vessel, but the vessel is the product of the conscious activity of the potter, not essentially a product of his human nature. A carpenter carves a piece of wood and makes a utensil, but the utensil is the product of the conscious activity of the carpenter, not essentially a product of his human nature. The sage gathers together his thoughts and ideas, experiments with various forms of conscious activity, and so produces ritual principles and sets forth laws and regulations. Hence, these ritual principles and laws are the products of the conscious activity of the sage, not essentially products of his human nature.

Phenomena such as the eye's fondness for beautiful forms, the ear's fondness for beautiful sounds, the mouth's fondness for delicious flavors, the mind's fondness for profit, or the body's fondness for pleasure and ease—these are all products of the emotional nature of man. They are instinctive and spontaneous; man does not have to do anything to produce them. But that which does not come into being instinctively but must wait for some activity to bring it into being is called the product of conscious activity. These are the products of the nature and of conscious activity respectively, and the proof that they are not the same. Therefore, the sage transforms his nature and initiates conscious activity; from this conscious activity he produces ritual principles, and when they have been produced he sets up rules and regulations. Hence, ritual principles and rules are produced by the sage. In respect to human nature the sage is the same as all other men and does not surpass them; it is only in his conscious activity that he differs from and surpasses other men.

It is man's emotional nature to love profit and desire gain. Suppose now that a man has some wealth to be divided. If he indulges his emotional nature, loving profit and desiring gain, then he will quarrel and wrangle even with his own brothers over the division. But if he has been transformed by the proper forms of ritual principle, then he will be capable of yielding even to a complete stranger. Hence, to indulge the emotional nature leads to the quarreling of brothers, but to be transformed by ritual principles makes a man capable of yielding to strangers.

Every man who desires to do good does so precisely because his nature is evil. A man whose accomplishments are meager longs for greatness; an ugly man longs for beauty; a man in cramped quarters longs for spaciousness; a poor man longs for wealth; a humble man longs for eminence. Whatever a man lacks in himself he will seek outside. But if a man is already rich, he will not long for wealth, and if he is already eminent, he will not long for greater power. What a man already possesses in himself he will not bother to look for outside. From this we can see that men desire to do good precisely because their nature is evil. Ritual principles are certainly not a part of man's original nature. Therefore, he forces himself to study and to seek to possess them. An understanding of ritual principles is not a part of man's original nature, and therefore he ponders and plans and thereby seeks to understand them. Hence, man in the state in which he is born neither possesses nor understands ritual principles. If he does not possess ritual principles, his behavior will be chaotic, and if he does not understand them, he will be wild and irresponsible. In fact, therefore, man in the state in which he is born possesses this tendency towards chaos and irresponsibility. From this it is obvious, then, that man's nature is evil, and that his goodness is the result of conscious activity.

Mencius states that man's nature is good, but I say that this view is wrong. All men in the world, past and present, agree in defining goodness as that which is upright, reasonable, and orderly, and evil as that which is prejudiced, irresponsible, and chaotic. This is the distinction between good and evil. Now suppose that man's nature was in fact intrinsically upright, reasonable, and orderly—then what need would there be for sage kings and ritual principles? The existence of sage kings and ritual principles could certainly add nothing to the situation. But because man's nature is in fact evil, this is not so. Therefore, in ancient times the sages, realizing that man's nature is evil, that it is prejudiced and not upright, irresponsible and lacking in order, for this reason established the authority of the ruler to control it, elucidated ritual principles to transform it, set up laws and standards to correct it, and meted out strict punishments to restrain it. As a result, all the world achieved order and conformed to goodness. Such is the orderly government of the sage kings and the transforming power of ritual principles. Now let someone try doing away with the authority of the ruler, ignoring the transforming power of ritual principles, rejecting the order that comes from laws and standards, and dispensing with the restrictive power of punishments, and then watch and see how the people of the world treat each other. He will find that the powerful impose upon the weak and rob them, the many terrorize the few and extort from them, and in no time the whole world will be given up to chaos and mutual destruction. It is obvious from this, then, that man's nature is evil, and that his goodness is the result of conscious activity.

Those who are good at discussing antiquity must demonstrate the validity of what they say in terms of modern times; those who are good at discussing Heaven must show proofs from the human world. In discussions of all kinds, men value what is in accord with the facts and what can be proved to be valid. Hence if a man sits on his mat propounding some theory, he should be able to stand right up and put it into practice, and show that it can be extended over a wide area with equal validity. Now Mencius states that man's nature is good, but this is neither in accord with the facts, nor can it be proved to be valid. One may sit down and propound such a theory, but he cannot stand up and put it into practice, nor can he extend it over a wide area with any success at all. How, then, could it be anything but erroneous?

If the nature of man were good, we could dispense with sage kings and forget about ritual principles. But if it is evil, then we must go along with the sage kings and honor ritual principles. The straightening board is made because of the warped wood; the plumb line is employed because things are crooked; rulers are set up and ritual principles elucidated because the nature of man is evil. From this it is obvious, then, that man's nature is evil, and that his goodness is the result of conscious activity. A straight piece of wood does not have to wait for the straightening board to become straight; it is straight by nature. But a warped piece of wood must wait until it has been laid against the straightening board, steamed, and forced into shape before it can become straight, because by nature it is warped. Similarly, since man's nature is evil, he must wait for the ordering power of the sage kings and the transforming power of ritual principles; only then can he achieve order and conform to goodness. From this it is obvious, then, that man's nature is evil, and that his goodness is the result of conscious activity.

Someone may ask whether ritual principles and concerted conscious activity are not themselves a part of man's nature, so that for that reason the sage is capable of producing them. But I would answer that this is not so. A potter may mold clay and produce an earthen pot, but surely molding pots out of clay is not a part of the potter's human nature. A carpenter may carve wood and produce a utensil, but surely carving utensils out of wood is not a part of the carpenter's human nature. The sage stands in the same relation to ritual principles as the potter to the things he molds and produces. How, then, could ritual principles and concerted conscious activity be a part of man's basic human nature? . . .

. . . A man, no matter how fine his nature or how keen his mind, must seek a worthy teacher to study under and good companions to associate with. If he studies under a worthy teacher, he will be able to hear about the ways of Yao, Shun, Yü, and T'ang, and if he associates with good companions, he will be able to observe conduct that is loyal and respectful. Then, although he is not aware of it, he will day by day progress in the practice of benevolence and righteousness, for the environment he is subjected to will cause him to progress. But if a man associates with men who are not good, then he will hear only deceit and lies and will see only conduct that is marked by wantonness, evil, and greed. Then, although he is not aware of it, he himself will soon be in danger of severe punishment, for the environment he is subjected to will cause him to be in danger. An old text says, "If you do not know a man, look at his friends; if you do not know a ruler, look at his attendants." Environment is the important thing! Environment is the important thing!

Plato

If Socrates is the patron saint of philosophy, his pupil Plato (c. 427–347 B.C.E.) is the first to have left behind substantial philosophical writings to influence posterity. Most of these take the form of dialogues in which the leading part is played by Socrates. Plato's style ranges from the vivid imagery of poetry and myth to puzzling technicalities of logical argument and linguistic wordplay. His most famous and lengthy dialogue is the *Republic,* in which he presents an intricately integrated account of metaphysics, theory of knowledge, and human psychology, together with recommendations for education, ethics, social and family life, and politics.

These extracts are from Robin Waterfield's translation, with his helpful section headings. In the first section (514–519), Plato presents his famous image of the unenlightened human condition as like prisoners chained in a cave. In the next section (433–444), he offers an analogy between "morality" (*dikaiosune*) in the community and in the individual (previous translators have used the term *justice* to translate this Greek word—the general idea is well-being, the best way for human beings to live, given their nature). Plato argues for his tripartite theory of the human mind as consisting of reason, spirit, and appetite, and concludes (588–591) that morality and well-being consist in harmony among the three.

The internal conflicts he memorably pictures are described in similar terms by Freud (see below).

Republic

Like all the great images of the world's greatest literature, Plato's Cave manages simultaneously to appear transparent and yet unexpectedly rich and surprising. Those readers who believe that philosophy is a dry academic pursuit will be surprised at its presentation here as a pursuit which frees us from a terrible slavery; but for Plato and his peers philosophy is a way of life, not just a course of study.

"Next," I said, "here's a situation which you can use as an analogy for the human condition—for our education or lack of it. Imagine people living in a cavernous cell down under the ground; at the far end of the cave, a long way off, there's an entrance open to the outside world. They've been there since childhood, with their legs and necks tied up in a way which keeps them in one place and allows them to look only straight ahead, but not to turn their heads. There's firelight burning a long way further up the cave behind them, and up the slope between the fire and the prisoners there's a road, beside which you should imagine a low wall has been built—like the partition which conjurors place between themselves and their audience and above which they show their tricks." *514a*

"All right," he said. *b*

"Imagine also that there are people on the other side of this wall who are carrying all sorts of artefacts. These artefacts, human statuettes, and animal models carved in stone and wood and all kinds of materials stick out over the wall; and as you'd expect, some of the people talk as they carry these objects along, while others are silent." *c 515a*

"This is a strange picture you're painting," he said, "with strange prisoners."

"They're no different from us," I said. "I mean, in the first place, do you think they'd see anything of themselves and one another except the shadows cast by the fire on to the cave wall directly opposite them?"

"Of course not," he said. "They're forced to spend their lives without moving their heads." *b*

Republic, translated by Robin Waterfield © Oxford University Press 1993.

"And what about the objects which were being carried along? Won't they only see their shadows as well?"

"Naturally."

"Now, suppose they were able to talk to one another: don't you think they'd assume that their words applied to what they saw passing by in front of them?"

"They couldn't think otherwise."

"And what if sound echoed off the prison wall opposite them? When any of the passers-by spoke, don't you think they'd be bound to assume that the sound came from a passing shadow?"

"I'm absolutely certain of it," he said.

c "All in all, then," I said, "the shadows of artefacts would constitute the only reality people in this situation would recognize."

"That's absolutely inevitable," he agreed.

"What do you think would happen, then," I asked, "If they were set free from their bonds and cured of their inanity? What would it be like if they found that happening to them? Imagine that one of them has been set free and is suddenly made to stand up, to turn his head and walk, and to look towards the firelight. It hurts him to do all this and he's too dazzled to be capable of making out the objects whose shadows he'd formerly *d* been looking at. And suppose someone tells him that what he's been seeing all this time has no substance, and that he's now closer to reality and is seeing more accurately, because of the greater reality of the things in front of his eyes—what do you imagine his reaction would be? And what do you think he'd say if he were shown any of the passing objects and had to respond to being asked what it was? Don't you think he'd be bewildered and would think that there was more reality in what he'd been seeing before than in what he was being shown now?"

"Far more," he said.

e "And if he were forced to look at the actual firelight, don't you think it would hurt his eyes? Don't you think he'd turn away and run back to the things he could make out, and would take the truth of the matter to be that these things are clearer than what he was being shown?"

"Yes," he agreed.

"And imagine him being dragged forcibly away from there up the rough, steep slope," I went on, "without being released until he's been *516a* pulled out into the sunlight. Wouldn't this treatment cause him pain and distress? And once he's reached the sunlight, he wouldn't be able to see a single one of the things which are currently taken to be real, would he, because his eyes would be overwhelmed by the sun's beams?"

"No, he wouldn't," he answered, "not straight away."

"He wouldn't be able to see things up on the surface of the earth, I suppose, until he'd got used to his situation. At first, it would be shadows that he could most easily make out, then he'd move on to the reflections of people and so on in water, and later he'd be able to see the actual things themselves. Next, he'd feast his eyes on the heavenly bodies and the heavens themselves, which would be easier at night: he'd look at the light of the stars and the moon, rather than at the sun and sunlight during *b* the daytime."

"Of course."

"And at last, I imagine, he'd be able to discern and feast his eyes on the sun—not the displaced image of the sun in water or elsewhere, but the sun on its own, in its proper place."

"Yes, he'd inevitably come to that," he said.

"After that, he'd start to think about the sun and he'd deduce that it is the source of the seasons and the yearly cycle, that the whole of the visible realm is its domain, and that in a sense everything which he and his *c* peers used to see is its responsibility."

"Yes, that would obviously be the next point he'd come to," he agreed.

"Now, if he recalled the cell where he'd originally lived and what passed for knowledge there and his former fellow prisoners, don't you think he'd feel happy about his own altered circumstances, and sorry for them?"

"Definitely,"

"Suppose that the prisoners used to assign prestige and credit to one another, in the sense that they rewarded speed at recognizing the shadows as they passed, and the ability to remember which ones normally come earlier and later and at the same time as which other ones, and expertise at using this as a basis for guessing which ones would arrive next. Do you *d* think our former prisoner would covet these honours and would envy the people who had status and power there, or would he much prefer, as Homer describes it, 'being a slave labouring for someone else—someone without property,' and would put up with anything at all, in fact, rather than share their beliefs and their life?"

"Yes, I think he'd go through anything rather than live that way," he *e* said.

"Here's something else I'd like your opinion about," I said. "If he went back underground and sat down again in the same spot, wouldn't the sudden transition from the sunlight mean that his eyes would be overwhelmed by darkness?"

"Certainly," he replied.

"Now, the process of adjustment would be quite long this time, and suppose that before his eyes had settled down and while he wasn't seeing well, he had once again to compete against those same old prisoners at identifying those shadows. Wouldn't he make a fool of himself? Wouldn't they say that he'd come back from his upward journey with his eyes ruined, and that it wasn't even worth trying to go up there? And wouldn't they—if they could—grab hold of anyone who tried to set them free and take them up there, and kill him?"

"They certainly would," he said.

"Well, my dear Glaucon," I said, "you should apply this allegory, as a whole, to what we were talking about before. The region which is accessible to sight should be equated with the prison cell, and the firelight there with the light of the sun. And if you think of the upward journey and the sight of things up on the surface of the earth as the mind's ascent to the intelligible realm, you won't be wrong—at least, *I* don't think you'd be wrong, and it's my impression that you want to hear. Only God knows if it's actually true, however. Anyway, it's my opinion that the last thing to be seen—and it isn't easy to see either—in the realm of knowledge is goodness; and the sight of the character of goodness leads one to deduce that it is responsible for everything that is right and fine, whatever the circumstances, and that in the visible realm it is the progenitor of light and of the source of light, and in the intelligible realm it is the source and provider of truth and knowledge. And I also think that the sight of it is a prerequisite for intelligent conduct either of one's own private affairs or of public business."

"I couldn't agree more," he said.

"All right, then," I said. "I wonder if you also agree with me in not finding it strange that people who've travelled there don't want to engage in human business: there's nowhere else their minds would ever rather be than in the upper region—which is hardly surprising, if our allegory has got this aspect right as well."

"No, it's not surprising," he agreed.

"Well, what about this?" I asked. "Imagine someone returning to the human world and all its misery after contemplating the divine realm. Do you think it's surprising if he seems awkward and ridiculous while he's still not seeing well, before he's had time to adjust to the darkness of his situation, and he's forced into a contest (in a lawcourt or wherever) about the shadows of morality or the statuettes which cast the shadows, and into a competition whose terms are the conceptions of morality held by people who have never seen morality itself?"

"No, that's not surprising in the slightest," he said.

" In fact anyone with any sense," I said, "would remember that the eyes *518a* can become confused in two different ways, as a result of two different sets of circumstances: it can happen in the transition from light to darkness, and also in the transition from darkness to light. If he took the same facts into consideration when he also noticed someone's mind in such a state of confusion that it was incapable of making anything out, his reaction wouldn't be unthinking ridicule. Instead, he'd try to find out whether this person's mind was returning from a mode of existence which involves greater lucidity and had been blinded by the unfamiliar darkness, or whether it was moving from relative ignorance to relative lucidity and had been overwhelmed and dazzled by the increased brightness. Once he'd distinguished between the two conditions and modes of existence, he'd congratulate anyone he found in the second state, and feel *b* sorry for anyone in the first state. If he did choose to laugh at someone in the second state, his amusement would be less absurd than when laughter is directed at someone returning from the light above."

"Yes," he said, "you're making a lot of sense."

Since the Cave was expressly introduced as being relevant to education, its immediate educational implications are now drawn out. We all have the capacity for knowledge (in the Platonic sense, not just information), and education should develop that potential. But since it requires knowledge of goodness to manage a community well, then those who gain such knowledge have to "return to the cave": paradoxically, those who least want power are the ones who should have it.

"Now, if this is true," I said, "we must bear in mind that education is not capable of doing what some people promise. They claim to introduce knowledge into a mind which doesn't have it, as if they were introducing sight into eyes which are blind." *c*

"Yes, they do," he said.

"An implication of what we're saying at the moment, however," I pointed out, "is that the capacity for knowledge is present in everyone's mind. If you can imagine an eye that can turn from darkness to brightness only if the body as a whole turns, then our organ of understanding is like that. Its orientation has to be accompanied by turning the mind as a whole away from the world of becoming, until it becomes capable of bearing the sight of real being and reality at its most bright, which we're saying is goodness. Yes?" *d*

"Yes."

"That's what education should be," I said, "the art of orientation. Educators should devise the simplest and most effective methods of turning minds around. It shouldn't be the art of implanting sight in the organ, but should proceed on the understanding that the organ already has the capacity, but is improperly aligned and isn't facing the right way."

"I suppose you're right," he said.

"So although the mental states which are described as good generally
e seem to resemble good physical states, in the sense that habituation and training do in fact implant them where they didn't use to be, yet understanding (as it turns out) is undoubtedly a property of something which is
519a more divine: it never loses its power, and it is useful and beneficial, or useless and harmful, depending on its orientation. For example, surely you've noticed how the petty minds of those who are acknowledged to be bad, but clever, are sharp-eyed and perceptive enough to gain insights into matters they direct their attention towards. It's not as if they weren't sharp-sighted, but their minds are forced to serve evil, and consequently the keener their vision is, the greater the evil they accomplish."

"Yes, I've noticed this," he said.

"However," I went on, "if this aspect of that kind of person is hammered at from an early age, until the inevitable consequences of incarna-
b tion have been knocked off it—the leaden weights, so to speak, which are grafted on to it as a result of eating and similar pleasures and indulgences and which turn the sight of the mind downwards—if it sheds these weights and is reoriented towards the truth, then (and we're talking about the same organ and the same people) it would see the truth just as clearly as it sees the objects it faces at the moment."

"Yes, that makes sense," he said.

"Well, doesn't this make sense as well?" I asked. "Or rather, isn't it an inevitable consequence of what we've been saying that uneducated peo-
c ple, who have no experience of truth, would make incompetent administrators of a community, and that the same goes for people who are allowed to spend their whole lives educating themselves? The first group would be no good because their lives lack direction: they've got no single point of reference to guide them in all their affairs, whether private or public. The second group would be no good because their hearts wouldn't be in the business: they think they've been transported to the Isles of the Blessed even while they're still alive."

"True," he said.

"Our job as founders, then," I said, "is to make sure that the best people come to that fundamental field of study (as we called it earlier): we must have them make the ascent we've been talking about and see goodness. And afterwards, once they've been up there and had a good look, we mustn't let them get away with what they do at the moment." *d*

"Which is what?"

"Staying there," I replied, "and refusing to come back down again to those prisoners, to share their work and their rewards, no matter whether those rewards are trivial or significant."

"But in that case," he protested, "we'll be wronging them: we'll be making the quality of their lives worse and denying them the better life they could be living, won't we?"

"You're again forgetting, my friend," I said, "that the point of legisla- *e* tion is not to make one section of a community better off than the rest, but to engineer this for the community as a whole. Legislators should persuade or compel the members of a community to mesh together, should make every individual share with his fellows the benefit which he is capable of contributing to the common welfare, and should ensure that the *520a* community does contain people with this capacity; and the purpose of all this is not for legislators to leave people to choose their own directions, but for them to use people to bind the community together."

"Yes, you're right," he said. "I was forgetting."

• • •

"From the outset, when we first started to found the community, there's *433a* a principle we established as a universal requirement—and this, or some version of it, is in my opinion morality. The principle we established, and then repeated time and again, as you'll remember, is that every individual has to do just one of the jobs relevant to the community, the one for which his nature has best equipped him."

"Yes, that's what we said."

"Furthermore, the idea that morality is doing one's own job and not intruding elsewhere is commonly voiced, and we ourselves have often *b* said it."

"Yes, we have."

"So, Glaucon," I said, "it seems likely that this is in a sense what morality is—doing one's own job. Do you know what makes me think so?"

"No," he answered. "Please tell me."

"We've examined self-discipline, courage, and wisdom," I said, "and it occurs to me that this principle is what is left in the community, because it is the principle which makes it possible for all those other qualities to

arise in the community, and its continued presence allows them to flourish in safety once they have arisen. And we did in fact say that if we found
c the other three, then whatever was left would be morality."

"Yes, that's necessarily so," he said.

"But if we had to decide which of these qualities it was whose presence is chiefly responsible for the goodness of the community," I said, "it would be hard to decide whether it's the unanimity between rulers and subjects, or the militia's retention of the lawful notion about what is and is not to be feared, or the wise guardianship which is an attribute of the
d rulers, or the fact that it is an attribute of every child, woman, slave, free person, artisan, ruler, and subject that each individual does his own job without intruding elsewhere, that is chiefly responsible for making it good."

"Yes, of course that would be a difficult decision," he said.

"When it comes to contributing to a community's goodness, then, there's apparently a close contest between the ability of everyone in a community to do their own jobs and its wisdom, self-discipline, and courage."

"There certainly is," he said.

"And wouldn't you say that anything which rivals these qualities in
e contributing towards a community's goodness must be morality?"

"Absolutely."

"See if you also agree when you look at it from this point of view. Won't you be requiring the rulers to adjudicate when lawsuits occur in the community?"

"Of course."

"And won't their most important aim in doing so be to ensure that people don't get hold of other people's property and aren't deprived of their own?"

"Yes."

"Because this is right?"

"Yes."

"So from this point of view too we are agreed that morality is keeping
434a one's own property and keeping to one's own occupation."

"True."

"See if you agree with me on this as well: if a joiner tried to do a shoemaker's job, or a shoemaker a carpenter's, or if they swapped tools or status, or even if the same person tried to do both jobs, with all the tools and so on of both jobs switched around, do you think that much harm would come to the community."

"Not really," he said.

"On the other hand, when someone whom nature has equipped to be an artisan or to work for money in some capacity or other gets so puffed up *b* by his wealth or popularity or strength or some such factor that he tries to enter the military class, or when a member of the militia tries to enter the class of policy-makers and guardians when he's not qualified to do so, and they swap tools and status, or when a single person tries to do all these jobs simultaneously, then I'm sure you'll agree that these inter-changes and intrusions are disastrous for the community."

"Absolutely."

"There's nothing more disastrous for the community, then, than the intrusion of any of the three classes into either of the other two, and the *c* interchange of roles among them, and there could be no more correct context for using the term criminal."

"Indubitably."

"And when someone commits the worst crimes against his own com-munity, wouldn't you describe this as immorality?"

"Of course."

"Then this is what immorality is. Here's an alternative way of putting it. Isn't it the case (to put it the other way round) that when each of the three classes—the one that works for a living, the auxiliaries, and the guardians—performs its proper function and does its own job in the com-munity, then this is morality and makes the community a moral one?"

"Yes, I think that's exactly right," he said. *d*

The existence of conflict within a person's mind proves that there are dif-ferent "parts" to the mind. On examination, we can claim that there are three parts. . . .

[Plato] *distinguishes a part which includes our desires or wants or instinctive appetites; our intellect, which uses both pure and applied thinking; and our passionate, assertive, proud, brave side, which (in non-Platonic terms) enhances or defends our "sense of I." This is Plato's famous theory of the tripartite mind, which recurs in* Phaedrus *and* Timaeus. . . .

"Let's not be too inflexible about it yet," I warned. "If we also conclude that this type of thing constitutes morality in the case of individual human beings as well, then we'll have no reservations. I mean, how could we under those circumstances? However, if we find that it doesn't apply to humans as well, then we'll have to take the enquiry into new areas. So

let's now wind up that aspect of the enquiry which is based on the idea we had that it would be easier to detect the nature of morality in an individual human being if we first tried to observe it in something larger and to watch its operation there. We decided that the larger thing was a commu-
e nity, and so we founded as good a community as we could, because we were well aware that it would have to be a good community for morality to exist in it. What we have to do now is apply the results we found in the case of the community to an individual. If there's a match, that will be fine; but if we find something different in the case of an individual, then we'll return to the community to test the new result. With luck, the fric-
435ᵃ tion of comparing the two cases will enable morality to flare up from these fire-sticks, so to speak, and once it's become visible we'll make it more of a force in our own lives."

"That's a viable notion," he said. "We should do as you suggest."

"Well," I said, "if a single property is predicated of two things of different sizes, then in so far as it's the same predicate, is it in fact dissimilar or similar in the two instances?"

"Similar," he said.

b "So in respect of the actual type of thing morality is, a moral person will be no different from a moral community, but will resemble it."

"Yes," he said.

"Now, we decided that a community was moral when each of the three natural classes that exist within it did its own job, and also that certain other states and conditions of the same three classes made it self-disciplined and courageous and wise."

"True."

c "It follows, my friend, that we should expect an individual to have the same three classes in himself, and that the same conditions make him liable to the same predicates as the community receives."

"That's absolutely inevitable," he said.

"Glaucon," I said, "now we're faced with another simple enquiry, to see whether or not the mind contains these three features."

"It hardly seems to me to be a simple one," he remarked. "But then it's probably a true saying, Socrates, that anything fine is difficult."

d "I think that's right," I said. "In fact, I have to tell you, Glaucon, that in my opinion we'll never completely understand this issue by relying on the kinds of methods we've employed so far in our discussion: a longer and fuller approach is needed. Still, we can hope to come up with something which is in keeping with what we've already said in the earlier stages of our enquiry."

"Shouldn't we be content with that?" he asked. "I for one would be satisfied with that for the time being."

"And it'll do perfectly well for me too," I said.

"No flagging, then," he said. "On with the enquiry."

"Well, here's something we're bound to agree on, aren't we?" I asked. *e* "That we do contain the same kinds of features and characteristics as the community. I mean, where else could it have got them from? When the general population of a community consists of people who are reputedly passionate—Thracians and Scythians, for example, and almost any northerner—it would be absurd to think that passion arises in this community from any other source. And the same goes for love of knowledge, for which our country has a strong reputation; and being mercenary might *436a* be claimed to be a particular characteristic of Phoenicians and Egyptians."

"Certainly."

"This is a matter of fact, then," I said, "and it wasn't hard to discover."

"No."

"But here's a hard one: is there just a single thing which we use for doing everything, or are there three and we use different things for different tasks? Do we learn with one of our aspects, get worked up with another, and with a third desire the pleasures of eating, sex, and so on, or do we use the whole of our mind for every task we actually get going on? These questions won't be easy to answer satisfactorily." *b*

"I agree," he said.

"Well, let's approach an answer by trying to see whether these aspects are the same as one another or are different."

"How?"

"It's clear that the same one thing cannot simultaneously either act or be acted on in opposite ways in the same respect and in the same context. And consequently, if we find this happening in the case of these aspects of ourselves, we'll know that there are more than one of them." *c*

"All right." . . .

"When someone is thirsty, then, the only thing—in so far as he is thirsty—that his mind wants is to drink. This is what it longs for and *b* strives for."

"Clearly."

"So imagine an occasion when something is making it resist the pull of its thirst: isn't this bound to be a different part of it from the thirsty part, which is impelling it towards drink as if it were an animal? I mean, we've already agreed that the same one thing cannot thanks to the same part of itself simultaneously have opposite effects in the same context."

"No, it can't."

"As an analogy, it isn't in my opinion right to say that an archer's hands are simultaneously pushing the bow away and pulling it closer. Strictly, one hand is pushing it away and the other is pulling it close."

c   "I quite agree," he said.

"Now, do we know of cases where thirsty people are unwilling to drink?"

"Certainly," he said. "It's a common occurrence."

"What could be the explanation for these cases?" I asked. "Don't we have to say that their mind contains a part which is telling them to drink, and a part which is telling them not to drink, and that this is a different part and overcomes the part which is telling them to drink?"

"I think so," he said.

"And those occasions when thirst and so on are countermanded occur
d thanks to rationality, whereas the pulls and impulses occur thanks to afflictions and diseased states, don't they?"

"I suppose so."

"So it wouldn't be irrational of us to expect that these are two separate parts," I said, "one of which we can describe as rational, and the other as irrational and desirous. The first is responsible for the mind's capacity to think rationally, and the second—which is an ally of certain satisfactions and pleasures—for its capacity to feel lust, hunger, and thirst, and in general to be stirred by desire."

e   "No, it wouldn't be irrational," he said. "This would be a perfectly reasonable view for us to hold."

"Let's have these, then," I said, "as two distinct aspects of our minds. What about the passionate part, however, which is responsible for the mind's capacity for passion? It is a third part, or might it be interchangeable with one of the other two?"

"I suppose it might be the same as the desirous part," he said.

"But there's a story I once heard which seems to me to be reliable," I said, "about how Leontius the son of Aglaeon was coming up from the Piraeus, outside the North Wall but close to it, when he saw some corpses with the public executioner standing near by. On the one hand, he experienced the desire to see them, but at the same time he felt disgust and averted his gaze. For a while, he struggled and kept his hands over his
440a eyes, but finally he was overcome by the desire; he opened his eyes wide, ran up to the corpses, and said, 'There you are, you wretches! What a lovely sight! I hope you feel satisfied!' "

"Yes, I've heard the story too," he said.

"Now, what it suggests," I said, "is that it's possible for anger to be at odds with the desires, as if they were different things."

"Yes, it does," he agreed.

"And that's far from being an isolated case, isn't it?" I asked. "It's not at all uncommon to find a person's desires compelling him to go against his reason, and to see him cursing himself and venting his passion on the *b* source of the compulsion within him. It's as if there were two warring factions, with passion fighting on the side of reason. But I'm sure you wouldn't claim that you had ever, in yourself or in anyone else, met a case of passion siding with the desires against the rational mind, when the rational mind prohibits resistance."

"No, I certainly haven't," he said.

"And what about when you feel you're in the wrong?" I asked. "If *c* someone who in your opinion has a right to do so retaliates by inflicting on you hunger and cold and so on, then isn't it the case that, in proportion to your goodness of character, you are incapable of getting angry at this treatment and your passion, as I say, has no inclination to get worked up against him?"

"True," he said.

"But suppose you feel you're being wronged. Under these circumstances, your passion boils and rages, and fights for what you regard as right. Then hunger, cold, and other sufferings make you stand firm and conquer them, and only success or death can stop it fighting the good fight, unless it is recalled by your rational mind and calmed down, as a *d* dog is by a shepherd."

"That's a very good simile," he said. "And in fact the part we've got the auxiliaries to play in our community is just like that of dogs, with their masters being the rulers, who are, as it were, the shepherds of the community."

"Yes, you've got it," I said. "That's exactly what I mean. But there's something else here too, and I wonder if you've noticed it as well."

"What is it?"

"That we're getting the opposite impression of the passionate part *e* from what we did before. Previously, we were thinking that it was an aspect of the desirous part, but now that seems to be way off the mark, and we're saying that when there's mental conflict, it is far more likely to fight alongside reason."

"Absolutely," he said.

"Is it different from the rational part, then, or is it a version of it, in

which case there are two, not three, mental categories—the rational and
the desirous? Or will the analogy with the community hold good? Three
441a classes constituted the community—the one which works for a living, the
auxiliaries, and the policy-makers—so is there in the mind as well a third
part, the passionate part, which is an auxiliary of the rational part, unless
it is corrupted by bad upbringing?"

"It must be a third part," he said.

"Yes," I said, "*if* we find that it's as distinct from the rational part as it
is from the desirous part."

"But that's easy," he said. "Just look at children. It's evident that from
the moment of their birth they have a copious supply of passion, but I'm
b not convinced that some of them ever acquire reason, and it takes quite a
time for most of them to do so."

"Yes, you've certainly put that well," I said. "And animals provide further evidence of the truth of what you're saying. Moreover, we can
adduce the passage from Homer we quoted earlier: 'He struck his breast
and spoke sternly to his heart.' Clearly, Homer here has one distinct part
c rebuking another distinct part—the part which has thought rationally
about what is better and worse rebuking the part whose passion is irrationally becoming aroused."

"You're absolutely right," he said.

"It's not been easy," I said, "but we've made it to the other shore: we've
reached the reasonable conclusion that the constituent categories of a community and of any individual's mind are identical in nature and number."

"Yes, they are."

*Since the three mental parts are precisely analogous to the three social
classes of Plato's community, Plato now analyses individual wisdom,
courage, self-discipline, and morality in ways which precisely parallel
his analysis of their civic manifestations. Morality, then, is an inner state
and has little to do with external appearances. It is harmony between the
parts of a person's mind under the leadership of his or her intellect;
immorality is anarchy and civil war between the parts . . .*

"Isn't it bound to follow that the manner and cause of a community's and
an individual's wisdom are identical?"

"Naturally."

d   "And that the manner and cause of a community's and an individual's
courage are identical, and that the same goes for every other factor which
contributes in both cases towards goodness?"

"Inevitably."

"So no doubt, Glaucon, we'll also be claiming that human morality is the same in kind as a community's morality."

"Yes, that's absolutely inevitable too."

"We can't have forgotten, however, that a community's morality consists in each of its three constituent classes doing its own job."

"No, I'm sure we haven't," he said.

"So we should impress upon our minds the idea that the same goes for human beings as well. Where each of the constituent parts of an individual does its own job, the individual will be moral and will do *his* own *e* job."

"Yes, we certainly should do that," he said.

"Since the rational part is wise and looks out for the whole of the mind, isn't it right for it to rule, and for the passionate part to be its subordinate and its ally?"

"Yes."

"Now—to repeat—isn't it the combination of culture and exercise which will make them attuned to each other? The two combined provide fine discussions and studies to stretch and educate the rational part, and music and rhythm to relax, calm, and soothe the passionate part." *442a*

"Absolutely."

"And once these two parts have received this education and have been trained and conditioned in their true work, then they are to be put in charge of the desirous part, which is the major constituent of an individual's mind and is naturally insatiably greedy for things. So they have to watch over it and make sure that it doesn't get so saturated with physical pleasures (as they are called) that in its bloated and strengthened state it stops doing its own job, and tries to dominate and rule over things which *b* it is not equipped by its hereditary status to rule over, and so plunges the whole of everyone's life into chaos."

"Yes, indeed," he said.

"Moreover, these two are perfect for guarding the entire mind and the body against external enemies, aren't they?" I asked. "The rational part will do the planning, and the passionate part the fighting. The passionate part will obey the ruling part and employ its courage to carry out the plans."

"True."

"I imagine, then, that it is the passionate part of a person which we are *c* taking into consideration when we describe him as courageous: we're saying that neither pain nor pleasure stops his passionate part retaining the pronouncements of reason about what is and is not to be feared."

"That's right," he agreed.

"And the part we take into consideration when we call him wise is that little part—his internal ruler, which made these pronouncements—which knows what is advantageous for each of the three parts and for their joint unity."

"Yes."

"And don't we call him self-disciplined when there's concord and attunement between these same parts—that is, when the ruler and its two *d* subjects unanimously agree on the necessity of the rational part being the ruler and when they don't rebel against it?"

"Yes, that's exactly what self-discipline is, in both a community and an individual," he said.

"And we're not changing our minds about the manner and cause of morality."

"Absolutely not."

"Well," I said, "have we blunted the edge of our notion of morality in any way? Do we have any grounds for thinking that our conclusions about its nature in a community don't apply in this context?"

"I don't think so," he replied.

e "If there's still any doubt in our minds," I said, "we can eradicate it completely by checking our conclusion against everyday cases."

"What cases?"

"Take this community of ours and a person who resembles it by virtue of both his nature and his upbringing, and suppose, for instance, we had to state whether, in our opinion, a person of this type would steal money which had been deposited with him. Is it conceivable to you that anyone *443a* would think our man capable of this, rather than any other type of person?"

"No one could think that," he said.

"And he could have nothing to do with temple-robbery, theft, and betrayal either of his personal friends or, on a public scale, of his country, could he?"

"No, he couldn't."

"Moreover, nothing could induce him to break an oath or any other kind of agreement."

"No, nothing."

"And he's the last person you'd expect to find committing adultery, neglecting his parents, and failing to worship the gods."

"Yes, of course," he said.

"And isn't the reason for all of this the fact that each of his constituent *b* parts does its own job as ruler or subject?"

"Yes, that's the only reason."

"Do you need to look any further for morality, then? Don't you think it can only be the capacity we've come up with, which enables both people and communities to be like this?"

"I for one certainly don't need to look any further," he said.

"Our dream has finally come true, then. We said we had a vague impression that we had probably—with the help of some god—stumbled across the origin and some kind of outline of morality right at the start of *c* our foundation of the community."

"Absolutely."

"It turns out, then, Glaucon—and this is why it was so useful—that the idea that a person who has been equipped by nature to be a shoemaker or a joiner or whatever should make shoes or do joinery or whatever was a dreamt image of morality."

"So it seems."

"And we've found that in real life morality is the same kind of property, apparently, though not in the field of external activities. Its sphere is a person's inner activity: it is really a matter of oneself and the parts of oneself. Once he has stopped his mental constituents doing any job which *d* is not their own or intruding on one another's work; once he has set his own house in order, which is what he really should be concerned with; once he is his own ruler, and is well regulated, and has internal concord; once he has treated the three factors as if they were literally the three defining notes of an octave—low high, and middle—and has created a harmony out of them and however many notes there may be in between; once he has bound all the factors together and made himself a perfect *e* unity instead of a plurality, self-disciplined and internally attuned: then and only then does he act—if he acts—to acquire property or look after his body or play a role in government or do some private business. In the course of this activity, it is conduct which preserves and promotes this inner condition of his that he regards as moral and describes as fine and it is the knowledge which oversees this conduct that he regards as wisdom; however, it is any conduct which disperses this condition that he regards *444a* as immoral, and the thinking which oversees this conduct that he regards as stupidity."

"You're absolutely right, Socrates," he said.

"All right," I said. "I imagine that we'd regard as no more than the truth the claim that we had found out what it is to be a moral person and a moral community, and had discovered what morality actually is when it occurs in them."

"Yes, we certainly would," he said.

"Shall we make the claim, then?"

"Yes."

"So be it" I said. "Next, I suppose, we should consider immorality."

"Obviously."

b   "Isn't it bound to involve these three factors being in conflict, intruding into one another's work, and exchanging roles, and one part rebelling against the mind as a whole in an improper attempt to usurp rulership—improper because its natural function is to be dominated unless it belongs to the ruling class. Our position, I'm sure, will be that it is disruption and disorder of the three parts along these lines that constitutes not only immorality, but also indiscipline, cowardice, and stupidity—in a word, badness of any kind."

"Precisely," he said.

c   "Now that morality and immorality are in plain view, doesn't that mean that wrongdoing and immoral conduct, and right conduct too, are as well?" I asked.

"Why?"

"Because their role in the mind happens to be identical to that of healthy or unhealthy factors in the body," I said.

"In what sense?"

"Healthy factors engender health, and unhealthy ones illness."

"Yes."

"Well, doesn't moral behaviour engender morality, while immoral
d behaviour engenders immorality?"

"Inevitably."

"But you create health by making the components of a body control and be controlled as nature intended, and you create disease by subverting this natural order."

"Yes."

"Doesn't it follow," I said, "that you create morality by making the components of a mind control and be controlled as nature intended, and immorality by subverting this natural order?"

"Absolutely," he said.

"Goodness, then, is apparently a state of mental health, bloom, and
e vitality; badness is a state of mental sickness, deformity, and infirmity."

"That's right."

"Isn't it the case, therefore, that goodness is a consequence of good conduct, badness of bad conduct?"

"Necessarily."

"Now we come to what is, I suppose, the final topic. We have to consider whether moral conduct, fine behaviour, and being moral (whether 445a or not the person is known to be moral) are rewarding, or whether it is wrongdoing and being immoral (provided that the immoral person doesn't have to pay for his crimes and doesn't become a better person as a result of being punished)."

• • •

"Yes, that's undoubtedly what a supporter of immorality would have to say," he agreed.

"So the alternative position, that morality is profitable, is equivalent to saying that our words and behaviour should be designed to maximize the *b* control the inner man has within us, and should enable him to secure the help of the leonine quality and then tend to the many-headed beast as a farmer tends to his crops—by nurturing and cultivating its tame aspects, and by stopping the wild ones growing. Then he can ensure that they're all compatible with one another, and with himself, and can look after them all equally, without favouritism."

"Yes, that's exactly what a supporter of morality has to say," he agreed.

"Whichever way you look at it, then, a supporter of morality is telling *c* the truth, and a supporter of immorality is wrong. Whether your criterion is pleasure, reputation, or benefit, a supporter of morality is right, and a critic of morality is unreliable and doesn't know what he's talking about."

"I quite agree: he doesn't in the slightest," he said.

"But he doesn't mean to make a mistake, so let's be gentle with him. Here's a question we can ask him, to try to win him over: 'My friend, don't you think that this is also what accounts for conventional standards of what is and is not acceptable? Things are acceptable when they subject the bestial aspects of our nature to the human—or, it might be more accu- *d* rate to say the divine—part of ourselves, but they're objectionable when they cause the oppression of our tame side under the savage side.' Will he agree, do you think?"

"Well, I'll be recommending him to," he answered.

"So what follows from this argument? Can there be any profit in the immoral acquisition of money, if this entails the enslavement of the best part of oneself to the worst part? The point is, if there's no profit in some- *e* one selling his son or daughter into slavery—slavery under savage and evil men—for even a great deal of money, then what happens if he cruelly enslaves the most divine part of himself to the vilest, most godless part? Isn't unhappiness the result? Isn't the deadly business he's being

590a paid for far more terrible than what Eriphyle did when she accepted the
      necklace as the price for her husband's death?"
          "Yes, by a long way," Glaucon said. "I mean, I'll answer on behalf of
      our supporter of immorality."
          "Now, do you think the reason for the traditional condemnation of
      licentiousness is the same—because it allows that fiend, that huge and
      many-faceted creature, greater freedom than it should have?"
          "Obviously," he said.
          "And aren't obstinacy and bad temper considered bad because they
   b distend and invigorate our leonine, serpentine side to a disproportionate
      extent?"
          "Yes."
          "Whereas a spoilt, soft way of life is considered bad because it makes
      this part of us so slack and loose that it's incapable of facing hardship?"
          "Of course."
          "And why are lack of independence and autonomy despised? Isn't it
      still to do with the passionate part, because we have to subordinate it to
      the unruly beast and, from our earliest years, get the lion used to being
      insulted and to becoming a monkey instead of a lion—and all for the sake
      of money and to satisfy our greed?"
   c "Yes."
          "What about mundane, manual labour? Why do you think it has a bad
      name? Isn't it precisely because there's an inherent weakness in the truly
      good part of the person which makes him incapable of controlling his
      internal beasts, so that all he does is pander to them, and all he can learn
      is their whims?"
          "I suppose that's right," he said.
          "The question is, how can a person in this condition become subject to
      the kind of rulership which is available to a truly good person? By being
      the slave, we suggest, of a truly good person, whose divine element rules
   d within him. But we're not suggesting, as Thrasymachus did about sub-
      jects, that his status as a subject should do him harm; we're saying that
      subjection to the principle of divine intelligence is to everyone's advan-
      tage. It's best if this principle is part of a person's own nature, but if it
      isn't, it can be imposed from outside, to foster as much unanimity and
      compatibility between us as might be possible when we're all governed
      by the same principle."
          "You're right," he said.
   e   "It's also clear," I continued, "that this is the function of law: this is
      why every member of a community has the law to fall back on. And it

explains why we keep children under control and don't allow them their freedom until we've formed a government within them, as we would in a community. What we do is use what is best in ourselves to cultivate the equivalent aspect of a child, and then we let him go free once the equivalent part within him has been established as his guardian and ruler." *591a*

"Yes, that's clear," he said.

"Is there any conceivable argument, then, Glaucon, which will enable us to claim that immorality or licentiousness is rewarding, when the result of any kind of shameful behaviour may be a richer or otherwise more powerful person, but is certainly a worse person?"

"No, there isn't," he replied.

• • •

Christianity
(the New Testament)

Like Socrates, the Jewish rabbi or religious teacher Jesus of Nazareth wrote nothing—nothing we know of, anyway. The new religion of Christianity rapidly developed out of the reactions of his followers to his life, his teaching, his trial and crucifixion—and his alleged resurrection and postmortem appearances to his disciples. The letters ("epistles") of St. Paul and other Christian leaders to the early Christian communities, written in the first generation after Jesus, predate the compilation of the gospel narratives of his life, ministry, and death.

In these extracts from St. Paul's Letter to the Romans (chapters 1:18–2:16; 3:19–31; 5–8), we find the earliest and most influential formulation of the doctrines of the divinity of Jesus Christ and his God-given power to redeem all of humanity from sin—Jews and Gentiles, men and women—and offer everlasting life. The opposition between spirit and flesh in St. Paul's writing seems to mean not so much a Platonic dualism of soul and body, but the difference between redeemed and sin-dominated life.

In his First Letter to the Corinthians, Chapter 15, St. Paul emphasizes the centrality of Christ's resurrection from the dead. He describes human life after death in terms of the resurrection of a new "spiritual body," not as the survival of a disembodied soul, which was a Greek idea, argued for by Plato. In the last extract here, from Chapter 11, St. Paul expresses a view about the secondary place of women, which for better or for worse, has been influential on much Christian thought ever since.

St. Paul, Letter to the Romans

God's Judgement on Sin

1 [18]DIVINE retribution is to be seen at work, falling from heaven on all the impiety and wickedness of men and women who in their wickedness suppress the truth. [19]For all that can be known of God lies plain before their eyes; indeed God himself has disclosed it to them. [20]Ever since the world began, his invisible attributes, that is to say his everlasting power and deity, have been visible to the eye of reason, in the things he has made. Their conduct, therefore, is indefensible; [21]knowing God, they have refused to honour him as God, or to render him thanks. Hence all their thinking has ended in futility, and their misguided minds are plunged in darkness. [22]They boast of their wisdom, but they have made fools of themselves, [23]exchanging the glory of the immortal God for an image shaped like mortal man, even for images like birds, beasts, and reptiles.

[24]For this reason God has given them up to their own vile desires, and the consequent degradation of their bodies. [25]They have exchanged the truth of God for a lie, and have offered reverence and worship to created things instead of to the Creator. Blessed is he for ever, Amen. [26]As a result God has given them up to shameful passions. Among them women have exchanged natural intercourse for unnatural, [27]and men too, giving up natural relations with women, burn with lust for one another; males behave indecently with males, and are paid in their own persons the fitting wage of such perversion.

[28]Thus, because they have not seen fit to acknowledge God, he has given them up to their own depraved way of thinking, and this leads them to break all rules of conduct. [29]They are filled with every kind of wicked-

Revised English Bible © Oxford University Press and Cambridge University Press 1989.

ness, villainy, greed, and malice; they are one mass of envy, murder, rivalry, treachery, and malevolence; gossips [30]and scandalmongers; and blasphemers, insolent, arrogant, and boastful; they invent new kinds of vice, they show no respect to parents, [31]they are without sense or fidelity, without natural affection or pity. [32]They know well enough the just decree of God, that those who behave like this deserve to die; yet they not only do these things themselves but approve such conduct in others.

2 You have no defence, then, whoever you may be, when you sit in judgement—for in judging others you condemn yourself, since you, the judge, are equally guilty. [2]We all know that God's judgement on those who commit such crimes is just; [3]and do you imagine—you that pass judgement on the guilty while committing the same crimes yourself—do you imagine that you, any more than they, will escape the judgement of God? [4]Or do you despise his wealth of kindness and tolerance and patience, failing to see that God's kindness is meant to lead you to repentance? [5]In the obstinate impenitence of your heart you are laying up for yourself a store of retribution against the day of retribution, when God's just judgement will be revealed, [6]and he will pay everyone for what he has done. [7]To those who pursue glory, honour, and immortality by steady persistence in well-doing, he will give eternal life, [8]but the retribution of his wrath awaits those who are governed by selfish ambition, who refuse obedience to truth and take evil for their guide. [9]There will be affliction and distress for every human being who is a wrongdoer, for the Jew first and for the Greek also, [10]but for everyone who does right there will be glory, honour, and peace, for the Jew first and also for the Greek. [11]God has no favourites.

[12]Those who have sinned outside the pale of the law of Moses will perish outside the law, and all who have sinned under that law will be judged by it. [13]None will be justified before God by hearing the law, but by doing it. [14]When Gentiles who do not possess the law carry out its precepts by the light of nature, then, although they have no law, they are their own law; [15]they show that what the law requires is inscribed on their hearts, and to this their conscience gives supporting witness, since their own thoughts argue the case, sometimes against them, sometimes even for them. [16]So it will be on the day when, according to my gospel, God will judge the secrets of human hearts through Christ Jesus.

• • •

[19]Now all the words of the law are addressed, as we know, to those who are under the law, so that no one may have anything to say in self-defence, and the whole world may be exposed to God's judgement. [20]For no human being can be justified in the sight of God by keeping the law: law brings only the consciousness of sin.

[21]But now, quite independently of law, though with the law and the prophets bearing witness to it, the righteousness of God has been made known; [22]it is effective through faith in Christ for all who have such faith—all, without distinction. [23]For all alike have sinned, and are deprived of the divine glory; [24]and all are justified by God's free grace alone, through his act of liberation in the person of Christ Jesus. [25]For God designed him to be the means of expiating sin by his death, effective through faith. God meant by this to demonstrate his justice, because in his forbearance he had overlooked the sins of the past—[26]to demonstrate his justice now in the present, showing that he is himself just and also justifies anyone who puts his faith in Jesus.

[27]What room then is left for human pride? It is excluded. And on what principle? The keeping of the law would not exclude it, but faith does. [28]For our argument is that people are justified by faith quite apart from any question of keeping the law.

[29]Do you suppose God is the God of the Jews alone? Is he not the God of Gentiles also? Certainly, of Gentiles also. [30]For if the Lord is indeed one, he will justify the circumcised by their faith and the uncircumcised through their faith. [31]Does this mean that we are using faith to undermine the law? By no means: we are upholding the law.

• • •

Life in Christ

5 THEREFORE, now that we have been justified through faith, we are at peace with God through our Lord Jesus Christ, [2]who has given us access to that grace in which we now live; and we exult in the hope of the divine glory that is to be ours. [3]More than this: we even exult in our present sufferings, because we know that suffering is a source of endurance, [4]endurance of approval, and approval of hope. [5]Such hope is no fantasy; through the Holy Spirit he has given us, God's love has flooded our hearts.

[6]It was while we were still helpless that, at the appointed time, Christ died for the wicked. [7]Even for a just man one of us would hardly die, though perhaps for a good man one might actually brave death; [8]but

Christ died for us while we were yet sinners, and that is God's proof of his love towards us. [9]And so, since we have now been justified by Christ's sacrificial death, we shall all the more certainly be saved through him from final retribution. [10]For if, when we were God's enemies, we were reconciled to him through the death of his Son, how much more, now that we have been reconciled, shall we be saved by his life! [11]But that is not all: we also exult in God through our Lord Jesus, through whom we have now been granted reconciliation.

[12]What does this imply? It was through one man that sin entered the world, and through sin death, and thus death pervaded the whole human race, inasmuch as all have sinned. [13]For sin was already in the world before there was law; and although in the absence of law no reckoning is kept of sin, [14]death held sway from Adam to Moses, even over those who had not sinned as Adam did, by disobeying a direct command—and Adam foreshadows the man who was to come. [15]But God's act of grace is out of all proportion to Adam's wrongdoing. For if the wrongdoing of that one man brought death upon so many, its effect is vastly exceeded by the grace of God and the gift that came to so many by the grace of the one man, Jesus Christ. [16]And again, the gift of God is not to be compared in its effect with that one man's sin; for the judicial action, following on the one offence, resulted in a verdict of condemnation, but the act of grace, following on so many misdeeds, resulted in a verdict of acquittal. [17]If, by the wrongdoing of one man, death established its reign through that one man, much more shall those who in far greater measure receive grace and the gift of righteousness live and reign through the one man, Jesus Christ.

[18]It follows, then, that as the result of one misdeed was condemnation for all people, so the result of one righteous act is acquittal and life for all. [19]For as through the disobedience of one man many were made sinners, so through the obedience of one man many will be made righteous.

[20]Law intruded into this process to multiply law-breaking. But where sin was multiplied, grace immeasurably exceeded it, [21]in order that, as sin established its reign by way of death, so God's grace might establish its reign in righteousness, and result in eternal life through Jesus Christ our Lord.

Baptism into Christ

6 WHAT are we to say, then? Shall we persist in sin, so that there may be all the more grace? [2]Certainly not! We died to sin: how can we live in it any

longer? [3]Have you forgotten that when we were baptized into union with Christ Jesus we were baptized into his death? [4]By that baptism into his death we were buried with him, in order that, as Christ was raised from the dead by the glorious power of the Father, so also we might set out on a new life.

[5]For if we have become identified with him in his death, we shall also be identified with him in his resurrection. [6]We know that our old humanity has been crucified with Christ, for the destruction of the sinful self, so that we may no longer be slaves to sin, [7]because death cancels the claims of sin. [8]But if we thus died with Christ, we believe that we shall also live with him, [9]knowing as we do that Christ, once raised from the dead, is never to die again: he is no longer under the dominion of death. [10]When he died, he died to sin, once for all, and now that he lives, he lives to God. [11]In the same way you must regard yourselves as dead to sin and alive to God, in union with Christ Jesus.

[12]Therefore sin must no longer reign in your mortal body, exacting obedience to the body's desires. [13]You must no longer put any part of it at sin's disposal, as an implement for doing wrong. Put yourselves instead at the disposal of God; think of yourselves as raised from death to life, and yield your bodies to God as implements for doing right. [14]Sin shall no longer be your master, for you are no longer under law, but under grace.

[15]What then? Are we to sin, because we are not under law but under grace? Of course not! [16]You know well enough that if you bind yourselves to obey a master, you are slaves of the master you obey; and this is true whether the master is sin and the outcome death, or obedience and the outcome righteousness. [17]Once you were slaves of sin, but now, thank God, you have yielded wholehearted obedience to that pattern of teaching to which you were made subject; [18]emancipated from sin, you have become slaves of righteousness [19](to use language that suits your human weakness). As you once yielded your bodies to the service of impurity and lawlessness, making for moral anarchy, so now you must yield them to the service of righteousness, making for a holy life.

[20]When you were slaves of sin, you were free from the control of righteousness. [21]And what gain did that bring you? Things that now make you ashamed, for their end is death. [22]But now, freed from the commands of sin and bound to the service of God, you have gains that lead to holiness, and the end is eternal life. [23]For sin pays a wage, and the wage is death, but God gives freely, and his gift is eternal life in union with Christ Jesus our Lord.

The Role of the Law

7 You must be aware, my friends—I am sure you have some knowledge of law—that a person is subject to the law only so long as he is alive. ²For example, a married woman is by law bound to her husband while he lives; but if the husband dies, she is released from the marriage bond. ³If, therefore, in her husband's lifetime she gives herself to another man, she will be held to be an adulteress; but if the husband dies, she is free of the law and she does not commit adultery by giving herself to another man. ⁴So too, my friends, through the body of Christ you died to the law and were set free to give yourselves to another, to him who rose from the dead so that we may bear fruit for God. ⁵While we lived on the level of mere human nature, the sinful passions evoked by the law were active in our bodies, and bore fruit for death. ⁶But now, having died to that which held us bound, we are released from the law, to serve God in a new way, the way of the spirit in contrast to the old way of a written code.

⁷What follows? Is the law identical with sin? Of course not! Yet had it not been for the law I should never have become acquainted with sin. For example, I should never have known what it was to covet, if the law had not said, 'You shall not covet.' ⁸Through that commandment sin found its opportunity, and produced in me all kinds of wrong desires. In the absence of law, sin is devoid of life. ⁹There was a time when, in the absence of law, I was fully alive; but when the commandment came, sin sprang to life and I died. ¹⁰The commandment which should have led to life proved in my experience to lead to death, ¹¹because in the commandment sin found its opportunity to seduce me, and through the commandment killed me. ¹²So then, the law in itself is holy and the commandment is holy and just and good.

¹³Are we therefore to say that this good thing caused my death? Of course not! It was sin that killed me, and thereby sin exposed its true character; it used a good thing to bring about my death, and so, through the commandment, sin became more sinful than ever. ¹⁴We know that the law is spiritual; but I am not: I am unspiritual, sold as a slave to sin. ¹⁵I do not even acknowledge my own actions as mine, for what I do is not what I want to do, but what I detest. ¹⁶But if what I do is against my will, then clearly I agree with the law and hold it to be admirable. ¹⁷This means that it is no longer I who perform the action, but sin that dwells in me. ¹⁸For I know that nothing good dwells in me—my unspiritual self, I mean—for though the will to do good is there, the ability to effect it is not. ¹⁹The good which I want to do, I fail to do; but what I do is the wrong which is against

my will; ²⁰and if what I do is against my will, clearly it is no longer I who am the agent, but sin that has its dwelling in me.

²¹I discover this principle, then: that when I want to do right, only wrong is within my reach. ²²In my inmost self I delight in the law of God, ²³but I perceive in my outward actions a different law, fighting against the law that my mind approves, and making me a prisoner under the law of sin which controls my conduct. ²⁴Wretched creature that I am, who is there to rescue me from this state of death? ²⁵Who but God? Thanks be to him through Jesus Christ our Lord! To sum up then: left to myself I serve God's law with my mind, but with my unspiritual nature I serve the law of sin.

Life through the Spirit

8 It follows that there is now no condemnation for those who are united with Christ Jesus. ²In Christ Jesus the life-giving law of the Spirit has set you free from the law of sin and death. ³ What the law could not do, because human weakness robbed it of all potency, God has done: by sending his own Son in the likeness of our sinful nature and to deal with sin, he has passed judgement against sin within that very nature, ⁴so that the commandment of the law may find fulfilment in us, whose conduct is no longer controlled by the old nature, but by the Spirit.

^{5–6}Those who live on the level of the old nature have their outlook formed by it, and that spells death; but those who live on the level of the spirit have the spiritual outlook, and that is life and peace. ⁷For the outlook of the unspiritual nature is enmity with God; it is not subject to the law of God and indeed it cannot be; ⁸those who live under its control cannot please God.

⁹But you do not live like that. You live by the spirit, since God's Spirit dwells in you; and anyone who does not posses the Spirit of Christ does not belong to Christ. ¹⁰But if Christ is in you, then although the body is dead because of sin, yet the Spirit is your life because you have been justified. ¹¹Moreover, if the Spirit of him who raised Jesus from the dead dwells in you, then the God who raised Christ Jesus from the dead will also give new life to your mortal bodies through his indwelling Spirit.

¹²It follows, my friends, that our old nature has no claim on us; we are not obliged to live in that way. ¹³If you do so, you must die. But if by the Spirit you put to death the base pursuits of the body, then you will live.

¹⁴For all who are led by the Spirit of God are sons of God. ¹⁵The Spirit

you have received is not a spirit of slavery, leading you back into a life of fear, but a Spirit of adoption, enabling us to cry "Abba! Father!" [16]The Spirit of God affirms to our spirit that we are God's children; [17]and if children, then heirs, heirs of God and fellow-heirs with Christ; but we must share his sufferings if we are also to share his glory.

[18]For I reckon that the sufferings we now endure bear no comparison with the glory, as yet unrevealed, which is in store for us. [19]The created universe is waiting with eager expectation for God's sons to be revealed. [20]It was made subject to frustration, not of its own choice but by the will of him who subjected it, yet with the hope [21]that the universe itself is to be freed from the shackles of mortality and is to enter upon the glorious liberty of the children of God. [22]Up to the present, as we know, the whole created universe in all its parts groans as if in the pangs of childbirth. [23]What is more, we also, to whom the Spirit is given as the first fruits of the harvest to come, are groaning inwardly while we look forward eagerly to our adoption, our liberation from mortality. [24]It was with this hope that we were saved. Now to see something is no longer to hope: why hope for what is already seen? [25]But if we hope for something we do not yet see, then we look forward to it eagerly and with patience.

[26]In the same way the Spirit comes to the aid of our weakness. We do not even know how we ought to pray, but through our inarticulate groans the Spirit himself is pleading for us, [27]and God who searches our inmost being knows what the Spirit means, because he pleads for God's people as God himself wills; [28]and in everything, as we know, he co-operates for good with those who love God and are called according to his purpose. [29]For those whom God knew before ever they were, he also ordained to share the likeness of his Son, so that he might be the eldest among a large family of brothers; [30]and those whom he foreordained, he also called, and those whom he called he also justified, and those whom he justified he also glorified.

[31]With all this in mind, what are we to say? If God is on our side, who is against us? [32]He did not spare his own Son, but gave him up for us all; how can he fail to lavish every other gift upon us? [33]Who will bring a charge against those whom God has chosen? Not God, who acquits! [34]Who will pronounce judgement? Not Christ, who died, or rather rose again; not Christ, who is at God's right hand and pleads our cause! [35]Then what can separate us from the love of Christ? Can affliction or hardship? Can persecution, hunger, nakedness, danger, or sword? [36]"We are being done to death for your sake all day long," as scripture says; "we have been treated like sheep for slaughter"—[37]and yet, throughout it all, over-

whelming victory is ours through him who loved us. [38]For I am convinced that there is nothing in death or life, in the realm of spirits or superhuman powers, in the world as it is or the world as it shall be, in the forces of the universe, [39]in heights or depths—nothing in all creation that can separate us from the love of God in Christ Jesus our Lord.

St. Paul, First Letter to the Corinthians

The Resurrection of the Dead

15 AND now, my friends, I must remind you of the gospel that I preached to you; the gospel which you received, on which you have taken your stand, [2]and which is now bringing you salvation. Remember the terms in which I preached the gospel to you—for I assume that you hold it fast and that your conversion was not in vain.

[3]First and foremost, I handed on to you the tradition I had received: that Christ died for our sins, in accordance with the scriptures; [4]that he was buried; that he was raised to life on the third day, in accordance with the scriptures; [5]and that he appeared to Cephas, and afterwards to the Twelve. [6]Then he appeared to over five hundred of our brothers at once, most of whom are still alive, though some have died. [7]Then he appeared to James, and afterwards to all the apostles.

[8]Last of all he appeared to me too; it was like a sudden, abnormal birth. [9]For I am the least of the apostles, indeed not fit to be called an apostle, because I had persecuted the church of God. [10]However, by God's grace I am what I am, and his grace to me has not proved vain; in my labours I have out-done them all—not I, indeed, but the grace of God working with me. [11]But no matter whether it was I or they! This is what we all proclaim, and this is what you believed.

[12]Now if this is what we proclaim, that Christ was raised from the dead, how can some of you say there is no resurrection of the dead? [13]If there is no resurrection, then Christ was not raised; [14]and if Christ was not raised, then our gospel is null and void, and so too is your faith; [15]and we turn out to have given false evidence about God, because we bore witness that he raised Christ to life, whereas, if the dead are not raised, he did not raise him. [16]For if the dead are not raised, it follows that Christ was not raised; [17]and if Christ was not raised, your faith has nothing to it and you are still

in your old state of sin. [18]It follows also that those who have died within Christ's fellowship are utterly lost. [19]If it is for this life only that Christ has given us hope, we of all people are most to be pitied.

[20]But the truth is, Christ was raised to life—the first fruits of the harvest of the dead. [21]For since it was a man who brought death into the world, a man also brought resurrection of the dead. [22]As in Adam all die, so in Christ all will be brought to life; [23]but each in proper order: Christ the first fruits, and afterwards, at his coming, those who belong to Christ. [24]Then comes the end, when he delivers up the kingdom to God the Father, after deposing every sovereignty, authority, and power. [25]For he is destined to reign until God has put all enemies under his feet; [26]and the last enemy to be deposed is death. [27]Scripture says, "He has put all things in subjection under his feet." But in saying "all things," it clearly means to exclude God who made all things subject to him; [28]and when all things are subject to him, then the Son himself will also be made subject to God who made all things subject to him, and thus God will be all in all.

[29]Again, there are those who receive baptism on behalf of the dead. What do you suppose they are doing? If the dead are not raised to life at all, what do they mean by being baptized on their behalf?

[30]And why do we ourselves face danger hour by hour? [31]Every day I die: I swear it by my pride in you, my friends—for in Christ Jesus our Lord I am proud of you. [32]With no more than human hopes, what would have been the point of my fighting those wild beasts at Ephesus? If the dead are never raised to life, "Let us eat and drink, for tomorrow we die."

[33]Make no mistake: "Bad company ruins good character." [34]Wake up, be sober, and stop sinning: some of you have no knowledge of God—to your shame I say it.

[35]But, you may ask, how are the dead raised? In what kind of body? [36]What stupid questions! The seed you sow does not come to life unless it has first died; [37]and what you sow is not the body that shall be, but a bare grain, of wheat perhaps, or something else; [38]and God gives it the body of his choice, each seed its own particular body. [39]All flesh is not the same: there is human flesh, flesh of beasts, of birds, and of fishes—all different. [40]There are heavenly bodies and earthly bodies; and the splendour of the heavenly bodies is one thing, the splendour of the earthly another. [41]The sun has a splendour of its own, the moon another splendour, and the stars yet another; and one star differs from another in brightness. [42]So it is with the resurrection of the dead: what is sown as a perishable thing is raised imperishable. [43]Sown in humiliation, it is raised in glory; sown in weak-

ness, it is raised in power; [44]sown a physical body, it is raised a spiritual body.

If there is such a thing as a physical body, there is also a spiritual body. [45]It is in this sense that scripture says, "The first man, Adam, became a living creature," whereas the last Adam has become a life-giving spirit. [46]Observe, the spiritual does not come first; the physical body comes first, and then the spiritual. [47]The first man is from earth, made of dust: the second man is from heaven. [48]The man made of dust is the pattern of all who are made of dust, and the heavenly man is the pattern of all the heavenly. [49]As we have worn the likeness of the man made of dust, so we shall wear the likeness of the heavenly man.

[50]What I mean, my friends, is this: flesh and blood can never possess the kingdom of God, the perishable cannot possess the imperishable. [51]Listen! I will unfold a mystery:we shall not all die, but we shall all be changed [52]in a flash, in the twinkling of an eye, at the last trumpet-call. For the trumpet will sound, and the dead will rise imperishable, and we shall be changed. [53]This perishable body must be clothed with the imperishable, and what is mortal with immortality. [54]And when this perishable body has been clothed with the imperishable and our mortality has been clothed with immortality, then the saying of scripture will come true: "Death is swallowed up; victory is won!" [55]"O Death, where is your victory? O Death, where is your sting?" [56]The sting of death is sin, and sin gains its power from the law. [57]But thanks be to God! He gives us victory through our Lord Jesus Christ.

• • •

Women and Public Worship

11   [2]I commend you for always keeping me in mind, and maintaining the tradition I handed on to you. [3]But I wish you to understand that, while every man has Christ for his head, a woman's head is man, as Christ's head is God. [4]A man who keeps his head covered when he prays or prophesies brings shame on his head; [5]but a woman brings shame on her head if she prays or prophesies bareheaded; it is as bad as if her head were shaved. [6]If a woman does not cover her head she might as well have her hair cut off; but if it is a disgrace for her to be cropped and shaved, then she should cover her head. [7]A man must not cover his head, because man is the image of God, and the mirror of his glory, whereas a woman reflects the glory of man. [8]For man did not originally spring from woman, but

woman was made out of man; [9]and man was not created for woman's sake, but woman for the sake of man; [10]and therefore a woman must have the sign of her authority on her head, out of regard for the angels. [11]Yet in the Lord's fellowship woman is as essential to man as man to woman. [12]If woman was made out of man, it is through woman that man now comes to be; and God is the source of all.

[13]Judge for yourselves: is it fitting for a woman to pray to God bare-headed? [14]Does not nature herself teach you that while long hair disgraces a man, [15]it is a woman's glory? For her hair was given as a covering.

[16]And if anyone still insists on arguing, there is no such custom among us, or in any of the congregations of God's people.

• • •

Islam

I wanted to represent an Islamic view of human nature, since Islam is the second world religion in terms of numbers, but it seemed difficult to select relevant passages from the Qur'an, so I have chosen a modern piece of writing instead. Although this piece dates from the twentieth century, it seems appropriate for several reasons to include it at this stage in this anthology, between the thought of the ancient and the early modern world.

Islamic civilization—not just the religion, but science and philosophy—enjoyed an immense flowering in the medieval period, especially between the ninth and thirteenth centuries. Islamic scholarship led the Christian West in many respects, and transmitted important knowledge to it. Intercultural comparisons are dangerously controversial, but contemporary Islamic thought seems rather like that of medieval Christianity—the "Age of Faith"—in assuming as an unquestionable premise the authority of a certain religious tradition based on a particular "revelation." The thought of scholarly ayatullahs such as Murtaza Mutahhari could be compared with that of medieval Christian philosophers such as St. Thomas Aquinas (1224–1274), in that both deploy wide knowledge and philosophical acumen to expound and defend what they see as the essential truths of their tradition.

Ayatullah Mutahhari (1920–1979) was one of the foremost

teachers and leaders of Islamic consciousness in Iran. He was a close associate of Ayatullah Khomeini, and an important figure in the events leading up to the Iranian revolution of 1978. Shortly afterward he was assassinated in a factional power struggle.

Readers should be aware that there was a schism in early Muslim history: Iranian Muslims follow the minority Shi'ite tradition, whereas the majority of world Muslims are Sunnis. Mutahhari cannot represent Islam as a whole, any more than any one post-Biblical figure can represent Christianity. But he does give a clear and readily intelligible exposition of a philosophical approach to religious faith, rooted in an understanding of human nature.

Ayatullah Murtaza Mutahhari, "Man and Faith"

Man and Animal

In the name of God, the Merciful, the Compassionate

Man is a species of animal and thus shares many features with other animals. But many differences distinguish man from animals, and grant him a special virtue, an elevation, that leaves him unrivaled. The basic difference between man and the other animals, the touchstone of his humanity, the source of what have come to be known as human civilization and culture, is the presence of insights and beliefs. Animals in general can perceive themselves and the external world and strive to attain their desires and objects in the light of their awareness and cognition. The same holds true of man, but he differs from the rest of the animals in the scope, extent, and breadth of his awareness and cognitions and in the level to which his desires and objects rise. This grants man a special virtue and elevation and separates him from the rest of the animals.

Awareness and Desire in Animals

First, the animal's awareness of the world comes solely through its external senses and is, accordingly, external and superficial; it does not reach

Ayatullah Murtaza Mutahhari, *Fundamentals of Islamic Thought: God, Man and the Universe* © Mizan Press 1985.

into the interiors and internal relationships of things. Second, it is individual and particular; it enjoys nothing of universality and generality. Third, it is localized, limited to the animal's environment. Fourth, it is immediate, confined to the present, divorced from past and future. The animal is not aware of its own history or that of the world and does not consider or relate its endeavors to the future.

The animal is thus confined in a fourfold prison. If it should perchance emerge, it does so not with awareness, by intelligence and choice, but captive to the compulsions of nature, instinctually, without awareness or intelligence.

The level of the animal's desires and objects is also limited. First, it is material, not rising above eating, drinking, sleeping, playing, nesting, and copulating. For the animal there is no question of abstract desires and objects, moral values, and so on. Second, it is private and individual, related to itself or at the most to its mate and offspring. Third, it is localized and related to its environment. Fourth, it is immediate and related to the present. The animal thus lives within certain confines in this respect as well.

If the animal pursues an object or moves toward an end that is beyond these confines, for instance, if it shows concern for the species rather than the individual or for the future rather than the present, as do such social animals as the honeybee, this behavior arises unconsciously and instinctually, by the direct command of the power that created it and administers the world.

Awareness and Desire in Man

Whether in the area of awareness, insights, and cognitions or desires and objects, the human domain reaches much further and higher than that of the animals. Human awareness and cognition traverse the exterior bounds of objects and phenomena to penetrate into their interiors, their essences and identities, their interrelationships and interdependencies, and the necessities governing them. Human awareness does not remain imprisoned within the limits of locale and place, nor does it remain chained to its moment; it journeys through both time and space. Accordingly, man grows aware both of what is beyond his environment and of his own past and future, discovering his own past history and that of the universe—the histories of the earth, the heavens, the mountains, the seas, the planets, plants and other animals—and contemplating the future to the far horizons. Beyond even this, man sends his thought racing after things limitless and eternal and gains a knowledge of some of them. One who transcends a cognition of the individual and the particular discovers general laws and universal truths that embrace the whole world. Thus, he establishes his dominion over nature.

Man can also attain an elevated level from the standpoint of desires and objects. Man is a being that seeks values and aspires to virtues and ideals that are not material or utilitarian, that are not restricted to self or at most to mate and offspring, that are general and inclusive and embrace the whole of humanity, that are unconfined to a particular environment, locale, or time period. Man is so devoted to ideals and beliefs that he may at times place them above all else and put service to others and their comfort ahead of his own comfort. It is as if the thorn that has pierced another's foot has pierced his own foot, or even his own eye. He commiserates with others; he rejoices in their joy and grieves at their grief. He may grow so attached to his sacred beliefs and ideals that he readily sacrifices to them not only his interests but his whole life and existence. The human dimension of civilization, the spirit of civilization, grows out of just such uniquely human feelings and desires.

The Touchstone of Man's Distinctiveness

Man's breadth of insight into the universe stems from humanity's collective efforts amassed and evolved over the centuries. This insight, expressed through special criteria, rules, and logical procedures, has come to be known as "science." Science in its most general sense means the sum total of human contemplations on the universe (including philosophy), the product of the collective efforts of humanity within a special system of logic.

The elevated and ideal aptitudes of humanity are born of its faith, belief, and attachment to certain realities in the universe that are both extraindividual, or general and inclusive, and extramaterial, or unrelated to advantage or profit. Such beliefs and attachments are in turn born of certain world views and cosmologies given to humanity by prophets of God or by certain philosophers who sought to present a kind of thought that would conduce to belief and idealism. As these elevated, ideal, supra-animal aptitudes in man find an ideational and credal infrastructure, they are designated "faith" (*iman*).

It is therefore my contention that the central difference between man and the other animals, the touchstone of man's humanity, on which humanity depends, consists in science and faith.

Much has been said about what distinguishes man from the other animals. Although some have denied there is any basic difference between man and other animals, asserting that the difference in awareness and cognition is quantitative or at the most qualitative, but not essential, these thinkers have passed over all the wonders and glories that have drawn the great philosophers of East and West to the question of cognition in man. They regard man as an animal entirely, from the standpoint of desires and objects, not differing from the animals in the least in this respect [Hobbes].

Others think that to have a psyche makes the difference; that is, they believe that only man has a psyche, or anima, that other animals have neither feelings nor appetites, know neither pain nor pleasure, that they are soulless machines only resembling animate beings. They think that the true definition of man is "the animate being" [Descautes].

Other thinkers who do not consider man the only animate being in the universe but maintain basic distinctions between man and the rest of the animals may be grouped according to which one of man's distinguishing features they have dwelt upon. They have defined man as the reasoning animal, the seeker after the Absolute, the unfinished, the idealist, the seeker after values, the metaphysical animal, the insatiable, the indeterminate, the committed and responsible, the provident, the free and empowered, the rebel, the social animal, the seeker after order, the seeker after beauty, the seeker after justice, the one facing two ways, the lover, the answerable, the conscientious, the one with two hearts, the creator, the solitary, the agitated, the devotee of creeds, the toolmaker, the seeker after the beyond, the visionary, the ideal, and the gateway to ideas.

Clearly, each of these distinctions is correct in its turn, but if we wish to advance a definition that comprehends all the basic differences, we can do no better than to speak of science and faith and to say that man is the animal distinguished from the other animals by the two features, "science" and "faith."

Relationship between Humanity and Animality

Those features man shares with the animal plus those features that distinguish him from the animal result in man having two lives, the animal life and the human life—in other words, the material life and the life of culture. What relationship exists between man's animality and his humanity, between his animal life and his human life, his material life and his cultural and spiritual life? Is one the basis and the other a reflection of it? Is one the infrastructure and the other the superstructure? Since we are considering this question from a sociological, not a psychological

point of view, we may express it this way: Among social structures is the
economic structure, related to production and production relations, the
principle and infrastructure? Do the remaining social structures, especially those in which man's humanity is manifested, all constitute something derivative, a superstructure, a reflection of the economic structure?
Have science, philosophy, literature, religion, law, morals, and art at all
times been manifestations of economic realities, having no substantive
reality?

This sociological discussion automatically leads to a psychological
conclusion and likewise to a philosophical argument that concerns
humanity, its objective and substantive realities—the question of what
today is called humanism. This conclusion is that man's humanity has no
substantive reality, that only his animality has any substantive reality.
Thus, any basic distinction between man and animal is denied.

According to this theory, not only is the substantive reality of human
beliefs denied, including the beliefs in truth, goodness, beauty, and God,
but the substantive reality of the desire to know the reality of the universe
from a human viewpoint is denied in that no viewpoint can be simply a
"viewpoint" and disinterested, but every viewpoint must reflect a particular material tendency. Things cannot be otherwise. Curiously, some
schools of thought offer this view and speak of humanity and humanism
in the same breath!

The truth is that the course of man's evolution begins with animality
and finds its culmination in humanity. This principle holds true for individual and society alike: Man at the outset of his existence is a material
body; through an essential evolutionary movement, he is transformed into
spirit or a spiritual substance. What is called the human spirit is born in
the lap of the body; it is there that it evolves and attains independence.
Man's animality amounts to a nest in which man's humanity grows and
evolves. It is a property of evolution that the more the organism evolves,
the more independent, self-subsistent, and governing of its own environment it becomes. The more man's humanity evolves, in the individual or
in society, the more it steps toward independence and governance over the
other aspects of his being. An evolved human individual has gained a relative ascendancy over his inner and outer environments. The evolved
individual is the one who has been freed of dominance by the inner and
outer environments, but depends upon belief and faith.

The evolution of society precisely corresponds to the evolution of the
spirit in the lap of the body or the evolution of the individual's humanity
in the lap of his animality. The germ of human society is economic structures; the cultural and ideal aspects of society amount to the spirit of soci-

ety. Just as there is an interaction between body and spirit, so there is one between the spirit and the body of society, that is, between its ideal structures and its material ones. Just as the evolution of the individual leads to greater freedom, autonomy, and sovereignty of the spirit, so does the evolution of society. That is, the more evolved human society becomes, the greater the autonomy of its cultural life and the sovereignty of that life over its material life. Man of the future is the cultural animal; he is the man of belief, faith, and method, not the man of stomach and waistline.

Human society, however, is not moving inexorably and directly to the perfection of human values. At every temporal stage, it is not necessarily one step more advanced than at the preceding stage. It is possible for humanity to pass through an era of social life in which, for all its scientific and technical progress, it declines with respect to human ideal values, as is said today of the humanity of our present century. This idea of human social evolution means rather that humanity is progressing in the sum total of its movements, whether material or ideal, but the movement sometimes twists to the right or left, sometimes stops, or occasionally even reverses itself. However, on the whole, it is a progressive, evolutionary movement. Thus, future man is the cultural animal, not the economic animal; future man is the man of belief and faith, not the man of stomach and waistline.

According to this theory, the evolution of the human aspect of man (because of its substantive reality) keeps step with, or rather anticipates, the evolution of the tools of production. It gradually reduces his dependency on and susceptibility to the natural and social environments and augments his freedom (which is equivalent to his dependence on belief, ideals, principle, and ideology), as well as his influence upon the natural and social environments. In the future, man will attain to ever more perfect spiritual freedom, that is, ever greater independence or ever greater dependence upon faith, belief, and ideology. Past man, while enjoying fewer of the blessings of nature and of his own being, was more captive to nature and to his own animality. But future man, while enjoying more of the blessings of nature and of his own being, will be proportionately freer from the captivities of nature and of his own animal potentials and better able to govern himself and nature.

According to this view, the human reality, despite having appeared along with and in the lap of animal and material evolution, is by no means a shadow, reflection, or function of these. It is itself an independent, evolving reality. Just as it is influenced by the material aspects of being, it influences them. It, not the evolution of the tools of production, determines man's ultimate destiny, his substantive cultural evolution, and his substantive reality. This substantive reality of the humanity of man keeps him in motion and evolves the tools of production along with the other concerns of life. The tools of production do not evolve of themselves, and man's humanity is not changed and transformed like the tools defining a system of production, such that it would be spoken of as evolving because it defined an evolving system of production.

Science and Faith

Relationship of Science and Faith

Now let us see what relationship to each other these two pillars or aspects of humanity bear, or can bear.

In the Christian world, owing to some textual corruptions in the Old Testament (the Torah), the idea of the opposition of science and faith has become widespread, an idea that has cost both of them dearly. This idea has its roots chiefly in the Book of Genesis. In Genesis 2:16–17, we find, regarding Adam, paradise, and the forbidden tree: "[The LORD God] told the man, 'You may eat from every tree in the garden, but not from the tree of the knowledge of good and evil; for on the day that you eat from it, you will certainly die.' " In Genesis 3:1–8, it is said:

> The Serpent was more crafty than any wild creature that the LORD God had made. He said to the woman, "Is it true that God has forbidden you to eat from any tree in the garden?" The woman answered the serpent, "We may eat the fruit of any tree in the garden, except for the tree in the middle of the garden; God has forbidden us either to eat or to touch the fruit of that; if we do, we shall die." The serpent said, "Of course you will not die. God knows that as soon as you eat it, your eyes will be opened and you will be like gods knowing both good and evil." When the woman saw that the fruit of the tree was good to eat, and that it was pleasing to the eye and tempting to contemplate, she took some and ate it. She also gave her husband some and he ate it. Then the eyes of both of them were opened and they discovered that they were naked; so they stitched fig-leaves together and made themselves loincloths.

In Genesis 3:23, it is said:

> [The LORD God] said, "The man has become like one of us, knowing good and evil; what if he now reaches out his hand and takes fruit from the tree of life also, eats it and lives forever?"

According to this conception of man and God, of consciousness and rebellion, God's command (*din*) is that man must not know good and evil, not grow conscious—the forbidden tree is the tree of consciousness. Man, in his rebellion, his mutiny, against God's command (his balking at the teachings of the revealed laws and prophets), attains consciousness and knowledge and so is driven from God's paradise. According to this conception, all satanic suggestions are the suggestions of consciousness; therefore, the suggestor, Satan, is reason itself.

To us Muslims, who have studied the Qur'an, God taught Adam all the names (realities) and then commanded the angels to prostrate themselves before him. Satan was expelled from the court for not prostrating before this viceregent of God, conscious of realities. And the *sunna* has taught us that the forbidden tree was that of greed, avidity, something of this sort, that is, something connected with the animality of Adam, not with his humanity, that Satan the suggestor always suggests things contrary to reason but conforming to the passions of the animal ego, and that what manifests Satan within man's being is the ego that incites to evil, not the Adamic reason. For us who are thus schooled, what we see in Genesis is quite astonishing.

It is this conception that divides the last fifteen hundred years of European history into the Age of Faith and the Age of Reason and sets faith and science at odds. But the history of Islamic civilization is divisible into the Age of Flowering, or the Age of Science and Faith, and the Age of Decline, in which science and faith together have declined. We Muslims must eschew this wrong conception that has inflicted irreparable injuries on science and on faith, indeed on humanity; we must not take this opposition of science and faith for granted.

Let us now proceed analytically and ask in a scholarly fashion whether these two aspects or bases of humanity actually each pertain to a certain era. Is man condemned ever to remain half-human, to have only half his humanity in a given era? Is he forever condemned to one of these two species of misfortune: the misfortunes arising from ignorance and the misfortunes arising from want of faith?

Every faith is inevitably based on a special mode of thought and a special conception of the universe and of being. Many conceptions and interpretations of the universe, although they can serve as bases for faith and devotion, are inconsistent with logical and scientific principles and so necessarily deserve rejection. But is there a mode of thought, a kind of conception and interpretation of the universe and of being, that both draws support from the region of science, philosophy, and logic and can be a firm foundation for a felicitous faith? If such a conception, mode of thought, or worldview exists, then it will be clear that man is not condemned to the misfortunes arising from either ignorance or want of faith.

One can address the relationship of science and faith from either of two standpoints. One standpoint is whether an interpretation or conception exists that is both productive of faith and idealism and supported by logic. Are all the ideas that science and philosophy impart to us contrary to faith, devotion, hope, and optimism? (This is a question that I will take up later in discussing the idea of a worldview.)

The other standpoint is that of the influences upon man of science on the one hand and faith on the other. Does science call us to one thing and faith to another, and opposed, thing? Does science seek to shape us one way and faith another, opposed, way? Does our science carry us in one direction and faith in another? Or do science and faith fulfill and complement one another? Does science shape half of us and faith the other half, harmoniously?

Science gives us enlightenment and power; faith gives us love, hope, and ardor. Science makes instruments; faith constructs purposes. Science gives speed; faith gives direction. Science is power; faith is benevolence. Science shows what is; faith inspires insight into what must be done. Science is the outer revolution; faith is the inner revolution. Science makes the universe the human universe; faith makes the psyche the psyche of humanity. Science expands man's being horizontally; faith conveys him upward. Science shapes nature; faith shapes man. Both science and faith empower man, but science gives a power of discrimination, and faith gives a power of integration. Both science and faith are beauty, but science is the beauty of the reason, and faith is the beauty of the spirit. Science is the beauty of thought, and faith is the beauty of feeling. Both science and faith give man security, but science gives outward security, and faith gives inward security. Science gives security against the onslaught of illness, floods, earthquakes, storms; faith, against worry, loneliness, feelings of helplessness, feelings of futility. Science brings the world into greater harmony with man, and faith brings man into greater harmony with himself.

• • •

Noninterchangeability of Science and Faith

Science cannot replace faith to give—besides illumination and power—love and hope. It cannot raise the level of our desires. Although it can help us attain objects and goals, to follow the road to them, it cannot take from us those objects, aspirations, and desires that by nature and instinct turn on individuality and self-interest and give us in their place objects and aspirations that turn on love and on ideal and spiritual bonds. Although it is a tool in our hands, it cannot transform our essence and identity. Likewise, faith cannot replace science, to enable us to understand nature, discover its laws, or learn about ourselves.

Historical experiences have shown that the separation of science from faith has brought about irremediable harm. Faith must be known in the light of science; faith must be kept far from superstition in the light of science. When science is removed from faith, faith is deformed into petrification and blind fanaticism; it turns on its own axis and goes nowhere. When there is no science and true knowledge, the faith of an ignorant believer becomes an instrument in the hands of the clever charlatans exemplified in early Islam by the Kharijites and seen in various forms in later times.

Conversely, science without faith is a sword in the hands of a maniac, or else a lamp at midnight in the hands of a thief, so he can pick out the choicest goods. Thus, the scientifically informed person of today without faith does not differ in the least from the ignoramus without faith of yesterday in the nature and essence of his behavior. What difference is there between the Churchills, Johnsons, Nixons, and Stalins of today and the Ghengises and Attilas of yesterday?

But, it might be said, is science not both light and power? Do the light and power of science not only apply to the external world, but also illuminate and reveal to us our inner world and so empower us to change it? If science can shape both the world and man, it can perform both its own function (world shaping) and that of faith (man shaping). The reply is, this is all correct, but the power of science is instrumental—that is, dependent upon man's will and command. In whatever area man wishes to carry out something, he can do it better with the tool of science. Thus, science is man's best aid in attaining the objects he has chosen, in traversing the roads he has decided to follow.

But when man puts the instrument to work, he already has an object in view; instruments are always employed in pursuit of objects. Where has he found these objects? Because man is animal by nature and human by acquisition, that is, because his human potentialities must be gradually nurtured in the light of faith, by nature he moves toward his natural, animal, individual, material, self-interested objects and employs his instruments accordingly. Therefore, man needs a power not among his own instruments and objects but that can rather impel man as an instrument in its own direction. He needs a power that can detonate him from within and activate his hidden potentialities. He needs a power that can produce a revolution in his heart and give him a new direction. This is not accomplished by science, by discovery of the laws governing nature and man. It is born of the sanctification and exaltation of certain values in one's spirit, which values in turn are born of a range of elevated aptitudes in man, which result further, from a particular conception and way of thinking about the universe and man that one can acquire neither in the laboratory nor from syllogism and deduction.

History shows the consequences of disjoining science and faith. Where faith has been, and science not, individuals' humanitarian efforts have produced no great effect—at times, no *good* effect. Sometimes they have given rise to fanaticisms, stagnations, and ruinous conflicts. Human history is filled with such events. Where science has been, with the place of faith left empty, as in some contemporary societies, all the power of science has been expended on selfishness, egoism, acquisitiveness, ambition, exploitation, subjugation, deceit, and guile.

• • •

Effects and Advantages of Religious Faith

Without ideals, aspirations, and faith, man can neither live a sane life nor accomplish anything useful or fruitful for humanity and human civilization. One lacking ideals and faith becomes either selfish, never emerging from his shell of private interests, or a wavering, bemused being who does not know his own duty in life, in moral and social questions. Man constantly confronts moral and social questions, and must necessarily respond. If one is attached to a teaching, a belief, a faith, one's duty is clear; but if no teaching or method has clarified one's duty, one lives ever in a state of irresolution, drawn sometimes this way, sometimes that, never in balance. So without any doubt, one must attach oneself to a teaching and an ideal.

Only religious faith, however, can make man truly "faithful"—can make faith, belief, and principle dominate selfishness and egoism, can create a kind of devotion and surrender in the individual such that he does not doubt the least point the teaching advances, and can render this belief something precious to him, to the extent that life without it is hollow and meaningless and that he will defend it with zeal and fervor.

Aptitudes to religious faith prompt man to struggle against his natural, individual inclinations and sometimes to sacrifice his reputation and very being for the sake of faith. This grows possible when his ideal takes on an aspect of sanctity and comes to rule his being completely. Only the power of religion can sanctify ideals and effect their rule in its fullest force over man.

Sometimes individuals make sacrifices and relinquish their fortunes, reputations, or lives not for ideals and religious belief but driven by obsessions, vindictiveness, and revengefulness, in short as a violent reaction to feelings of stress and oppression. We see this sort of thing in various parts of the world. The difference between a religious ideal and a nonreligious one is that when religious belief appears and sanctifies an ideal, sacrifices take place naturally and with complete contentment. There is a difference between an act accomplished in contentment and faith—a kind of choice—and an act accomplished under the impact of obsessions and disturbing internal stresses—a kind of explosion.

If man's world view is a purely materialistic one founded on the restriction of reality to sense objects, any sort of social and humane idealism will prove contrary to the sensible realities through which man then feels related to the world.

What results from a sensual world-view is egoism, not idealism. If idealism is founded upon a world-view of which it is not the logical consequence, it amounts to nothing more than fantasy. That is, man must figuratively make a separate world of the realities existing within him, from his imagination, and be content with them. But if idealism stems from religion, it rests on a kind of world-view whose logical consequence is to live by social ideals and aspirations. Religious faith is a loving bond between man and the universe, or to put it differently, is a harmony between man and the universal ideals of being. Nonreligious faith and aspirations, on the other hand, constitute a kind of "severance" from the universe and an imaginary construction of a world of one's own that is in no way reinforced by the outer world.

Religious faith does more than specify a set of duties for man contrary to his natural propensities; it changes the mien of the universe in man's eyes. It demonstrates the existence of elements in the structure of the universe other than the sensible ones. It transforms a cold, desiccated, mechanical, and material universe into one living, intelligent, and conscious. Religious faith transforms man's conception of the universe and creation. William James, the American philosopher and psychologist whose life extended into the early part of the present Christian century, says: "The world interpreted religiously is not the materialistic world over again, with an altered expression; it must have, over and above the altered expression, *a natural constitution* different at some point from that which a materialistic world would have."

Beyond all this, there is an aspiration to sacred truths and realities that can be worshipped innate in every human individual. Man is the focus of a range of potential extramaterial aptitudes and capacities waiting to be nurtured. Man's aptitudes are not confined to the material and his ideal aspirations are not solely inculcated and acquired. This is a truth science affirms. William James says: "So far as our ideal impulses originate in this [mystical or supernatural] region (and most of them do originate in it, for we find them possessing us in a way for which we cannot articulately account), we belong to it in a more intimate way than that in which we belong to the visible world, for we belong in the most intimate sense wherever our ideals belong."

Because these impulses exist, they should be nurtured. If they are not rightly nurtured and rightly profited from, they will deviate and cause unimaginable harm leading to idolatry, anthropolatry, nature worship, and a thousand other forms of false worship. Erich Fromm says:

> There is no one without a religious need, a need to have a frame of ori-entation and an object of devotion. . . .
> He may be aware of his system as being a religious one, different from those of the secular realm, or he may think that he has no religion and inter-pret his devotion to certain allegedly secular aims like power, money or success as nothing but his concern for the practical and expedient. The question is not *religion* or *not* but *which kind of religion.*

What this psychologist means is that man cannot live without worship and a sense of the sacred. If he does not know and worship the One God, he will erect something else as the higher reality and make it the object of his faith and worship.

Therefore, because it is imperative for humanity to have an ideal, an aspiration, and a faith and because, on the one hand, religious faith is the only faith that can really penetrate us and, on the other hand, by our nature we seek for something to hold sacred and to worship, the only road open to us is to affirm religious faith.

The Noble Qur'an was the first book:

1. To speak explicitly of religious faith as a kind of harmony with the creation: "Do they seek for other than God's religion, while all in the heavens and on earth bow to Him?" (3:83)
2. To present religious faith as part of the makeup of human beings: "So set your face toward religion as one upright—such is the disposition with which God has created man." (30:30)

René Descartes

The Frenchman René Descartes (1596–1650) was a central figure in the scientific revolution of the seventeenth century. He contributed to the development of mathematics, physics, physiology, and philosophy. His scientific work has been superseded, but his philosophical writings remain standard reading, for they express fundamental conceptions that any would-be philosopher must address.

The part of his philosophy that most concerns us here is his metaphysical account of human nature as consisting of body and soul—two distinct but interacting substances, each of which can exist without the other. In this dualism Descartes follows a long tradition of philosophers including Plato, but he put a new gloss on the distinction, and gave new arguments for it. According to Descartes, the body occupies space and is subject to the same laws of nature that science studies, but it has no mental properties. It is the mind or soul that, properly speaking, thinks, feels, perceives, and decides what to believe and what to do (thereby exercising free will). The soul is incorporeal, that is, not made of matter—it does not occupy space (although it exists in time), and it cannot be studied by the methods of science. Descartes was thus led to make an absolute distinction between humans as possessing souls, and other animals, who in his view lack all consciousness, even sensations, perceptions, or emotions. In the *Discourse on Method* (1637) Descartes gave a preliminary exposition of his ideas in semiautobiographical form. In the first of these excerpts (from Part IV) he gives a rather compressed account of his main argument for dualism, starting from the reflection that whatever else one may doubt, one cannot doubt one's own existence as a conscious being. This is one example of his "rationalist" approach: his assumption that by the use of our pure unaided reason in a reflective, self-conscious way we can prove some fundamental truths about ourselves and the universe. In his masterpiece, the *Meditations,* Descartes gives his full, subtly argued account of how he thinks the immateriality of the soul can be proved by reason (see Meditations II and VI).

In the second extract here, from Part V of the *Discourse,* Descartes offers rather different, empirically based (a posteriori) arguments for dualism as the hypothesis that best explains the observed behavior of people and animals. He argues that there is a sharp distinction—of kind rather than degree—between the innate mental faculties of humans and all other creatures, picking out language as a distinctive component of human rationality. He here writes more as a natural scientist than as a rationalist philosopher. It is this empirically based sort of rationalism that Chomsky has defended in the twentieth century (see below).

Discourse on Method

Consciousness, and Dualism of Body and Soul

I do not know whether I should tell you of the first meditations that I had there, for they are perhaps too metaphysical and uncommon for everyone's taste. And yet, to make it possible to judge whether the foundations I have chosen are firm enough, I am in a way obliged to speak of them. For a long time I had observed, as noted above, that in practical life it is sometimes necessary to act upon opinions which one knows to be quite uncer-

Discourse on Method, in *The Philosophical Writings of Descartes,* Vol. 1, translated by John Cottingham, Robert Stoothof, and Dugald Murdoch © Cambridge University Press 1985.

tain just as if they were indubitable. But since I now wished to devote myself solely to the search for truth, I thought it necessary to do the very opposite and reject as if absolutely false everything in which I could imagine the least doubt, in order to see if I was left believing anything that was entirely indubitable. Thus, because our senses sometimes deceive us, I decided to suppose that nothing was such as they led us to imagine. And since there are men who make mistakes in reasoning, committing logical fallacies concerning the simplest questions in geometry, and because I judged that I was as prone to error as anyone else, I rejected as unsound all the arguments I had previously taken as demonstrative proofs. Lastly, considering that the very thoughts we have while awake may also occur while we sleep without any of them being at that time true, I resolved to pretend that all the things that had ever entered my mind were no more true than the illusions of my dreams. But immediately I noticed that while I was trying thus to think everything false, it was necessary that I, who was thinking this, was something. And observing that this truth "*I am thinking, therefore I exist*" was so firm and sure that all the most extravagant suppositions of the sceptics were incapable of shaking it, I decided that I could accept it without scruple as the first principle of the philosophy I was seeking.

Next I examined attentively what I was. I saw that while I could pretend that I had no body and that there was no world and no place for me to be in, I could not for all that pretend that I did not exist. I saw on the contrary that from the mere fact that I thought of doubting the truth of other things, it followed quite evidently and certainly that I existed; whereas if I had merely ceased thinking, even if everything else I had ever imagined had been true, I should have had no reason to believe that I existed. From this I knew I was a substance whose whole essence or nature is simply to think, and which does not require any place, or depend on any material thing, in order to exist. Accordingly this "I"—that is, the soul by which I am what I am—is entirely distinct from the body, and indeed is easier to know than the body, and would not fail to be whatever it is, even if the body did not exist.

After this I considered in general what is required of a proposition in order for it to be true and certain; for since I had just found one that I knew to be such, I thought that I ought also to know what this certainty consists in. I observed that there is nothing at all in the proposition "*I am thinking, therefore I exist*" to assure me that I am speaking the truth, except that I see very clearly that in order to think it is necessary to exist. So I decided that I could take it as a general rule that the things we conceive very clearly and very distinctly are all true; only there is some difficulty in recognizing which are the things that we distinctly conceive.

• • •

Language and Rationality

. . . I showed what structure the nerves and muscles of the human body must have in order to make the animal spirits inside them strong enough to move its limbs—as when we see severed heads continue to move about and bite the earth although they are no longer alive. I also indicated what changes must occur in the brain in order to cause waking, sleep and dreams; how light, sounds, smells, tastes, heat and the other qualities of external objects can imprint various ideas on the brain through the mediation of the senses; and how hunger, thirst, and the other internal passions can also send their ideas there. And I explained which part of the brain must be taken to be the "common" sense, where these ideas are received; the memory, which preserves them; and the corporeal imagination, which can change them in various ways, form them into new ideas, and, by distributing the animal spirits to the muscles, make the parts of this body move in as many different ways as the parts of our bodies can move without being guided by the will, and in a manner which is just as appropriate to the objects of the senses and the internal passions. This will not seem at all strange to those who know how many kinds of automatons, or moving machines, the skill of man can construct with the use of very few parts, in comparison with the great multitude of bones, muscles, nerves, arteries, veins and all the other parts that are in the body of any animal. For they will regard this body as a machine which, having been made by the hands of God, is incomparably better ordered than any machine that can be devised by man, and contains in itself movements more wonderful than those in any such machine.

I made special efforts to show that if any such machines had the organs and outward shape of a monkey or of some other animal that lacks reason, we should have no means of knowing that they did not possess entirely the same nature as these animals; whereas if any such machines bore a resemblance to our bodies and imitated our actions as closely as possible for all practical purposes, we should still have two very certain means of recognizing that they were not real men. The first is that they could never use words, or put together other signs, as we do in order to declare our thoughts to others. For we can certainly conceive of a machine so constructed that it utters words, and even utters words which correspond to bodily actions causing a change in its organs (e.g. if you touch it in one spot it asks what you want of it, if you touch it in another it cries out that you are hurting it, and so on). But it is not conceivable that such a machine should produce different arrangements of words so as to give an appropriately meaningful answer to whatever is said in its presence, as the dullest of men can do. Secondly, even though such machines might do some things as well as we do them, or perhaps even better, they would inevitably fail in others, which would reveal that they were acting not through understanding but only from the disposition of their organs. For whereas reason is a universal instrument which can be used in all kinds of situations, these organs need some particular disposition for each particular action; hence it is for all practical purposes impossible for a machine to have enough different organs to make it act in all the contingencies of life in the way in which our reason makes us act.

Now in just these two ways we can also know the difference between man and beast. For it is quite remarkable that there are no men so dull-witted or stupid—and this includes even madmen—that they are incapable of arranging various words together and forming an utterance from them in order to make their thoughts understood; whereas there is no other animal, however perfect and well-endowed it may be, that can do the like. This does not happen because they lack the necessary organs, for we see that magpies and parrots can utter words as we do, and yet they cannot speak as we do: that is, they cannot show that they are thinking what they are saying. On the other hand, men born deaf and dumb, and thus deprived of speech-organs as much as the beasts or even more so, normally invent their own signs to make themselves understood by those who, being regularly in their company, have the time to learn their language. This shows not merely that the beasts have less reason than men, but that they have no reason at all. For it patently requires very little reason to be able to speak; and since as much inequality can be observed among the animals of a given species as among human beings, and some animals are more easily trained than others, it would be incredible that a superior specimen of the monkey or parrot species should not be able to speak as well as the stupidest child—or at least as well as a child with a defective brain—if their souls were not completely different in nature from ours. And we must not confuse speech with the natural movements which express passions and which can be imitated by machines as well as by animals. Nor should we think, like some of the ancients, that the beasts speak, although we do not understand their language. For if that were true, then since they have many organs that correspond to ours, they could make themselves understood by us as well as by their fellows. It is also a very remarkable fact that although many animals show more skill than we do in some of their actions, yet the same animals show none at all in many others; so what they do better does not prove that they have any intelligence, for if it did then they would have more intelligence than any of us and would excel us in everything. It proves rather that they have no intelligence at all, and that it is nature which acts in them according to the disposition of their organs. In the same way a clock, consisting only of wheels and springs, can count the hours and measure time more accurately than we can with all our wisdom.

After that, I described the rational soul, and showed that, unlike the other things of which I had spoken, it cannot be derived in any way from the potentiality of matter, but must be specially created. And I showed how it is not sufficient for it to be lodged in the human body like a helmsman in his ship, except perhaps to move its limbs, but that it must be more closely joined and united with the body in order to have, besides this power of movement, feelings and appetites like ours and so constitute a real man. Here I dwelt a little upon the subject of the soul, because it is of the greatest importance. For after the error of those who deny God, which I believe I have already adequately refuted, there is none that leads weak minds further from the straight path of virtue than that of imagining that the souls of the beasts are of the same nature as ours, and hence that after this present life we have nothing to fear or to hope for, any more than flies and ants. But when we know how much the beasts differ from us, we understand much better the arguments which prove that our soul is of a nature entirely independent of the body, and consequently that it is not bound to die with it. And since we cannot see any other causes which destroy the soul, we are naturally led to conclude that it is immortal. . . .

Thomas Hobbes

The Englishman Thomas Hobbes (1588–1679) published his *Leviathan* in 1651, in the period of the English civil war. It is famous as one of the classics of political philosophy, arguing the need for a sovereign authority with an effective monopoly of the use of force, to save people from the evils of "the state of nature" in which every individual is at risk from others. So it is in each person's self-interest for there to be such a government, able to enforce security.

This political conclusion is derived from premises about individual human nature. Hobbes rejected Cartesian dualism and claimed that the very notion of incorporeal substance is self-contradictory. As we see in these excerpts, he espoused an uncompromising metaphysical materialism about human nature, treating life as a motion of the limbs, sensation as motion within the bodily organs, and desire as whatever state or process inside the body causes bodily movement.

Human nature in Hobbes' view is fundamentally selfish—each person's desires are for his own survival and reproduction. There is an anticipation here of a crude Darwinism. However, recent biological theories have recognized some instinctual tendencies toward cooperation in social animals like ourselves (see the passage from Ridley below).

Leviathan

Materialism and Desire

Concerning the thoughts of man, I will consider them first singly, and afterwards in train, or dependence upon one another. Singly, they are every one a *representation* or *appearance,* of some quality, or other accident of a body without us, which is commonly called an *object.* Which object worketh on the eyes, ears, and other parts of a man's body; and by diversity of working, produceth diversity of appearances.

The original of them all, is that which we call SENSE, for there is no conception in a man's mind, which hath not at first, totally, or by parts, been begotten upon the organs of sense. The rest are derived from that original.

To know the natural cause of sense, is not very necessary to the business now in hand; and I have elsewhere written of the same at large. Nevertheless, to fill each part of my present method, I will briefly deliver the same in this place.

The cause of sense, is the external body, or object, which presseth the organ proper to each sense, either immediately, as in the taste and touch; or mediately, as in seeing, hearing, and smelling; which pressure, by the mediation of the nerves, and other strings and membranes of the body, continued inwards to the brain and heart, causeth there a resistance, or counter-pressure, or endeavour of the heart to deliver itself, which endeavour, because *outward,* seemeth to be some matter without. And this *seeming,* or *fancy,* is that which men call *sense;* and consisteth, as to the eye, in a *light,* or *colour figured;* to the ear, in a *sound;* to the nostril, in an *odour;* to the tongue and palate, in a *savour;* and to the rest of the body, in *heat, cold, hardness, softness,* and such other qualities as we discern by *feeling.* All which qualities, called *sensible,* are in the object, that causeth them, but so many several motions of the matter, by which it presseth our organs diversely. Neither in us that are pressed, are they any thing else, but divers motions; for motion produceth nothing but motion. But their appearance to us is fancy, the same waking, that dreaming. And as pressing, rubbing, or striking the eye, makes us fancy a light; and pressing the ear, produceth a din; so do the bodies also we see, or hear, produce the same by their strong, though unobserved action. For if those colours

Leviathan, edited by John Plamenatz © Fontana 1962.

and sounds were in the bodies, or objects that cause them, they could not be severed from them, as by glasses, and in echoes by reflection, we see they are; where we know the thing we see is in one place, the appearance in another. And though at some certain distance, the real and very object seem invested with the fancy it begets in us; yet still the object is one thing, the image or fancy is another. So that sense, in all cases, is nothing else but original fancy, caused, as I have said, by the pressure, that is, by the motion, of external things upon our eyes, ears, and other organs thereunto ordained. . . .

There be in animals, two sorts of *motions* peculiar to them: one called *vital;* begun in generation, and continued without interruption through their whole life; such as are the *course* of the *blood,* the *pulse,* the *breathing,* the *concoction, nutrition, excretion,* etc. to which motions there needs no help of imagination: the other is *animal motion,* otherwise called *voluntary motion;* as to *go,* to *speak,* to *move* any of our limbs, in such manner as is first fancied in our minds. That sense is motion in the organs and interior parts of man's body, caused by the action of the things we see, hear, etc.; and that fancy is but the relics of the same motion, remaining after sense, has been already said in the first and second chapters. And because *going, speaking,* and the like voluntary motions, depend always upon a precedent thought of *whither, which way,* and *what;* it is evident, that the imagination is the first internal beginning of all voluntary motion. And although unstudied men do not conceive any motion at all to be there, where the thing moved is invisible; or the space it is moved in is, for the shortness of it, insensible; yet that doth not hinder, but that such motions are. For let a space be never so little, that which is moved over a greater space, whereof that little one is part, must first be moved over that. These small beginnings of motion, within the body of man, before they appear in walking, speaking, striking, and other visible actions, are commonly called ENDEAVOUR.

This endeavour, when it is toward something which causes it, is called APPETITE, or DESIRE; the latter, being the general name; and the other oftentimes restrained to signify the desire of food, namely *hunger* and *thirst.* And when the endeavour is fromward something, it is generally called AVERSION. . . .

That which men desire, they are also said to LOVE: and to HATE those things for which they have aversion. So that desire and love are the same thing; save that by desire, we always signify the absence of the object; by love, most commonly the presence of the same. So also by aversion, we signify the absence; and by hate, the presence of the object.

Of appetites and aversions, some are born with men; as appetite of food, appetite of excretion, and exoneration, which may also and more properly be called aversions, from somewhat they feel in their bodies; and some other appetites, not many. The rest, which are appetites of particular things, proceed from experience, and trial of their effects upon themselves or other men. For of things we know not at all, or believe not to be, we can have no further desire, than to taste and try. But aversion we have for things, not only which we know have hurt us, but also that we do not know whether they will hurt us, or not.

Those things which we neither desire, nor hate, we are said to *contemn;* CONTEMPT being nothing else but an immobility, or contumacy of the heart, in resisting the action of certain things; and proceeding from that the heart is already moved otherwise, by other more potent objects; or from want of experience of them.

And because the constitution of a man's body is in continual mutation, it is impossible that all the same things should always cause in him the same appetites, and aversions: much less can all men consent, in the desire of almost any one and the same object.

But whatsoever is the object of any man's appetite or desire, that is it which he for his part calleth *good:* and the object of his hate and aversion, *evil;* and of his contempt, *vile* and *inconsiderable.* For these words of good, evil, and contemptible, are ever used with relation to the person that useth them: there being nothing simply and absolutely so; nor any common rule of good and evil, to be taken from the nature of the objects themselves; but from the person of the man, where there is no commonwealth; or, in a commonwealth, from the person that representeth it; or from an arbitrator or judge, whom men disagreeing shall by consent set up, and make his sentence the rule thereof.

• • •

Of the Natural Condition of Mankind as Concerning Their Felicity, and Misery

Nature hath made men so equal, in the faculties of the body, and mind; as that though there be found one man sometimes manifestly stronger in body, or of quicker mind than another; yet when all is reckoned together, the difference between man, and man, is not so considerable, as that one man can thereupon claim to himself any benefit, to which another may not pretend, as well as he. For as to the strength of body, the weakest has strength enough to kill the strongest, either by secret machination, or by confederacy with others, that are in the same danger with himself.

And as to the faculties of the mind, setting aside the arts grounded upon words, and especially that skill of proceeding upon general, and infallible rules, called science; which very few have, and but in few things; as being not a native faculty, born with us; nor attained, as prudence, while we look after somewhat else, I find yet a greater equality amongst men, than that of strength. For prudence, is but experience; which equal time, equally bestows on all men, in those things they equally apply themselves unto. That which may perhaps make such equality incredible, is but a vain conceit of one's own wisdom, which almost all men think they have in a greater degree, than the vulgar; that is, than all men but themselves, and a few others, whom by fame, or for concurring with themselves, they approve. For such is the nature of men, that howsoever they may acknowledge many others to be more witty, or more eloquent, or more learned; yet they will hardly believe there be many so wise as themselves; for they see their own wit at hand, and other men's at a distance. But this proveth rather that men are in that point equal, than unequal. For there is not ordinarily a greater sign of the equal distribution of any thing, than that every man is contented with his share.

From this equality of ability, ariseth equality of hope in the attaining of our ends. And therefore if any two men desire the same thing, which nevertheless they cannot both enjoy, they become enemies; and in the way to their end, which is principally their own conservation, and sometimes their delectation only, endeavour to destroy, or subdue one another. And from hence it comes to pass, that where an invader hath no more to fear, than another man's single power; if one plant, sow, build, or possess a convenient seat, others may probably be expected to come prepared with forces united, to dispossess, and deprive him, not only of the fruit of his labour, but also of his life, or liberty. And the invader again is in the like danger of another.

And from this diffidence of one another, there is no way for any man to secure himself, so reasonable, as anticipation; that is, by force, or wiles, to master the persons of all men he can, so long, till he see no other power great enough to endanger him: and this is no more than his own conservation requireth, and is generally allowed. Also because there be some, that taking pleasure in contemplating their own power in the acts of conquest, which they pursue farther than their security requires; if others, that otherwise would be glad to be at ease within modest bounds, should not by invasion increase their power, they would not be able, long time, by standing only on their defence, to subsist. And by consequence, such augmentation of dominion over men being necessary to a man's conservation, it ought to be allowed him.

Again, men have no pleasure, but on the contrary a great deal of grief, in keeping company, where there is no power able to over-awe them all. For every man looketh that his companion should value him, at the same rate he sets upon himself: and upon all signs of contempt, or undervaluing, naturally endeavours, as far as he dares, (which amongst them that have no common power to keep them in quiet, is far enough to make them destroy each other), to extort a greater value from his contemners, by damage; and from others, by the example.

So that in the nature of man, we find three principal causes of quarrel. First, competition; secondly, diffidence; thirdly, glory.

The first, maketh men invade for gain; the second, for safety; and the third, for reputation. The first use violence, to make themselves masters of other men's persons, wives, children, and cattle; the second, to defend them; the third, for trifles, as a word, a smile, a different opinion, and any other sign of undervalue, either direct in their persons, or by reflection in their kindred, their friends, their nation, their profession, or their name.

Hereby it is manifest, that during the time men live without a common power to keep them all in awe, they are in that condition which is called war; and such a war, as is of every man, against every man. For WAR, consisteth not in battle only, or the act of fighting; but in a tract of time, wherein the will to contend by battle is sufficiently known: and therefore the notion of *time,* is to be considered in the nature of war; as it is in the nature of weather. For as the nature of foul weather, lieth not in a shower or two of rain; but in an inclination thereto of many days together: so the nature of war, consisteth not in actual fighting; but in the known disposition thereto, during all the time there is no assurance to the contrary. All other time is PEACE.

Whatsoever therefore is consequent to a time of war, where every man is enemy to every man; the same is consequent to the time, wherein men live without other security, than what their own strength, and their own invention shall furnish them withal. In such condition, there is no place for industry; because the fruit thereof is uncertain: and consequently no culture of the earth; no navigation, nor use of the commodities that may be imported by sea; no commodious building; no instruments of moving, and removing, such things as require much force; no knowledge of the face of the earth; no account of time; no arts; no letters; no society; and which is worst of all, continual fear, and danger of violent death; and the life of man, solitary, poor, nasty, brutish, and short.

It may seem strange to some man, that has not well weighed these things; that nature should thus dissociate, and render men apt to invade, and destroy one another: and he may therefore, not trusting to this inference, made from the passions, desire perhaps to have the same confirmed by experience. Let him therefore consider with himself, when taking a journey, he arms himself, and seeks to go well accompanied; when going to sleep, he locks his doors; when even in his house he locks his chests; and this when he knows there be laws, and public officers, armed, to revenge all injuries shall be done him; what opinion he has of his fellow-subjects, when he rides armed; of his fellow citizens, when he locks his doors; and of his children, and servants, when he locks his chests. Does he not there as much accuse mankind by his actions, as I do by my words? But neither of us accuse man's nature in it. The desires, and other passions of man, are in themselves no sin. No more are the actions, that proceed from those passions, till they know a law that forbids them: which till laws be made they cannot know: nor can any law be made, till they have agreed upon the person that shall make it.

It may peradventure be thought, there was never such a time, nor condition of war as this; and I believe it was never generally so, over all the world: but there are many places, where they live so now. For the savage people in many places of America, except the government of small families, the concord whereof dependeth on natural lust, have no government at all; and live at this day in that brutish manner, as I said before. Howsoever, it may be perceived what manner of life there would be, where there were no common power to fear, by the manner of life, which men that have formerly lived under a peaceful government, use to degenerate into, in a civil war.

But though there had never been any time, wherein particular men were in a condition of war one against another; yet in all times, kings, and persons of sovereign authority, because of their independency, are in continual jealousies, and in the state and posture of gladiators; having their weapons pointing, and their eyes fixed on one another; that is, their forts, garrisons, and guns upon the frontiers of their kingdoms; and continual spies upon their neighbours; which is a posture of war. But because they uphold thereby, the industry of their subjects; there does not follow from it, that misery, which accompanies the liberty of particular men.

To this war of every man, against every man, this also is consequent; that nothing can be unjust. The notions of right and wrong, justice and injustice have there no place. Where there is no common power, there is no law: where no law, no injustice. Force, and fraud, are in war the two cardinal virtues. Justice, and injustice are none of the faculties neither of the body, nor mind. If they were, they might be in a man that were alone in the world, as well as his senses, and passions. They are qualities, that relate to men in society, not in solitude. It is consequent also to the same condition, that there be no propriety, no dominion, no *mine* and *thine* distinct; but only that to be every man's, that he can get; and for so long, as he can keep it. And thus much for the ill condition, which man by mere nature is actually placed in; though with a possibility to come out of it, consisting partly in the passions, partly in his reason.

The passions that incline men to peace, are fear of death; desire of such things as are necessary to commodious living; and a hope by their industry to obtain them. And reason suggesteth convenient articles of peace, upon which men may be drawn to agreement. These articles, are they, which otherwise are called the Laws of Nature: whereof I shall speak more particularly, in the two following chapters.

David Hume

The Scotsman David Hume (1711–1776) was a seminal figure in the Enlightenment, the eighteenth-century movement of thought that proposed to reform traditional thought and practice by the application of reason to human affairs. Hume wrote on many topics, including politics and history, but it is as a philosopher that he is now most famous. His magnum opus is the three-volume *Treatise of Human Nature,* written in his twenties; later he wrote more popular expositions of his ideas in his two *Enquiries,* concerning human understanding, and the principles of morals.

Hume's philosophy is strictly empiricist: he holds that all knowledge about the world (including about human nature) must be based on experience. Pure reason can prove results only about the abstractions of logic and mathematics. His *Treatise* is significantly subtitled "An Attempt to Introduce the Experimental (i.e. Experiential, or Empirical) Method of Reasoning into Moral Subjects (i.e. Theorizing About Human Nature)." In the first excerpt here, from the introduction, he boldly sketches his general strategy.

In Book I, Part I, Hume lays down his fundamental premise, that all ideas are derived from experience. In this concept—empiricism—he was anticipated by John Locke's *Essay* of 1690, but Hume tries to improve on Locke's rather vague use of the term *idea* by distinguishing "ideas" as general concepts from "impressions" as particular perceptions. He deduces that we have no idea of substance, except as a bundle of perceptible qualities. And in Book I, Part IV, he applies this principle to argue that we have no notion of soul or mental substance. Locke had also opened up this ground in his treatment of personal identity (*Essay,* Book II, Ch. 27) as depending on memory rather than on the continued existence of a mental substance.

In a selection reprinted below, Henry Bracken argues that this empiricist approach to the nature of persons as a bundle of qualities—in contrast to the rationalist doctrine of rational soul—made it easier to make racial discriminations, and he quotes a passage in which Hume does just that.

Treatise of Human Nature

The Empirical Study of Human Nature

. . .'Tis evident, that all the sciences have a relation, greater or less, to human nature; and that however wide any of them may seem to run from it, they still return back by one passage or another. Even *Mathematics, Natural Philosophy,* and *Natural Religion,* are in some measure dependent on the science of Man; since they lie under the cognizance of men, and are judged of by their powers and faculties. 'Tis impossible to tell what changes and improvements we might make in these sciences were we thoroughly acquainted with the extent and force of human understanding, and cou'd explain the nature of the ideas we employ, and of the operations we perform in our reasonings. And these improvements are the more to be hoped for in natural religion, as it is not content with instructing us in the nature of superior powers, but carries its views farther, to their disposition towards us, and our duties towards them; and consequently we ourselves are not only the beings, that reason, but also one of the objects, concerning which we reason.

If therefore the sciences of Mathematics, Natural Philosophy, and Natural Religion, have such a dependence on the knowledge of man, what may be expected in the other sciences, whose connexion with human

A Treatise of Human Nature, edited by L. A. Selby-Bigge © Oxford University Press 1888.

nature is more close and intimate? The sole end of logic is to explain the principles and operations of our reasoning faculty, and the nature of our ideas: morals and criticism regard our tastes and sentiments: and politics consider men as united in society, and dependent on each other. In these four sciences of *Logic, Morals, Criticism,* and *Politics,* is comprehended almost every thing, which it can any way import us to be acquainted with, or which can tend either to the improvement or ornament of the human mind.

Here then is the only expedient, from which we can hope for success in our philosophical researches, to leave the tedious lingring method, which we have hitherto followed, and instead of taking now and then a castle or village on the frontier, to march up directly to the capital or center of these sciences, to human nature itself; which being once masters of, we may every where else hope for an easy victory. From this station we may extend our conquests over all those sciences, which more intimately concern human life, and may afterwards proceed at leisure to discover more fully those, which are the objects of pure curiosity. There is no question of importance, whose decision is not compriz'd in the science of man; and there is none, which can be decided with any certainty, before we become acquainted with that science. In pretending therefore to explain the principles of human nature, we in effect propose a compleat system of the sciences, built on a foundation almost entirely new, and the only one upon which they can stand with any security.

And as the science of man is the only solid foundation for the other sciences, so the only solid foundation we can give to this science itself must be laid on experience and observation. 'Tis no astonishing reflection to consider, that the application of experimental philosophy to moral subjects should come after that to natural at the distance of above a whole century; since we find in fact, that there was about the same interval betwixt the origins of these sciences; and that reckoning from Thales to Socrates, the space of time is nearly equal to that betwixt my Lord Bacon and some late philosophers in *England,* who have begun to put the science of man on a new footing, and have engaged the attention, and excited the curiosity of the public. So true it is, that however other nations may rival us in poetry, and excel us in some other agreeable arts, the improvements in reason and philosophy can only be owing to a land of toleration and of liberty.

Nor ought we to think, that this latter improvement in the science of man will do less honour to our native country than the former in natural philosophy, but ought rather to esteem it a greater glory, upon account of the greater importance of that science, as well as the necessity it lay under of such a reformation. For to me it seems evident, that the essence of the mind being equally unknown to us with that of external bodies, it must be equally impossible to form any notion of its powers and qualities otherwise than from careful and exact experiments, and the observation of those particular effects, which result from its different circumstances and situations. And tho' we must endeavour to render all our principles as universal as possible, by tracing up our experiments to the utmost, and explaining all effects from the simplest and fewest causes, 'tis still certain we cannot go beyond experience; and any hypothesis, that pretends to discover the ultimate original qualities of human nature, ought at first to be rejected as presumptuous and chimerical.

I do not think a philosopher, who would apply himself so earnestly to the explaining the ultimate principles of the soul, would show himself a great master in that very science of human nature, which he pretends to explain, or very knowing in what is naturally satisfactory to the mind of man. For nothing is more certain, than that despair has almost the same effect upon us with enjoyment, and that we are no sooner acquainted with the impossibility of satisfying any desire, than the desire itself vanishes. When we see, that we have arrived at the utmost extent of human reason, we sit down contented; tho' we be perfectly satisfied in the main of our ignorance, and perceive that we can give no reason for our most general and most refined principles, beside our experience of their reality; which is the reason of the mere vulgar, and what it required no study at first to have discovered for the most particular and most extraordinary phænomenon. And as this impossibility of making any farther progress is enough to satisfy the reader, so the writer may derive a more delicate satisfaction from the free confession of his ignorance, and from his prudence in avoiding that error, into which so many have fallen, of imposing their conjectures and hypotheses on the world for the most certain principles. When this mutual contentment and satisfaction can be obtained betwixt the master and scholar, I know not what more we can require of our philosophy.

But if this impossibility of explaining ultimate principles should be esteemed a defect in the science of man, I will venture to affirm, that 'tis a defect common to it with all the sciences, and all the arts, in which we can employ ourselves, whether they be such as are cultivated in the schools of the philosophers, or practised in the shops of the meanest artizans. None of them can go beyond experience, or establish any principles which are not founded on that authority. Moral philosophy has, indeed, this peculiar disadvantage, which is not found in natural, that in collecting its experiments, it cannot make them purposely, with premeditation, and after such a manner as to satisfy itself concerning every particular difficulty which may arise. When I am at a loss to know the effects of one body upon another in any situation, I need only put them in that situation, and observe what results from it. But should I endeavour to clear up after the same manner any doubt in moral philosophy, by placing myself in the same case with that which I consider, 'tis evident this reflection and premeditation would so disturb the operation of my natural principles, as must render it impossible to form any just conclusion from the phænomenon. We must therefore glean up our experiments in this science from a cautious observation of human life, and take them as they appear in the common course of the world, by men's behaviour in company, in affairs, and in their pleasures. Where experiments of this kind are judiciously collected and compared, we may hope to establish on them a science, which will not be inferior in certainty, and will be much superior in utility to any other of human comprehension.

Of the Origin of Our Ideas

All the perceptions of the human mind resolve themselves into two distinct kinds, which I shall call *Impressions* and *Ideas.* The difference betwixt these consists in the degrees of force and liveliness with which they strike upon the mind, and make their way into our thought or consciousness. Those perceptions, which enter with most force and violence, we may name *impressions;* and under this name I comprehend all our sensations, passions and emotions, as they make their first appearance in the soul. By *ideas* I mean the faint images of these in thinking and reasoning; such as, for instance, are all the perceptions excited by the present discourse, excepting only, those which arise from the sight and touch, and excepting the immediate pleasure or uneasiness it may occasion. I believe it will not be very necessary to employ many words in explaining this distinction. Every one of himself will readily perceive the difference betwixt feeling and thinking. The common degrees of these are easily distinguished; tho' it is not impossible but in particular instances they may very nearly approach to each other. Thus in sleep, in a fever, in madness, or in any very violent emotions of soul, our ideas may approach to our impressions: As on the other hand it sometimes happens, that our impressions are so faint and low, that we cannot distinguish them from our ideas. But notwithstanding this near resemblance in a few instances, they are in general so very different, that no-one can make a scruple to rank them under distinct heads, and assign to each a peculiar name to mark the difference.

There is another division of our perceptions, which it will be convenient to observe, and which extends itself both to our impressions and ideas. This division is into Simple and Complex. Simple perceptions or impressions and ideas are such as admit of no distinction nor separation. The complex are the contrary to these, and may be distinguished into parts. Tho' a particular colour, taste, and smell are qualities all united together in this apple, 'tis easy to perceive they are not the same, but are at least distinguishable from each other. . . .

Thus we find, that all simple ideas and impressions resemble each other; and as the complex are formed from them, we may affirm in general, that these two species of perception are exactly correspondent. Having discover'd this relation, which requires no farther examination, I am curious to find some other of their qualities. Let us consider how they stand with regard to their existence, and which of the impressions and ideas are causes, and which effects.

The *full* examination of this question is the subject of the present treatise; and therefore we shall here content ourselves with establishing one general proposition, *That all our simple ideas in their first appearance are deriv'd from simple impressions, which are correspondent to them, and which they exactly represent.* . . .

This then is the first principle I establish in the science of human nature; nor ought we to despise it because of the simplicity of its appearance. For 'tis remarkable, that the present question concerning the precedency of our impressions or ideas, is the same with what has made so much noise in other terms, when it has been disputed whether there be any *innate ideas,* or whether all ideas be derived from sensation and reflexion. We may observe, that in order to prove the ideas of extension and colour not to be innate, philosophers do nothing but shew, that they are conveyed by our senses. To prove the ideas of passion and desire not to be innate, they observe that we have a preceding experience of these emotions in ourselves. Now if we carefully examine these arguments, we shall find that they prove nothing but that ideas are preceded by other more lively perceptions, from which they are derived, and which they represent. I hope this clear stating of the question will remove all disputes concerning it, and will render this principle of more use in our reasonings, than it seems hitherto to have been. . . .

Of Substances

I wou'd fain ask those philosophers, who found so much of their reasonings on the distinction of substance and accident, and imagine we have clear ideas of each, whether the idea of *substance* be deriv'd from the impressions of sensation or reflexion? If it be convey'd to us by our senses, I ask, which of them; and after what manner? If it be perceiv'd by the eyes, it must be a colour; if by the ears, a sound; if by the palate, a taste; and so of the other senses. But I believe none will assert, that substance is either a colour, or sound, or a taste. The idea of substance must therefore be deriv'd from an impression or reflexion, if it really exist. But the impressions of reflexion resolve themselves into our passions and emotions; none of which can possibly represent a substance. We have therefore no idea of substance, distinct from that of a collection of particular qualities, nor have we any other meaning when we either talk or reason concerning it.

The idea of a substance as well as that of a mode, is nothing but a collection of simple ideas, that are united by the imagination, and have a particular name assigned them, by which we are able to recall, either to ourselves or others, that collection. But the difference betwixt these ideas consists in this, that the particular qualities, which form a substance, are commonly refer'd to an unknown *something,* in which they are supposed to inhere; or granting this fiction should not take place, are at least supposed to be closely and inseparably connected by the relations of contiguity and causation. The effect of this is, that whatever new simple quality we discover to have the same connexion with the rest, we immediately comprehend it among them, even tho' it did not enter into the first conception of the substance. Thus our idea of gold may at first be a yellow colour, weight, malleableness, fusibility; but upon the discovery of its dissolubility in *aqua regia,* we join that to the other qualities, and suppose it to belong to the substance as much as if its idea had from the beginning made a part of the compound one. The principle of union being regarded as the chief part of the complex idea, gives entrance to whatever quality afterwards occurs, and is equally comprehended by it, as are the others, which first presented themselves.

• • •

Of the Immateriality of the Soul

Having found such contradictions and difficulties in every system concerning external objects, and in the idea of matter, which we fancy so clear and determinate, we shall naturally expect still greater difficulties and contradictions in every hypothesis concerning our internal perceptions, and the nature of the mind, which we are apt to imagine so much more obscure, and uncertain. But in this we shou'd deceive ourselves. The intellectual world, tho' involv'd in infinite obscurities, is not perplex'd with any such contradictions, as those we have discover'd in the natural. What is known concerning it, agrees with itself; and what is unknown, we must be contented to leave so.

'Tis true, wou'd we hearken to certain philosophers, they promise to diminish our ignorance; but I am afraid 'tis at the hazard of running us into contradictions, from which the subject is of itself exempted. These philosophers are the curious reasoners concerning the material or immaterial substances, in which they suppose our perceptions to inhere. In order to put a stop to these endless cavils on both sides, I know no better method, than to ask these philosophers in a few words, *What they mean by substance and inhesion?* And after they have answer'd this question, 'twill then be reasonable, and not till then, to enter seriously into the dispute.

This question we have found impossible to be answer'd with regard to matter and body: But besides that in the case of the mind, it labours under all the same difficulties, 'tis burthen'd with some additional ones, which are peculiar to that subject. As every idea is deriv'd from a precedent impression, had we any idea of the substance of our minds, we must also have an impression of it; which is very difficult, if not impossible, to be conceiv'd. For how can an impression represent a substance, otherwise than by resembling it? And how can an impression resemble a substance, since, according to this philosophy, it is not a substance, and has none of the peculiar qualities or characteristics of a substance?

But leaving the question *of what may or may not be,* for that other *what actually is,* I desire those philosophers, who pretend that we have an idea of the substance of our minds, to point out the impression that produces it, and tell distinctly after what manner that impression operates, and from what object it is deriv'd. Is it an impression of sensation or of reflection? Is it pleasant, or painful, or indifferent? Does it attend us at all times, or does it only return at intervals? If at intervals, at what times principally does it return, and by what causes is it produc'd?

If instead of answering these questions, any one shou'd evade the difficulty, by saying, that the definition of a substance is *something which may exist by itself;* and that this definition ought to satisfy us: Shou'd this be said, I shou'd observe, that this definition agrees to every thing, that can possibly be conceiv'd; and never will serve to distinguish substance from accident, or the soul from its perceptions. For thus I reason. Whatever is clearly conceiv'd may exist; and whatever is clearly conceiv'd, after any manner, may exist after the same manner. This is one principle, which has been already acknowledg'd. Again, every thing, which is different, is distinguishable, and every thing which is distinguishable, is separable by the imagination. This is another principle. My conclusion from both is, that since all our perceptions are different from each other, and from every thing else in the universe, they are also distinct and separable, and may be consider'd as separately existent, and may exist separately, and have no need of any thing else to support their existence. They are, therefore, substances, as far as this definition explains a substance.

· · ·

Of Personal Identity

There are some philosophers, who imagine we are every moment intimately conscious of what we call our *Self;* that we feel its existence and its continuance in existence; and are certain, beyond the evidence of a demonstration, both of its perfect identity and simplicity. The strongest sensation, the most violent passion, say they, instead of distracting us from this view, only fix it the more intensely, and make us consider their influence on *self* either by their pain or pleasure. To attempt a farther proof of this were to weaken its evidence; since no proof can be deriv'd from any fact, of which we are so intimately conscious; nor is there any thing, of which we can be certain, if we doubt of this.

Unluckily all these positive assertions are contrary to that very experience, which is pleaded for them, nor have we any idea of *self,* after the manner it is here explain'd. For from what impression cou'd this idea be deriv'd? This question 'tis impossible to answer without a manifest contradiction and absurdity; and yet 'tis a question, which must necessarily be answer'd, if we wou'd have the idea of self pass for clear and intelligible. It must be some one impression, that gives rise to every real idea. But self or person is not any one impression, but that to which our several impressions and ideas are suppos'd to have a reference. If any impression gives rise to the idea of self, that impression must continue invariably the same, thro' the whole course of our lives; since self is suppos'd to exist after that manner. But there is no impression constant and invariable. Pain and pleasure, grief and joy, passions and sensations succeed each other, and never all exist at the same time. It cannot, therefore, be from any of these impressions, or from any other, that the idea of self is deriv'd; and consequently there is no such idea.

But farther, what must become of all our particular perceptions upon this hypothesis? All these are different, and distinguishable, and separable from each other, and may be separately consider'd, and may exist separately, and have no need of any thing to support their existence. After what manner, therefore, do they belong to self; and how are they connected with it? For my part, when I enter most intimately into what I call *myself,* I always stumble on some particular perception or other, of heat or cold, light or shade, love or hatred, pain or pleasure. I never can catch *myself* at any time without a perception, and never can observe any thing but the perception. When my perceptions are remov'd for any time, as by sound sleep; so long am I insensible of *myself,* and may truly be said not to exist. And were all my perceptions remov'd by death, and cou'd I neither think, nor feel, nor see, nor love, nor hate after the dissolution of my body, I shou'd be entirely annihilated, nor do I conceive what is farther requisite to make me a perfect non-entity. If any one upon serious and unprejudic'd reflexion, thinks he has a different notion of *himself,* I must confess I can reason no longer with him. All I can allow him is, that he may be in the right as well as I, and that we are essentially different in this particular. He may, perhaps, perceive something simple and continu'd, which he calls *himself;* tho' I am certain there is no such principle in me.

But setting aside some metaphysicians of this kind, I may venture to affirm of the rest of mankind, that they are nothing but a bundle or collection of different perceptions, which succeed each other with an inconceivable rapidity, and are in a perpetual flux and movement. Our eyes cannot turn in their sockets without varying our perceptions. Our thought is still more variable than our sight; and all our other senses and faculties contribute to this change; nor is there any single power of the soul, which remains unalterably the same, perhaps for one moment. *The mind is a kind of theatre,* where several perceptions successively make their appearance; pass, re-pass, glide away, and mingle in an infinite variety of postures and situations. There is properly no *simplicity* in it at one time, nor *identity* in different; whatever natural pro-pension we may have to imagine that simplicity and identity. The comparison of the theatre must not mislead us. They are the successive perceptions only, that constitute the mind; nor have we the most distant notion of the place, where these scenes are represented, or of the materials, of which it is compos'd. . . .

Jean-Jacques Rousseau

Jean-Jacques Rousseau (1712–1778), born in the city-state of Geneva in Switzerland, was another of the seminal thinkers of the Enlightenment. He contributed to the ferment of ideas questioning traditional authority and power structures, leading up to the French Revolution of 1789. His political philosophy is summed up in *The Social Contract* (1762). He was an eccentric, restless, and intensely personal figure, who got involved in famous quarrels and wrote a famous set of *Confessions* in 1770.

Like that of Hobbes, Rousseau's political analysis is based on an account of human nature, but he has a rather different theory to offer. In his *Discourse on Inequality* (1755) he argued for the original goodness of human nature. Rousseau offers a highly speculative history of society, claiming to show how the growth of what is called civilization has corrupted people's natural happiness and freedom and allowed unnatural, unjust inequalities to develop.

The following extracts are taken from the beginning and end of Rousseau's influential treatise on education, *Emile* (1762). The first gives a short expression of his idealistic vision of the essential goodness of human nature. The second, from Book V on marriage, gives us his views on the natural differences of the sexes. Many of his statements here will evoke contemporary scorn as mere statements of male prejudice, typical of his time and long afterward.

However, it is worth asking ourselves which, if any, of his statements are true and false, in view of the continuing controversies about how much of the observed differences between men and women are innate. (In this connection see the selections from Mill and Holmstrom below, and the introductions to Wilson and to Rose et al.)

Emile

The Meaning of Education

Everything is good as it comes from the hands of the Maker of the world but degenerates once it gets into the hands of man. Man makes one land yield the products of another, disregards differences of climates, elements and seasons, mutilates his dogs and horses, perverts and disfigures everything. Not content to leave anything as nature has made it, he must needs shape man himself to his notions, as he does the trees in his garden.

But under present conditions, human beings would be even worse than they are without this fashioning. A man left entirely to himself from birth would be the most misshapen of creatures. Prejudices, authority, necessity, example, the social institutions in which we are immersed, would crush out nature in him without putting anything in its place. He would fare like a shrub that has grown up by chance in the middle of a road, and got trampled under foot by the passers-by.

Plants are fashioned by cultivation, men by education. We are born feeble and need strength; possessing nothing, we need assistance; beginning without intelligence, we need judgment. All that we lack at birth and need when grown up is given us by education. This education comes to us from nature, from men, or from things. The internal development of our faculties and organs is the education of nature. The use we learn to make of this development is the education of men. What comes to us from our experience of the things that affect us is the education of things. Each of us therefore is fashioned by three kinds of teachers. When their lessons are at variance the pupil is badly educated, and is never at peace with himself. When they coincide and lead to a common goal he goes straight to his

Emile, selected and translated by William Boyd, in *Emile for Today* © Heinemann 1956.

mark and lives single-minded. Now, of these three educations the one due to nature is independent of us, and the one from things only depends on us to a limited extent. The education that comes from men is the only one within our control, and even that is doubtful. Who can hope to have the entire direction of the words and deeds of all the people around a child? It is only by good luck that the goal can be reached. What is this goal? It is nature's own goal. Since the three educations must work together for a perfect result, the one that can be modified determines the course of the other two. But perhaps "nature" is too vague a word. We must try to fix its meaning. Nature, it has been said, is only habit. Is that really so? Are there not habits which are formed under pressure, leaving the original nature unchanged? One example is the habit of plants which have been forced away from the upright direction. When set free, the plant retains the bent forced upon it; but the sap has not changed its first direction and any new growth the plant makes returns to the vertical. It is the same with human inclinations. So long as there is no change in conditions the inclinations due to habits, however unnatural, remain unchanged, but immediately the restraint is removed the habit vanishes and nature reasserts itself.

We are born capable of sensation and from birth are affected in diverse ways by the objects around us. As soon as we become conscious of our sensations we are inclined to seek or to avoid the objects which produce them: at first, because they are agreeable or disagreeable to us, later because we discover that they suit or do not suit us, and ultimately because of the judgments we pass on them by reference to the idea of happiness or perfection we get from reason. These inclinations extend and strengthen with the growth of sensibility and intelligence, but under the pressure of habit they are changed to some extent with our opinions. The inclinations before this change are what I call our nature. In my view everything ought to be in conformity with these original inclinations.

There would be no difficulty if our three educations were merely different. But what is to be done when they are at cross purposes? Consistency is plainly impossible when we seek to educate a man for others, instead of for himself. If we have to combat either nature or society, we must choose between making a man or making a citizen. We cannot make both. There is an inevitable conflict of aims, from which come two opposing forms of education: the one communal and public, the other individual and domestic.

To get a good idea of communal education, read Plato's *Republic*. It is not a political treatise, as those who merely judge books by their titles think. It is the finest treatise on education ever written. Communal education in this sense, however, does not and can not now exist. There are no longer any real fatherlands and therefore no real citizens. The words "fatherland" and "citizen" should be expunged from modern languages. I do not regard the instruction given in those ridiculous establishments called colleges as "public," any more than the ordinary kind of education. This education makes for two opposite goals and reaches neither. The men it turns out are double-minded, seemingly concerned for others, but really only concerned for themselves. From this contradiction comes the conflict we never cease to experience in ourselves. We are drawn in different directions by nature and by man, and take a midway path that leads us nowhere. In this state of confusion we go through life and end up with our contradictions unsolved, never having been any good to ourselves or to other people.

There remains then domestic education, the education of nature. But how will a man who has been educated entirely for himself get on with other people? If there were any way of combining in a single person the twofold aim, and removing the contradictions of life, a great obstacle to happiness would be removed. But before passing judgment on this kind of man it would be necessary to follow his development and see him fully formed. It would be necessary, in a word, to make the acquaintance of the natural man. This is the subject of our quest in this book.

What can be done to produce this very exceptional person? In point of fact all we have to do is to prevent anything being done. When it is only a matter of sailing against the wind it is enough to tack, but when the sea runs high and you want to stay where you are, you must throw out the anchor.

In the social order where all stations in life are fixed, every one needs to be brought up for his own station. The individual who leaves the place for which he has been trained is useless in any other. In Egypt, where the son was obliged to follow in his father's footsteps, education had at least an assured aim: in our country where social ranks are fixed, but the men in them are constantly changing, nobody knows whether he is doing his son a good or a bad turn when he educates him for his own rank.

In the natural order where all men are equal, manhood is the common vocation. One who is well educated for that will not do badly in the duties that pertain to it. The fact that my pupil is intended for the army, the church or the bar, does not greatly concern me. Before the vocation determined by his parents comes the call of nature to the life of human kind. Life is the business I would have him learn. When he leaves my hands, I admit he will not be a magistrate, or a soldier, or a priest. First and foremost, he will be a man. All that a man must be he will be when the need arises, as well as anyone else. Whatever the changes of fortune he will always be able to find a place for himself.

• • •

The Differences between the Sexes

Sophie should be as typically woman as Emile is man. She must possess all the characteristics of humanity and of womanhood which she needs for playing her part in the physical and the moral order. Let us begin by considering in what respects her sex and ours agree and differ.

In everything that does not relate to sex the woman is as the man: they are alike in organs, needs and capacities. In whatever way we look at them the difference is only one of less or more. In everything that relates to sex there are correspondences and differences. The difficulty is to determine what in their constitution is due to sex and what is not. All we know with certainty is that the common features are due to the species and the differences to sex. From this twofold point of view we find so many likenesses and so many contrasts that we cannot but marvel that nature has been able to create two beings so much alike with constitutions so different.

The sameness and the difference cannot but have an effect on mentality. This is borne out by experience and shows the futility of discussions about sex superiorities and inequalities. A perfect man and a perfect woman should no more resemble each other in mind than in countenance: and perfection does not admit of degrees.

In the mating of the sexes each contributes in equal measure to the common end but not in the same way. From this diversity comes the *first* difference which has to be noted in their personal relations. It is the part of the one to be active and strong, and of the other to be passive and weak. Accept this principle and it follows in the *second* place that woman is intended to please man. If the man requires to please the woman in turn the necessity is less direct. Masterfulness is his special attribute. He pleases by the very fact that he is strong. This is not the law of love, I admit. But it is the law of nature, which is more ancient than love.

If woman is made to please and to be dominated, she ought to make herself agreeable to man and avoid provocation. Her strength is in her charms and through them she should constrain him to discover his powers and make use of them. The surest way of bringing these powers into active operation is to make it necessary by her resistance. In this way self-esteem is added to desire and the man triumphs in the victory which the woman has compelled him to achieve. Out of this relation comes attack and defence, boldness on the one side and timidity on the other, and in the end the modesty and sense of shame with which nature has armed the weak for the subjugation of the strong.

Hence as a *third* consequence of the different constitution of the sexes, the stronger may appear to be master, and yet actually be dependent on the weaker: not because of a superficial practice of gallantry or the prideful generosity of the protective sex, but by reason of an enduring law of nature. By giving woman the capacity to stimulate desires greater than can be satisfied, nature has made man dependent on woman's good will and constrained him to seek to please her as a condition of her submission. Always there remains for man in his conquest the pleasing doubt whether strength has mastered weakness, or there has been a willing subjection; and the woman has usually the guile to leave the doubt unresolved.

Men and women are unequally affected by sex. The male is only a male at times; the female is a female all her life and can never forget her sex.

Plato in his *Republic* gives women the same physical training as men. That is what might be expected. Having made an end of private families in his state and not knowing what to do with the women, he found himself compelled to make men of them. That wonderful genius provided for everything in his plans, and went out of his way to meet an objection that nobody was likely to make, while missing the real objection. I am not speaking about the so-called community of wives, so often charged against him by people who have not read him. What I refer to is the social promiscuity which ignored the differences of sex by giving men and women the same occupations, and sacrificed the sweetest sentiments of nature to the artificial sentiment of loyalty which could not exist without them. He did not realise that the bonds of convention always develop from some natural attachment: that the love one has for his neighbours is the basis of his devotion to the state; that the heart is linked with the great fatherland through the little fatherland of the home; that it is the good son, the good husband, the good father, that makes the good citizen.

Differences in Education

Once it has been shown that men and women are essentially different in character and temperament, it follows that they ought not to have the same education. In accordance with the direction of nature they ought to co-operate in action, but not to do the same things. To complete the attempt we have been making to form the man of nature, we must now go on to consider how the fitting mate for him is to be formed.

If you want right guidance, always follow the leadings of nature. Everything that characterises sex should be respected as established by nature. Men's pride leads them astray when, comparing women with themselves, they say, as they are continually doing, that women have this or that defect, which is absent in men. What would be defects in men are good qualities in women, which are necessary to make things go on well. Women on their side never stop complaining that we men make coquettes of them and keep amusing them with trifles in order to maintain our ascendency. What a foolish idea! When have men ever had to do with the education of girls? Who prevents the mothers bringing up their daughters as they please? Are we men to blame if girls please us by their beauty and attract us by the art they have learned from their mothers? Well, try to educate them like men. They will be quite willing. But the more they resemble men the less will be their power over men, and the greater their own subjection.

The faculties common to the sexes are not equally shared between them; but take them all in all, they are well balanced. The more womanly a woman is, the better. Whenever she exercises her own proper powers she gains by it: when she tries to usurp ours she becomes our inferior. Believe me, wise mother, it is a mistake to bring up your daughter to be like a good man. Make her a good woman, and you can be sure that she will be worth more for herself and for us. This does not mean that she should be brought up in utter ignorance and confined to domestic tasks. A man does not want to make his companion a servant and deprive himself of the peculiar charms of her company. That is quite against the teaching of nature, which has endowed women with quick pleasing minds. Nature means them to think, to judge, to love, to know and to cultivate the mind as well as the countenance. This is the equipment nature has given them to compensate for their lack of strength and enable them to direct the strength of men.

As I see it, the special functions of women, their inclinations and their duties, combine to suggest the kind of education they require. Men and women are made for each other but they differ in the measure of their dependence on each other. We could get on better without women than women could get on without us. To play their part in life they must have our willing help, and for that they must earn our esteem. By the very law of nature women are at the mercy of men's judgments both for themselves and for their children. It is not enough that they should be estimable: they must be esteemed. It is not enough that they should be beautiful: they must be pleasing. It is not enough that they should be wise: their wisdom must be recognised. Their honour does not rest on their conduct but on their reputation. Hence the kind of education they get should be the very opposite of men's in this respect. Public opinion is the tomb of a man's virtue but the throne of a woman's.

On the good constitution of the mothers depends that of the children and the early education of men is in their hands. On women too depend the morals, the passions, the tastes, the pleasures, aye and the happiness of men. For this reason their education must be wholly directed to their relations with men. To give them pleasure, to be useful to them, to win their love and esteem, to train them in their childhood, to care for them when they grow up, to give them counsel and consolation, to make life sweet and agreeable for them: these are the tasks of women in all times for which they should be trained from childhood.

Immanuel Kant

The German thinker Immanuel Kant (1724–1804) is one of the greatest philosophers of all time. He wrote on almost every aspect of theoretical and practical philosophy, from theory of knowledge, philosophy of science and mathematics, to ethics, law, politics, history, and religion. His three major works are *Critique of Pure Reason* (1781), *Critique of Practical Reason* (1788), and *Critique of Judgment* (1790). He wrote two shorter books to introduce his philosophy—*Prolegomena* (1783) and *Groundwork* (1785). The latter (sometimes known in English as *The Moral Law*) is a standard text in ethics; it conveys something of the sublimity of his conception of moral obligation and the respect due to all persons as ends in themselves, but it is not easy reading, as generations of students will attest.

These extracts focus on Kant's account of human nature in two of his less well-known works. They are from *Anthropology from a Pragmatic Point of View,* which he published in 1798 after many years of giving popular lectures on the topic, and his *Religion within the Boundaries of Mere Reason* (1793). The first passage (*Anthropology,* Part II.E) ends with an expression of Kant's hopes for the future historical development of human culture and civilization. In the second, which is taken from Part 1 of the *Religion,* Kant expresses the view that only a religious approach involving divine grace as well as human choice can overcome the evil tendencies in human nature.

It should be noted that, despite his noble philosophy of treating all persons with equal respect, Kant was a man of his time in that he did not recognize women, or members of nonwhite races, as full rational persons with equal civic rights. One of various places where he asserts the inequality of women is in the *Anthropology*, Part II.B; and in an essay, "The Different Races of Mankind" (1775), he asserted "the immutability and permanence of race." According to Charles Mills (*The Racial Contract,* 1997, pp. 69–72), Kant was one of the foundational thinkers for subsequent conceptions of racial distinction. Feminist issues are taken up in the selections from Mill and Holmstrom below, and the dark racial side of European intellectual history is taken up in the selection by Bracken.

Anthropology from a Pragmatic Point of View

On the Character of the Species

In order to characterize a species of beings, two things are required: we have to apprehend it together with other species we are acquainted with under one concept, and to state its characteristic property (*proprietas*)— the quality by which it differs from the other species—and use this as our basis for distinguishing it from them. But if we are comparing a kind of being that we know (A) with another that we do not know (non-A), how can we expect or demand to state the character of the one we know, when we have no middle term for the comparison (*tertium comparationis*)? Let the highest specific concept be that of a *terrestrial* rational being: we cannot name its character because we have no knowledge of *non-terrestrial* rational beings that would enable us to indicate their characteristic property and so to characterize terrestrial rational beings among rational beings in general. It seems, then, that the problem of indicating the character of the human species is quite insoluble; for to set about solving it,

Anthropology from a Pragmatic Point of View, translated by Mary J. Gregor © Martinus Nijhoff 1974.

we should have to compare two *species* of rational beings through *experience,* and experience does not present us with a second such species.

All we have left, then, for assigning man his class in the system of animate nature and so characterizing him is this: that he has a character which he himself creates, insofar as he is capable of perfecting himself according to the ends that he himself adopts. Because of this, man, as an animal endowed with the *capacity for reason* (*animal rationabilis*), can make of himself a *rational animal* (*animal rationale*)—and as such he first *preserves* himself and his species; secondly, he trains, instructs and *educates* his species for domestic society; and thirdly, he *governs* it as a systematic whole (that is, a whole ordered by principles of reason) as is necessary for society. But in comparison with the Idea of possible rational beings on earth, the characteristic of his species is this: that nature implanted in it the seeds of *discord,* and willed that man's own reason bring *concord,* or at least a constant approximation to it, out of this. In the *Idea,* this *concord* is the *end;* but in *actuality,* discord is the *means,* in nature's schema, of a supreme and, to us, inscrutable wisdom which uses cultural progress to realize man's perfection, even at the price of much of his enjoyment of life.

Among the living beings *that inhabit the earth,* man is easily distinguished from all other natural beings by his *technical* predisposition for manipulating things (a mechanical predisposition joined with consciousness), by his *pragmatic* predisposition (for using other men skilfully for his purposes), and by the *moral* predisposition in his being (to treat himself and others according to the principle of freedom under laws). And any one of these three levels can, itself, already distinguish man characteristically from the other inhabitants of the earth.

I. THE TECHNICAL PREDISPOSITION. As for the questions: whether man was originally destined to walk on two feet or on four (as Moscati proposed, perhaps merely as a thesis for a dissertation); whether the Gibbon, the Orang-Utang, the Chimpanzee and so on are destined [to walk upright or on all fours] (here Linné and Camper disagree with each other); whether man is a herbivorous or (since he has a membranous stomach) a carnivorous animal; whether, having neither claws nor fangs, and so no weapons (were it not for reason), he is by nature a predator or a peaceable animal: the answer to them is of no consequence. In any case, this question could still be raised: is man by nature a *sociable* animal or a solitary one who shies away from his neighbors? The latter, most probably.

[The hypothesis of] a first human couple whom nature put, already fully developed, in the midst of what could be eaten, without also giving them a natural instinct that we, in our present natural state, do not have is hard to reconcile with nature's provision for the preservation of the species. The first man would drown in the first pond he saw before him, since swimming is a skill that must be learned; or he would eat poisonous roots and fruits and so be in constant danger of death. But if nature *did implant* this instinct in the first human couple, how could they have failed to pass it on to their children—something that never happens now?

It is true that songbirds teach their young certain songs and transmit them by tradition, so that a bird taken from the nest while still blind and brought up in isolation has no song when it is grown up, but only a certain innate sound of its vocal organs. But where did the first song come from? It was not learned; and if instinct was its origin, why did the young not inherit it?

The characterization of man as a rational animal is already present in the form and organization of the human *hand,* partly by the structure and partly by the sensitive feeling of the *fingers* and *fingertips.* By this nature made him fit for manipulating things not in one particular way but in any way whatsoever, and so for using reason, and indicated the technical predisposition—or the predisposition for skill—of his species as a *rational* animal.

II. THE PRAGMATIC PREDISPOSITION is a step higher. It is man's predisposition to become civilized by culture, especially the cultivation of social qualities, and his natural tendency in social relations to leave the crude state of mere private force and to become a well-bred (if not yet moral) being destined for concord. Man can be and needs to be educated, as much by instruction as by training (discipline). The question here is (with or against Rousseau): whether the character of man's species, in terms of its natural predisposition, fares better in the *crude state* of its nature than *with the arts of culture,* where there is no end in sight? It must be noted, first of all, that when any other animal [species] is left to its own devices, each individual attains its complete destiny; but in man's case only the *species,* at most, achieves it. So the human race can work its way up to its destiny only by *progress* throughout a series of innumerable generations. In the course of it, the goal remains always in prospect for him; but while his *tendency* to this final end can often be obstructed, it can never be completely reversed.

III. THE MORAL PREDISPOSITION. The question here is: whether man is *good* by nature, or *evil* by nature, or whether he is by nature equally receptive to good or evil, according as one or another hand happens to mould him (*cereus in vitium flecti* etc.)—in which case the *species* itself would have no character. But this [last] situation is self-contradictory. For man is a being who has the power of practical reason and is conscious that his choice is free (a person); and in his consciousness of freedom and in his feeling (which is called moral feeling) that justice or injustice is done to him or, by him, to others, he sees himself as subject to a law of duty, no matter how obscure his ideas about it may be. This in itself is the *intelligible* character of humanity as such, and insofar as he has it man is *good* in his inborn predispositions (good by nature). But experience also shows that there is in man a tendency to actively desire what is *unlawful* even though he knows that it is unlawful—that is, a tendency to *evil*— which makes itself felt as inevitably and as soon as he begins to exercise his freedom, and which can therefore be considered innate. And so we must judge that man, according to his *sensible* character, is also evil (by nature). It is not self-contradictory to do this if we are talking about the *character of the species;* for we can assume that its natural destiny consists in continual progress toward the better.

The sum total of what pragmatic anthropology has to say about man's destiny and the character of his development is this: man is destined by his reason to live in a society with men and in it to *cultivate* himself, to *civilize* himself, and to make himself *moral* by the arts and sciences. No matter how strong his animal tendency to yield *passively* to the attractions of comfort and well-being, which he calls happiness, he is still destined to make himself worthy of humanity by *actively* struggling with the obstacles that cling to him because of the crudity of his nature.

Man must, therefore, be *educated* to the good. But those who are supposed to educate him are again men who are themselves still involved in the crudity of nature and are supposed to bring about what they themselves are in need of. This explains why man is constantly deviating from his destiny and always returning to it. Let us cite the difficulties in the solution of this problem and the obstacles to solving it.

A

On the physical side, man's first calling is his impulse to preserve his species as an animal species. But even here, the natural phases of his development refuse to coincide with the civil. According to the first, man in his natural state, by the age of fifteen in any case, is *impelled* by his *sexual instinct* to procreate and maintain his kind, and is also *capable* of doing it. According to the second, he can hardly venture upon it before he is twenty (on the average). For even if, as a citizen of the world, a young man is able soon enough to satisfy his own inclination and his wife's, it is only much later that, as a citizen of a state, he can maintain his wife and children. In order to set up a household with a wife, he must learn a trade and acquire a clientele; and in the more refined classes he may be twenty-five before he is ready for his vocation. How does he fill this interval of forced and unnatural celibacy? With vices, most often.

B

In the whole human species, the drive to acquire scientific knowledge, as a form of culture that ennobles humanity, is completely out of proportion to a man's life span. When a scholar has forged ahead in his own field to the point where he can make an original contribution to it, death calls him away, and his place is taken by a neophyte who, shortly before his own death, after he too has taken one step forward, in turn yields his place to another. What a mass of information, what inventions in the way of new methods would we now have on hand had nature let an Archimedes, a Newton, or a Lavoisier, with their diligence and talent, live to be a hundred with their vigor undiminished! But the scientific progress of the species is never more than fragmentary (according to time), and has no guarantee against regression, with which it is always threatened by intervals of revolutionary barbarism.

C

Our species seems to fare no better in achieving its destiny with respect to *happiness,* which man's nature constantly impels him to strive for, while reason imposes the limiting condition of worthiness to be happy—that is, of morality. As for Rousseau's hypochondriac (gloomy) portrayal of the human species when it ventures out of the state of nature, we need not take this as a recommendation to re-enter the state of nature and return to the woods. What he really wants to do is to show the difficulty that reaching our destiny by way of continually approximating to it involves for our species. And he is not pulling this view out of thin air. The experience of ancient and modern times must disconcert every thinking person and make him doubt whether our species will ever fare better.

Rousseau devoted three works to the damage done to our species by (1) leaving nature for *culture,* which weakened our forces, (2) *becoming civilized,* which produced inequality and mutual oppression, (3) supposedly *becoming moral,* which involved unnatural education and distortion of our way of thinking. These three writings, which present the state of nature as a state of *innocence* (a paradise guarded against our return by a sentinel with a fiery sword), should serve his *Social Contract, Emile,* and the *Vicar of Savoy* only as a guiding thread for finding our way out of the labyrinth of evil with which our species has surrounded itself by its own fault. Rousseau did not really want man to *go* back to the state of nature, but rather to *look* back at it from the step where he now stands. He assumed that man is good *by nature* (as it is bequeathed to him), but good in a negative way: that is, he is not evil of his own accord and on purpose, but only in danger of being contaminated and corrupted by evil or inept guides and examples. But since he needs, for his moral education, *good* men who must themselves have been educated for it, and since none of these are free from (innate or acquired) corruption, the problem of moral education for our *species* remains unsolved even in principle and not merely in degree. For an innate evil propensity in our species is indeed censured by ordinary human reason and perhaps even restrained, but still not eradicated.

A civil constitution artificially raises to its highest power the human species' good predisposition to the final end of its destiny. But even under a civil constitution, *animality* manifests itself earlier and, at bottom, more powerfully than pure *humanity:* domestic animals are more useful to man than wild beasts only because they have been *weakened.* Man's self-will is always ready to break forth in hostility toward his neighbors, and always presses him to claim unconditional freedom, not merely independence of others but even mastery of other beings that are his equal by nature—something we can already see in even the smallest child. This is because nature within man tries to lead him from culture to morality and not (as reason prescribes) from morality and its law, as the starting point, to a culture designed to conform with morality. And this course inevitably *perverts* his tendency and *turns it against* its end—as when, for example, scriptural teaching, which ought of necessity to be [a form of] *moral* culture, begins with *historical* culture, which is merely cultivation of memory, and tries in vain to deduce morality from it.

It is *only from Providence* that man anticipates the education of the human race, taking the species as a *whole*—that is, *collectively (universorum)* and not in terms of all its individual members *(singulorum),* where the multitude does not form a system but only an aggregate gathered together. Only from Providence does he expect his species to tend toward the civil constitution it envisages, which is to be based on the principle of freedom but at the same time on the principle of constraint in accordance with law. That is, he expects it from a wisdom that is not *his,* but is yet the Idea of his own reason, an Idea that is impotent (by his own fault). This education from above is salutary but harsh and stern; nature works it out by way of great hardships, to the extent of nearly destroying the whole race. It consists in bringing forth the *good*—which man does not intend but which, once it is there, continues to maintain itself—from *evil*, which is intrinsically self-vitiating. Providence means precisely the same wisdom that we observe with admiration in the preservation of species of organic natural beings, constantly working toward their destruction and yet always protecting them; and we do not assume a higher principle in its provisions for man than we suppose it is already using in the preservation of plants and animals. For the rest, the human race should and can create its own good fortune; but that it *will* do so, we cannot infer a priori from what we have seen of its natural predispositions. We can infer it only from experience and history; and our expectation is as well based as is necessary for us not to despair of our race's progress toward the better, but to promote its approach to this goal with all our prudence and moral illumination (each to the best of his ability).

We can therefore say: the first characteristic of the human species is man's power, as a rational being, to acquire character as such for his own person as well as for the society in which nature has placed him. This characteristic already presupposes a propitious natural predisposition and a tendency to the good in him; for evil is really without character (since it involves conflict with itself and does not permit any permanent principle within itself).

The character of a living being is what enables us to know in advance its destiny. For the ends of nature, we can assume the principle that nature wants every creature to achieve its destiny through the appropriate development of all the predispositions of its nature, so that at least the species, if not every *individual*, fulfills nature's purpose. In the case of irrational animals, each individual actually attains its destiny by the wisdom of nature. But with man, only the species achieves this. We know of only one species of rational beings on earth: namely, the human race; and in the human race we know, again, only one tendency of nature to this end: namely, the tendency some day to bring about, by its own activity, the development of the good out of evil. This is a prospect that we can anticipate with moral *certainty* (with certainty sufficient for the duty of working toward that end), unless natural upheavals suddenly cut it short. For men are rational beings who, though indeed wicked, are still resourceful and also endowed with a moral predisposition. As culture advances they feel ever more keenly the injuries their egoism inflicts on one another; and since they see no other remedy for it than to subject the private interest (of the individual) to the public interest (of all united), they submit, though reluctantly, to a discipline (of civil constraint). But in doing this they subject themselves only to constraint according to laws they themselves have given, and feel themselves ennobled by their consciousness of it: namely, by their awareness of belonging to a species that lives up to man's vocation, as reason represents it to him in the ideal.

Main Features of the Description of the Human Species' Character

I. Man was not meant to belong to a herd, like cattle, but to a hive, like bees. *Necessity* to be a member of some civil society or other.

The simplest, least artificial way of establishing a civil society is to have one sage in this hive (monarchy). But when there are many such hives near one another, they soon attack one another, as robber bees (make war), not, however, as men do, to strengthen their own group by uniting the other one with it—here the comparison ends—but only to use the *others'* hard work *themselves,* by cunning or force. Each people tries to strengthen itself by subjugating neighboring peoples, whether from a desire for aggrandizement or from fear of being swallowed up by others unless it steals a march of them. So in our species, civil or foreign war, though it is a great misfortune, is also the incentive to pass from the crude state of nature to the civil state. It is a mechanical device of Providence, in which the antagonistic forces do impede each other by their friction, but are still maintained in regular motion for a long time through the push and pull of other incentives.

II. *Freedom* and *law* (which limits freedom) are the two pivots around which civil legislation turns. But in order for law to be efficacious and not merely an empty recommendation, a middle term must be added, namely power, which, when it is connected with the principles of freedom, provides the principles of law with effect.

There are four conceivable combinations of power with freedom and law:

a) Law and freedom without power (anarchy)
b) Law and power without freedom (despotism)
c) Power without freedom and law (barbarism)
d) Power with freedom and law (republic)

We see that only the last combination deserves to be called a true civil constitution. But by a republic we do not mean one of the three forms of state (democracy), but only a state as such. And the ancient dictum of Brocard: *Salus civitatis* (not *civium*) *suprema lex esto* does not mean that the material good of the community (the *happiness* of the citizens) should serve as the supreme principle of the state constitution; for this well-being, which each individual pictures to himself in his own way, according to his personal inclination, has not at all the value of an objective principle, which requires universality. The dictum says only that the *rational good*, the preservation of the *state constitution* once it exists, is the highest law of a civil society as such; for it is only by the state constitution that civil society maintains itself.

The character of the species, as it is indicated by the experience of all ages and of all peoples, is this: that, taken collectively (the human race as one whole), it is a multitude of persons, existing successively and side by side, who cannot *do without* associating peacefully and yet cannot *avoid* constantly offending one another. Hence they feel destined by nature to [form], through mutual compulsion under laws that proceed from themselves, a coalition in a *cosmopolitan* society *(cosmopolitismus)*—a coalition which, though constantly threatened by dissension, makes progress on the whole. This Idea is, in itself, unattainable: it is not a constitutive principle (the principle of anticipating lasting peace amid the most vigorous actions and reactions of men). It is only a regulative principle, [directing us] to pursue this diligently as the destiny of the human race, not without solid grounds for supposing that man has a natural tendency toward it.

The question can be raised, whether our species should be considered a *good* race or an *evil* one (for we can also call it a *race*, if we conceive of it as a species of rational *beings on earth* in comparison with rational beings on other planets, as a multitude of creatures originating from one demiurge); and then I must admit that there is not much to boast about in it. If we look at man's behavior not only in ancient history but also in contemporary events, we are often tempted to take the part of *Timon* the misanthropist in our judgments; but far more often, and more to the point, that of *Momus,* who considers foolishness rather than evil as the most striking trait of character in our species. But since foolishness combined with a lineament of evil (which is then called offensive folly) is an unmistakable feature in the moral physiognomy of our species, the mere fact that any prudent man finds it necessary to conceal a good part of his thoughts makes it clear enough that every member of our race is well advised to be on his guard and not to reveal himself *completely.* And this already betrays the propensity of our species to be ill disposed toward one another.

It could well be that some other planet is inhabited by rational beings who have to think aloud—who, whether awake or dreaming, in company with others or alone, can have no thoughts they do not *utter.* How would their behavior toward one another then differ from that of the human race? Unless they were all as *pure as angels,* we cannot conceive how they could live together peacefully, have any respect at all for one another, and get on well together. So it already belongs to the basic composition of a human creature and to the concept of his species to explore the thoughts of others but to withhold one's own—a nice quality that does not fail to progress gradually from *dissimulation* to *deception* [*vorsetzlichen Täuschung*] and finally to *lying.* This would give a caricature of our species that would warrant, not mere good-natured *laughter* at it, but *contempt* for what constitutes its character, and the admission that this race of terrestrial rational beings deserves no honorable place among the other races (which we do not know). And this would be correct, were it not that our very judgment of condemnation reveals a moral predisposition in us, an innate demand of reason to counteract this tendency. So it presents the human species, not as evil, but as a species of rational beings that strives, in the face of obstacles, to rise out of evil in constant progress toward the good. In this, our volition is generally good; but we find it hard to accomplish what we will, because we cannot expect the end to be attained by the free accord of *individuals,* but only by a progressive organization of citizens of the earth into and towards the species, as a system held together by cosmopolitan bonds.

Religion within the Boundaries of Mere Reason

Concerning the Indwelling of the Evil Principle Alongside the Good or Of the Radical Evil in Human Nature

That "the world lieth in evil" is a complaint as old as history, even as old as the older art of poetic fiction; indeed, just as old as that oldest among all fictions; the religion of the priests. All allow that the world began with

Religion within the Boundaries of Mere Reason, translated by George di Giovanni, in *Religion and Rational Theology,* in *The Cambridge Edition of the Works of Immanuel Kant* © Cambridge University Press 1996.

something good: with the Golden Age, with life in Paradise, or an even happier life in communion with heavenly beings. But then they make this happiness disappear like a dream, and they spitefully hasten the decline into evil (moral evil, with which the physical always went hand in hand) in an accelerating fall, so that now (this "now" is, however, as old as history) we live in the final age; the Last Day and the destruction of the world are knocking at the door, and in certain regions of India the Judge and Destroyer of the world, Rutra (otherwise known as Shiva or Shiwa), already is worshipped as the God now holding power, after Vishnu, the Sustainer of the World, grown weary of the office he had received from Brahma the Creator, resigned it centuries ago.

More recent, though far less widespread, is the opposite heroic opinion, which has gained standing only among philosophers and, in our days, especially among the pedagogues: that the world steadfastly (though hardly noticeably) forges ahead in the very opposite direction, namely 6:20 from bad to better; that at least there is in the human being the predisposition to move in this direction. But surely, if the issue is *moral* good or evil (not just growth in civilization), they have not drawn this view from experience, for the history of all times attests far too powerfully against it; and we may presume that it is, rather, just an optimistic presupposition on the part of the moralists, from Seneca to Rousseau, intended to encourage the indefatigable cultivation of that seed of goodness that perhaps lies in us, if one could only count on any such natural foundation of goodness in the human kind. Yet this is also to be said: Since we must assume that the human being is sound of body by nature (i.e., in the way he is usually born), there is no cause not to assume that he is equally sound and good of soul by nature as well. Nature itself would then be promoting the cultivation in us of this ethical predisposition toward goodness. As Seneca says: "We are sick with curable diseases, and if we wish to be cured, nature comes to our aid, *for we are born to health."*

But since it well may be that we have erred in both these ways of reading experience, the question arises whether a middle ground may not at least be possible, namely that, as a species, the human being can neither be good nor evil, or, at any rate, that he can be the one just as much as the other, partly good, partly evil. We call a human being evil, however, not because he performs actions that are evil (contrary to law), but because these are so constituted that they allow the inference of evil maxims in him. Now through experience we can indeed notice unlawful actions, and also notice (at least within ourselves) that they are consciously contrary to law. But we cannot observe maxims, we cannot do so unproblematically even within ourselves; hence the judgment that an agent is an evil human being cannot reliably be based on experience. In order, then, to call a human being evil, it must be possible to infer *a priori* from a number of consciously evil actions, or even from a single one, an underlying evil maxim, and, from this, the presence in the subject of a common ground, itself a maxim, of all particular morally evil maxims.

But lest anyone be immediately scandalized by the expression *nature,*   6:21 which would stand in direct contradiction to the predicates *morally* good or *morally* evil if taken to mean (as it usually does) the opposite of the ground of actions [arising] from *freedom,* let it be noted that by "the nature of a human being" we only understand here the subjective ground—wherever it may lie—of the exercise of the human being's freedom in general (under objective moral laws) antecedent to every deed that falls within the scope of the senses. But this subjective ground must, in turn, itself always be a deed of freedom (for otherwise the use or abuse of the human being's power of choice with respect to the moral law could not be imputed to him, nor could the good or evil in him be called "moral"). Hence the ground of evil cannot lie in any object *determining* the power of choice through inclination, not in any natural impulses, but only in a rule that the power of choice itself produces for the exercise of its freedom, i.e., in a maxim. One cannot, however, go on asking what, in a human being, might be the subjective ground of the adoption of this maxim rather than its opposite. For if this ground were ultimately no longer itself a maxim, but merely a natural impulse, the entire exercise of freedom could be traced back to a determination through natural causes—and this would contradict freedom. Whenever we therefore say, "The human being is by nature good," or, "He is by nature evil," this only means that he holds within himself a first ground (to us inscrutable) for the adoption of good or evil (unlawful) maxims, and that he holds this ground *qua* human, universally—in such a way, therefore, that by his maxims he expresses at the same time the character of his species.

We shall say, therefore, of one of these [two] characters (which distinguish the human being from other possible rational beings) that it is *innate* in him; and yet we shall always be satisfied that nature is not to blame for it (if the character is evil), nor does it deserve praise (if it is good), but that the human being is alone its author. But since the first ground of the adoption of our maxims, which must itself again lie in the   6:22 free power of choice, cannot be any fact possibly given in experience, the good or the evil in the human being is said to be innate (as the subjective first ground of the adoption of this or that maxim with respect to the moral law) only *in the sense* that it is posited as the ground antecedent to every use of freedom given in experience (from the earliest youth as far back as birth) and is thus represented as present in the human being at the moment of birth—not that birth itself is its cause.

• • •

I. Concerning the Original Predisposition to Good in Human Nature

We may justifiably bring this predisposition, with reference to its end, under three headings, as elements of the determination of the human being:

1. The predisposition to the *animality* of the human being, as a *living being;*
2. To the *humanity* in him, as a living and at the same time *rational* being;
3. To his *personality,* as a rational and at the same time *responsible* being.

1. The predisposition to animality in the human being may be brought under the general title of physical or merely *mechanical* self-love, i.e. a love for which reason is not required. It is threefold: *first,* for self-preservation; *second,* for the propagation of the species, through the sexual drive, and for the preservation of the offspring thereby begotten through breeding; *third,* for community with other human beings, i.e. the social drive. On these three can be grafted all sorts of vices (which, however, do not of themselves issue from this predisposition as a root). They can be named vices of the *savagery* of nature, and, at their greatest deviation 6:27 from the natural ends, are called the *bestial vices of gluttony, lust and wild lawlessness* (in relation to other human beings).

2. The predispositions to humanity can be brought under the general title of a self-love which is physical and yet *involves comparison* (for which reason is required); that is, only in comparison with others does one judge oneself happy or unhappy. Out of this self-love originates the inclination *to gain worth in the opinion of others,* originally, of course, merely *equal worth:* not allowing anyone superiority over oneself, bound up with the constant anxiety that others might be striving for ascendancy; but from this arises gradually an unjust desire to acquire superiority for

oneself over others. Upon this, namely, upon *jealousy* and *rivalry*, can be grafted the greatest vices of secret or open hostility to all whom we consider alien to us. These vices, however, do not really issue from nature as their root but are rather inclinations, in the face of the anxious endeavor of others to attain a hateful superiority over us, to procure it for ourselves over them for the sake of security, as preventive measure; for nature itself wanted to use the idea of such a competitiveness (which in itself does not exclude reciprocal love) as only an incentive to culture. Hence the vices that are grafted upon this inclination can also be named vices of *culture*, and in their extreme degree of malignancy (where they are simply the idea of a maximum of evil that surpasses humanity), e.g., in *envy, ingratitude, joy in others' misfortunes*, etc., they are called *diabolical vices*.

3. The predisposition to personality is the susceptibility to respect for the moral law *as of itself a sufficient incentive to the power of choice*. This susceptibility to simple respect for the moral law within us would thus be the moral feeling, which by itself does not yet constitute an end of the natural predisposition but only insofar as it is an incentive of the power of choice. But now this is possible only because the free power of choice incorporates moral feeling into its maxim: so a power of choice so constituted is a good character, and this character, as in general every character of the free power of choice, is something that can only be acquired; yet, for its possibility there must be present in our nature a predisposition onto which nothing evil can be grafted. The idea of the moral law alone, 6:28 together with the respect that is inseparable from it, cannot be properly called a *predisposition to personality;* it is personality itself (the idea of humanity considered wholly intellectually). The subjective ground, however, of our incorporating this incentive into our maxims seems to be an addition to personality, and hence seems to deserve the name of a predisposition on behalf of it.

If we consider the three predispositions just named according to the conditions of their possibility, we find that the *first* does not have reason at its root at all; that the *second* is rooted in a reason which is indeed practical, but only as subservient to other incentives; and that the *third* alone is rooted in reason practical of itself, i.e. in reason legislating unconditionally. All these predispositions in the human being are not only (negatively) *good* (they do not resist the moral law) but they are also predispositions *to the good* (they demand compliance with it). They are *original*, for they belong to the possibility of human nature. The human being can indeed use the first two inappropriately, but cannot eradicate either of the two. By the predispositions of a being we understand the constituent parts required for it as well as the forms of their combination that make for such a being. They are *original* if they belong with necessity to the possibility of this being, but *contingent* if the being in question is possible in itself also without them. It should be noted, finally, that there is no question here of other predispositions except those that relate immediately to the faculty of desire and the exercise of the power of choice.

II. Concerning the Propensity to Evil in Human Nature

6:29 By *propensity (propensio)* I understand the subjective ground of the possibility of an inclination (habitual desire, *concupiscentia*), insofar as this possibility is contingent for humanity in general. It is distinguished from a predisposition in that a propensity can indeed be innate yet *may* be represented as not being such: it can rather be thought of (if it is good) as *acquired*, or (if evil) as *brought* by the human being *upon* himself. Here, however, we are only talking of a propensity to genuine evil, i.e. moral evil, which, since it is only possible as the determination of a free power of choice and this power for its part can be judged good or evil only on the basis of its maxims, must reside in the subjective ground of the possibility of the deviation of the maxims from the moral law. And, if it is legitimate to assume that this propensity belongs to the human being universally (and hence to the character of the species), the propensity will be called a *natural* propensity of the human being to evil. We can further add that the will's capacity or incapacity arising from this natural propensity to adopt or not to adopt the moral law in its maxims can be called *the good or the evil heart*.

We can think of three different grades of this natural propensity to evil. *First,* it is the general weakness of the human heart in complying with the adopted maxims, or the *frailty* of human nature; *second,* the propensity to adulterate moral incentives with immoral ones (even when it is done with good intention, and under maxims of the good), i.e. *impurity; third,* the propensity to adopt evil maxims, i.e. the *depravity* of human nature, or of the human heart.

First, the frailty (*fragilitas*) of human nature is expressed even in the complaint of an Apostle: "What I would, that I do not!" i.e. I incorporate the good (the law) into the maxim of my power of choice; but this good, which is an irresistible incentive objectively or ideally (*in thesi*), is subjectively (*in hypothesi*) the weaker (in comparison with inclination) whenever the maxim is to be followed.

Second, the impurity (*impuritas, improbitas*) of the human heart con-

sists in this, that although the maxim is good with respect to its object (the   6:30
intended compliance with the law) and perhaps even powerful enough in
practice, it is not purely moral, i.e. it has not, as it should be [the case],
adopted the law *alone* as its *sufficient* incentive but, on the contrary, often
(and perhaps always) needs still other incentives besides it in order to
determine the power of choice for what duty requires; in other words,
actions conforming to duty are not done purely from duty.

Third, the depravity (*vitiositas, pravitas*) or, if one prefers, the *corruption (corruptio)* of the human heart is the propensity of the power of
choice to maxims that subordinate the incentives of the moral law to others (not moral ones). It can also be called the *perversity (perversitas)* of
the human heart, for it reverses the ethical order as regards the incentives
of a *free* power of choice; and although with this reversal there can still be
legally good (*legale*) actions, yet the mind's attitude is thereby corrupted
at its root (so far as the moral disposition is concerned), and hence the
human being is designated as evil.

It will be noted that the propensity to evil is here established (as regards
actions) in the human being, even the best; and so it also must be if it is to
be proved that the propensity to evil among human beings is universal, or,
which here amounts to the same thing, that it is woven into human nature.

III. The Human Being Is by Nature Evil

In view of what has been said above, the statement, "The human being is
evil," cannot mean anything else than that he is conscious of the moral
law and yet has incorporated into his maxim the (occasional) deviation
from it. "He is evil *by nature*" simply means that being evil applies to him
considered in his species; not that this quality may be inferred from the
concept of his species ([i.e.] from the concept of a human being in general, for then the quality would be necessary), but rather that, according to
the cognition we have of the human being through experience, he cannot
be judged otherwise, in other words, we may presuppose evil as subjectively necessary in every human being, even the best. Now, since this
propensity must itself be considered morally evil, hence not a natural predisposition but something that a human being can be held accountable
for, consequently must consist in maxims of the power of choice contrary
to the law and yet, because of freedom, such maxims must be viewed as
accidental, a circumstance that would not square with the universality of
the evil at issue unless their supreme subjective ground were not in all
cases somehow entwined with humanity itself and, as it were, rooted in it:

so we can call this ground a natural propensity to evil, and, since it must nevertheless always come about through one's own fault, we can further even call it a *radical* innate *evil* in human nature (not any the less brought upon us by ourselves).

6:33   We can spare ourselves the formal proof that there must be such a corrupt propensity rooted in the human being, in view of the multitude of woeful examples that the experience of human *deeds* parades before us. If we wish to draw our examples from that state in which many a philosopher especially hoped to meet the natural goodliness of human nature, namely from the so-called *state of nature,* let one but compare with this hypothesis the scenes of unprovoked cruelty in the ritual murders of Tofoa, New Zealand, and the Navigator Islands, and the never-ending cruelty (which Captain Hearne reports) in the wide wastes of northwestern America from which, indeed, no human being derives the least benefit, and we find vices of savagery more than sufficient to distance us from any such opinion. If we are however disposed to the opinion that we can have a better cognition of human nature known in its civilized state (where its predispositions can be more fully developed), we must then hear out a long melancholy litany of charges against humankind—of secret falsity even in the most intimate friendship, so that a restraint on trust in the mutual confidence of even the best friends is reckoned a universal maxim of prudence in social dealings; of a propensity to hate him to whom we are indebted, to which a benefactor must always heed; of a hearty goodwill that nonetheless admits the remark that "in the misfortunes of our best friends there is something that does not altogether displease us", and of many other vices yet hidden under the appearance of virtue, let alone those of which no secret is made, for to us someone already counts as good when *his evil is common to a class*—and we shall have enough of the vices of *culture* and civilization (the most offensive of all) to make us rather turn our eyes away from the doings of human

6:34   beings, lest we be dragged ourselves into another vice, namely that of misanthropy. And if we are not satisfied yet, we need but consider a state wondrously compounded from both the others, namely that of a people in its external relations, where civilized peoples stand vis-à-vis one another in the relation of raw nature (the state of constant war) and have also firmly taken it into their heads not to get out of it, and we shall become aware of fundamental principles in the great societies we call *states* directly in contradiction to official policy yet never abandoned, principles which no philosopher has yet been able to bring into agreement with morality or else (what is terrible) suggest [how to replace with] better ones, reconcilable with human nature: So *philosophical chiliasm,* which hopes for a state of perpetual peace based on a federation of nations united in a world-republic, is universally derided as sheer fantasy as much as *theological chiliasm,* which awaits for the completed moral improvement of the human race.

• • •

IV. Concerning the Origin of Evil in Human Nature

Origin (the first origin) is the descent of an effect from its first cause, i.e. from that cause which is not in turn the effect of another cause of the same kind. It can be considered as either *origin according to reason,* or *origin according to time.* In the first meaning, only the effect's *being* is considered; in the second, its *occurrence,* and hence, as an event, it is referred to its *cause in time.* If an effect is referred to a cause which is however bound to it according to the laws of freedom, as is the case with moral evil, then the determination of the power of choice to the production of this effect is thought as bound to its determining ground not in time but merely in the representation of reason; it cannot be derived from some *preceding* state or other, as must always occur, on the other hand, whenever the evil action 6:40 is referred to its natural cause as *event* in the world. To look for the temporal origin of free actions as free (as though they were natural effects) is therefore a contradiction; and hence also a contradiction to look for the temporal origin of the moral constitution of the human being, so far as this constitution is considered as contingent, for constitution here means the ground of the *exercise* of freedom which (just like the determining ground of the free power of choice in general) must be sought in the representations of reason alone.

Whatever the nature, however, of the origin of moral evil in the human being, of all the ways of representing its spread and propagation through the members of our species and in all generations, the most inappropriate is surely to imagine it as having come to us by way of *inheritance* from our first parents; for then we could say of moral evil exactly what the poet says of the good: "Race and ancestors, and those things which we did not make ourselves, I scarcely consider as our own." We should note further that, when we enquire into the origin of evil, at the beginning we still do not take into account the propensity to it (as *peccatum in potentia*) but only consider the actual evil of given actions according to the evil's inner 6:41 possibility, and according to all that must conspire within the power of choice for such actions to be performed.

Every evil action must be so considered, whenever we seek its rational origin, as if the human being had fallen into it directly from the state of innocence. For whatever his previous behavior may have been, whatever the natural causes influencing him, whether they are inside or outside them, his action is yet free and not determined through any of these causes; hence the action can and must always be judged as an *original* exercise of his power of choice. He should have refrained from it, whatever his temporal circumstances and entanglements; for through no cause in the world can he cease to be a free agent. It is indeed rightly said that to the human being are also imputed the *consequences* originating from his previous free but lawless actions. All that is thereby meant, however, is this: It is not necessary to get sidetracked into the prevarication of establishing whether such actions may have been free or not, since there is already sufficient ground for the imputation in the admittedly free action which was their cause. However evil a human being has been right up to the moment of an impending free action (evil even habitually, as second nature), his duty to better himself was not just in the past: it still is his duty *now;* he must therefore be capable of it and, should he not do it, he is at the moment of action just as accountable, and stands just as condemned, as if, though endowed with a natural predisposition to the good (which is inseparable from freedom), he had just stepped out of the state of innocence into evil. Hence we cannot inquire into the origin in time of this deed but must inquire only into its origin in reason, in order thereby to determine and, where possible, to explain the propensity [to it], if there is one, i.e. the subjective universal ground of the adoption of a transgression into our maxim.

Now, the mode of representation which the Scriptures use to depict the origin of evil, as having a *beginning* in human nature, well agrees with the foregoing; for the Scriptures portray this beginning in a narrative, where what must be thought as objectively first by nature (without regard to the condition of time) appears as a first in time. Evil begins, according to the Scriptures, not from a fundamental propensity to it, for otherwise its 6:42 beginning would not result from freedom, but from *sin* (by which is understood the transgression of the moral law as *divine command*); the state of human beings prior to any propensity to evil is however called the state of innocence. The moral law moved forward in the form of *prohibition* (Genesis II:16–17), as befits a being who, like the human, is not pure but is tempted by inclinations. But, instead of following this law absolutely as sufficient incentive (which alone is unconditionally good, and with which there cannot be further hesitation), the human being looked about for yet other incentives (III:6) which can be good only conditionally (i.e. so far as they do not infringe the law). And he made it his maxim—if one thinks of action as originating from freedom with consciousness—to follow the law of duty, not from duty but, if need be, also with an eye to other aims. He thereby began to question the stringency of the command that excludes the influence of every other incentive, and thereupon to rationalize downgrading his obedience to the command to the status of the merely conditional obedience as a means (under the principle of self-love), until, finally, the preponderance of the sensory inducements over the incentive of the law was incorporated into the maxim of action, and thus sin came to be (III:6). "Change but the name, of you the tale is told."

• • •

GENERAL REMARK CONCERNING THE RESTORATION TO ITS POWER OF THE ORIGINAL PREDISPOSITION TO THE GOOD. The human being must make or have made *himself* into whatever he is or should become in a moral sense, good or evil. These two [characters] must be an effect of his free power of choice, for otherwise they could not be imputed to him and, consequently, he could be neither *morally* good nor evil. If it is said, The human being is created good, this can only mean nothing more than: He has been created for the *good* and the original *predisposition* in him is good; the human being is not thereby good as such, but he brings it about that he becomes either good or evil, according as he either incorporates or does not incorporate into his maxims the incentives contained in that predisposition (and this must be left entirely to his free choice). Granted that some supernatural cooperation is also needed to his becoming good or better, whether this cooperation only consist in the diminution of obstacles or be also a positive assistance, the human being must nonetheless make himself antecedently worthy of it; and he must *accept* this help (which is no small matter), i.e. he must incorporate this positive increase of force into his maxim: in this way alone is it possible that the good be imputed to him, and that he be acknowledged a good human being.

How it is possible that a naturally evil human being should make himself into a good human being surpasses every concept of ours. For how can an evil tree bear good fruit? But, since by our previous admission a tree which was (in its predisposition) originally good but did bring forth bad fruits, and since the fall from good into evil (if we seriously consider that evil originates from freedom) is no more comprehensible than the   6:45

ascent from evil back to the good, then the possibility of this last cannot be disputed. For, in spite of that fall, the command that we *ought* to become better human beings still resounds unabated in our souls; consequently, we must also be capable of it, even if what we can do is of itself insufficient and, by virtue of it, we only make ourselves receptive to a higher assistance inscrutable to us. Surely we must presuppose in all this that there is still a germ of goodness left in its entire purity, a germ that cannot be extirpated or corrupted.

• • •

Against this expectation of self-improvement, reason, which by nature finds moral labor vexing, now conjures up, under the pretext of natural impotence, all sorts of impure religious ideas (among which belongs falsely imputing to God the principle of happiness as the supreme condition of his commands). All religions, however, can be divided into *religion of rogation* (of mere cult) and *moral religion,* i.e. the religion of *good life-conduct.* According to the first, the human being either flatters himself that God can make him eternally happy (through the remissions of his debts) without any necessity on his part *to become a better human being;* or else, if this does not seem possible to him, that *God* himself *can make him a better human being* without his having to contribute more than to *ask* for it, and, since before an omniscient being asking is no more than *wishing,* this would amount in fact to doing nothing, for, if improvement were a matter of mere wishing, every human being would be good. According to moral religion, however (and, of all the public religions so
6:52 far known, the Christian alone is of this type), it is a fundamental principle that, to become a better human being, everyone must do as much as it is in his powers to do; and only then, if a human being has not buried his innate talent (Luke 19:12–16), if he has made use of the original predisposition to the good in order to become a better human being, can he hope that what does not lie in his power will be made good by cooperation from above. Nor is it absolutely necessary that the human being know in what this cooperation consists; indeed, it is perhaps unavoidable that, were the way it occurs revealed at a given time, different people would, at some other time, form different conceptions of it, and that in all sincerity. For here too the principle holds, "It is not essential, and hence not necessary, that every human being know what God does, or has done, for his salvation"; but it is essential to know *what a human being has to do himself* in order to become worthy of this assistance.

Karl Marx

After Kant there arose a generation of thinkers, many of them influenced by the philosophy of Hegel, who became vividly aware of the long developmental processes of human history. Karl Marx (1818–1883) developed his ideas in the shadow of Hegel and his successors. But he combined their view of human development through many stages with a thoroughly realistic sense of the crucial importance of economic facts—how people produce their livelihood at each stage of society.

Like Freud after him, Marx claimed to have found a new science of human nature (based respectively on socioeconomic or psychobiological foundations). And both were concerned not merely to explain human phenomena, but to apply their theory to liberate people from the social or mental forces that prevented their free development. Marx had a very strong sense of social justice; in his famous words, the point of philosophy is not just to interpret the world, but to change it. The first of these excerpts is the famous summary of the "materialist theory of history" in the preface to Marx's *Contribution to the Critique of Political Economy* (1859); the rest are from *The German Ideology* (written with Engels in 1845–1846).

Some issues about Marx's theory of human nature are taken up

in connection with feminism in the selection by Holmstrom
below.

The Materialist Theory of History

From *Contribution to the Critique of Political Economy*

. . . The general result at which I arrived and which, once won, served as
a guiding thread for my studies, can be briefly formulated as follows: In
the social production of their life, men enter into definite relations that are
indispensable and independent of their will; these relations of production
correspond to a definite stage of development of their material forces of
production. The sum total of these relations of production constitutes the
economic structure of society—the real foundation, on which rises a legal
and political superstructure and to which correspond definite forms of
social consciousness. The mode of production of material life determines
the social, political and intellectual life process in general. It is not the
consciousness of men that determines their being, but, on the contrary,
their social being that determines their consciousness. At a certain stage
of their development, the material productive forces in society come in
conflict with the existing relations of production, or—what is but a legal
expression for the same thing—with the property relations within which
they have been at work before. From forms of development of the productive forces these relations turn into their fetters. Then begins an epoch
of social revolution. With the change of the economic foundation the
entire immense superstructure is more or less rapidly transformed. In
considering such transformations a distinction should always be made
between the material transformation of the economic conditions of production, which can be determined with the precision of natural science,
and the legal, political, religious, aesthetic or philosophic—in short, ideological forms in which men become conscious of this conflict and fight
it out. Just as our opinion of an individual is not based on what he thinks
of himself, so can we not judge of such a period of transformation by its
own consciousness; on the contrary, this consciousness must be
explained rather from the contradictions of material life, from the existing conflict between the social productive forces and the relations of pro-

From *The Portable Marx*, edited by Eugene Kamenka © Viking and Penguin 1983.

duction. No social order ever disappears before all the productive forces for which there is room in it have been developed; and new, higher relations of production never appear before the material conditions of their existence have matured in the womb of the old society itself. Therefore, mankind always sets itself only such tasks as it can solve; since, looking at the matter more closely, we will always find that the task itself arises only when the material conditions necessary for its solution already exist or are at least in the process of formation. In broad outlines we can designate the Asiatic, the ancient, the feudal, and the modern bourgeois modes of production as so many progressive epochs in the economic formation of society. The bourgeois relations of production are the last antagonistic form of the social process of production—antagonistic not in the sense of individual antagonism, but of one arising from the social conditions of life of the individuals; at the same time the productive forces developing in the womb of bourgeois society create the material conditions for the solution of that antagonism. This social formation constitutes, therefore, the closing chapter of the prehistoric stage of human society.

• • •

From *The German Ideology*

. . . The premises from which we begin are not arbitrary ones, not dogmas, but real premises from which abstraction can only be made in the imagination. They are the real individuals, their activity and the material conditions under which they live, both those which they find already existing and those produced by their activity. These premises can thus be verified in a purely empirical way.

The first premise of all human history is, of course, the existence of living human individuals. Thus the first fact to be established is the physical organization of these individuals and their consequent relation to the rest of nature. Of course, we cannot here go either into the actual physical nature of man, or into the natural conditions in which man finds himself—geological, orohydrographical, climatic and so on. The writing of history must always set out from these natural bases and their modification in the course of history through the action of man.

Men can be distinguished from animals by consciousness, by religion or anything else you like. They themselves begin to distinguish themselves from animals as soon as they begin to *produce* their means of subsistence, a step which is conditioned by their physical organization. By producing their means of subsistence men are indirectly producing their actual material life.

The way in which men produce their means of subsistence depends first of all on the nature of the actual means they find in existence and have to reproduce. This mode of production must not be considered simply as being the reproduction of the physical existence of the individuals. Rather it is a definite form of activity of these individuals, a definite form of expressing their life, a definite *mode of life* on their part. As individuals express their life, so they are. What they are, therefore, coincides with their production, both with *what* they produce and with *how* they produce. The nature of individuals thus depends on the material conditions determining their production.

This production only makes its appearance with the increase of population. In its turn this presupposes the intercourse of individuals with one another. The form of this intercourse is again determined by production.

The relations of different nations among themselves depend upon the extent to which each has developed its productive forces, the division of labour and internal intercourse. This statement is generally recognized. But not only the relation of one nation to others, but also the whole internal structure of the nation itself depends on the stage of development reached by its production and its internal and external intercourse. How far the productive forces of a nation are developed is shown most manifestly by the degree to which the division of labour has been carried. Each new productive force, in so far as it is not merely a quantitative extension of productive forces already known (for instance the bringing into cultivation of fresh land), brings about a further development of the division of labour.

The division of labour inside a nation leads at first to the separation of industrial and commercial from agricultural labour, and hence to the separation of town and country and a clash of interests between them. Its further development leads to the separation of commercial from industrial labour. At the same time through the division of labour there develop further, inside these various branches, various divisions among the individuals cooperating in definite kinds of labour. The relative position of these individual groups is determined by the methods employed in agriculture, industry and commerce (patriarchalism, slavery, estates, classes). These same conditions are to be seen (given a more developed intercourse) in the relations of different nations to one another.

The various stages of development in the division of labour are just so many different forms of ownership; i.e. the existing stage in the division of labour determines also the relations of individuals to one another with reference to the material, instrument, and product of labour. The first form of ownership is tribal ownership. It corresponds to the undeveloped stage of production, during which a people lives by hunting and fishing, by the rearing of beasts or, in the highest stage, agriculture. In the latter case it presupposes a great mass of uncultivated stretches of land. The division of labour is at this stage still very elementary and is confined to a further extension of the natural division of labour imposed by the family. The social structure is therefore limited to an extension of the family; patriarchal family chieftains; below them the members of the tribe; finally slaves. The slavery latent in the family only develops gradually with the increase of population, the growth of wants, and with the extension of external relations, of war or of trade.

The second form is the ancient communal and state ownership which proceeds especially from the union of several tribes into a city by agreement or by conquest, and which is still accompanied by slavery. Beside communal ownership we already find movable, and later also immovable, private property developing, but as an abnormal form subordinate to communal ownership. It is only as a community that the citizens hold power over their labouring slaves, and on this account alone, therefore, they are bound to the form of communal ownership. It is communal private property which compels the active citizens to remain in this natural form of association over against their slaves. For this reason the whole structure of society based on this communal ownership, and with it the power of the people, decays in the same measure as immovable private property evolves. The division of labour is already more developed. We already find the antagonism of town and country; later the antagonism between those states which represent town interests and those which represent country, and inside the towns themselves the antagonism between industry and maritime commerce. The class relation between citizens and slaves is now completely developed.

With the development of private property, we find here for the first time the same conditions which we shall find again, only on a more extensive scale, with modern private property. On the one hand the concentration of private property, which began very early in Rome (as the Licinian agrarian law proves), and proceeded very rapidly from the time of the civil wars and especially under the Emperors; on the other hand, coupled with this, the transformation of the plebeian small peasantry into a proletariat, which, however, owing to its intermediate position between propertied citizens and slaves, never achieved an independent development.

The third form of ownership is feudal or estate-property. If antiquity started out from the town and its little territory, the Middle Ages started out from the country. This different starting-point was determined by the sparseness of the population at that time, which was scattered over a large area and which received no large increase from the conquerors. In contrast to Greece and Rome, feudal development therefore extends over a much wider field, prepared by the Roman conquests and the spread of agriculture at first associated with them. The last centuries of the declining Roman Empire and its conquest by the barbarians destroyed a number of productive forces; agriculture had declined, industry had decayed for want of a market, trade had died out or been violently suspended, the rural and urban population had decreased. From these conditions and the mode of organization of the conquest determined by them, feudal property developed under the influence of the Germanic military constitution. Like tribal and communal ownership, it is based again on a community; but the directly producing class standing over against it is not, as in the case of the ancient community, the slaves, but the enserfed small peasantry. As soon as feudalism is fully developed, there also arises antagonism to the towns. The hierarchical system of land-ownership, and the armed bodies of retainers associated with it, gave the nobility power over the serfs. This feudal organization was, just as much as the ancient communal ownership, an association against a subjected producing class; but the form of association and the relation to the direct producers were different because of the different conditions of production.

This feudal organization of land-ownership had its counterpart in the towns in the shape of corporative property, the feudal organization of trades. Here property consisted chiefly in the labour of each individual person. The necessity for association against the organized robber-nobility, the need for communal covered markets in an age when the industrialist was at the same time a merchant, the growing competition of the escaped serfs swarming into the rising towns, the feudal structure of the whole country: these combined to bring about the guilds. Further, the gradually accumulated capital of individual craftsmen and their stable numbers, as against the growing population, evolved the relation of journeyman and apprentice, which brought into being in the towns a hierarchy similar to that in the country.

Thus the chief form of property during the feudal epoch consisted on the one hand of landed property with serf-labour chained to it, and on the other of individual labour with small capital commanding the labour of journeymen. The organization of both was determined by the restricted conditions of production—the small-scale and primitive cultivation of the land, and the craft type of industry. There was little division of labour in the heyday of feudalism. Each land bore in itself the conflict of town and country and the division into estates was certainly strongly marked; but apart from the differentiation of princes, nobility, clergy and peasants in the country, and masters, journeymen, apprentices and soon also the rabble of casual labourers in the towns, no division of importance took place. In agriculture it was rendered difficult by the strip-system, beside which the cottage industry of the peasants themselves emerged as another factor. In industry there was no division of labour at all in the individual trades themselves, and very little between them. The separation of industry and commerce was found already in existence in older towns; in the newer it only developed later, when the towns entered into mutual relations.

The grouping of larger territories into feudal kingdoms was a necessity for the landed nobility as for the towns. The organization of the ruling class, the nobility, had, therefore, everywhere a monarch at its head.

The fact is, therefore, that definite individuals who are productively active in a definite way enter into these definite social and political relations. Empirical observation must in each separate instance bring out empirically, and without any mystification and speculation, the connection of the social and political structure with production. The social structure and the state are continually evolving out of the life-process of definite individuals, but of individuals, not as they may appear in their own or other people's imagination, but as they really are; i.e. as they are effective, produce materially, and are active under definite material limits, presuppositions and conditions independent of their will.

The production of ideas, of conceptions, of consciousness, is at first directly interwoven with the material activity and the material intercourse of men, the language of real life. Conceiving, thinking, the mental intercourse of men, appear at this stage as the direct efflux of their material behaviour. The same applies to mental production as expressed in the language of the politics, laws, morality, religion, metaphysics of a people. Men are the producers of their conceptions, ideas, etc.—real, active men, as they are conditioned by a definite development of their productive forces and of the intercourse corresponding to these, up to its furthest forms. Consciousness can never be anything else than conscious existence, and the existence of men is their actual life-process. If in all ideology men and their circumstances appear upside down as in a *camera obscura*, this phenomenon arises just as much from their historical life-process as the inversion of objects on the retina does from their physical life-process.

In direct contrast to German philosophy, which descends from heaven to earth, here we ascend from earth to heaven. That is to say, we do not set out from what men say, imagine, conceive, nor from men as narrated, thought of, imagined, conceived, in order to arrive at men in the flesh. We set out from real, active men, and on the basis of their real life-process we demonstrate the development of the ideological reflexes and echoes of this life-process. The phantoms formed in the human brain are also, necessarily, sublimates of their material life-process, which is empirically verifiable and bound to material premises. Morality, religion, metaphysics, all the rest of ideology and their corresponding forms of consciousness, thus no longer retain the semblance of independence. They have no history, no development; but men, developing their material production and their material intercourse, alter, along with this their real existence, their thinking and the products of their thinking. Life is not determined by consciousness, but consciousness by life. In the first method of approach the starting-point is consciousness taken as the living individual; in the second it is the real living individuals themselves, as they are in actual life, and consciousness is considered solely as *their* consciousness.

This method of approach is not devoid of premises. It starts out from the real premises and does not abandon them for a moment. Its premises are men, not in any fantastic isolation or abstract definition, but in their actual, empirically perceptible process of development under definite conditions. As soon as this active life-process is described, history ceases to be a collection of dead facts as it is with the empiricists (themselves still abstract), or an imagined activity of imagined subjects, as with the idealists.

Where speculation ends—in real life—there real, positive science begins: the representation of the practical activity, of the practical process of development of men. Empty talk about consciousness ceases, and real knowledge has to take its place. When reality is depicted, philosophy as an independent branch of activity loses its medium of existence. At the best its place can only be taken by a summing-up of the most general results, abstractions which arise from the observation of the historical development of men. . . .

Consciousness and the Division of Labour

From *The German Ideology*

Only now, after having considered four moments, four aspects of the fundamental historical relationships, do we find that man also possesses "consciousness"; but, even so, not inherent, not "pure" consciousness. From the start the "spirit" is afflicted with the curse of being "burdened" with matter, which here makes its appearance in the form of agitated layers of air, sounds, in short, of language. Language is as old as consciousness, language is practical consciousness, as it exists for other men, and for that reason is really beginning to exist for me personally as well; for language, like consciousness, only arises from the need, the necessity, of intercourse with other men. Where there exists a relationship, it exists for me: the animal has no "relations" with anything, cannot have any. For the animal, its relation to others does not exist as a relation. Consciousness is therefore from the very beginning a social product, and remains so as long as men exist at all. Consciousness is at first, of course, merely consciousness concerning the immediate sensuous environment and consciousness of the limited connection with other persons and things outside the individual who is growing self-conscious. At the same time it is consciousness of nature, which first appears to men as a completely alien, all-powerful and unassailable force, with which men's relations are purely animal and by which they are overawed like beasts; it is thus a purely animal consciousness of nature (natural religion).

We see here immediately: this natural religion or animal behaviour towards nature is determined by the form of society and vice versa. Here, as everywhere, the identity of nature and man appears in such a way that the restricted relation of men to nature determines their restricted relation to one another, and their restricted relation to one another determines men's restricted relation to nature, just because nature is as yet hardly modified historically; and, on the other hand, man's consciousness of the necessity of associating with the individuals around him is the beginning of the consciousness that he is living in society at all. This beginning is as animal as social life itself at this stage. It is mere herd-consciousness, and at this point man is only distinguished from sheep by the fact that with him consciousness takes the place of instinct or that his instinct is a conscious one.

This sheep-like or tribal consciousness receives its further development and extension through increased productivity, the increase of needs, and, what is fundamental to both of these, the increase of population. With these there develops the division of labour, which was originally nothing but the division of labour in the sexual act, then that division of labour which develops spontaneously or "naturally" by virtue of natural predisposition (e.g. physical strength), needs, accidents, etc., etc. Division of labour only becomes truly such from the moment when a division of material and mental labour appears. From this moment onwards consciousness *can* really flatter itself that it is something other than consciousness of existing practice, that it is *really* conceiving something without conceiving something *real;* from now on consciousness is in a position to emancipate itself from the world and to proceed to the formation of "pure" theory, theology, philosophy, ethics, etc. But even if this theory, theology, philosophy, ethics, etc. comes into contradiction with the existing relations, this can only occur as a result of the fact that existing social relations have come into contradiction with existing forces of production; this, moreover, can also occur in a particular national sphere of relations through the appearance of the contradiction, not within the national orbit, but between this national consciousness and the practice of other nations, i.e. between the national and the general consciousness of a nation.

Moreover, it is quite immaterial what consciousness starts to do on its own; out of all such muck we get only the one inference that these three moments, the forces of production, the state of society, and consciousness, can and must come into contradiction with one another, because the division of labour implies the possibility, nay the fact that intellectual and material activity—enjoyment and labour, production and consumption— devolve on different individuals, and that the only possibility of their not coming into contradiction lies in the negation in its turn of the division of labour. It is self-evident, moreover, that "spectres," "bonds," "the higher being," "concept," "scruple," are merely the idealistic, spiritual expression, the conception apparently of the isolated individual, the image of very empirical fetters and limitations, within which the mode of production of life, and the form of intercourse coupled with it, move.

With the division of labour, in which all these contradictions are implicit, and which in its turn is based on the natural division of labour in the family and the separation of society into individual families opposed to one another, is given simultaneously the distribution, and indeed the unequal distribution (both quantitative and qualitative), of labour and its products, hence property: the nucleus, the first form, of which lies in the family, where wife and children are the slaves of the husband. This latent slavery in the family, though still very crude, is the first property, but even at this early stage it corresponds perfectly to the definition of modern economists who call it the power of disposing of the labour-power of others. Division of labour and private property are, moreover, identical expressions: in the one the same thing is affirmed with reference to activity as is affirmed in the other with reference to the product of the activity.

Further, the division of labour implies the contradiction between the interest of the separate individual or the individual family and the communal interest of all individuals who have intercourse with one another. And indeed, this communal interest does not exist merely in the imagination, as "the general good," but first of all in reality, as the mutual interdependence of the individuals among whom the labour is divided. And out of this very contradiction between the interest of the individual and that of the community the latter takes an independent form as the State, divorced from the real interests of individual and community, and at the same time as an illusory communal life, always based, however, on the real ties existing in every family and tribal conglomeration (such as flesh and blood, language, division of labour on a larger scale, and other interests) and especially, as we shall enlarge upon later, on the classes, already determined by the division of labour, which in every such mass of men separate out, and of which one dominates all the others. It follows from this that all struggles within the state, the struggle between democracy, aristocracy and monarchy, the struggle for the franchise, etc., etc., are merely the illusory forms in which the real struggles of the different classes are fought out among one another. . . .

And finally, the division of labour offers us the first example of how, as long as man remains in natural society, that is as long as a cleavage exists between the particular and the common interest, as long therefore as activity is not voluntarily, but naturally, divided, man's own deed becomes an alien power opposed to him, which enslaves him instead of being controlled by him. For as soon as labour is distributed, each man has a particular, exclusive sphere of activity, which is forced upon him and from which he cannot escape. He is a hunter, a fisherman, a shepherd, or a critical critic, and must remain so if he does not want to lose his means of livelihood; while in communist society, where nobody has one exclusive sphere of activity but each can become accomplished in any branch he wishes, society regulates the general production and thus makes it possible for me to do one thing to-day and another to-morrow, to hunt in the morning, fish in the afternoon, rear cattle in the evening, criticize after dinner, just as I have a mind, without ever becoming hunter, fisherman, shepherd or critic.

This crystallization of social activity, this consolidation of what we ourselves produce into an objective power above us, growing out of our control, thwarting our expectations, bringing to naught our calculations, is one of the chief factors in historical development up till now. The social power, i.e. the multiplied productive force, which arises through the co-operation of different individuals as it is determined by the division of labour, appears to come about naturally, not as their own united power, but as an alien force existing outside them, of the origin and goal of which they are ignorant, which they thus cannot control, which on the contrary passes through a peculiar series of phases and stages independent of the will and action of man, nay even being the prime governor of these. . . .

This "estrangement" [or "alienation"] (to use a term which will be comprehensible to the philosophers) can, of course, only be abolished given two *practical* premises. For it to become an "intolerable" power, i.e. a power against which men make a revolution, it must necessarily have rendered the great mass of humanity "propertyless," and produced, at the same time, the contradiction of an existing world of wealth and culture, both of which conditions presuppose a great increase in productive power, a high degree of its development. And, on the other hand, this development of productive forces (which itself implies the actual empirical existence of men in their *world-historical,* instead of local, being) is absolutely necessary as a practical premise: firstly, for the reason that without it only *want* is made general, and with want the struggle for necessities and all the old filthy business would necessarily be reproduced; and secondly, because only with this universal development of productive forces is a *universal* intercourse between men established, which produces in all nations simultaneously the phenomenon of the "propertyless" mass (universal competition), makes each nation dependent on the revolutions of the others, and finally has put *world-historical,* empirically universal individuals in place of local ones. Without this, (1) Communism could only exist as a local even; (2) The forces of intercourse themselves could not have developed as universal, hence intolerable powers: they would have remained home-bred superstitious conditions; and (3) Each extension of intercourse would abolish local communism. Empirically, communism is only possible as the act of the dominant peoples "all at once" or simultaneously, which presupposes the universal development of productive forces and the world-intercourse bound up with them.

Moreover, the world-market is presupposed by the mass of propertyless workers—labour-power cut off as a mass from capital or from even a limited satisfaction—and therefore no longer by the mere precariousness of labour, which, not giving an assured livelihood, is often lost through competition. The proletariat can thus only exist *world-historically,* just as communism, its movement, can only have a "world-historical" existence. World-historical existence of individuals, i.e. existence of individuals which is directly linked up with world history.

Communism is for us not a stable state which is to be established, an *ideal* to which reality will have to adjust itself. We call communism the *real* movement which abolishes the present state of things. The conditions of this movement result from the premises now in existence.

• • •

This conception of history depends on our ability to expound the real process of production, starting out from the material production of life itself, and to comprehend the form of intercourse connected with this and created by this mode of production (i.e., civil society in its various stages), as the basis of all history; and to show it in its action as state, to explain all the different theoretical products and forms of consciousness, religion, philosophy, ethics, etc., etc., and trace their origins and growth from that basis; by which means, of course, the whole thing can be depicted in its totality (and therefore, too, the reciprocal action of these various sides on one another). It has not, like the idealistic view of history, in every period to look for a category, but remains constantly on the real *ground* of history; it does not explain practice from the idea but explains the formation of ideas from material practice and accordingly it comes to the conclusion that all forms and products of consciousness cannot be dissolved by mental criticism, by resolution into "self-consciousness" or transformation into "apparitions," "spectres," "fancies," etc., but only by the practical overthrow of the actual social relations which give rise to this idealistic humbug; that not criticism but revolution is the driving force of history, also of religion, of philosophy and all other types of theory. It shows that history does not end by being resolved into "self-consciousness" as "spirit of the spirit," but that in it at each stage there is found a material result: a sum of productive forces, a historically created relation of individuals to nature and to one another, which is handed down to each generation from its predecessor; a mass of productive forces, capital funds and conditions, which, on the one hand, is indeed modified by the new generation, but also on the other prescribes for it its conditions of life and gives it a definite development, a special character. It shows that circumstances make men just as much as men make circumstances.

This sum of productive forces, capital funds and social forms of intercourse, which every individual and generation finds in existence as something given, is the real basis of what the philosophers have conceived as "substance" and "essence of man," and what they have deified and attacked: a real basis which is not in the least disturbed, in its effect and influence on the development of men, by the fact that these philosophers revolt against it as "self-consciousness" and the "Unique." These conditions of life, which different generations find in existence, decide also whether or not the periodically recurring revolutionary convulsion will be strong enough to overthrow the basis of the entire existing system. And if these material elements of a complete revolution are not present (namely, on the one hand the existing productive forces, on the other the formation of a revolutionary mass, which revolts not only against separate conditions of society up till then, but against the very "production of life" till then, the "total activity" on which it was based), then, as far as practical development is concerned, it is absolutely immaterial whether the *idea* of this revolution has been expressed a hundred times already, as the history of communism proves.

John Stuart Mill

John Stuart Mill (1806–1873) was arguably the greatest English philosopher of the nineteenth century. In *A System of Logic* (1843) he expounded a sophisticated defense of an empiricist view of knowledge, science, and mathematics. In Book VI of that work he argues that there can be a science of human nature, based on observed correlations of mental states of consciousness with bodily states, and with each other. This involved the introspectionist approach that was to be rejected by the behaviorist movement in the early twentieth century (see Skinner below).

Mill is probably most famous for his ethical and political philosophy, expressed mainly in *On Liberty* (1859) and *Utilitarianism* (1863). He also argued, unusually and courageously for his time, for the legal and social equality of women. He gives considerable credit for his own intellectual achievements to Harriet Taylor, who became his wife in 1852. Mary Wollstonecraft had already argued for a similar view in 1792 in her pioneering essay *Vindication of the Rights of Woman,* but it was difficult to find succinct extracts to fit into this volume. The following passage is from Mill's *The Subjection of Women,* a lengthily eloquent essay published in 1869. He makes some good methodological remarks about talk of "natures," which are further developed in Holmstrom's paper below. He briefly suggests how similar criticisms apply to the question of supposed national or racial characters—but it has to be pointed out that Mill was not consistent on the question of racial differences (see Bracken's selection below).

The Subjection of Women

• • •

At present, in the more improved countries, the disabilities of women are the only case, save one, in which laws and institutions take persons at their birth, and ordain that they shall never in all their lives be allowed to compete for certain things. The one exception is that of royalty. Persons still are born to the throne; no one, not of the reigning family, can ever occupy it, and no one even of that family can, by any means but the course of hereditary succession, attain it. All other dignities and social advantages are open to the whole male sex: many indeed are only attainable by wealth, but wealth may be striven for by any one, and is actually obtained by many men of the very humblest origin. The difficulties, to the majority, are indeed insuperable without the aid of fortunate accidents; but no male human being is under any legal ban: neither law nor opinion superadd artificial obstacles to the natural ones. Royalty, as I have said, is excepted: put in this case every one feels it to be an exception—an anomaly in the modern world, in marked opposition to its customs and principles, and to be justified only by extraordinary special expediencies, which, though individuals and nations differ in estimating their weight, unquestionably do in fact exist. But in this exceptional case, in which a high social function is, for important reasons, bestowed on birth instead of being put up to competition, all free nations contrive to adhere in substance to the principle from which they nominally derogate; for they circumscribe this high function by conditions avowedly intended to prevent the person to whom it ostensibly belongs from really performing it; while the person by whom it is performed, the responsible minister, does obtain the post by a competition from which no full-grown citizen of the male sex is legally excluded. The disabilities, therefore, to which women are subject from the mere fact of their birth, are the solitary examples of the kind in modern legislation.

The Subjection of Women, in Three Essays © Oxford University Press 1912 (new edition 1975).

In no instance except this, which comprehends half the human race, are the higher social functions closed against any one by a fatality of birth which no exertions, and no change of circumstances, can overcome; for even religious disabilities (besides that in England and in Europe they have practically almost ceased to exist) do not close any career to the disqualified person in case of conversion.

The social subordination of women thus stands out an isolated fact in modern social institutions; a solitary breach of what has become their fundamental law; a single relic of an old world of thought and practice exploded in everything else, but retained in the one thing of most universal interest; as if a gigantic dolmen, or a vast temple of Jupiter Olympius, occupied the site of St. Paul's and received daily worship, while the surrounding Christian churches were only resorted to on fasts and festivals. This entire discrepancy between one social fact and all those which accompany it, and the radical opposition between its nature and the progressive movement which is the boast of the modern world, and which has successively swept away everything else of an analogous character, surely affords, to a conscientious observer of human tendencies, serious matter for reflection. It raises a prima facie presumption on the unfavourable side, far outweighing any which custom and usage could in such circumstances create on the favourable; and should at least suffice to make this, like the choice between republicanism and royalty, a balanced question.

The least that can be demanded is, that the question should not be considered as prejudged by existing fact and existing opinion, but open to discussion on its merits, as a question of justice and expediency: the decision on this, as on any of the other social arrangements of mankind, depending on what an enlightened estimate of tendencies and consequences may show to be most advantageous to humanity in general, without distinction of sex. And the discussion must be a real discussion, descending to foundations, and not resting satisfied with vague and general assertions. It will not do, for instance, to assert in general terms, that the experience of mankind has pronounced in favour of the existing system. Experience cannot possibly have decided between two courses, so long as there has only been experience of one. If it be said that the doctrine of the equality of the sexes rests only on theory, it must be remembered that the contrary doctrine also has only theory to rest upon. All that is proved in its favour by direct experience, is that mankind have been able to exist under it, and to attain the degree of improvement and prosperity which we now see; but whether that prosperity has been attained sooner, or is now greater, than it would have been under the other system, experience does not say. On the other hand, experience does say, that every step in improvement has been so invariably accompanied by a step made in raising the social position of women, that historians and philosophers have been led to adopt their elevation or debasement as on the whole the surest test and most correct measure of the civilization of a people or an age. Through all the progressive period of human history, the condition of women has been approaching nearer to equality with men. This does not of itself prove that the assimilation must go on to complete equality; but it assuredly affords some presumption that such is the case.

Neither does it avail anything to say that the *nature* of the two sexes adapts them to their present functions and position, and renders these appropriate to them. Standing on the ground of common sense and the constitution of the human mind, I deny that any one knows, or can know, the nature of the two sexes, as long as they have only been seen in their present relation to one another. If men had ever been found in society without women, or women without men, or if there had been a society of men and women in which the women were not under the control of the men, something might have been positively known about the mental and moral differences which may be inherent in the nature of each. What is now called the nature of women is an eminently artificial thing—the result of forced repression in some directions, unnatural stimulation in others. It may be asserted without scruple, that no other class of dependents have had their character so entirely distorted from its natural proportions by their relation with their masters; for, if conquered and slave races have been, in some respects, more forcibly repressed, whatever in them has not been crushed down by an iron heel has generally been let alone, and if left with any liberty of development, it has developed itself according to its own laws; but in the case of women, a hot-house and stove cultivation has always been carried on of some of the capabilities of their nature, for the benefit and pleasure of their masters. Then, because certain products of the general vital force sprout luxuriantly and reach a great development in this heated atmosphere and under this active nurture and watering, while other shoots from the same root, which are left outside in the wintry air, with ice purposely heaped all round them, have a stunted growth, and some are burnt off with fire and disappear; men, with that inability to recognize their own work which distinguishes the unanalytic mind, indolently believe that the tree grows of itself in the way they have made it grow, and that it would die if one half of it were not kept in a vapour bath and the other half in the snow.

Of all difficulties which impede the progress of thought, and the formation of well-grounded opinions on life and social arrangements, the greatest is now the unspeakable ignorance and inattention of mankind in respect to the influences which form human character. Whatever any portion of the human species now are, or seem to be, such, it is supposed, they have a natural tendency to be: even when the most elementary knowledge of the circumstances in which they have been placed, clearly points out the causes that made them what they are. Because a cottier deeply in arrears to his landlord is not industrious, there are people who think that the Irish are naturally idle. Because constitutions can be overthrown when the authorities appointed to execute them turn their arms against them, there are people who think the French incapable of free government. Because the Greeks cheated the Turks, and the Turks only plundered the Greeks, there are persons who think that the Turks are naturally more sincere: and because women, as is often said, care nothing about politics except their personalities, it is supposed that the general good is naturally less interesting to women than to men. History, which is now so much better understood than formerly, teaches another lesson: if only by showing the extraordinary susceptibility of human nature to external influences, and the extreme variableness of those of its manifestations which are supposed to be most universal and uniform. But in history, as in travelling, men usually see only what they already had in their own minds; and few learn much from history, who do not bring much with them to its study.

Hence, in regard to that most difficult question, what are the natural differences between the two sexes—a subject on which it is impossible in the present state of society to obtain complete and correct knowledge—while almost everybody dogmatizes upon it, almost all neglect and make light of the only means by which any partial insight can be obtained into it. This is, an analytic study of the most important department of psychology, the laws of the influence of circumstances on character. For, however great and apparently ineradicable the moral and intellectual differences between men and women might be, the evidence of their being natural differences could only be negative. Those only could be inferred to be natural which could not possibly be artificial—the residuum, after deducting every characteristic of either sex which can admit of being explained from education or external circumstances. The profoundest knowledge of the laws of the formation of character is indispensable to entitle any one to affirm even that there is any difference, much more what the difference is, between the two sexes considered as moral and rational beings; and since no one, as yet, has that knowledge (for there is hardly any subject which, in proportion to its importance, has been so little studied), no one is thus far entitled to any positive opinion on the subject. Conjectures are all that can at present be made; conjectures more or less probable, according as more or less authorized by such knowledge as we yet have of the laws of psychology, as applied to the formation of character.

Even the preliminary knowledge, what the differences between the sexes now are, apart from all question as to how they are made what they are, is still in the crudest and most incomplete state. Medical practitioners and physiologists have ascertained, to some extent, the differences in bodily constitution; and this is an important element to the psychologist: but hardly any medical practitioner is a psychologist. Respecting the mental characteristics of women; their observations are of no more worth than those of common men. It is a subject on which nothing final can be known, so long as those who alone can really know it, women themselves, have given but little testimony, and that little, mostly suborned. It is easy to know stupid women. Stupidity is much the same all the world over. A stupid person's notions and feelings may confidently be inferred from those which prevail in the circle by which the person is surrounded. Not so with those whose opinions and feelings are an emanation from their own nature and faculties. It is only a man here and there who has any tolerable knowledge of the character even of the women of his own family. I do not mean, of their capabilities; these nobody knows, not even themselves, because most of them have never been called out. I mean their actually existing thoughts and feelings. Many a man thinks he perfectly understands women, because he has had amatory relations with several, perhaps with many of them. If he is a good observer, and his experience extends to quality as well as quantity, he may have learnt something of one narrow department of their nature—an important department, no doubt. But of all the rest of it, few persons are generally more ignorant, because there are few from whom it is so carefully hidden. The most favourable case which a man can generally have for studying the character of a woman, is that of his own wife: for the opportunities are greater, and the cases of complete sympathy not so unspeakably rare. And in fact, this is the source from which any knowledge worth having on the subject has, I believe, generally come. But most men have not had the opportunity of studying in this way more than a single case: accordingly one can, to an almost laughable degree, infer what a man's wife is like, from his opinions about women in general. To make even this one case yield any result, the woman must be worth knowing, and the man not only a competent judge, but of a character so sympathetic in itself, and so well adapted to hers, that he can either read her mind by sympathetic intuition, or has nothing in himself which makes her shy of disclosing it. Hardly anything, I believe, can be more rare than this conjunction. It often happens that there is the most complete unity of feeling and community of interests as to all external things, yet the one has as little admission into the internal life of the other as if they were common acquaintance. Even with true affection, authority on the one side and subordination on the other prevent perfect confidence. Though nothing may be intentionally withheld, much is not shown. In the analogous relation of parent and child, the corresponding phenomenon must have been in the observation of every one. As between father and son, how many are the cases in which the father, in spite of real affection on both sides, obviously to all the world does not know, nor suspect, parts of the son's character familiar to his companions and equals. The truth is, that the position of looking up to another is extremely unpropitious to complete sincerity and openness with him. The fear of losing ground in his opinion or in his feelings is so strong, that even in an upright character, there is an unconscious tendency to show only the best side, or the side which, though not the best, is that which he most likes to see: and it may be confidently said that thorough knowledge of one another hardly ever exists, but between persons who, besides being intimates, are equals. How much more true, then, must all this be, when the one is not only under the authority of the other, but has it inculcated on her as a duty to reckon everything else subordinate to his comfort and pleasure, and to let him neither see nor feel anything coming from her, except what is agreeable to him. All these difficulties stand in the way of a man's obtaining any thorough knowledge even of the one woman whom alone, in general, he has sufficient opportunity of studying. When we further consider that to understand one woman is not necessarily to understand any other woman; that even if he could study many women of one rank, or of one country, he would not thereby understand women of other ranks or countries; and even if he did, they are still only the women of a single period of history; we may safely assert that the knowledge which men can acquire of women, even as they have been and are, without reference to what they might be, is wretchedly imperfect and superficial, and always will be so, until women themselves have told all that they have to tell.

And this time has not come; nor will it come otherwise than gradually. It is but of yesterday that women have either been qualified by literary accomplishments, or permitted by society, to tell anything to the general public. As yet very few of them dare tell anything, which men, on whom their literary success depends, are unwilling to hear. Let us remember in what manner, up to a very recent time, the expression, even by a male author, of uncustomary opinions, or what are deemed eccentric feelings, usually was, and in some degree still is, received; and we may form some faint conception under what impediments a woman, who is brought up to think custom and opinion her sovereign rule, attempts to express in books anything drawn from the depths of her own nature. The greatest woman who has left writings behind her sufficient to give her an eminent rank in the literature of her country, thought it necessary to prefix as a motto to her boldest work, 'Un homme peut braver l'opinion; une femme doit s'y soumettre.' [title-page of Mme. de Staël's *Delphine.*] The greater part of what women write about women is mere sycophancy to men. In the case of unmarried women, much of it seems only intended to increase their chance of a husband. Many, both married and unmarried, overstep the mark, and inculcate a servility beyond what is desired or relished by any man, except the very vulgarest. But this is not so often the case as, even at a quite late period, it still was. Literary women are becoming more freespoken, and more willing to express their real sentiments. Unfortunately, in this country especially, they are themselves such artificial products, that their sentiments are compounded of a small element of individual observation and consciousness, and a very large one of acquired associations. This will be less and less the case, but it will remain true to a great extent, as long as social institutions do not admit the same free development of originality in women which is possible to men. When that time comes, and not before, we shall see, and not merely hear, as much as it is necessary to know of the nature of women, and the adaptation of other things to it.

I have dwelt so much on the difficulties which at present obstruct any real knowledge by men of the true nature of women, because in this as in so many other things "opinio copiae inter maximas causas inopiae est"; and there is little chance of reasonable thinking on the matter, while people flatter themselves that they perfectly understand a subject of which most men know absolutely nothing, and of which it is at present impossible that any man, or all men taken together, should have knowledge which can qualify them to lay down the law to women as to what is, or is not, their vocation. Happily, no such knowledge is necessary for any practical purpose connected with the position of women in relation to society and life. For, according to all the principles involved in modern society, the question rests with women themselves—to be decided by their own experience, and by the use of their own faculties. There are no means of finding what either one person or many can do, but by trying—and no means by which any one else can discover for them what it is for their happiness to do or leave undone.

One thing we may be certain of—that what is contrary to women's nature to do, they never will be made to do by simply giving their nature free play. The anxiety of mankind to interfere in behalf of nature, for fear lest nature should not succeed in effecting its purpose, is an altogether unnecessary solicitude. What women by nature cannot do, it is quite superfluous to forbid them from doing. What they can do, but not so well as the men who are their competitors, competition suffices to exclude them from; since nobody asks for protective duties and bounties in favour of women; it is only asked that the present bounties and protective duties in favour of men should be recalled. If women have a greater natural inclination for some things than for others, there is no need of laws or social inculcation to make the majority of them do the former in preference to the latter. Whatever women's services are most wanted for, the free play of competition will hold out the strongest inducements to them to undertake. And, as the words imply, they are most wanted for the things for which they are most fit; by the apportionment of which to them, the collective faculties of the two sexes can be applied on the whole with the greatest sum of valuable result.

Charles Darwin

The thought of Charles Darwin (1809–1882) is crucial to all theorizing about human nature. His fundamental work was *The Origin of Species,* which he was eventually provoked into publishing in 1859, after much hesitation due to his painful awareness of the controversy it would cause. In that book he outlined his theory of evolution of species by natural selection, and he surveyed the widespread evidence for it. But he cagily confined himself to just one sentence about human beings: "Light will be thrown on the origin of man and his history."

The implication that human beings have gradually evolved from more primitive creatures was obvious, however. Controversy duly ensued, and has hardly stopped since. Darwin went on to address the question of human evolution directly in *The Descent of Man,* published in 1871. In the passage excerpted here he speculates about the development of human moral and intellectual faculties. This is a classic source of the strong current of evolutionary approaches to human nature that has flowed ever since, and has taken new scientific forms in the sociobiology and evolutionary psychology of the late twentieth century (see the readings from Lorenz, Wilson, and Ridley below).

The Descent of Man

On the Development of the Intellectual and Moral Faculties During Primeval and Civilized Times

The subjects to be discussed in this chapter are of the highest interest, but are treated by me in a most imperfect and fragmentary manner. Mr Wallace, in an admirable paper . . . argues that man after he had partially acquired those intellectual and moral faculties which distinguish him from the lower animals, would have been but little liable to have had his bodily structure modified through natural selection or any other means. For man is enabled through his mental faculties "to keep with an unchanged body in harmony with the changing universe." He has great power of adapting his habits to new conditions of life. He invents weapons, tools and various stratagems, by which he procures food and defends himself. When he migrates into a colder climate he uses clothes, builds sheds, and makes fires; and, by the aid of fire, cooks food otherwise indigestible. He aids his fellow-men in many ways, and anticipates future events. Even at a remote period he practised some subdivision of labour.

The lower animals, on the other hand, must have their bodily structure modified in order to survive under greatly changed conditions. They must be rendered stronger, or acquire more effective teeth or claws, in order to defend themselves from new enemies; or they must be reduced in size so as to escape detection and danger. When they migrate into a colder climate they must become clothed with thicker fur, or have their constitutions altered. If they fail to be thus modified, they will cease to exist.

The case, however, is widely different, as Mr. Wallace has with justice insisted, in relation to the intellectual and moral faculties of man. These faculties are variable; and we have every reason to believe that the variations tend to be inherited. Therefore, if they were formerly of high importance to primeval man and to his ape-like progenitors, they would have been perfected or advanced through natural selection. Of the high importance of the intellectual faculties there can be no doubt, for man mainly owes to them his pre-eminent position in the world. We can see that, in the rudest state of society, the individuals who were the most sagacious, who

From *The Descent of Man*, in *A Darwin Selection*, edited by Mark Ridley © Harper Collins Publishers 1994.

invented and used the best weapons or traps, and who were best able to defend themselves, would rear the greatest number of offspring. The tribes which included the largest number of men thus endowed would increase in number and supplant other tribes. Numbers depend primarily on the means of subsistence, and this, partly on the physical nature of the country, but in a much higher degree on the arts which are there practised. As a tribe increases and is victorious, it is often still further increased by the absorption of other tribes. The stature and strength of the men of a tribe are likewise of some importance for its success, and these depend in part on the nature and amount of the food which can be obtained. In Europe the men of the Bronze period were supplanted by a more powerful and, judging from their sword-handles, larger-handed race; but their success was probably due in a much higher degree to their superiority in the arts.

All that we know about savages, or may infer from their traditions and from old monuments, the history of which is quite forgotten by the present inhabitants, shews that from the remotest times successful tribes have supplanted other tribes. Relics of extinct or forgotten tribes have been discovered throughout the civilized regions of the earth, on the wild plains of America, and on the isolated islands in the Pacific Ocean. At the present day civilized nations are everywhere supplanting barbarous nations, excepting where the climate opposes a deadly barrier; and they succeed mainly, though not exclusively, through their arts, which are the products of the intellect. It is, therefore, highly probable that with mankind the intellectual faculties have been gradually perfected through natural selection; and this conclusion is sufficient for our purpose. Undoubtedly it would have been very interesting to have traced the development of each separate faculty from the state in which it exists in the lower animals to that in which it exists in man; but neither my ability nor knowledge permit the attempt.

It deserves notice that as soon as the progenitors of man became social (and this probably occurred at a very early period), the advancement of the intellectual faculties will have been aided and modified in an important manner, of which we see only traces in the lower animals, namely, through the principle of imitation, together with reason and experience. Apes are much given to imitation, as are the lowest savages; and the simple fact previously referred to, that after a time no animal can be caught in the same place by the same sort of trap, shews that animals learn by experience, and imitate each others' caution. Now, if some one man in a tribe, more sagacious than the others, invented a new snare or weapon, or other means of attack or defence, the plainest self-interest, without the assistance of much reasoning power, would prompt the other members to imitate him; and all would thus profit. The habitual practice of each new art must likewise in some slight degree strengthen the intellect. If the new invention were an important one, the tribe would increase in number, spread, and supplant other tribes. In a tribe thus rendered more numerous there would always be a rather better chance of the birth of other superior and inventive members. If such men left children to inherit their mental superiority, the chance of the birth of still more ingenious members would be somewhat better, and in a very small tribe decidedly better. Even if they left no children, the tribe would still include their blood-relations; and it has been ascertained by agriculturists that by preserving and breeding from the family of an animal, which when slaughtered was found to be valuable, the desired character has been obtained.

Turning now to the social and moral faculties. In order that primeval men, or the ape-like progenitors of man, should have become social, they must have acquired the same instinctive feelings which impel other animals to live in a body; and they no doubt exhibited the same general disposition. They would have felt uneasy when separated from their comrades, for whom they would have felt some degree of love; they would have warned each other of danger, and have given mutual aid in attack or defence. All this implies some degree of sympathy, fidelity, and courage. Such social qualities, the paramount importance of which to the lower animals is disputed by no one, were no doubt acquired by the progenitors of man in a similar manner, namely, through natural selection, aided by inherited habit. When two tribes of primeval man, living in the same country, came into competition, if the one tribe included (other circumstances being equal) a greater number of courageous, sympathetic, and faithful members, who were always ready to warn each other of danger, to aid and defend each other, this tribe would without doubt succeed best and conquer the other. Let it be borne in mind how all-important, in the never-ceasing wars of savages, fidelity and courage must be. The advantage which disciplined soldiers have over undisciplined hordes follows chiefly from the confidence which each man feels in his comrades. Obedience, as Mr. Bagehot has well shewn, is of the highest value, for any form of government is better than none. Selfish and contentious people will not cohere, and without coherence nothing can be effected. A tribe possessing the above qualities in a high degree would spread and be victorious over other tribes; but in the course of time it would, judging from all past history, be in its turn overcome by some other and still more highly endowed tribe. Thus the social and moral qualities would tend slowly to advance and be diffused throughout the world.

But it may be asked, how within the limits of the same tribe did a large number of members first become endowed with these social and moral qualities, and how was the standard of excellence raised? It is extremely doubtful whether the offspring of the more sympathetic and benevolent parents, or of those which were the most faithful to their comrades, would be reared in greater number than the children of selfish and treacherous parents of the same tribe. He who was ready to sacrifice his life, as many a savage has been, rather than betray his comrades, would often leave no offspring to inherit his noble nature. The bravest men, who were always willing to come to the front in war, and who freely risked their lives for others, would on an average perish in larger number than other men. Therefore it seems scarcely possible (bearing in mind that we are not here speaking of one tribe being victorious over another) that the number of men gifted with such virtues, or that the standard of their excellence, could be increased through natural selection, that is, by the survival of the fittest.

Although the circumstances which lead to an increase in the number of men thus endowed within the same tribe are too complex to be clearly followed out, we can trace some of the probable steps. In the first place, as the reasoning powers and foresight of the members became improved, each man would soon learn from experience that if he aided his fellow-men, he would commonly receive aid in return. From this low motive he might acquire the habit of aiding his fellows; and the habit of performing benevolent actions certainly strengthens the feeling of sympathy, which gives the first impulse to benevolent actions. Habits, moreover, followed during many generations probably tend to be inherited.

But there is another and much more powerful stimulus to the development of the social virtues, namely, the praise and the blame of our fellow-men. The love of approbation and the dread of infamy, as well as the bestowal of praise or blame, are primarily due, as we have seen in the third chapter, to the instinct of sympathy; and this instinct no doubt was originally acquired, like all the other social instincts, through natural selection. At how early a period the progenitors of man, in the course of their development, became capable of feeling and being impelled by the praise or blame of their fellow-creatures, we cannot, of course, say. But it appears that even dogs appreciate encouragement, praise and blame. The rudest savages feel the sentiment of glory, as they clearly show by preserving the trophies of their prowess, by their habit of excessive boasting, and even by the extreme care which they take of their personal appearance and decorations; for unless they regarded the opinion of their comrades, such habits would be senseless.

They certainly feel shame at the breach of some of their lesser rules; but how far they experience remorse is doubtful. I was at first surprised that I could not recollect any recorded instances of this feeling in savages; and Sir J. Lubbock states that he knows of none. But if we banish from our minds all cases given in novels and plays and in death-bed confessions made to priests, I doubt whether many of us have actually witnessed remorse; though we may have often seen shame and contrition for smaller offences. Remorse is a deeply hidden feeling. It is incredible that a savage, who will sacrifice his life rather than betray his tribe, or one who will deliver himself up as a prisoner rather than break his parole, would not feel remorse in his inmost soul, though he might conceal it, if he had failed in a duty which he held sacred.

We may therefore conclude that primeval man, at a very remote period, would have been influenced by the praise and blame of his fellows. It is obvious, that the members of the same tribe would approve of conduct which appeared to them to be for the general good, and would reprobate that which appeared evil. To do good unto others—to do unto others as ye would they should do unto you,—is the foundation-stone of morality. It is, therefore, hardly possible to exaggerate the importance during rude times of the love of praise and the dread of blame. A man who was not impelled by any deep, instinctive feeling, to sacrifice his life for the good of others, yet was roused to such actions by a sense of glory, would by his example excite the same wish for glory in other men, and would strengthen by exercise the noble feeling of admiration. He might thus do far more good to his tribe than by begetting offspring with a tendency to inherit his own high character.

With increased experience and reason, man perceives the more remote consequences of his actions, and the self-regarding virtues, such as temperance, chastity, etc. which during early times are, as we have before seen, utterly disregarded, come to be highly esteemed or even held sacred.... Ultimately a highly complex sentiment, having its first origin in the social instincts, largely guided by the approbation of our fellow-men, ruled by reason, self-interest, and in later times by deep religious feelings, confirmed by instruction and habit, all combined, constitute our moral sense or conscience.

It must not be forgotten that although a high standard of morality gives but a slight or no advantage to each individual man and his children over the other men of the same tribe, yet that an advancement in the standard of morality and in increase in the number of well-endowed men will certainly give an immense advantage to one tribe over another. There can be no doubt that a tribe including many members who, from possessing in a high degree the spirit of patriotism, fidelity, obedience, courage, and sympathy, were always ready to give aid to each other and to sacrifice themselves for the common good, would be victorious over most other tribes; and this would be natural selection. At all times throughout the world tribes have supplanted other tribes; and as morality is one element in their success, the standard of morality and the number of well-endowed men will thus everywhere tend to rise and increase.

It is, however, very difficult to form any judgment why one particular tribe and not another has been successful and has risen in the scale of civilization. Many savages are in the same condition as when first discovered several centuries ago. As Mr. Bagehot has remarked, we are apt to look at progress as the normal rule in human society; but history refutes this. The ancients did not even entertain the idea; nor do the oriental nations at the present day. According to another high authority, Mr. Maine "the greatest part of mankind has never shewn a particle of desire that its civil institutions should be improved." Progress seems to depend on many concurrent favourable conditions, far too complex to be followed out. But it has often been remarked, that a cool climate leading to industry and the various arts has been highly favourable, or even indispensable for this end. The Esquimaux, pressed by hard necessity, have succeeded in many ingenious inventions, but their climate has been too severe for continued progress. Nomadic habits, whether over wide plains, or through the dense forests of the tropics, or along the shores of the sea, have in every case been highly detrimental. Whilst observing the barbarous inhabitants of Tierra del Fuego, it struck me that the possession of some property, a fixed abode, and the union of many families under a chief, were the indispensable requisites for civilization. Such habits almost necessitate the cultivation of the ground; and the first steps in cultivation would probably result . . . from some such accident as the seeds of a fruit-tree falling on a heap of refuse and producing an unusually fine variety. The problem, however, of the first advance of savages towards civilization is at present much too difficult to be solved.

Sigmund Freud

Sigmund Freud (1856–1939) developed his theory and treatment (both of which bear the name *psychoanalysis*) in the last years of the nineteenth century, and he amended them over the next forty years. He changed some of his ideas considerably, but there is a strong continuity of basic themes running through all his work.

As well as his lengthy theoretical books, he wrote several short, stylish popular expositions of his theory of human mental functioning and the therapeutic practice he based on it. Three of these stand out as good introductions to his thought—the *Five Lectures on Psycho-Analysis* delivered at Clark University in Massachusetts in 1909 (expounding his early theory), *The Question of Lay-Analysis* of 1926 (which expounds a later version of his theory), and *An Outline of Psycho-Analysis,* (a final summing up, written in the last years of his life in 1938–9 in exile in London after his escape from the Nazi take-over of his native Austria). Unfortunately, the publishers do not now permit reprints of these works, so instead we offer here a "reconstruction" of Freud's mature theory by Brian Farrell, which will serve almost as well as an introduction to Freud's theory of human nature.

In his later period (after 1920), Freud explained his theory of the mind in terms of the tripartite structure of id, ego, and superego (reminiscent of Plato's three parts of the soul). Earlier, Freud had used only the rather different distinction between conscious, pre-conscious, and unconscious mental states. His theory of instincts also underwent change. In the later versions he distinguished life and death instincts (preservative and destructive), where earlier he had talked in terms of hunger (self-preservation) and love (species-preservation). Farrell's reconstruction uses Freud's later theoretical formulations, which presuppose the more fundamental notion of the unconscious.

At the end of *An Outline of Psycho-Analysis,* Freud refers to the difficulties in justifying interpretations of mental phenomena, and to the frequent lack of agreement amongst psycho-analysts. He brings up the question of emotional prejudice, and rather patronizingly suggests that women analysts who have not been convinced of his theory of "penis envy" are liable to make mistakes in interpretation. But one wonders what entitled Freud to be so sure of his own view on this and other matters—especially given he had written (in *The Question of Lay-Analysis*) that "the sexual life of adult women is a 'dark continent' for psychology"! Methodological and epistemological issues about psycho-analysis have been the subject of much controversy ever since.

B. A. Farrell, "A Reconstruction of Freud's Mature Theory"

Let us begin our inquiry into the standing of psychoanalysis by reminding ourselves of the gist, or core, of Freud's view of human nature, as reconstructed.

I

Consider the new born infants, Joe, a boy, and Sue, a girl. The mind of each is powered by two basic forces or instincts—Eros and the Death instinct (or Thanatos). The instincts are manifested in the energy the mind displays. Eros is itself composed of two instincts—self-preservation and

B. A. Farrell, *The Standing of Psycho-Analysis* (Oxford, Oxford University Press). © Oxford University Press 1981.

sexuality; and the energy of the sexual instinct is called "libido." The Death instinct manifests itself in the aggressive and destructive activity of the mind, including the wish to destroy oneself. No name is given in the theory to the energy of the Death instinct.

To begin with, the mind of Joe (or Sue) has no internal structure, and Joe goes into action, without inhibitions, to satisfy the demands of the instincts. In other words, his mind operates in accordance with "the pleasure principle." But little Joe soon finds that he has to wait, for example, for his Mummy to come to him, and even to give up demanding that she attend to him when (say) she has to go into hospital. That is to say, he soon discovers that it is better for him not merely to act according to the pleasure principle, but also to take the real world into account, and so act in accordance with "the reality principle." As he comes to act in this way, his mind becomes differentiated into two parts, or structures—the Id (which contains the instincts) and the Ego, which does the job of mediating between the demands of the Id and the demands of the real world. The Ego therefore works in accordance with the reality principle. When some threat looms up, Joe reacts with anxiety; and this is the danger signal that sends the Ego into self-preservative action to deal with the danger.

However, the differentiation of Ego and Id is only one change that happens quite early in Joe's life. Another is the development of his sexual instinct.

This instinct has its source in a process of excitation in an organ, namely an erotogenic zone of the body. The instinct has an aim, which is to obtain satisfaction by means of the appropriate stimulation of an erotogenic zone. It also has an object, which is the person to whom the sexual attraction is directed. The zone of the body which first predominates in Joe's life is the mouth. This is followed by the anus; and the anal phase or stage (or, more correctly, as we shall see below, the anal-sadistic stage) is followed in turn by the phallic stage. But little Sue does not possess a penis, and the excitations of this last stage come from her clitoris, which is the dominant erotogenic zone for her at this stage. From this point onward the sexual histories of Joe and Sue begin to diverge.

How does this divergence come about? As the Ego starts differentiating itself from the Id, the energy of the sexual instinct in Joe and Sue— their libido—is directed towards themselves. This is the stage of primary narcissism, in which the object of their sexual impulse is themselves. But the Ego soon starts to invest libido in, or to "cathect," mental items that in some way represent other objects. Its first cathexis of other objects enables the child to become sexually interested in objects other than itself—first the breast, and then later the mother. The phallic stage in both Joe and Sue is contemporaneous with a period in which their early libidinal interest in the mother comes to dominate the scene.

The boy Joe becomes sexually attracted to the mother, wishes to have bedroom access to her and becomes sexually jealous of the father. In short, he develops the well-known Oedipus Complex. But he now takes in that his mother has no penis, unlike himself, and his fear grows (as the result, for example, of masturbation prohibitions) that, if he pursues his interest in his mother, his penis too will be cut off. This conflict is resolved by repressing his libidinal interest in his mother; by his Ego absorbing, or introjecting, (in particular) the standards of the father, which prohibit incest; and by identifying himself with the father. All this has two results.

(i) His libidinal interests in his mother are transformed by being desexualised and inhibited in their aim—so that they now appear as affection for the mother. If Joe can sublimate his libidinal interests at this point, then he will be successful in destroying his Oedipus Complex. (See page 175 below for an explanation of the word "sublimation.")

(ii) By introjecting parental and, especially, paternal standards, and by identifying himself with the father, Joe's mind undergoes a further differentiation. It acquires a new structure, the Super-Ego, which serves to control his own activity by means, in particular, of the imperatives that issue from what we ordinarily call his "conscience."

The history of little Sue at this stage is very different. In her phallic phase, Sue, like Joe, develops a wish to give the mother a child. But then she comes to recognise that she has no penis and holds her mother responsible for this lack. So her strong early attachment to the mother begins to break down. She becomes ready to give up her clitoral interest, she develops "penis envy," and turns to her father to satisfy her wish for a penis. The pets and dolls she has been playing with now fuse with the penis into a wish for a child-penis from the father. At this stage she enters upon her Oedipus Complex. Her mother becomes her rival for the father, and she remains Oedipally attached to the father for an indefinite period of her life. Because of this fact, the Super-Ego she acquires is not as strong and clear cut as Joe's.

After the drama of the Oedipal stage and at about the age of five, both Joe and Sue enter a period of relative libidinal calm—called the latency period. With the changes at puberty, the genitals now achieve primacy as the erotogenic zone, with Joe developing a new sex aim—namely penetration, and with Sue transferring her susceptibility to stimulation from her clitoris to the vaginal orifice. They both bring together the affectionate and sensual currents of their sexuality, and each directs them, with the normal genital aim of copulation, to one person of the opposite sex.

It is clear from this history that normal adult sexuality is not a "simple" instinct, but is a sort of synthesis out of the component instincts, which, as we have seen, are at work from birth. In the course of development, the instinct may undergo a more or less serious failure to pass through some given stage. The instinct will then be "fixated" at this stage, and this will have important consequences in later life. Moreover, the infant and child live in a particular family, with its own social milieu; and this setting can give the child experiences which produce—through the fixation of instinct—all manner of perverted sexual aberrations in adulthood.

The child's development is further complicated by hereditary and constitutional differences, in, for example, the strength or weakness of some component instincts, the sexual precocity of the child, or his (her) capacity to deal with excessive sexual excitation by sublimation. Moreover, and very important, it is quite misleading to distinguish Joe as a male and Sue as a female in the simple way we have done. For Joe's libido is also partly female in character, and Sue's partly male. That is to say, they are each bisexually disposed, the proportions and strengths varying widely between different children. We must also remember that this whole, schematically presented history is open to wide and subtle variations from child to child; and, in any case, an analyst may say, our knowledge of it is still incomplete and uncertain in a number of respects.

A still further complication in the development of the sexual instinct is produced by the role of our other fundamental instinct, namely destructiveness. This interacts with Eros and the growth of psychic structure in a number of ways and places. Thus, initially the libido neutralises the destructive impulses. The latter emerge strikingly in the anal-sadistic phase, when Joe's destructiveness comes out in his aggressive behaviour, and in the use to which he puts his excretory functions (by, for example, asserting his own will against the parents by defiantly refusing to part with his faeces). Joe's sadism, therefore, is a fusion of his libidinal and destructive impulses, and he comes to view the sexual intercourse of his parents as a violent and sadistic interchange. With the development of his Super-Ego, Joe becomes able, for example, to feel personally unworthy and useless (having failed to live up to parental standards); and hence his destructive impulse can now be directed against the Ego itself. Again, just as with Eros, the destructive impulse develops in ways that vary widely—depending on heredity and the family situation and social milieu of the child.

II

We have seen that the job of the Ego is to take account of reality. How, in outline, does it go about doing this? Suppose the mother of little Joe has great difficulties in breast-feeding him, and handles the whole situation somewhat ineptly. Suppose that for purely biological reasons Joe reacts very badly to his frustrations at this time, and develops great tension and anxiety about feeding. This anxiety may threaten to grow beyond the limits of what he can tolerate. Joe's Ego will then react by exerting counter, or anti-cathectic, energy to repress the impulses responsible for his growing tension. He may then begin to show lack of interest in feeding and the activity of the oral stage. This is an instance of "primal repression;" and it is the way the child's Ego deals with the anxiety produced by all childhood traumas involved in the development of sexuality, including the resolution of the Oedipus Complex. Primal repression also works against anxieties produced by the destructive instinct, but only where the activity of the latter is associated with the sexual instinct, as, for example, in sadism.

In the post-Oedipal child, and in the adult, the Ego works in a somewhat different way. When the boy Joe comes to adolescence and adulthood, he is likely, for instance, to develop a wish to fondle and suck the breasts of Sibyl, his girlfriend or fiancée. But this wish may generate anxiety, because it threatens to reactivate the anxiety of the oral trauma he experienced as a child. Joe's Ego then exerts anti-cathexes on the idea of the wish; and this makes the wish an unconscious one for Joe. But this wish has all manner of associations—with ideas of his wishing to suck sweets, to chew gum, and so on. Most of us are able to recognise such wishes, should we have them, and partly, for this reason, they can be said to be "preconscious" in character. But for Joe to have such wishes preconsciously (for example, that he would like to chew gum) is to retain dangerous links (for him) between his power consciously to recognise this preconscious wish and his unconscious wish to suck Sibyl's breasts. Therefore his Ego also withdraws sufficient energy from all such associations, or derivatives, as to make these unconscious. Joe cannot now recognise, by any ordinary means, that he wishes to suck sweets or

Sibyl's breasts. When the Ego works in this way, it is carrying out "Actual Repression" or "Repression Proper." Both types of repression, Primal and Actual, involve the constant expenditure of energy by the Ego. Furthermore, what is unconscious for Joe includes much more than what has been repressed. The Ego's way of controlling excitation which we have just described, namely repression, is itself unconscious to Joe.

However, repression is only one way, though a critically important one, of controlling the excitation to which the mind is subject. There are a number of other unconscious ways of doing so; and, along with repression, they are usually referred to as Mechanisms of Defence. Some of these are well-known. Thus, when Sue at seven runs into trouble at school, she may try to cope, in part, by regression—for example, by thumb-sucking and playing the role of a small child. Joe may try to deal with his guilt about some piece of misbehaviour by blaming his older brother for leading him on, and thereby projecting his guilt on to the latter. Some other well-known mechanisms are displacement, reaction formation, identification, destruction in the Id and sublimation. Most Mechanisms of Defence are unsuccessful, in that they do not eliminate the dangerous impulses, but only keep them at bay at the price of a steady, never-ending expenditure of energy. Some defences, however, are successful, not in the weak sense of producing temporary or uneasy stability, but in the stronger sense of ensuring that the dangerous impulse ceases to exist. Thus, when a boy begins to turn away from his Oedipal wishes, he uses repression; but in normal cases the child goes on to achieve the complete destruction of the wishes. Again, at the beginning of her latency period, Sue may deal with her pregenital sexual impulses by sublimating them, that is, she may replace them altogether with one or more other impulses, with new aims, and ones which are socially acceptable—for example, a passionate interest in scientific discovery, or artistic expression.

Though we have listed and discussed some of the defences one by one, we have to remember that these mechanisms work jointly and in an interlocking way to enable the Ego to control the excitation affecting the whole mind of Joe or Sue. The single most important aspect of this activity of the Ego is the control by the unconscious Mechanisms of Defence of the relations between the mental structure containing unconscious items, and the structure containing preconscious ones. The mechanisms work, overall, so as to allow only such items from the unconscious through into the preconscious that each mind is in a position to tolerate. When, therefore, a person's mind is not in a position to tolerate recognising that he, or she, has a wish (say) to injure the married partner, unconscious defensive manoeuvres will be taken to keep this wish unconscious.

But in ordinary life the Ego is not wholly able to stop the unconscious getting through to consciousness. Where some derivative of the repressed material is sufficiently remote from the latter, or is sufficiently distorted by the Mechanisms of Defence, then the Ego does not recognise the true significance of the derivative, and it can emerge into the light of consciousness. It can come out in various, very familiar ways. Thus when Sue, as a child, had a dream, this was the undisguised expression of an unrepressed wish. But when Sue, as an adult, has a dream, it is in most cases the disguised revelation of a repressed wish. As the latter cannot get through directly in its real guise, it is transformed by the unconscious mechanisms, more especially condensation and displacement, into something unrecognisably different. This then gets past the censorship barrier, and appears as the manifest content of the dream; and this is what Sue reports. If Sue becomes aware of the real significance of her dream, she becomes aware of its latent content, and of her repressed wish, which came out in disguised form in the manifest content of the dream. It is no surprise, given the history of the sexual instinct, that in a great many dreams of the type we are considering, the repressed and disguised wish is sexual in character.

In a somewhat similar way the unconscious also gets through to consciousness in our daytime fantasies. The unconscious is also at work in an analogous way in humour and jokes with a point to them. Moreover, the unconscious is also operating in our lapses of memory, slips of the tongue and the like. These are not accidental events, but the manifestation of unconscious motives. Then, again, the unconscious also gets past the Ego in the quite different field of belief in God. When Joe grows into adulthood, he may develop the unconscious wish to have his strong and loving father with him to protect him always. Because he cannot keep his real and earthly father, he cathects the fantasy of a substitute father in Heaven. Because of the influence of his unconscious wishes here he comes to believe in this God, when in reality he is believing in an illusion.

III

Now let us look at the adult whose Ego has been able to deal fairly satisfactorily with the demands made upon it. Such an adult belongs to the vast majority. In him (or her) the genitals have primacy erotogenically; the components of the sexual instinct have been synthesised; and the affectionate and sensual aspects of sexuality have fused in the manner we have already outlined. In this sort of adult the Ego itself is strong, since the adult has developed normally; his Ego has not had to develop extensive defensive measures to dam up instinctual energy; and therefore the energies available to the Ego have not been greatly curtailed.

Of course, normal adults differ from one another in countless and subtle ways. Nevertheless, amid all these differences, one can discern some patterns of uniformity in certain types of character which they display. Thus when the individual as a child becomes fixated at a certain sexual stage, say the anal, he is liable to develop as an adult certain character traits, which reflect his difficulties in getting through the anal stage as a child. He is liable to exhibit the trio of traits—orderliness, parsimony, and obstinacy. Experiences at the oral stage may be such as to contribute to him developing into an oral character. Furthermore, the normal adult in the course of his development from the latency period will also have dealt with his sexual impulses by sublimating them, so that as an adult he may have a deep interest in, for example, science or art. But again individuals vary widely in their capacity for sublimation, for biological reasons about which psychoanalysis can say nothing.

However, even though he and she are quite normal human beings, it does not follow that they are free from conflict and contented. Rather the contrary. For in the course of their individual development, they have had to repress their sexuality and to restrict their innate destructiveness and aggression. They have had to do so in order to become members of a civilised community. It is only because this happens generally to the young that a civilised community is possible at all. But this process is liable to generate and maintain all manner of conflicts in individuals; and, in Freud's words,[1] "the fateful question of the human species seems to me to be whether and to what extent the cultural process developed in it will succeed in mastering the derangements of communal life caused by the human instinct of aggression and self-destruction." Will Eros be able to keep Death or Thanatos at bay?

IV

But what of the many adults whose Ego has not managed to deal fairly satisfactorily with the demands made upon it, and who therefore exhibit, or suffer from, some manifestly pathological condition? How does this come about? What has gone wrong in these instances? It follows very obviously from what has been said already that matters can go wrong in an indefinite variety of ways. On the other hand, this variety does exhibit—so it is alleged—certain patterns of regularity. Let us concentrate on the putative pattern which is central for psychoanalysis, namely that of neurotic disorder.

Consider again the adult Joe, who, we supposed, has had a history of oral difficulties as a child. Let Joe now have some experience (such as, for example, the death of his mother) that produces excitation which his Ego is not strong enough to master. Joe's Ego cannot master it, because in the course of his development the Ego has had to expend a great deal of energy on building and maintaining defences against Joe's impulses. This has left the Ego in a weakened condition. The reason the excitation has to be mastered is that it threatens to revive the anxiety of infantile and childhood traumas. Because the Ego cannot control the situation, Joe's experience (of his mother's death) precipitates a regression—that is to say, in this instance, instinctual impulses appropriate to an earlier stage of Joe's development are reactivated. Since the resolution of the Oedipus Complex is the climax of the infantile development of sexuality, Joe's impulse regresses to the Oedipal period. But, because of Joe's earlier oral history, his Oedipus Complex, far from being destroyed, was poorly resolved and influenced by his earlier difficulties. The fixation points in his sexual development are pre-Oedipal and pregenital in character, and are to be found in the oral stage. Hence, under the impact of the precipitating experience of his mother's death, Joe regresses to fixation points in the oral stage. Joe is now threatened by the return of what he had repressed as an infant.

But if the ghastly anxieties of the infantile traumas were to get through to consciousness, Joe would be flooded and overwhelmed by agitation. Now, though the Ego has not been strong enough to prevent the threat arising, it still has the strength to resort to a variety of defences to stop the threat materialising—displacement, reaction formation, and so forth. Therefore, when the repressed material does emerge into consciousness, it does so in such a heavily disguised form that Joe does not recognise its significance. What emerges is a compromise between the unconscious material really present, and what the mind of Joe can tolerate in consciousness. This compromise constitutes the symptoms of Joe's neurotic disorder. Since Joe, on our supposition, suffered oral traumas, his symptoms will be some array characteristic of adults who had severe oral difficulties as infants. For example, feelings of depression, feeling that he is unloved and neglected, difficulties in eating anything, oscillating, perhaps, with bouts of gormandising which disgust him.

From all this it is clear that before an event (for example, the death of

Joe's mother) can serve to precipitate a neurotic collapse, a whole complex set of predisposing conditions has to be realised. Thus, Joe's oral libido was strong and liable to get stuck at this stage; he was not good at "taking" frustration; his early experiences with the mother and others were traumatically frightening, and he developed libidinal fixations; the Ego had to defend against the ensuing anxiety by means of primal repression at this stage, and also right through the Oedipal period, thereby leaving itself very weak. If Joe's oral libido had been strong and liable to get stuck at this stage, but if, on the other hand, he had been a placid baby, or if the mother had not been so frustrating, then his predisposition to neurotic disorder of the sort he showed would not have existed, or would have been less strong. Alternatively, if his capacity for sublimation after latency had been very great, then, in spite of his predisposition, his Ego might have been able to master the disturbance set up by the death of his mother.

Joe exhibits one specific type of neurotic disorder. There are other forms, and whether a person's collapse takes one form or another depends on a variety of other conditions. Thus, if a male infant fixates at the anal-sadistic stage and resolves the Oedipus Complex by, in particular, developing and repressing intense anger at the father, then he is predisposed to this extent to collapse into an obsessional neurosis. Or, again, if the infant libidinises some bodily organ or function excessively, and fixation occurs in respect of it, then he is predisposed, to this extent, to break down into what is called a conversion neurosis—one in which the central symptoms are physical complaints involving the organ or function concerned. On the other hand, if Sue suffers, not from excessive frustration as Joe did, but from overgratification of her impulses, at some stage or stages, then she will be disposed to exhibit a different pattern of disorder (for example, that of a spoilt immature individual who is incapable of standing on her own feet).

The different forms of disorder we have been considering go to constitute one pattern of neurosis which is standard and central for psychoanalysis. There are other patterns. For example, the Ego of a war-time bomber pilot may suffer, after a number of flying missions, from an inability to master the excessive excitation produced by the stress of his work; and he collapses into what is called a traumatic neurosis. It is important to note that in all the examples mentioned so far, the Ego *opposes* the regression that occurs. But if the Ego *accepts* it, then the person's disordered conduct will not constitute typical neurotic symptoms (which are "desexualised"), but will be the manifestation of a perversion, which will help to bring about its own sort of sexual satisfaction and orgasm.

What goes wrong when a person suffers from a neurosis is different from what happens when he develops a psychosis. In the latter, the Ego splits into two—a part which is reality-facing, and a part which withdraws from reality completely. If the latter part is the stronger, then a necessary condition is satisfied for the development of psychotic disorder—whether schizophrenia, where the world of real objects is denied, or psychotic depression, where the person gives up altogether trying to realise his desires in the real world.

V

From the account we have given so far of psychoanalytic theory, it is clear that it falls into certain sections or parts, or sub-theories—the theories of instincts, psychic structure, development, defence, dreams, errors and lapses, and psychopathology. It is also clear that the theory is not a unified one, in the way that, for instance, the theory of Mechanics, or Mendelian genetics, are unified theories. However, psychoanalytic theory is more unified than our account so far may suggest. For the theory also contains what can be called a High Level theory, which is closely involved with the various sub-theories we have sketched above, and which serves to unify them to some extent. This High Level account contains what analysts refer to as "Metapsychology," and can be sketched as follows.

What psychoanalysis as a theory is fundamentally about is the way in which the mind works. The mind consists of a set of 'elements' in very complicated interrelations. An element is a mental presentation, and, in their mutual interrelations, the elements go to constitute what can be called a psychic or mental system. Now a mental element has a charge of energy attached to it, and it may also have an "idea" or "ideational presentation" attached to it. Hence, the system as a whole contains a quantity of excitation, coming both from the instincts (in the Id) and from the external world. The system controls this excitation in accordance with certain interconnected principles. In particular, it functions so as to keep the total quantity of excitation in the system as low as possible (the principle of inertia), and also (under other circumstances) so as to keep the quantity constant (the principle of constancy). Consequently, when little Joe, or Sue, wants the breast, the mental system seeks to discharge the tension or excitation by feeding, and thereby keep the quantity of excitation as low as possible. But when little Joe's frustrations over feeding generate excitation that the system cannot tolerate, then the latter works to keep the quantity of excitation constant, and therefore stable and within tolerable bounds. It does so by exerting force against the mental presentations involved, thereby primarily repressing the impulses responsible for the threat of excessive excitation. Later in life, when Joe develops a "dangerous" wish, the system exerts a counter-force against the ideational aspect of the mental element involved, and withdraws energy from the ideational aspects of all derivative elements—thereby actually repressing the wish, as we saw above. The part of the mental system that does this work is the Ego, which is sometimes aided and sometimes hindered by another part, the Super-Ego. What the Ego has to do, in particular, is to keep away from consciousness those mental presentations, whose recognition by the person would raise excitation to an intolerable level. As we have seen above, the different ways in which the Ego achieves this result are known as the Mechanisms of Defence. When the adult system is faced by a threat to its defensive position, excitation is generated, which serves as a signal of danger—called anxiety—and this feeds back to set going protective measures. It is orthodox to say, following Freud, that the unconscious part of Joe's mind is regulated by "primary processes," which are mainly concerned to discharge energy; whereas the preconscious part is governed by "secondary processes," which only allow for discharge in ways that are consonant with the capacities of the Ego and the nature of the real world.

In psychoanalytic theory, therefore, the mind of a person is a self-regulating control system. The specific form the system takes, and how it actually works in the case of any given individual, Joe or Sue, depends on a very large number of conditions. Its specific form and manner of functioning is the outcome, in particular, both of biologically given material and the experience the system has undergone, especially in its early years. This experience comes to the system through its own family, and the way this functioned during the early years of the system. The family, in turn, is the important agent by which the community exerts its influence on, and control over, each individual mental system, and so enables the person concerned to grow up and function as a member of the community to which it belongs.

VI

So much for an outline of Freud's mature position as reconstructed. In order to examine its standing, it is necessary to take note of the other main traditions in psychodynamics.

Two of Freud's early associates to break away were Carl Jung and Alfred Adler. Jung argued that the concept of libido should be widened to cover all forms of psychic energy, not merely the sexual; he presented a view of development which differed from Freud's; he made important use of the concept of the Collective Unconscious (which embraced items common to all mankind, because they are biologically inherited); and he used the concepts of the Unconscious and the Ego in new ways. He also offered his own account of psychic structure, which led on to a complex differentiation of personality types. Though he regarded the psyche, like Freud, as a selfregulating system, this worked for him in a non-Freudian sort of way (for example, with a different concept of repression); and he had non-Freudian views about treatment. Adler took a very different stance from both Freud and Jung. He appeared to offer no theory of instincts, no biologically fixed stages of development, no concept of libido or psychic energy, and little about psychic structure. He concentrated on the ways the individual child and person adapts to the problems of living, and the relative success or failure of these modes of adaptation. The child begins from a state of helplessness, for which it strives to compensate; the way it does so becomes its "life style." If the child develops Oedipal difficulties and castration fears, for example, these are evidence of failure to adapt brought about by defective personal relations within the family. Neurotic difficulties in the adult are the outcome of early failures, which have produced a life style that no longer works.

Jung began the tradition in Psychodynamics known as "Analytical Psychology," Adler began "Individual Psychology." This happened before the First World War. Between the wars new psychoanalytic doctrines and traditions developed vigorously, more especially perhaps in the United States.

One such development took an Adlerian-like stance, rejected Freud's libido theory, and emphasised the importance of the inter-personal environment and the task of the child and adult in having to deal with it. This development is associated, in particular, with the names of Horney and Sullivan. In contrast, there were others who kept the libido theory and developed Freud's own later emphasis on the Ego, in order to develop what is known as "Ego-Psychology." The chief names associated with this development are Anna Freud and Heinz Hartmann. The latter concentrated on an effort to incorporate the Ego functions (for example, thinking and perception) within a Freudian type of scheme.

However, there were still other analysts who modified the Freudian theory in quite different ways. Thus, Melanie Klein pushed the story back to the very first experiences of the infant at the breast, when it mentally splits the breast into the good, feeding one, and the bad, frustrating one, and develops a world of unconscious fantasies about the part and whole objects it encounters. Otto Rank had previously pushed the story even further back, namely to the trauma of birth and the related problem of separation. In great contrast with these trends Wilhelm Reich was concerned in his early years with an attempt to bring together or reconcile Freudian and Marxist theory—an attempt which led him to reject what he took to be Freud's views about the repression of sexuality as a necessary condition for the growth and maintenance of a civilised culture. Later on, Erich Fromm applied a Marxist-oriented sociology in an endeavour to explore the interactions between psychological forces within the individual and different kinds of social structure—interactions that issue in different types of personality.

After the Second World War, Western countries—and especially the United States—witnessed a boom in psychotherapies of various kinds, psychodynamic and non-psychodynamic in character, with their connected doctrines. During this period the West also saw the development of therapies and theories which concentrated on the behavior of patients and its modification. These post-War theories are too numerous to outline here.

VII

It is obvious that our glance at the history of psychodynamic theories is so sketchy as to be very arbitrary. For this history is full of contributions from a large number of analysts, and our sketch has only named a few of them. It is also clear that these contributions, from Freud onwards, present collectively a great variety of different views.

It is important, however, that these differences should not be exaggerated. For behind them lie, in most instances, certain common themes which these views all share, and which unite them as specifically psychodynamic in character. These common themes are not open to precise formulation; different analysts would probably state them somewhat differently; and analysts make use of them in dissimilar ways. Still, it is very necessary to state these themes and to bear them in mind.

1. Psychic Determinism. No item in mental life and in conduct and behaviour is "accidental"; it is the outcome of antecedent conditions.

2. Much mental activity and behaviour is purposive or goal-directed in character.
3. Much of mental activity and behaviour, and its determinants, is unconscious in character.
4. The early experience of the individual, as a child, is very potent, and tends to be pre-potent over later experience.

We do not need to ask whether these common themes actually form part of psychoanalytic theory and other psychodynamic theories. For, irrespective of whether they do so or not, it is clear that they do serve as principles to regulate or guide the thought and work of analysts. It is by the use of these themes, in conjunction with the theories, that psychodynamic psychologists claim to be able to make sense out of much of human functioning that was previously inexplicable. If, when we examine the validity of psychodynamic theories, we find that they are weak and poorly supported, then *ipso facto* we also throw doubt on the value of these four themes as guides to research and to the truth about human nature. Conversely, the better supported we find the theories to be, the more do we establish the value of these themes, or Regulative principles.

Jean-Paul Sartre

Jean-Paul Sartre (1905–1980) is famous as a philosopher, novelist, playwright, and biographer. He was a leading figure of French intellectual life in the postwar period. His name is forever associated with existentialism—the philosophy that places supreme value on the freedom of the individual to decide the meaning of his or her own life. The existentialist movement included such diverse figures as the eccentric Danish Protestant Kierkegaard, the atheist Nietsche, who proclaimed "the death of God," and Heidegger, who explored the human condition in the ponderous Germanic abstractions of *Being and Time*.

Sartre's position involves a resolute assertion of the human being's essential freedom as not open to any kind of scientific explanation. In his analysis, consciousness and freedom are inseparable. This extract consists of most of Sartre's lecture *Existentialism and Humanism,* delivered to great public acclaim in 1946. This is the easiest introduction to his thought, but it is relatively superficial compared with his magnum opus, the lengthy and difficult *Being and Nothingness* (1943).

The view of human nature developed in that work involves a very Cartesian distinction between "being-for-itself" (consciousness) and "being-in-itself" (the inanimate world). Sartre emphasizes that all action must be an attempt to change the world, to bring about what the agent desires. So it implies the ability to consider, desire, or fear what may or may not be the case. Sartre argues that there is a mode of consciousness, which he calls by the dramatic name *anguish,* in which we are peculiarly aware of our radical freedom, of the insufficiency of all desires, decisions, or values to determine our conduct. But we normally do our best to avoid this unsettling awareness, and live most of our lives in what Sartre calls "bad faith" or "self-deception," pretending (even to ourselves) not to be free.

Existentialism and Humanism

My purpose here is to offer a defence of existentialism against several reproaches that have been laid against it. . . .

It is to these various reproaches that I shall endeavour to reply to-day; that is why I have entitled this brief exposition "Existentialism and Humanism." Many may be surprised at the mention of humanism in this connection, but we shall try to see in what sense we understand it. . . .

Atheistic Existentialism

• • •

The question is only complicated because there are two kinds of existentialists. There are, on the one hand, the Christians, amongst whom I shall name Jaspers and Gabriel Marcel, both professed Catholics; and on the other the existential atheists, amongst whom we must place Heidegger as well as the French existentialists and myself. What they have in common is simply the fact that they believe that *existence* comes before *essence*—or, if you will, that we must begin from the subjective. What exactly do we mean by that?

If one considers an article of manufacture—as, for example, a book or a paper-knife—one sees that it has been made by an artisan who had a conception of it; and he has paid attention, equally, to the conception of a paper-knife and to the pre-existent technique of production which is a

From *Existentialism and Humanism,* translated by P. Mairet, © Methuen & Co. 1948.

part of that conception and is, at bottom, a formula. Thus the paper-knife is at the same time an article producible in a certain manner and one which, on the other hand, serves a definite purpose, for one cannot suppose that a man would produce a paper-knife without knowing what it was for. Let us say, then, of the paper-knife that its essence—that is to say the sum of the formulae and the qualities which made its production and its definition possible—precedes its existence. The presence of such-and-such a paper-knife or book is thus determined before my eyes. Here, then, we are viewing the world from a technical standpoint, and we can say that production precedes existence.

When we think of God as the creator, we are thinking of him, most of the time, as a supernal artisan. Whatever doctrine we may be considering, whether it be a doctrine like that of Descartes, or of Leibnitz himself, we always imply that the will follows, more or less, from the understanding or at least accompanies it, so that when God creates he knows precisely what he is creating. Thus, the conception of man in the mind of God is comparable to that of the paper-knife in the mind of the artisan: God makes man according to a procedure and a conception, exactly as the artisan manufactures a paper-knife, following a definition and a formula. Thus each individual man is the realisation of a certain conception which dwells in the divine understanding. In the philosophic atheism of the eighteenth century, the notion of God is suppressed, but not, for all that, the idea that essence is prior to existence; something of that idea we still find everywhere, in Diderot, in Voltaire and even in Kant. Man possesses a human nature; that "human nature," which is the conception of human being, is found in every man; which means that each man is a particular example of an universal conception, the conception of Man. In Kant, this universality goes so far that the wild man of the woods, man in the state of nature and the bourgeois are all contained in the same definition and have the same fundamental qualities. Here again, the essence of man precedes that historic existence which we confront in experience.

Atheistic existentialism, of which I am a representative, declares with greater consistency that if God does not exist there is at least one being whose existence comes before its essence, a being which exists before it can be defined by any conception of it. That being is man or, as Heidegger has it, the human reality. What do we mean by saying that existence precedes essence? We mean that man first of all exists, encounters himself, surges up in the world—and defines himself afterwards. If man as the existentialist sees him is not definable, it is because to begin with he is nothing. He will not be anything until later, and then he will be what he makes of himself. Thus, there is no human nature, because there is no God to have a conception of it. Man simply is. Not that he is simply what he conceives himself to be, but he is what he wills, and as he conceives himself after already existing—as he wills to be after that leap towards existence. Man is nothing else but that which he makes of himself. That is the first principle of existentialism. And this is what people call its "subjectivity," using the word as a reproach against us. But what do we mean to say by this, but that man is of a greater dignity than a stone or a table? For we mean to say that man primarily exists—that man is, before all else, something which propels itself towards a future and is aware that it is doing so. Man is, indeed, a project which possesses a subjective life, instead of being a kind of moss, or a fungus or a cauliflower. Before that projection of the self nothing exists; not even in the heaven of intelligence: man will only attain existence when he is what he purposes to be. Not, however, what he may wish to be. For what we usually understand by wishing or willing is a conscious decision taken—much more often than not—after we have made ourselves what we are. I may wish to join a party, to write a book or to marry—but in such a case what is usually called my will is probably a manifestation of a prior and more spontaneous decision. If, however, it is true that existence is prior to essence, man is responsible for what he is. Thus, the first effect of existentialism is that it puts every man in possession of himself as he is, and places the entire responsibility for his existence squarely upon his own shoulders. And, when we say that man is responsible for himself, we do not mean that he is responsible only for his own individuality, but that he is responsible for all men. The word "subjectivism" is to be understood in two senses, and our adversaries play upon only one of them. Subjectivism means, on the one hand, the freedom of the individual subject and, on the other, that man cannot pass beyond human subjectivity. It is the latter which is the deeper meaning of existentialism. When we say that man chooses himself, we do mean that every one of us must choose himself; but by that we also mean that in choosing for himself he chooses for all men. For in effect, of all the actions a man may take in order to create himself as he wills to be, there is not one which is not creative, at the same time, of an image of man such as he believes he ought to be. To choose between this or that is at the same time to affirm the value of that which is chosen; for we are unable ever to choose the worse. What we choose is always the better; and nothing can be better for us unless it is better for all. If, moreover, existence precedes essence and we will to exist at the same time as we fashion our image, that image is valid for all and for the entire epoch in which we find ourselves. Our responsibility is thus much greater than we had supposed, for it concerns mankind as a whole. If I am a worker, for instance, I may choose to join a Christian rather than a Communist trade union. And if, by that membership, I choose to signify that resignation is, after all, the attitude that best becomes a man, that man's kingdom is not upon this earth, I do not commit myself alone to that view. Resignation is my will for everyone, and my action is, in consequence, a commitment on behalf of all mankind. Or if, to take a more personal case, I decide to marry and to have children, even though this decision proceeds simply from my situation, from my passion or my desire, I am thereby committing not only myself, but humanity as a whole, to the practice of monogamy. I am thus responsible for myself and for all men, and I am creating a certain image of man as I would have him to be. In fashioning myself I fashion man.

Anguish

This may enable us to understand what is meant by such terms—perhaps a little grandiloquent—as anguish, abandonment and despair. As you will soon see, it is very simple. First, what do we mean by anguish? The existentialist frankly states that man is in anguish. His meaning is as follows—When a man commits himself to anything, fully realising that he is not only choosing what he will be, but is thereby at the same time a legislator deciding for the whole of mankind—in such a moment a man cannot escape from the sense of complete and profound responsibility. There are many, indeed, who show no such anxiety. But we affirm that they are merely disguising their anguish or are in flight from it. Certainly, many people think that in what they are doing they commit no one but themselves to anything: and if you ask them, "What would happen if everyone did so?" they shrug their shoulders and reply, "Everyone does not do so." But in truth, one ought always to ask oneself what would happen if everyone did as one is doing; nor can one escape from that disturbing thought except by a kind of self-deception. The man who lies in self-excuse, by saying "Everyone will not do it" must be ill at ease in his conscience, for the act of lying implies the universal value which it denies. By its very disguise his anguish reveals itself. This is the anguish that Kierkegaard called "the anguish of Abraham." You know the story: An angel commanded Abraham to sacrifice his son: and obedience was obligatory, if it really was an angel who had appeared and said, "Thou, Abraham, shalt sacrifice thy son." But anyone in such a case would wonder, first, whether it was indeed an angel and secondly, whether I am really Abraham. Where are the proofs? A certain mad woman who suffered from hallucinations said that people were telephoning to her, and giving her orders. The doctor asked, "But who is it that speaks to you?" She replied: "He says it is God." And what, indeed, could prove to her that it was God? If an angel appears to me, what is the proof that it is an angel; or, if I hear voices, who can prove that they proceed from heaven and not from hell, or from my own subconsciousness or some pathological condition? Who can prove that they are really addressed to me?

Who, then, can prove that I am the proper person to impose, by my own choice, my conception of man upon mankind? I shall never find any proof whatever; there will be no sign to convince me of it. If a voice speaks to me, it is still I myself who must decide whether the voice is or is not that of an angel. If I regard a certain course of action as good, it is only I who choose to say that it is good and not bad. There is nothing to show that I am Abraham: nevertheless I also am obliged at every instant to perform actions which are examples. Everything happens to every man as though the whole human race had its eyes fixed upon what he is doing and regulated its conduct accordingly. So every man ought to say, "Am I really a man who has the right to act in such a manner that humanity regulates itself by what I do." If a man does not say that, he is dissembling his anguish. Clearly, the anguish with which we are concerned here is not one that could lead to quietism or inaction. It is anguish pure and simple, of the kind well known to all those who have borne responsibilities. When, for instance, a military leader takes upon himself the responsibility for an attack and sends a number of men to their death, he chooses to do it and at bottom he alone chooses. No doubt he acts under a higher command, but its orders, which are more general, require interpretation by him and upon that interpretation depends the life of ten, fourteen or twenty men. In making the decision, he cannot but feel a certain anguish. All leaders know that anguish. It does not prevent their acting, on the contrary it is the very condition of their action, for the action presupposes that there is a plurality of possibilities, and in choosing one of these, they realise that it has value only because it is chosen. Now it is anguish of that kind which existentialism describes, and moreover, as we shall see, makes explicit through direct responsibility towards other men who are concerned. Far from being a screen which could separate us from action, it is a condition of action itself.

Abandonment

And when we speak of "abandonment"—a favourite word of Heidegger—we only mean to say that God does not exist, and that it is necessary to draw the consequences of his absence right to the end. The existentialist is strongly opposed to a certain type of secular moralism which seeks to suppress God at the least possible expense. Towards 1880, when the French professors endeavoured to formulate a secular morality, they said something like this:—God is a useless and costly hypothesis, so we will do without it. However, if we are to have morality, a society and a law-abiding world, it is essential that certain values should be taken seriously; they must have an a priori existence ascribed to them. It must be considered obligatory a priori to be honest, not to lie, not to beat one's wife, to bring up children and so forth; so we are going to do a little work on this subject, which will enable us to show that these values exist all the same, inscribed in an intelligible heaven although, of course, there is no God. In other words—and this is, I believe, the purport of all that we in France call radicalism—nothing will be changed if God does not exist; we shall rediscover the same norms of honesty, progress and humanity, and we shall have disposed of God as an out-of-date hypothesis which will die away quietly of itself. The existentialist, on the contrary, finds it extremely embarrassing that God does not exist, for there disappears with Him all possibility of finding values in an intelligible heaven. There can no longer be any good a priori, since there is no infinite and perfect consciousness to think it. It is nowhere written that "the good" exists, that one must be honest or must not lie, since we are now upon the plane where there are only men. Dostoievsky once wrote "If God did not exist, everything would be permitted"; and that, for existentialism, is the starting point. Everything is indeed permitted if God does not exist, and man is in consequence forlorn, for he cannot find anything to depend upon either within or outside himself. He discovers forthwith, that he is without excuse. For if indeed existence precedes essence, one will never be able to explain one's action by reference to a given and specific human nature; in other words, there is no determinism—man is free, man *is* freedom. Nor, on the other hand, if God does not exist, are we provided with any values or commands that could legitimise our behaviour. Thus we have neither behind us, nor before us in a luminous realm of values, any means of justification or excuse. We are left alone, without excuse. That is what I mean when I say that man is condemned to be free. Condemned, because he did not create himself, yet is nevertheless at liberty, and from the moment that he is thrown into this world he is responsible for everything he does. The existentialist does not believe in the power of passion. He will never regard a grand passion as a destructive torrent upon which a man is swept into certain actions as by fate, and which, therefore, is an excuse for them. He thinks that man is responsible for his passion. Neither will an existentialist think that a man can find help through some sign being vouchsafed upon earth for his orientation: for he thinks that the man himself interprets the sign as he chooses. He thinks that every man, without any support or help whatever, is condemned at every instant to invent man. As Ponge has written in a very fine article, "Man is the future of man." That is exactly true. Only, if one took this to mean that the future is laid up in Heaven, that God knows what it is, it would be false, for then it would no longer even be a future. If, however, it means that, whatever man may now appear to be, there is a future to be fashioned, a virgin future that awaits him—then it is a true saying. But in the present one is forsaken.

As an example by which you may the better understand this state of abandonment, I will refer to the case of a pupil of mine, who sought me out in the following circumstances. His father was quarrelling with his mother and was also inclined to be a "collaborator"; his elder brother had been killed in the German offensive of 1940 and this young man, with a sentiment somewhat primitive but generous, burned to avenge him. His mother was living alone with him, deeply afflicted by the semitreason of his father and by the death of her eldest son, and her one consolation was in this young man. But he, at this moment, had the choice between going to England to join the Free French Forces or of staying near his mother and helping her to live. He fully realised that this woman lived only for him and that his disappearance—or perhaps his death—would plunge her into despair. He also realised that, concretely and in fact, every action he performed on his mother's behalf would be sure of effect in the sense of aiding her to live, where as anything he did in order to go and fight would be an ambiguous action which might vanish like water into sand and serve no purpose. For instance, to set out for England he would have to wait indefinitely in a Spanish camp on the way through Spain; or, on arriving in England or in Algiers he might be put into an office to fill up forms. Consequently, he found himself confronted by two very different modes of action; the one concrete, immediate, but directed towards only one individual; and the other an action addressed to an end infinitely greater, a national collectivity, but for that very reason ambiguous—and it might be frustrated on the way. At the same time, he was hesitating between two kinds of morality; on the one side the morality of sympathy, of personal devotion and, on the other side, a morality of wider scope but of more debatable validity. He had to choose between those two. What could help him to choose? Could the Christian doctrine? No. Christian doctrine says: Act with charity, love your neighbour, deny yourself for others, choose the way which is hardest, and so forth. But which is the harder road? To whom does one owe the more brotherly love, the patriot or the mother? Which is the more useful aim, the general one of fighting in and for the whole community, or the precise aim of helping one particular person to live? Who can give an answer to that a priori? No one. Nor is it given in any ethical scripture. The Kantian ethic says, Never regard another as a means, but always as an end. Very well; if I remain with my mother, I shall be regarding her as the end and not as a means: but by the same token I am in danger of treating as means those who are fighting on my behalf; and the converse is also true, that if I go to the aid of the combatants I shall be treating them as the end at the risk of treating my mother as a means.

If values are uncertain, if they are still too abstract to determine the particular, concrete case under consideration, nothing remains but to trust in our instincts. That is what this young man tried to do; and when I saw him he said, "In the end, it is feeling that counts; the direction in which it is really pushing me is the one I ought to choose. If I feel that I love my mother enough to sacrifice everything else for her—my will to be avenged, all my longings for action and adventure—then I stay with her. If, on the contrary, I feel that my love for her is not enough, I go." But how does one estimate the strength of a feeling? The value of his feeling for his mother was determined precisely by the fact that he was standing by her. I may say that I love a certain friend enough to sacrifice such or such a sum of money for him, but I cannot prove that unless I have done it. I may say, "I love my mother enough to remain with her," if actually I have remained with her. I can only estimate the strength of this affection if I have performed an action by which it is defined and ratified. But if I then appeal to this affection to justify my action, I find myself drawn into a vicious circle.

Moreover, as Gide has very well said, a sentiment which is play-acting and one which is vital are two things that are hardly distinguishable one from another. To decide that I love my mother by staying beside her, and to play a comedy the upshot of which is that I do so—these are nearly the same thing. In other words, feeling is formed by the deeds that one does;

therefore I cannot consult it as a guide to action. And that is to say that I can neither seek within myself for an authentic impulse to action, nor can I expect, from some ethic, formulae that will enable me to act. You may say that the youth did, at least, go to a professor to ask for advice. But if you seek counsel—from a priest, for example—you have selected that priest; and at bottom you already knew, more or less, what he would advise. In other words, to choose an adviser is nevertheless to commit oneself by that choice. If you are a Christian, you will say, Consult a priest; but there are collaborationists, priests who are resisters and priests who wait for the tide to turn: which will you choose? Had this young man chosen a priest of the resistance, or one of the collaboration, he would have decided beforehand the kind of advice he was to receive. Similarly, in coming to me, he knew what advice I should give him, and I had but one reply to make. You are free, therefore choose—that is to say, invent. No rule of general morality can show you what you ought to do: no signs are vouchsafed in this world. The Catholics will reply, "Oh, but they are!" Very well; still, it is I myself, in every case, who have to interpret the signs. Whilst I was imprisoned, I made the acquaintance of a somewhat remarkable man, a Jesuit, who had become a member of that order in the following manner. In his life he had suffered a succession of rather severe setbacks. His father had died when he was a child, leaving him in poverty, and he had been awarded a free scholarship in a religious institution, where he had been made continually to feel that he was accepted for charity's sake, and, in consequence, he had been denied several of those distinctions and honours which gratify children. Later, about the age of eighteen, he came to grief in a sentimental affair; and finally, at twenty-two—this was a trifle in itself, but it was the last drop that overflowed his cup—he failed in his military examination. This young man, then, could regard himself as a total failure: it was a sign—but a sign of what? He might have taken refuge in bitterness or despair. But he took it—very cleverly for him—as a sign that he was not intended for secular successes, and that only the attainments of religion, those of sanctity and of faith, were accessible to him. He interpreted his record as a message from God, and became a member of the Order. Who can doubt but that this decision as to the meaning of the sign was his, and his alone? One could have drawn quite different conclusions from such a series of reverses—as, for example, that he had better become a carpenter or a revolutionary. For the decipherment of the sign, however, he bears the entire responsibility. That is what "abandonment" implies, that we ourselves decide our being. And with this abandonment goes anguish.

Despair

As for "despair," the meaning of this expression is extremely simple. It merely means that we limit ourselves to a reliance upon that which is within our wills, or within the sum of the probabilities which render our action feasible. Whenever one wills anything, there are always these elements of probability. If I am counting upon a visit from a friend, who may be coming by train or by tram, I presuppose that the train will arrive at the appointed time, or that the tram will not be derailed. I remain in the realm of possibilities; but one does not rely upon any possibilities beyond those that are strictly concerned in one's action. Beyond the point at which the possibilities under consideration cease to affect my action, I ought to disinterest myself. For there is no God and no prevenient design, which can adapt the world and all its possibilities to my will. When Descartes said, "Conquer yourself rather than the world," what he meant was, at bottom, the same—that we should act without hope.

Marxists, to whom I have said this, have answered: "Your action is limited, obviously, by your death; but you can rely upon the help of others. That is, you can count both upon what the others are doing to help you elsewhere, as in China and in Russia, and upon what they will do later, after your death, to take up your action and carry it forward to its final accomplishment which will be the revolution. Moreover you must rely upon this; not to do so is immoral." To this I rejoin, first, that I shall always count upon my comrades-in-arms in the struggle, in so far as they are committed, as I am, to a definite, common cause; and in the unity of a party or a group which I can more or less control—that is, in which I am enrolled as a militant and whose movements at every moment are known to me. In that respect, to rely upon the unity and the will of the party is exactly like my reckoning that the train will run to time or that the tram will not be derailed. But I cannot count upon men whom I do not know, I cannot base my confidence upon human goodness or upon man's interest in the good of society, seeing that man is free and that there is no human nature which I can take as foundational. I do not know whither the Russian revolution will lead. I can admire it and take it as an example in so far as it is evident, to-day, that the proletariat plays a part in Russia which it has attained in no other nation. But I cannot affirm that this will necessarily lead to the triumph of the proletariat: I must confine myself to what I can see. Nor can I be sure that comrades-in-arms will take up my work after my death and carry it to the maximum perfection, seeing that those men are free agents and will freely decide, to-morrow, what man is then to be. To-morrow, after my death, some men may decide to establish Fascism, and the others may be so cowardly or so slack as to let them do so. If so, Fascism will then be the truth of man, and so much the worse for us. In reality, things will be such as men have decided they shall be. Does that mean that I should abandon myself to quietism? No. First I ought to commit myself and then act my commitment, according to the time-honoured formula that "one need not hope in order to undertake one's work." Nor does this mean that I should not belong to a party, but only that I should be without illusion and that I should do what I can. For instance, if I ask myself "Will the social ideal as such, ever become a reality?" I cannot tell, I only know that whatever may be in my power to make it so, I shall do; beyond that, I can count upon nothing.

Quietism is the attitude of people who say, "let others do what I cannot do." The doctrine I am presenting before you is precisely the opposite of this, since it declares that there is no reality except in action. It goes further, indeed, and adds, "Man is nothing else but what he purposes, he exists only in so far as he realises himself, he is therefore nothing else but the sum of his actions, nothing else but what his life is." Hence we can well understand why some people are horrified by our teaching. For many have but one resource to sustain them in their misery, and that is to think, "Circumstances have been against me, I was worthy to be something much better than I have been. I admit I have never had a great love or a great friendship; but that is because I never met a man or a woman who were worthy of it; if I have not written any very good books, it is because I had not the leisure to do so; or, if I have had no children to whom I could devote myself it is because I did not find the man I could have lived with. So there remains within me a wide range of abilities, inclinations and potentialities, unused but perfectly viable, which endow me with a worthiness that could never be inferred from the mere history of my actions." But in reality and for the existentialist, there is no love apart from the deeds of love; no potentiality of love other than that which is manifested in loving; there is no genius other than that which is expressed in works of art. The genius of Proust is the totality of the works of Proust; the genius of Racine is the series of his tragedies, outside of which there is nothing. Why should we attribute to Racine the capacity to write yet another tragedy when that is precisely what he did not write? In life, a man commits himself, draws his own portrait and there is nothing but that portrait. No doubt this thought may seem comfortless to one who has not made a success of his life. On the other hand, it puts everyone in a position to understand that reality alone is reliable; that dreams, expectations and hopes serve to define a man only as deceptive dreams, abortive hopes, expectations unfulfilled; that is to say, they define him negatively, not positively. Nevertheless, when one says, "You are nothing else but what you live," it does not imply that an artist is to be judged solely by his works of art, for a thousand other things contribute no less to his definition as a man. What we mean to say is that a man is no other than a series of undertakings, that he is the sum, the organisation, the set of relations that constitute these undertakings.

In the light of all this, what people reproach us with is not, after all, our pessimism, but the sternness of our optimism. If people condemn our works of fiction, in which we describe characters that are base, weak, cowardly and sometimes even frankly evil, it is not only because those characters are base, weak, cowardly or evil. For suppose that, like Zola, we showed that the behaviour of these characters was caused by their heredity, or by the action of their environment upon them, or by determining factors, psychic or organic. People would be reassured, they would say, "You see, that is what we are like, no one can do anything about it." But the existentialist, when he portrays a coward, shows him as responsible for his cowardice. He is not like that on account of a cowardly heart or lungs or cerebrum, he has not become like that through his physiological organism; he is like that because he has made himself into a coward by his actions. There is no such thing as a cowardly temperament. There are nervous temperaments; there is what is called impoverished blood, and there are also rich temperaments. But the man whose blood is poor is not a coward for all that, for what produces cowardice is the act of giving up or giving way; and a temperament is not an action. A coward is defined by the deed that he has done. What people feel obscurely, and with horror, is that the coward as we present him is guilty of being a coward. What people would prefer would be to be born either a coward or a hero. One of the charges most often laid against the *Chemins de la Liberté* is something like this—"But, after all, these people being so base, how can you make them into heroes?" That objection is really rather comic, for it implies that people are born heroes: and that is, at bottom, what such people would like to think. If you are born cowards, you can be quite content, you can do nothing about it and you will be cowards all your lives whatever you do; and if you are born heroes you can again be quite content; you will be heroes all your lives, eating and drinking heroically. Whereas the existentialist says that the coward makes himself cowardly, the hero makes himself heroic; and that there is always a possibility for the coward to give up cowardice and for the hero to stop being a hero.

What counts is the total commitment, and it is not by a particular case or particular action that you are committed altogether.

Optimism, Action, and Morality

We have now, I think, dealt with a certain number of the reproaches against existentialism. You have seen that it cannot be regarded as a philosophy of quietism since it defines man by his action; nor as a pessimistic description of man, for no doctrine is more optimistic, the destiny of man is placed within himself. Nor is it an attempt to discourage man from action since it tells him that there is no hope except in his action, and that the one thing which permits him to have life is the deed. Upon this level therefore, what we are considering is an ethic of action and self-commitment. However, we are still reproached, upon these few data, for confining man within his individual subjectivity. There again people badly misunderstand us.

Our point of departure is, indeed, the subjectivity of the individual; and that for strictly philosophic reasons. It is not because we are bourgeois, but because we seek to base our teaching upon the truth, and not upon a collection of fine theories, full of hope but lacking real foundations. And at the point of departure there cannot be any other truth than this, *I think, therefore I am,* which is the absolute truth of consciousness as it attains to itself. Every theory which begins with man, outside of this moment of self-attainment, is a theory which thereby suppresses the truth, for outside of the Cartesian *cogito,* all objects are no more than probable, and any doctrine of probabilities which is not attached to a truth will crumble into nothing. In order to define the probable one must possess the true. Before there can be any truth whatever, then, there must be an absolute truth, and there is such a truth which is simple, easily attained and within the reach of everybody; it consists in one's immediate sense of one's self.

In the second place, this theory alone is compatible with the dignity of man, it is the only one which does not make man into an object. All kinds of materialism lead one to treat every man including oneself as an object—that is, as a set of pre-determined reactions, in no way different from the patterns of qualities and phenomena which constitute a table, or a chair or a stone. Our aim is precisely to establish the human kingdom as a pattern of values in distinction from the material world. But the subjectivity which we thus postulate as the standard of truth is no narrowly individual subjectivism, for as we have demonstrated, it is not only one's own self that one discovers in the *cogito,* but those of others too. Contrary to the philosophy of Descartes, contrary to that of Kant, when we say "I think" we are attaining to ourselves in the presence of the other, and we are just as certain of the other as we are of ourselves. Thus the man who discovers himself directly in the *cogito* also discovers all the others, and discovers them as the condition of his own existence. He recognises that he cannot be anything (in the sense in which one says one is spiritual, or that one is wicked or jealous) unless others recognise him as such. I cannot obtain any truth whatsoever about myself, except through the mediation of another. The other is indispensable to my existence, and equally so to any knowledge I can have of myself. Under these conditions, the intimate discovery of myself is at the same time the revelation of the other as a freedom which confronts mine, and which cannot think or will without doing so either for or against me. Thus, at once, we find ourselves in a world which is, let us say, that of "inter-subjectivity." It is in this world that man has to decide what he is and what others are.

Furthermore, although it is impossible to find in each and every man a universal essence that can be called human nature, there is nevertheless a human universality of *condition.* It is not by chance that the thinkers of today are so much more ready to speak of the condition than of the nature of man. By his condition they understand, with more or less clarity, all the *limitations* which a priori define man's fundamental situation in the universe. His historical situations are variable: man may be born a slave in a pagan society, or may be a feudal baron, or a proletarian. But what never vary are the necessities of being in the world, of having to labour and to die there. These limitations are neither subjective nor objective, or rather there is both a subjective and an objective aspect of them. Objective, because we meet with them everywhere and they are everywhere recognisable: and subjective because they are *lived* and are nothing if man does not live them—if, that is to say, he does not freely determine himself and his existence in relation to them. And, diverse though man's purposes may be, at least none of them is wholly foreign to me, since every human purpose presents itself as an attempt either to surpass these limitations, or to widen them, or else to deny or to accommodate oneself to them. Consequently every purpose, however individual it may be, is of universal value. Every purpose, even that of a Chinese, an Indian or a Negro, can be understood by a European. To say it can be understood, means that the European of 1945 may be striving out of a certain situation towards the same limitations in the same way, and that he may re-conceive in himself the purpose of the Chinese, of the Indian or the African. In every purpose

there is universality, in this sense that every purpose is comprehensible to
every man. Not that this or that purpose defines man for ever, but that it
may be entertained again and again. There is always some way of understanding an idiot, a child, a primitive man or a foreigner if one has sufficient information. In this sense we may say that there is a human universality, but it is not something given; it is being perpetually made. I make
this universality in choosing myself; I also make it by understanding the
purpose of any other man, of whatever epoch. This absoluteness of the act
of choice does not alter the relativity of each epoch.

What is at the very heart and center of existentialism, is the absolute
character of the free commitment, by which every man realises himself in
realising a type of humanity—a commitment always understandable, to
no matter whom in no matter what epoch—and its bearing upon the relativity of the cultural pattern which may result from such absolute commitment. One must observe equally the relativity of Cartesianism and the
absolute character of the Cartesian commitment. In this sense you may
say, if you like, that every one of us makes the absolute by breathing, by
eating, by sleeping or by behaving in any fashion whatsoever. There is no
difference between free being—being as self-committal, as existence
choosing its essence—and absolute being. And there is no difference
whatever between being as an absolute, temporarily localised—that is,
localised in history—and universally intelligible being.

This does not completely refute the charge of subjectivism. Indeed that
objection appears in several other forms, of which the first is as follows.
People say to us, "Then it does not matter what you do," and they say this
in various ways. First they tax us with anarchy; then they say, "You cannot judge others, for there is no reason for preferring one purpose to
another"; finally, they may say, "Everything being merely voluntary in
this choice of yours, you give away with one hand what you pretend to
gain with the other." These three are not very serious objections. As to the
first, to say that it matters not what you choose is not correct. In one sense
choice is possible, but what is not possible is not to choose. I can always
choose, but I must know that if I do not choose, that is still a choice. This,
although it may appear merely formal, is of great importance as a limit to
fantasy and caprice. For, when I confront a real situation—for example,
that I am a sexual being, able to have relations with a being of the other
sex and able to have children—I am obliged to choose my attitude to it,
and in every respect I bear the responsibility of the choice which, in committing myself, also commits the whole of humanity. Even if my choice
is determined by no a priori value whatever, it can have nothing to do with

caprice: and if anyone thinks that this is only Gide's theory of the *acte gratuit* over again, he has failed to see the enormous difference between this theory and that of Gide. Gide does not know what a situation is, his "act" is one of pure caprice. In our view, on the contrary, man finds himself in an organised situation in which he is himself involved: his choice involves mankind in its entirety, and he cannot avoid choosing. Either he must remain single, or he must marry without having children, or he must marry and have children. In any case, and whichever he may choose, it is impossible for him, in respect of this situation, not to take complete responsibility. Doubtless he chooses without reference to any pre-established values, but it is unjust to tax him with caprice. Rather let us say that the moral choice is comparable to the construction of a work of art.

But here I must at once digress to make it quite clear that we are not propounding an aesthetic morality, for our adversaries are disingenuous enough to reproach us even with that. I mention the work of art only by way of comparison. That being understood, does anyone reproach an artist when he paints a picture for not following rules established a priori? Does one ever ask what is the picture that he ought to paint? As everyone knows, there is no pre-defined picture for him to make; the artist applies himself to the composition of a picture, and the picture that ought to be made is precisely that which he will have made. As everyone knows, there are no aesthetic values a priori, but there are values which will appear in due course in the coherence of the picture, in the relation between the will to create and the finished work. No one can tell what the painting of tomorrow will be like; one cannot judge a painting until it is done. What has that to do with morality? We are in the same creative situation. We never speak of a work of art as irresponsible; when we are discussing a canvas by Picasso, we understand very well that the composition became what it is at the time when he was painting it, and that his works are part and parcel of his entire life.

It is the same upon the plane of morality. There is this in common between art and morality, that in both we have to do with creation and invention. We cannot decide a priori what it is that should be done. I think it was made sufficiently clear to you in the case of that student who came to see me, that to whatever ethical system he might appeal, the Kantian or any other, he could find no sort of guidance whatever; he was obliged to invent the law for himself. Certainly we cannot say that this man, in choosing to remain with his mother—that is, in taking sentiment, personal devotion and concrete charity as his moral foundations—would be making an irresponsible choice, nor could we do so if he preferred the sacrifice of going away to England. Man makes himself; he is not found ready-made; he makes himself by the choice of his morality, and he cannot but choose a morality, such is the pressure of circumstances upon him. We define man only in relation to his commitments; it is therefore absurd to reproach us for irresponsibility in our choice.

In the second place, people say to us, "You are unable to judge others." This is true in one sense and false in another. It is true in this sense, that whenever a man chooses his purpose and his commitment in all clearness and in all sincerity, whatever that purpose may be it is impossible to prefer another for him. It is true in the sense that we do not believe in progress. Progress implies amelioration; but man is always the same, facing a situation which is always changing, and choice remains always a choice in the situation. The moral problem has not changed since the time when it was a choice between slavery and anti-slavery—from the time of the war of Secession, for example, until the present moment when one chooses between the Mouvement Républicain Populaire and the Communists.

We can judge, nevertheless, for, as I have said, one chooses in view of others, and in view of others one chooses himself. One can judge, first—and perhaps this is not a judgment of value, but it is a logical judgment—that in certain cases choice is founded upon an error, and in others upon the truth. One can judge a man by saying that he deceives himself. Since we have defined the situation of man as one of free choice, without excuse and without help, any man who takes refuge behind the excuse of his passions, or by inventing some deterministic doctrine, is a self-deceiver. One may object: "But why should he not choose to deceive himself?" I reply that it is not for me to judge him morally, but I define his self-deception as an error. Here one cannot avoid pronouncing a judgment of truth. The self-deception is evidently a falsehood, because it is a dissimulation of man's complete liberty of commitment. Upon this same level, I say that it is also a self-deception if I choose to declare that certain values are incumbent upon me; I am in contradiction with myself if I will these values and at the same time say that they impose themselves upon me. If anyone says to me, "And what if I wish to deceive myself?" I answer, "There is no reason why you should not, but I declare that you are doing so, and that the attitude of strict consistency alone is that of good faith. Furthermore, I can pronounce a moral judgment. For I declare that freedom, in respect of concrete circumstances, can have no other end and aim but itself; and when once a man has seen that values depend upon himself, in that state of forsakenness he can will only one thing, and that is freedom as the foundation of all values. That does not mean that he wills it in the abstract: it simply means that the actions of men of good faith have, as their ultimate significance, the quest of freedom itself as such. A man who belongs to some communist or revolutionary society wills certain concrete ends, which imply the will to freedom, but that freedom is willed in community. We will freedom for freedom's sake, and in and through particular circumstances. And in thus willing freedom, we discover that it depends entirely upon the freedom of others and that the freedom of others depends upon our own. Obviously, freedom as the definition of a man does not depend upon others, but as soon as there is a commitment, I am obliged to will the liberty of others at the same time as mine. I cannot make liberty my aim unless I make that of others equally my aim. Consequently, when I recognise, as entirely authentic, that man is a being whose existence precedes his essence, and that he is a free being who cannot, in any circumstances, but will his freedom, at the same time I realise that I cannot not will the freedom of others. Thus, in the name of that will to freedom which is implied in freedom itself, I can form judgments upon those who seek to hide from themselves the wholly voluntary nature of their existence and its complete freedom. Those who hide from this total freedom, in a guise of solemnity or with deterministic excuses, I shall call cowards. Others, who try to show that their existence is necessary, when it is merely an accident of the appearance of the human race on earth,—I shall call scum. But neither cowards nor scum can be identified except upon the plane of strict authenticity. Thus, although the content of morality is variable, a certain form of this morality is universal. Kant declared that freedom is a will both to itself and to the freedom of others. Agreed: but he thinks that the formal and the universal suffice for the constitution of a morality. We think, on the contrary, that principles that are too abstract break down when we come to defining action. To take once again the case of that student; by what authority, in the name of what golden rule of morality, do you think he could have decided, in perfect peace of mind, either to abandon his mother or to remain with her ? There are no means of judging. The content is always concrete, and therefore unpredictable; it has always to be invented. The one thing that counts, is to know whether the invention is made in the name of freedom.

Let us, for example, examine the two following cases, and you will see how far they are similar in spite of their difference. Let us take *The Mill on the Floss*. We find here a certain young woman, Maggie Tulliver, who is an incarnation of the value of passion and is aware of it. She is in love with a young man, Stephen, who is engaged to another, an insignificant young woman. This Maggie Tulliver, instead of heedlessly seeking her own happiness, chooses in the name of human solidarity to sacrifice herself and to give up the man she loves. On the other hand, La Sanseverina in Stendhal's *Chartreuse de Parme,* believing that it is passion which endows man with his real value, would have declared that a grand passion justifies its sacrifices, and must be preferred to the banality of such conjugal love as would unite Stephen to the little goose he was engaged to marry. It is the latter that she would have chosen to sacrifice in realising her own happiness, and, as Stendhal shows, she would also sacrifice herself upon the plane of passion if life made that demand upon her. Here we are facing two clearly opposed moralities; but I claim that they are equivalent, seeing that in both cases the overruling aim is freedom. You can imagine two attitudes exactly similar in effect, in that one girl might prefer, in resignation, to give up her lover whilst the other preferred, in fulfilment of sexual desire, to ignore the prior engagement of the man she loved; and, externally, these two cases might appear the same as the two we have just cited, while being in fact entirely different. The attitude of La Sanseverina is much nearer to that of Maggie Tulliver than to one of careless greed. Thus, you see, the second objection is at once true and false. One can choose anything, but only if it is upon the plane of free commitment.

The third objection, stated by saying, "You take with one hand what you give with the other," means, at bottom, "your values are not serious, since you choose them yourselves." To that I can only say that I am very sorry that it should be so; but if I have excluded God the Father, there must be somebody to invent values. We have to take things as they are. And moreover, to say that we invent values means neither more nor less than this; that there is no sense in life a priori. Life is nothing until it is lived; but it is yours to make sense of, and the value of it is nothing else but the sense that you choose. Therefore, you can see that there is a possibility of creating a human community. I have been reproached for suggesting that existentialism is a form of humanism: people have said to me, "But you have written in your *Nauseé* that the humanists are wrong, you have even ridiculed a certain type of humanism, why do you now go back upon that?" In reality, the word humanism has two very different meanings. One may understand by humanism a theory which upholds man as the end-in-itself and as the supreme value. Humanism in this sense appears, for instance, in Cocteau's story *Round the World in 80 Hours,* in which one of the characters declares, because he is flying over mountains in an aeroplane, "Man is magnificent!" This signifies that although I, personally, have not built aeroplanes I have the benefit of those particular inventions and that I personally, being a man, can consider myself responsible for, and honoured by, achievements that are peculiar to some men. It is to assume that we can ascribe value to man according to the most distinguished deeds of certain men. That kind of humanism is absurd, for only the dog or the horse would be in a position to pronounce a general judgment upon man and declare that he is magnificent, which they have never been such fools as to do—at least, not as far as I know. But neither is it admissible that a man should pronounce judgment upon Man. Existentialism dispenses with any judgment of this sort: an existentialist will never take man as the end, since man is still to be determined. And we have no right to believe that humanity is something to which we could set up a cult, after the manner of Auguste Comte. The cult of humanity ends in Comtian humanism, shut-in upon itself, and—this must be said—in Fascism. We do not want a humanism like that.

But there is another sense of the word, of which the fundamental meaning is this: Man is all the time outside of himself: it is in projecting and losing himself beyond himself that he makes man to exist; and, on the other hand, it is by pursuing transcendent aims that he himself is able to exist. Since man is thus self-surpassing, and can grasp objects only in relation to his self-surpassing, he is himself the heart and centre of his transcendence. There is no other universe except the human universe, the universe of human subjectivity. This relation of transcendence as constitutive of man (not in the sense that God is transcendent, but in the sense of self-surpassing) with subjectivity (in such a sense that man is not shut up in himself but forever present in a human universe)—it is this that we call existential humanism. This is humanism, because we remind man that there is no legislator but himself; that he himself, thus abandoned, must decide for himself; also because we show that it is not by turning back upon himself, but always by seeking, beyond himself, an aim which is one of liberation or of some particular realisation, that man can realise himself as truly human.

You can see from these few reflections that nothing could be more unjust than the objections people raise against us. Existentialism is nothing else but an attempt to draw the full conclusions from a consistently atheistic position. Its intention is not in the least that of plunging men into despair. And if by despair one means—as the Christians do—any attitude of unbelief, the despair of the existentialists is something different. Existentialism is not atheist in the sense that it would exhaust itself in demonstrations of the non-existence of God. It declares, rather, that even if God existed that would make no difference from its point of view. Not that we believe God does exist, but we think that the real problem is not that of His existence; what man needs is to find himself again and to understand that nothing can save him from himself, not even a valid proof of the existence of God. In this sense existentialism is optimistic, it is a doctrine of action, and it is only by self-deception, by confusing their own despair with ours that Christians can describe us as without hope.

B. F. Skinner

The American John B. Watson earned a lasting place in the history of psychology by founding the behaviorist movement in 1913. Toward the end of the nineteenth century, Wilhelm Wundt and William James had tried to establish psychology as an experimental science, seeking to find laws governing states of consciousness. Freud extended the range of the term *mental* to cover states and processes that are not available to consciousness, but he still assumed that introspectable phenomena such as dreams were *among* the data for psychological explanation. Watson attracted ready support for the view that the data of the science of psychology should be completely objective and publicly observable, and should therefore be defined to be the behavior of living creatures. (He also assumed that all learning could be explained by a few simple laws of conditioning.)

B. F. Skinner, who became Professor of Psychology at Harvard, took up these behaviorist themes, Besides his technical scientific papers, he published a number of popular works: *Walden Two* (1948), a novel about a Utopian community; *Science and Human Behavior* (1953); and *Beyond Freedom and Dignity* (1971). He repeats the oft-made suggestion to apply the methods of science to human affairs, promising a new "technology of behavior," an answer to many social problems in his strictly behavioristic approach to psychology. He blamed much of "the present unhappy condition of the world" on what he saw as our confusion between a "scientific conception of human behavior" and a "philosophy of personal freedom."

In these extracts from his late book *About Behaviorism* (1974), Skinner continues to maintain his hopes for both a science and a technology of human behavior.

About Behaviorism

Behaviorism is not the science of human behavior; it is the philosophy of that science. Some of the questions it asks are these: Is such a science really possible? Can it account for every aspect of human behavior? What methods can it use? Are its laws as valid as those of physics and biology? Will it lead to a technology, and if so, what role will it play in human affairs? Particularly important is its bearing on earlier treatments of the same subject. Human behavior is the most familiar feature of the world in which people live, and more must have been said about it than about any other thing; how much of what has been said is worth saving?

Some of these questions will eventually be answered by the success or failure of scientific and technological enterprises, but current issues are raised, and provisional answers are needed now. A great many intelligent people believe that answers have already been found and that they are all unpromising. Here, for example, are some of the things commonly said about behaviorism or the science of behavior. They are all, I believe, wrong.

1. It ignores consciousness, feelings, and states of mind.
2. It neglects innate endowment and argues that all behavior is acquired during the lifetime of the individual.
3. It formulates behavior simply as a set of responses to stimuli, thus representing a person as an automaton, robot, puppet, or machine.
4. It does not attempt to account for cognitive processes.
5. It has no place for intention or purpose.
6. It cannot explain creative achievements—in art, for example, or in music, literature, science, or mathematics.

From *About Behaviorism* by B. F. Skinner. Copyright © 1974 by B. F. Skinner. Reprinted by permission of Alfred A. Knopf Inc.

7. It assigns no role to a self or sense of self.
8. It is necessarily superficial and cannot deal with the depths of the mind or personality.
9. It limits itself to the prediction and control of behavior and misses the essential nature or being of man.
10. It works with animals, particularly with white rats, but not with people, and its picture of human behavior is therefore confined to those features which human beings share with animals.
11. Its achievements under laboratory control cannot be duplicated in daily life, and what it has to say about human behavior in the world at large is therefore unsupported metascience.
12. It is oversimplified and naïve and its facts are either trivial or already well known.
13. It is scientistic rather than scientific. It merely emulates the sciences.
14. Its technological achievements could have come about through the use of common sense.
15. If its contentions are valid, they must apply to the behavioral scientist himself, and what he says is therefore only what he has been conditioned to say and cannot be true.
16. It dehumanizes man; it is reductionistic and destroys man *qua* man.
17. It is concerned only with general principles and therefore neglects the uniqueness of the individual.
18. It is necessarily antidemocratic because the relation between experimenter and subject is manipulative, and its results can therefore be used by dictators but not by men of good will.
19. It regards abstract ideas such as morality or justice as fictions.
20. It is indifferent to the warmth and richness of human life, and it is incompatible with the creation and enjoyment of art, music, and literature and with love for one's fellow men.

These contentions represent, I believe, an extraordinary misunderstanding of the achievements and significance of a scientific enterprise. How can it be explained? The early history of the movement may have caused trouble. The first explicit behaviorist was John B. Watson, who in 1913 issued a kind of manifesto called *Psychology as the Behaviorist Views It.* As the title shows, he was not proposing a new science but arguing that psychology should be redefined as the study of behavior. This may have been a strategic mistake. Most of the psychologists at the time believed they were studying mental processes in a mental world of consciousness, and they were naturally not inclined to agree with Watson. Early behaviorists wasted a good deal of time, and confused an important central issue, by attacking the introspective study of mental life.

Watson himself had made important observations of instinctive behavior and was, indeed, one of the first ethologists in the modern spirit, but he was greatly impressed by new evidence of what an organism could learn to do, and he made some rather extreme claims about the potential of a newborn human infant. He himself called them exaggerations, but they have been used to discredit him ever since. His new science was also, so to speak, born prematurely. Very few scientific facts about behavior— particularly human behavior—were available. A shortage of facts is always a problem in a new science, but in Watson's aggressive program in a field as vast as human behavior it was especially damaging. He needed more factual support than he could find, and it is not surprising that much of what he said seemed oversimplified and naïve.

Among the behavioral facts at hand were reflexes and conditioned reflexes, and Watson made the most of them, but the reflex suggested a push-pull type of causality not incompatible with the nineteenth-century conception of a machine. The same impression was given by the work of the Russian physiologist Pavlov, published at about the same time, and it was not corrected by the stimulus-response psychology which emerged during the next three or four decades.

Watson naturally emphasized the most reproducible results he could find, and most of them had been obtained from animals—the white rats of animal psychology and Pavlov's dogs. It seemed to be implied that human behavior had no distinguishing characteristics. And to bolster his claim that psychology was a science, and to fill out his textbook, he borrowed from anatomy and physiology, and Pavlov took the same line by insisting that his experiments on behavior were really "an investigation of the physiological activity of the cerebral cortex," although neither man could point to any direct observations of the nervous system which threw light on behavior. They were also forced into hasty interpretations of complex behavior, Watson arguing that thinking was merely subvocal speech and Pavlov that language was simply a "second signal system." Watson had little or nothing to say about intention or purpose or creativity. He emphasized the technological promise of a science of behavior, but his examples were not incompatible with a manipulative control.

More than sixty years have passed since Watson issued his manifesto, and a great deal has happened in that time. The scientific analysis of behavior has made dramatic progress, and the shortcomings in Watson's account are now, I believe, chiefly of historical interest. Nevertheless, criticism has not greatly changed. All the misunderstandings listed above are to be found in current publications by philosophers, theologians, social scientists, historians, men and women of letters, psychologists, and many others. The vagaries of the early history of the movement can hardly suffice as an explanation.

Some trouble no doubt arises from the fact that human behavior is a sensitive field. Much is at stake in the way in which we look at ourselves, and a behavioristic formulation certainly calls for some disturbing changes. Moreover, terms originating in earlier formulations are deeply imbedded in our language, and they have had a place in both technical and nontechnical literature for centuries. Nevertheless, it would be unfair to argue that the critic has not been able to free himself from these historical prejudices. There must be some other reason why behaviorism as the philosophy of a science of behavior is still so seriously misunderstood.

I believe the explanation is this: the science itself is misunderstood. There are many different kinds of behavioral science, and some of them, as I shall show later, formulate the field in ways which do not raise important behavioristic issues. The criticisms listed above are most effectively answered by a special discipline, which has come to be called the experimental analysis of behavior. The behavior of individual organisms is studied in carefully controlled environments, and the relation between behavior and environment then formulated. Unfortunately, very little is known about this analysis outside the field. Its most active investigators, and there are hundreds of them, seldom make any effort to explain themselves to nonspecialists. As a result, few people are familiar with the scientific underpinnings of what, I believe, is the most cogent statement of the behavioristic position.

The behaviorism I present in this book is the philosophy of this special version of a science of behavior. The reader should know that not all behaviorists will agree with everything I say. Watson spoke for "the behaviorist," and in his time he *was* the behaviorist, but no one can assume that mantle today. What follows is admittedly—and, as a behaviorist, I must say necessarily—a personal view. I believe, however, that it is a consistent and coherent account, which satisfactorily answers the criticisms listed above.

I also believe in its importance. The major problems facing the world today can be solved only if we improve our understanding of human behavior. Traditional views have been around for centuries, and I think it is fair to say that they have proved to be inadequate. They are largely responsible for the situation in which we now find ourselves. Behaviorism offers a promising alternative, and I have written this book in an effort to make its position clear.

The Explanation of Behavior

• • •

Why do people behave as they do? It was probably first a practical question: How could a person anticipate and hence prepare for what another person would do? Later it would become practical in another sense: How could another person be induced to behave in a given way? Eventually it became a matter of understanding and explaining behavior. It could always be reduced to a question about causes.

We tend to say, often rashly, that if one thing follows another, it was probably caused by it—following the ancient principle of *post hoc, ergo propter hoc* (after this, therefore because of this). Of many examples to be found in the explanation of human behavior, one is especially important here. The person with whom we are most familiar is ourself; many of the things we observe just before we behave occur within our body, and it is easy to take them as the causes of our behavior. If we are asked why we have spoken sharply to a friend, we may reply, "Because I felt angry." It is true that we felt angry before, or as, we spoke, and so we take our anger to be the cause of our remark. Asked why we are not eating our dinner, we may say, "Because I do not feel hungry." We often feel hungry when we eat and hence conclude that we eat because we feel hungry. Asked why we are going swimming, we may reply, "Because I feel like swimming." We seem to be saying, "When I have felt like this before, I have behaved in such and such a way." Feelings occur at just the right time to serve as causes of behavior, and they have been cited as such for centuries. We assume that other people feel as we feel when they behave as we behave.

But where are these feelings and states of mind? Of what stuff are they made? The traditional answer is that they are located in a world of non-physical dimensions called the mind and that they are mental. But another question then arises: How can a mental event cause or be caused by a physical one? If we want to predict what a person will do, how can we discover the mental causes of his behavior, and how can we produce the feelings and states of mind which will induce him to behave in a given way? Suppose, for example, that we want to get a child to eat a nutritious but not very palatable food. We simply make sure that no other food is available, and eventually he eats. It appears that in depriving him of food (a physical event) we have made him feel hungry (a mental event), and that because he has felt hungry, he has eaten the nutritious food (a physical event). But how did the physical act of deprivation lead to the feeling of hunger, and how did the feeling move the muscles involved in ingestion? There are many other puzzling questions of this sort. What is to be done about them?

The commonest practice is, I think, simply to ignore them. It is possible to believe that behavior expresses feelings, to anticipate what a person will do by guessing or asking him how he feels, and to change the environment in the hope of changing feelings while paying little if any attention to theoretical problems. Those who are not quite comfortable about such a strategy sometimes take refuge in physiology. Mind, it is said, will eventually be found to have a physical basis. As one neurologist recently put it, "Everyone now accepts the fact that the brain provides the physical basis of human thought." Freud believed that his very complicated mental apparatus would eventually be found to be physiological, and early introspective psychologists called their discipline Physiological Psychology. The theory of knowledge called Physicalism holds that when we introspect or have feelings we are looking at states or activities of our brains. But the major difficulties are practical: we cannot anticipate what a person will do by looking directly at his feelings *or* his nervous system, nor can we change his behavior by changing his mind *or* his brain. But in any case we seem to be no worse off for ignoring philosophical problems.

Structuralism

A more explicit strategy is to abandon the search for causes and simply describe what people do. Anthropologists can report customs and manners, political scientists can take the line of "behavioralism" and record political action, economists can amass statistics about what people buy and sell, rent and hire, save and spend, and make and consume, and psychologists can sample attitudes and opinions. All this may be done through direct observation, possibly with the help of recording systems, and with interviews, questionnaires, tests, and polls. The study of literature, art, and music is often confined to the forms of these products of human behavior, and linguists may confine themselves to phonetics, semantics, and syntax. A kind of prediction is possible on the principle that what people have often done they are likely to do again; they follow customs because it is customary to follow them, they exhibit voting or buying habits, and so on. The discovery of organizing principles in the structure of behavior—such as "universals" in cultures or languages, archetypal patterns in literature, or psychological types—may make it possible to predict instances of behavior that have not previously occurred.

The structure or organization of behavior can also be studied as a function of time or age, as in the development of a child's verbal behavior or his problem-solving strategies or in the sequence of stages through which a person passes on his way from infancy to maturity, or in the stages through which a culture evolves. History emphasizes changes occurring in time, and if patterns of development or growth can be discovered, they may also prove helpful in predicting future events.

Control is another matter. Avoiding mentalism (or "psychologism") by refusing to look at causes exacts its price. Structuralism and developmentalism do not tell us why customs are followed, why people vote as they do or display attitudes or traits of character, or why different languages have common features. Time or age cannot be manipulated; we can only wait for a person or a culture to pass through a developmental period.

In practice the systematic neglect of useful information has usually meant that the data supplied by the structuralist are acted upon by others—for example, by decision-makers who in some way manage to take the causes of behavior into account. In theory it has meant the survival of mentalistic concepts. When explanations are demanded, primitive cultural practices are attributed to "the mind of the savage," the acquisition of language to "innate rules of grammar," the development of problem-solving strategies to the "growth of mind," and so on. In short, structuralism tells us how people behave but throws very little light on why they behave as they do. It has no answer to the question with which we began.

Methodological Behaviorism

The mentalistic problem can be avoided by going directly to the prior physical causes while bypassing intermediate feelings or states of mind. The quickest way to do this is to confine oneself to what an early behaviorist, Max Meyer, called the "psychology of the other one": consider only those facts which can be objectively observed in the behavior of one person in its relation to his prior environmental history. If all linkages are lawful, nothing is lost by neglecting a supposed nonphysical link. Thus, if we know that a child has not eaten for a long time, and if we know that he therefore feels hungry and that because he feels hungry he then eats, then we know that if he has not eaten for a long time, he will eat. And if by making other food inaccessible, we make him feel hungry, and if because he feels hungry he then eats a special food, then it must follow that by making other food inaccessible, we induce him to eat the special food.

Similarly, if certain ways of teaching a person lead him to notice very small differences in his "sensations," and if because he sees these differences he can classify colored objects correctly, then it should follow that we can use these ways of teaching him to classify objects correctly. Or, to take still another example, if circumstances in a white person's history generate feelings of aggression toward blacks, and if those feelings make him behave aggressively, then we may deal simply with the relation between the circumstances in his history and his aggressive behavior.

There is, of course, nothing new in trying to predict or control behavior by observing or manipulating prior public events. Structuralists and developmentalists have not entirely ignored the histories of their subjects, and historians and biographers have explored the influences of climate, culture, persons, and incidents. People have used practical techniques of predicting and controlling behavior with little thought to mental states. Nevertheless, for many centuries there was very little systematic inquiry into the role of the physical environment, although hundreds of highly technical volumes were written about human understanding and the life of the mind. A program of methodological behaviorism became plausible only when progress began to be made in the scientific observation of behavior, because only then was it possible to override the powerful effect of mentalism in diverting inquiry away from the role of the environment.

Mentalistic explanations allay curiosity and bring inquiry to a stop. It is so easy to observe feelings and states of mind at a time and in a place which make them seem like causes that we are not inclined to inquire further. Once the environment begins to be studied, however, its significance cannot be denied.

Methodological behaviorism might be thought of as a psychological version of logical positivism or operationism, but they are concerned with different issues. Logical positivism or operationism holds that since no two observers can agree on what happens in the world of the mind, then from the point of view of physical science mental events are "unobservables"; there can be no truth by agreement, and we must abandon the examination of mental events and turn instead to how they are studied. We cannot measure sensations and perceptions as such, but we can measure a person's capacity to discriminate among stimuli, and the *concept* of sensation or perception can then be reduced to the *operation* of discrimination.

The logical positivists had their version of "the other one." They argued that a robot which behaved precisely like a person, responding in the same way to stimuli, changing its behavior as a result of the same operations, would be indistinguishable from a real person, even though it would not have feelings, sensations, or ideas. If such a robot could be built, it would prove that none of the supposed manifestations of mental life demanded a mentalistic explanation.

With respect to its own goals, methodological behaviorism was successful. It disposed of many of the problems raised by mentalism and freed itself to work on its own projects without philosophical digressions. By directing attention to genetic and environmental antecedents, it offset an unwarranted concentration on an inner life. It freed us to study the behavior of lower species, where introspection (then regarded as exclusively human) was not feasible, and to explore similarities and differences between man and other species. Some concepts previously associated with private events were formulated in other ways.

But problems remained. Most methodological behaviorists granted the existence of mental events while ruling them out of consideration. Did they really mean to say that they did not matter, that the middle stage in that three-stage sequence of physical-mental-physical contributed nothing—in other words, that feelings and states of mind were merely epiphenomena? It was not the first time that anyone had said so. The view that a purely physical world could be self-sufficient had been suggested centuries before, in the doctrine of psychophysical parallelism, which held that there were two worlds—one of mind and one of matter—and that neither had any effect on the other. Freud's demonstration of the unconscious, in which an awareness of feelings or states of mind seemed unnecessary, pointed in the same direction.

But what about other evidence? Is the traditional *post hoc, ergo propter hoc* argument entirely wrong? Are the feelings we experience just before we behave wholly unrelated to our behavior? What about the power of mind over matter in psychosomatic medicine? What about psychophysics and the mathematical relation between the magnitudes of stimuli and sensations? What about the stream of consciousness? What about the intrapsychic processes of psychiatry, in which feelings produce or suppress other feelings and memories evoke or mask other memories? What about the cognitive processes said to explain perception, thinking, the construction of sentences, and artistic creation? Must all this be ignored because it cannot be studied objectively?

Radical Behaviorism

The statement that behaviorists deny the existence of feelings, sensations, ideas, and other features of mental life needs a good deal of clarification. Methodological behaviorism and some versions of logical positivism ruled private events out of bounds because there could be no public agreement about their validity. Introspection could not be accepted as a scientific practice, and the psychology of people like Wilhelm Wundt and Edward B. Titchener was attacked accordingly. Radical behaviorism, however, takes a different line. It does not deny the possibility of self-observation or self-knowledge or its possible usefulness, but it questions the nature of what is felt or observed and hence known. It restores introspection but not what philosophers and introspective psychologists had believed they were "specting," and it raises the question of how much of one's body one can actually observe.

Mentalism kept attention away from the external antecedent events which might have explained behavior, by seeming to supply an alternative explanation. Methodological behaviorism did just the reverse: by dealing exclusively with external antecedent events it turned attention away from self-observation and self-knowledge. Radical behaviorism restores some kind of balance. It does not insist upon truth by agreement and can therefore consider events taking place in the private world within the skin. It does not call these events unobservable, and it does not dismiss them as subjective. It simply questions the nature of the object observed and the reliability of the observations.

The position can be stated as follows: what is felt or introspectively observed is not some nonphysical world of consciousness, mind, or mental life but the observer's own body. This does not mean, as I shall show later, that introspection is a kind of physiological research, nor does it mean (and this is the heart of the argument) that what are felt or introspectively observed are the causes of behavior. An organism behaves as it does because of its current structure, but most of this is out of reach of introspection. At the moment we must content ourselves, as the methodological behaviorist insists, with a person's genetic and environmental histories. What are introspectively observed are certain collateral products of those histories.

The environment made its first great contribution during the evolution of the species, but it exerts a different kind of effect during the lifetime of the individual, and the combination of the two effects is the behavior we observe at any given time. Any available information about either contribution helps in the prediction and control of human behavior and in its interpretation in daily life. To the extent that either can be changed, behavior can be changed.

Our increasing knowledge of the control exerted by the environment makes it possible to examine the effect of the world within the skin and the nature of self-knowledge. It also makes it possible to interpret a wide range of mentalistic expressions. For example, we can look at those features of behavior which have led people to speak of an act of will, of a sense of purpose, of experience as distinct from reality, of innate or acquired ideas, of memories, meanings, and the personal knowledge of the scientist, and of hundreds of other mentalistic things or events. Some can be "translated into behavior," others discarded as unnecessary or meaningless.

In this way we repair the major damage wrought by mentalism. When what a person does is attributed to what is going on inside him, investigation is brought to an end. Why explain the explanation? For twenty-five hundred years people have been preoccupied with feelings and mental life, but only recently has any interest been shown in a more precise analysis of the role of the environment. Ignorance of that role led in the first place to mental fictions, and it has been perpetuated by the explanatory practices to which they gave rise.

• • •

On the Positive Side

Behaviorism has so often been defined in terms of its supposed shortcomings—of what it is said to ignore or neglect—that setting the record straight often appears to destroy what was meant to be saved. In answering these charges I may seem to have "abandoned the very basis of behaviorism," but what I have abandoned are the vestiges of early statements of the position, subjected to various elaborations and criticisms over a period of some sixty years. What survives can be put in a positive form:

1. The position I have taken is based, as the reader was warned, on a particular kind of behavioral science. I have chosen it in part no doubt

because of my familiarity with it but mainly because it has certain features especially relevant to the behavioristic argument. It offers, I believe, the clearest possible statement of the causal relations between behavior and environment. It analyzes individual data rather than group averages. The complexity of the experimental environment has gradually increased until it now approaches the complexity of daily life—in which, therefore, extrapolations from the laboratory become increasingly useful.

2. What we have learned from the experimental analysis of behavior suggests that the environment performs the functions previously assigned to feelings and introspectively observed inner states of the organism. This fact has been only slowly recognized. Only very strong evidence of the role of the environment could offset the effects of mentalism in directing attention to supposed inner causes.

3. A behavioral analysis acknowledges the importance of physiological research. What an organism does will eventually be seen to be due to what it is, at the moment it behaves, and the physiologist will someday give us all the details. He will also tell us how it has arrived at that condition as a result of its previous exposure to the environment as a member of the species and as an individual.

4. A crucial step in the argument can then be taken: what is felt or seen through introspection is only a small and relatively unimportant part of what the physiologist will eventually discover. In particular it is not the system which mediates the relation between behavior and the environment revealed by an experimental analysis.

As the philosophy of a science of behavior, behaviorism calls for probably the most drastic change ever proposed in our way of thinking about man. It is almost literally a matter of turning the explanation of behavior inside out.

The Future of Behaviorism

A good deal of what is called behavioral science is not behavioristic in the present sense. Some of it, as we have seen, avoids theoretical issues by confining itself to the form, topography, or structure of behavior. Some of it appeals to the "conceptual nervous systems" of mathematical models and systems theories. Much of it remains frankly mentalistic. Perhaps this diversity is healthful: different approaches could be regarded as mutations, from which a truly effective behavioral science will eventually be selected. Nevertheless, the present condition is not promising. Even in a single part of the field it is unusual to find two authorities talking about precisely the same things, and although nothing could be more relevant to the problems of the world today, the actual accomplishments of behavioral science do not seem to be extensive. (It has been suggested that the science is "too young" to solve our problems. This is a curious example of developmentalism, in which immaturity offers a kind of exoneration. We forgive the baby for not walking because he is not yet old enough, and by analogy we forgive the asocial or disturbed adult because he has not quite grown up, but must we then wait until the behavioral sciences *grow* more effective?)

I contend that behavioral science has not made a greater contribution just because it is not very behavioristic. It has recently been pointed out that an International Congress on Peace was composed of statesmen, political scientists, historians, economists, physicists, biologists—and not a single behaviorist in the strict sense. Evidently behaviorism was regarded as useless. But we must ask what the conference achieved. It was composed of specialists from many different fields, who probably spoke the commonsense lingua franca of the layman, with its heavy load of references to inner causation. What might the conference have achieved if it could have abandoned this false scent? The currency of mentalism in discussions of human affairs may explain why conferences on peace are held with such monotonous regularity year after year.

To assert that a thoroughgoing behaviorism could make a great difference is almost inevitably to be asked: "Well, then, what do you suggest? What would *you* do about war, or population, or pollution, or racial discrimination, or the revolt of the young?" Unfortunately, to understand the principles involved in solving a problem is not to have the solution. To know aerodynamics is not at once to know how to design a plane, to know plate tectonics is not at once to know how to predict earthquakes, to understand the double helix is not at once to be able to create a new species. The details of a problem must be studied. Knowing the basic principles without knowing the details of a practical problem is no closer to a solution than knowing the details without knowing the basic principles. But problems can be solved, even the big ones, if those who are familiar with the details will also adopt a workable conception of human behavior.

When we say that science and technology have created more problems than they have solved, we mean physical and biological science and technology. It does not follow that a technology of behavior will mean further trouble. On the contrary, it may be just what is needed to salvage the other contributions. We cannot say that a science of behavior has failed, for it has scarcely been tried. And it will not be given a fair trial until its philosophy has been clearly understood. A distinguished social philosopher has said, "It is only through a change of consciousness that the world will be saved. Everyone must begin with himself." But no one can *begin* with himself; and if he could, it would certainly not be by changing his consciousness.

If it were true that "an ever greater danger than nuclear war arises from within man himself in the form of smouldering fears, contagious panics, primitive needs for cruel violence, and raging suicidal destructiveness," then we should be lost. Fortunately, the point of attack is more readily accessible. It is the environment which must be changed. A way of life which furthers the study of human behavior in its relation to that environment should be in the best possible position to solve its major problems. This is not jingoism, because the great problems are now global. In the behavioristic view, man can now control his own destiny because he knows what must be done and how to do it.

Konrad Lorenz

The Austrian biologist Konrad Lorenz won a Nobel Prize for his work in the new discipline of ethology. The ethologists accepted the behaviorists' definition of their common subject of study—the behavior of living creatures—but they disagreed sharply about the kind of explanation of behavior to be expected, and about the appropriate methods of research. Whereas the behaviorists hoped to find some laws of conditioning by the environment that would apply to *all* animals, including humans, the ethologists backed the more plausible hunch that there are innate behavioral differences among species. They therefore concentrated on observing what different animals do *spontaneously,* before intervening to experiment, and they proposed to explain much animal behavior in terms of instincts whose existence is in turn to be explained by evolution.

Like Skinner, Lorenz was ready and eager to apply his theories to try to diagnose human problems. Besides his technical scientific papers, he published a number of popular works, of which the most famous is *On Aggression* (1963). I include here his summarizing Introduction and the main argument of his Chapter 13 about human aggression.

On Aggression

The subject of this book is *aggression*, that is to say the fighting instinct in beast and man which is directed *against* members of the same species. The decision to write it came about through a chance combination of two circumstances. I was in the United States, first in order to give some lectures to psychiatrists, psycho-analysts and psychologists about some comparable behavioural theories and behavioural physiology and secondly to verify through field observation on the coral reefs of Florida a hypothesis I had formed, on the basis of aquarium observations, about the aggressive behaviour of certain fish and the function of their colouring in the preservation of the species. It was at the clinical hospitals that for the first time in my life I came into conversation with psycho-analysts who did not treat the theories of Freud as inviolable dogmas but, as is appropriate in every scientific field, working hypotheses. Viewing them in this way I came to understand much in Sigmund Freud's theories that I had previously rejected as far too audacious. Discussions of his theories of motivation revealed unexpected correspondences between the findings of psychoanalysis and behavioural physiology, which seemed all the more significant because of the differences in approach, methods and above all inductive basis between the two disciplines.

I had expected unbridgeable differences of opinion over the concept of the death wish which, according to one of Freud's theories, is a destructive principle which exists as an opposite pole to all instincts of self-preservation. In the eyes of the behavioural scientist this hypothesis, which is foreign to biology, is not only unnecessary but false. Aggression, the effects of which are frequently equated with those of the death wish, is an instinct like any other and in natural conditions it helps just as much as any other to ensure the survival of the individual and the species. In man, whose own efforts have caused an over-rapid change in the conditions of his life, the aggressive impulse often has destructive results. But so, too, do his other instincts, if in a less dramatic way. When I expressed these views on the theory of the death wish to my psycho-analytical friends I was surprised to find myself in the position of someone trying to force a door which is already open. They pointed out to me many passages in the writings of Freud which show how little reliance he himself

Excerpts from *On Aggression* by Konrad Lorenz, copyright © 1963 by Dr. G. Bortha-Schoeler Verlag, Wein, English translation by Marjorie Kerr Wilson, copyright © 1966 by Konrad Lorenz, reprinted by permission of Harcourt, Inc.

had placed on his dualistic hypothesis, which must have been fundamentally alien and repugnant to him as a good monist and mechanistically thinking natural scientist.

It was shortly afterwards, when I was making a field study of coral fish in warm seas, amongst which the function of aggression in the preservation of the species is plain, that the impulse to write this book came to me. For behavioural science really knows so much about the natural history of aggression that it does become possible to make statements about the causes of much of its malfunctioning in man. To achieve insight into the origins of a disease is by no means the same as to discover an effective therapy but it is certainly one of the necessary conditions for this.

I am aware that the task I have set myself makes excessive demands upon my pen. It is almost impossible to portray in words the functioning of a system in which every part is related to every other in such a way that each has a causal influence on the others. Even if one is only trying to explain a petrol engine it is hard to know where to begin, because the person to whom one seeks to explain it can only understand the nature of the crank-shaft if he has first grasped that of the connecting rods, the pistons, the valves, the camshaft and so on. Unless one understands the elements of a complete system as a whole one cannot understand them at all. The more complex the structure of a system is, the greater this difficulty becomes—and it must be surmounted both in one's research and one's teaching. Unfortunately the working structure of the instinctive and culturally acquired patterns of behaviour which make up the social life of man seems to be one of the most complicated systems we know on this earth. In order to make comprehensible the few causal connections which I believe I can trace right through this tangle of reciprocal effects, I must, for good or ill, go back a long way.

Fortunately the observed facts which are my starting point are fascinating in themselves. I hope that the territorial fights of the coral fish, the "quasi-moral" urges and inhibitions of social animals, the loveless married and social life of the night heron, the bloody mass battles of the brown rat and many other remarkable behaviour patterns of animals will engage the reader's interest up to the point when he reaches an understanding of the deeper connections between them.

I intend to lead him to it by following as closely as possible the route which I took myself, and this is for reasons of principle. Inductive natural science always starts without preconceptions from the observation of individual cases and proceeds from this towards the abstract law which they all obey. Most textbooks take the opposite course for the sake of brevity and clarity and set down the general before the particular. The presentation is thereby made more lucid but less convincing. It is only too easy first to evolve a theory and then to under-pin it with examples, for nature is so diverse that with diligent searching one can find apparently convincing examples to support wholly abstruse hypotheses. My book would really be convincing if the reader reached the same conclusion as myself solely on the basis of the facts which I set before him. But as I cannot expect him to follow such a thorny path, let me offer in advance, by way of a signpost, a brief account of the contents of each chapter.

I start in the first two chapters with the description of simple observations of typical forms of aggressive behaviour. Then in the third I proceed to the discussion of its function in the preservation of the species. In the fourth I say enough about the physiology of instinctual motivation in general and the aggressive impulse in particular to explain the spontaneity of the irresistible outbreaks which recur with rhythmical regularity. In the fifth chapter I illustrate the process of ritualization and show how the instinctive impulse newly created by it is made independent—in so far as is necessary for the later understanding of its effects in inhibiting aggression. The sixth chapter serves the same purpose: here I have tried to give a general picture of the way instinctive impulses function. In the seventh chapter concrete examples are given to show what mechanisms evolution has "invented" in order to channel aggression along harmless paths, the role played by ritual in this process and the similarity between the patterns of behaviour which arise in this way and those which in man are guided by responsible morality. These chapters give the basis for an understanding of the functioning of four very different types of social organization. The first is the anonymous crowd, which is free of all kinds of aggression but also lacks the personal awareness and cohesion of individuals. The second is the family and social life of the night heron and other birds which nest in colonies, the only structural basis of which is territorial—the defence of a given area. The third is the remarkable "large family" of rats, the members of which do not recognize one another as individuals but by the tribal smell and whose social behaviour towards one another is exemplary, whilst they attack with bitter factional hatred every member of the species that belongs to a different tribe. The fourth type of social organization is that in which it is the bond of love and friendship between individuals which prevents the members of the society from fighting and harming one another. This form of society, the structure of which is in many ways analogous to that of men, is shown in detail by the example of the greylag goose.

After what has been said in these eleven chapters I think I can help to explain the causes of many of the ways in which aggression in man goes wrong. The twelfth chapter, "Sermon on Humility," should provide a further basis by disposing of certain inner obstacles which prevent many people from seeing themselves as a part of the universe and recognizing that their own behaviour too obeys the laws of nature. These obstacles come first of all from rejection of the idea of causality, which is thought to contradict the fact of free will, and secondly from man's spiritual pride. The thirteenth chapter seeks to depict the present situation of mankind objectively, somewhat as a biologist from Mars might see it. In the fourteenth chapter I try to propose certain counter-measures against those malfunctions of aggression, the causes of which I believe I have identified.

● ● ●

Let us imagine that an absolutely unbiased observer on another planet, perhaps on Mars, is examining human behaviour on earth, with the aid of a telescope whose magnification is too small to enable him to discern individuals and follow their separate behaviour, but large enough for him to observe occurrences such as migration of peoples, wars and similar great historical events. He would never gain the impression that human behaviour was dictated by intelligence, still less by responsible morality. If we suppose our extraneous observer to be a being of pure reason, devoid of instincts himself and unaware of the way in which all instincts in general and aggression in particular can miscarry, he would be at a complete loss how to explain history at all. The ever-recurrent phenomena of history do not have reasonable causes. It is a mere commonplace to say that they are caused by what common parlance so aptly terms "human nature." Unreasoning and unreasonable human nature causes two nations to compete, though no economic necessity compels them to do so; it induces two political parties or religions with amazingly similar programmes of salvation to fight each other bitterly and it impels an Alexander or a Napoleon to sacrifice millions of lives in his attempt to unite the world under his sceptre. We have been taught to regard some of the persons who have committed these and similar absurdities with respect, even as "great" men, we are wont to yield to the political wisdom of those in charge, and we are all so accustomed to these phenomena that most of us fail to realize how abjectly stupid and undesirable the historical mass behaviour of humanity actually is.

Having realized this, however, we cannot escape the question why reasonable beings do behave so unreasonably. Undeniably, there must be superlatively strong factors which are able to overcome the commands of individual reason so completely and which are so obviously impervious to experience and learning. As Hegel said, "What experience and history teach us is this—that people and governments have never learnt anything from history, or acted on principles deduced from it."

All these amazing paradoxes, however, find an unconstrained explanation, falling into place like the pieces of a jigsaw puzzle, if one assumes that human behaviour, and particularly human social behaviour, far from being determined by reason and cultural tradition alone, is still subject to all the laws prevailing in all phylogenetically adapted instinctive behaviour. Of these laws we posses a fair amount of knowledge from studying the instincts of animals. Indeed, if our extramundane observer were a knowledgeable ethologist, he would unavoidably draw the conclusion that man's social organization is very similar to that of rats which, like humans, are social and peaceful beings within their clans, but veritable devils towards all fellow-members of their species not belonging to their own community. If, furthermore, our Martian naturalist knew of the explosive rise in human populations, the ever-increasing destructiveness of weapons, and the division of mankind into a few political camps, he would not expect the future of humanity to be any rosier than that of several hostile clans of rats on a ship almost devoid of food. And this prognosis would even be optimistic, for in the case of rats reproduction stops automatically when a certain state of overcrowding is reached, while man as yet has no workable system for preventing the so-called population explosion. Furthermore, in the case of the rats it is likely that after the wholesale slaughter enough individuals would be left over to propagate the species. In the case of man, this would not be so certain after the use of the hydrogen bomb.

It is a curious paradox that the greatest gifts of man, the unique faculties of conceptual thought and verbal speech which have raised him to a level high above all other creatures and given him mastery over the globe, are not altogether blessings, or at least are blessings that have to be paid for very dearly indeed. All the great dangers threatening humanity with extinction are direct consequences of conceptual thought and verbal speech. They drove man out of the paradise in which he could follow his instincts with impunity and do or not do whatever he pleased. There is much truth in the parable of the tree of knowledge and its fruit, though I want to make an addition to it to make it fit into my own picture of Adam: that apple was thoroughly unripe! Knowledge springing from conceptual thought robbed man of the security provided by his well-adapted instincts long, long before it was sufficient to provide him with an equally safe adaptation. Man is, as Arnold Gehlen has so truly said, by nature a jeopardized creature.

Conceptual thought and speech changed all man's evolution by achieving something which is equivalent to the inheritance of acquired characters. We have forgotten that the verb inherit had a juridical connotation long before it acquired a biological one. When a man invents, let us say, bow and arrow, not only his progeny but his entire community will inherit the knowledge and the use of these tools and possess them just as surely as organs grown on the body. Nor is their loss any more likely than the rudimentation of an organ of equal survival value. Thus, within one or two generations a process of ecological adaptation can be achieved which in normal phylogeny and without the interference of conceptual thought, would have taken a time of an altogether different, much greater order of magnitude. Small wonder indeed if the evolution of social instincts and, what is even more important, social inhibitions could not keep pace with the rapid development forced on human society by the growth of traditional culture, particularly material culture.

Obviously, instinctive behaviour mechanisms failed to cope with the new circumstances which culture unavoidably produced even at its very dawn. There is evidence that the first inventors of pebble tools, the African Australopithecines, promptly used their new weapon to kill not only game, but fellow-members of their species as well. Peking Man, the Prometheus who learned to preserve fire, used it to roast his brothers: beside the first traces of the regular use of fire lie the mutilated and roasted bones of *Sinanthropus pekinenis* himself.

One is tempted to believe that every gift bestowed on man by his power of conceptual thought has to be paid for with a dangerous evil as the direct consequence of it. Fortunately for us, this is not so. Besides the faculty of conceptual thought, another constituent characteristic of man played an important role in gaining a deeper understanding of his environment, and this is curiosity. Insatiable curiosity is the root of exploration and experimentation, and these activities, even in their most primitive form, imply a function akin to asking questions. Explorative experimentation is a sort of dialogue with surrounding nature. Asking a question and recording the answer lead to anticipating the latter, and, given conceptual thought, to the linking of cause and effect. From hence it is but a step to consciously foreseeing the consequences of one's actions. Thus, the same human faculties which supplied man with tools and with power dangerous to himself, also gave him the means to prevent their misuse: rational responsibility. I shall now proceed to discuss, one by one, the dangers which humanity incurs by rising above the other animals by virtue of its great specific gifts. Subsequently I shall try to show in what way the greatest gift of all, rational, responsible morality, functions in banning these dangers. Most important of all, I shall have to expound the functional limitation of morality.

In the chapter on behaviour mechanisms functionally analogous to morality I have spoken of the inhibitions controlling aggression in various social animals, preventing it from injuring or killing fellow-members of the species. As I explained, these inhibitions are most important and consequently most highly differentiated in those animals which are capable of killing living creatures of about their own size. A raven can peck out the eye of another with one thrust of its beak, a wolf can rip the jugular vein of another with a single bite. There would be no more ravens and no more wolves if reliable inhibitions did not prevent such actions. Neither a dove nor a hare nor even a chimpanzee is able to kill its own kind with a single peck or bite; in addition, animals with relatively poor defensive weapons have a correspondingly great ability to escape quickly, even from specially armed predators which are more efficient in chasing, catching and killing than even the strongest of their own species. Since there rarely is, in nature, the possibility of such an animal seriously injuring one of its own kind, there is no selection pressure at work to breed inhibitions against killing. The absence of such inhibitions is apparent to the animal keeper—to his own and to his animals' disadvantage—if he does not take seriously the intra-specific fights of completely "harmless" animals. Under the unnatural conditions of captivity, where a defeated animal cannot escape from its victor, it may be killed slowly and cruelly. In my book *King Solomon's Ring,* I have described in the chapter "Morals and Weapons" how the symbol of peace, the dove, can torture one of its own kind to death, without any inhibition being aroused.

Anthropologists concerned with the habits of Australopithecus have repeatedly stressed that these hunting progenitors of man have left humanity with the dangerous heritage of what they term "carnivorous mentality." This statement confuses the concept of the carnivore and the cannibal which are, to a large extent, mutually exclusive. One can only deplore the fact that man has definitely not got a carnivorous mentality! All his trouble arises from his being a basically harmless, omnivorous creature, lacking in natural weapons with which to kill big prey, and, therefore, also devoid of the built-in safety devices which prevent "professional" carnivores from abusing their killing power to destroy fellow-members of their own species. A lion or a wolf may, on extremely rare occasions, kill another by one angry stroke, but, as I have already explained in the chapter on behaviour mechanisms functionally analogous to morality, all heavily armed carnivores possess sufficiently reliable inhibitions which prevent the self-destruction of the species.

In human evolution, no inhibitory mechanisms preventing sudden manslaughter were necessary, because quick killing was impossible anyhow; the potential victim had plenty of opportunity to elicit the pity of the aggressor by submissive gestures and appeasing attitudes. No selection pressure arose in the prehistory of mankind to breed inhibitory mechanisms preventing the killing of conspecifics until, all of a sudden, the invention of artificial weapons upset the equilibrium of killing potential and social inhibitions. . . .

Aggressive behaviour and killing inhibitions represent only one special case among many in which phylogenetically adapted behaviour mechanisms are thrown out of balance by the rapid change wrought in human ecology and sociology by cultural development. In order to explain the function of responsible morality in re-establishing a tolerable equilibrium between man's instincts and the requirements of a culturally evolved social order, a few words must first be said about social instincts in general. It is a widely held opinion, shared by some contemporary philosophers, that all human behaviour patterns which serve the welfare of the community, as opposed to that of the individual, are dictated by specifically human rational thought. Not only is this opinion erroneous, but the very opposite is true. If it were not for a rich endowment of social instincts, man could never have risen above the animal world. All specifically human faculties, the power of speech, cultural tradition, moral responsibility could have evolved only in a being which, before the very dawn of conceptual thinking, lived in well-organized communities. Our prehuman ancestor was indubitably as true a friend to his friend as a chimpanzee or even a dog, as tender and solicitous to the young of his community and as self-sacrificing in its defence, aeons before he developed conceptual thought and became aware of the consequences of his actions.

According to Immanuel Kant's teachings on morality, it is human reason (*Vernunft*) alone which supplies the categorical imperative "thou shalt" as an answer to responsible self-questioning concerning any possible consequences of a certain action. However, it is doubtful whether "reason" is the correct translation of Kant's use of the word Vernunft which also implies the connotation of common sense and of understanding and appreciation of another "reasonable" being. For Kant it is self-evident that one reasonable being cannot possibly want to hurt another. This unconscious acceptance of what he considered self-evident, in other words, of common sense, represents the chink in the great philosopher's shining armour of pure rationality, through which emotion, which always means an instinctive urge, creeps into his considerations and makes them more acceptable to the biologically minded than they would otherwise be. It is hard to believe that a man will refrain from a certain action which natural inclination urges him to perform only because he has realized that it involves a logical contradiction. To assume this one would have to be an even more unworldly German professor and an even more ardent admirer of reason than Immanuel Kant was.

In reality, even the fullest rational insight into the consequences of an action and into the logical consistency of its premise would not result in an imperative or in a prohibition, were it not for some emotional, in other words instinctive, source of energy supplying motivation. Like power steering in a modern car, responsible morality derives the energy which it needs to control human behaviour from the same primal powers which it was created to keep in rein. Man as a purely rational being, divested of his animal heritage of instincts, would certainly not be an angel—the opposite.

· · ·

In the growth of human cultures, as in that of arthropods, there is a built-in mechanism providing for graduated change. During and shortly after puberty human beings have an indubitable tendency to loosen their allegiance to all traditional rites and social norms of their culture, allowing conceptual thought to cast doubt on their value and to look around for new and perhaps more worthy ideals. There probably is, at that time of life, a definite sensitive period for a new object-fixation, much as in the case of the object-fixation found in animals and called imprinting. If at that critical time of life old ideals prove fallacious under critical scrutiny and new ones fail to appear, the result is that complete aimlessness, the utter boredom which characterizes the young delinquent. If, on the other hand, the clever demagogue, well versed in the dangerous art of producing supra-normal stimulus situations, gets hold of young people at the susceptible age, he finds it easy to guide their object-fixation in a direction subservient to his political aims. At the post-puberal age some human beings seem to be driven by an over-powering urge to espouse a cause, and, failing to find a worthy one, may become fixated on astonishingly inferior substitutes. The instinctive need to be the member of a closely knit group fighting for common ideals may grow so strong that it becomes inessential what these ideals are and whether they possess any intrinsic value. This, I believe, explains the formation of juvenile gangs whose social structure is very probably a rather close reconstruction of that prevailing in primitive human society.

Apparently this process of object-fixation can take its full effect only once in an individual's life. Once the valuation of certain social norms or the allegiance to a certain cause is fully established, it cannot be erased again, at least not to the extent of making room for a new, equally strong one. Also it would seem that once the sensitive period has elapsed, a man's ability to embrace ideals at all is considerably reduced. All this helps to explain the hackneyed truth that human beings have to live through a rather dangerous period at and shortly after puberty. The tragic paradox is that the danger is greatest for those who are by nature best fitted to serve the noble cause of humanity.

The process of object-fixation has consequences of an importance that can hardly be overestimated. It determines neither more nor less than that which a man will live for, struggle for and, under certain circumstances, blindly go to war for. It determines the conditioned stimulus situation releasing a powerful phylogenetically evolved behaviour which I propose to call that of militant enthusiasm.

Militant enthusiasm is particularly suited for the paradigmatic illustration of the manner in which a phylogenetically evolved pattern of behaviour interacts with culturally ritualized social norms and rites, and in which, though absolutely indispensable to the function of the compound system, it is prone to miscarry most tragically if not strictly controlled by rational responsibility based on causal insight. The Greek word *enthousiasmos* implies that a person is possessed by a god, the German word *Begeisterung* means that he is controlled by a spirit, a *Geist*, more or less holy.

In reality, militant enthusiasm is a specialized form of communal aggression, clearly distinct from and yet functionally related to the more primitive forms of petty individual aggression. Every man of normally strong emotions knows, from his own experience, the subjective phenomena that go hand in hand with the response of militant enthusiasm. A shiver runs down the back, and, as more exact observation shows, along the outside of both arms. One soars elated above all the ties of everyday life, one is ready to abandon all for the call of what, in the moment of this specific emotion, seems to be a sacred duty. All obstacles in its path become unimportant, the instinctive inhibitions against hurting or killing one's fellows lose, unfortunately, much of their power. Rational considerations, criticism, and all reasonable arguments against the behaviour dictated by militant enthusiasm are silenced by an amazing reversal of all values, making them appear not only untenable but base and dishonourable. Men may enjoy the feeling of absolute righteousness even while they commit atrocities. Conceptual thought and moral responsibility are at their lowest ebb. As an Ukrainian proverb says: "When the banner is unfurled, all reason is in the trumpet."

The subjective experiences just described are correlated with the following, objectively demonstrable phenomena. The tone of the entire striated musculature is raised, the carriage is stiffened, the arms are raised from the sides and slightly rotated inwards so that the elbows point outwards. The head is proudly raised, the chin stuck out, and the facial muscles mime the "hero face," familiar from the films. Down the back and along the outer surface of the arms the hair stands on end. This is the objectively observed aspect of the shiver!

Anybody who has ever seen the corresponding behaviour of the male chimpanzee defending his band or family with self-sacrificing courage, will doubt the purely spiritual character of human enthusiasm. The chimp, too, sticks out his chin, stiffens his body, and raises his elbows; his hair stands on end producing a terrifying magnification of his body contours as seen from the front. The inward rotation of his arms obviously has the purpose of turning the longest-haired side outwards to enhance the effect. The whole combination of body attitude and hair-raising constitutes a bluff. This is also seen when a cat humps its back, and is calculated to make the animal appear bigger and more dangerous than it really is. Our shiver which, in German poetry, is called a *heiliger Schauer,* which means a "holy shiver," turns out to be the vestige of a pre-human vegetative response of causing to bristle a fur which we no longer have.

To the humble seeker of biological truth there cannot be the slightest doubt that human militant enthusiasm evolved out of a communal defence response of our pre-human ancestors. The unthinking single-mindedness of the response must have been of high survival value even in a tribe of fully evolved human beings. It was necessary for the individual male to forget all his other allegiances in order to be able to dedicate himself, body and soul, to the cause of the communal battle. *"Was schert mich Weib, was schert mich Kind"*—"What do I care for wife or child" says the Napoleonic soldier in a famous poem by Heinrich Heine, and it is highly characteristic of the reaction that this poet, otherwise a caustic critic of emotional romanticism, was so unreservedly enraptured by his enthusiasm for the "great" conqueror as to find this supremely apt expression.

The object which militant enthusiasm tends to defend has changed with cultural development. Originally it was certainly the community of concrete, individually known members of a group, held together by the bond of personal love and friendship. With the growth of the social unit, the social norms and rites held in common by all its members became the main factor holding it together as an entity, and therewith they became automatically the symbol of the unit. By a process of true Pavlovian conditioning plus a certain amount of irreversible imprinting these rather abstract values have in every human culture been substituted for the primal, concrete object of the communal defence reaction.

This traditionally conditioned substitution of object has important consequences for the function of militant enthusiasm. On the one hand, the abstract nature of its object can give it a definitely inhuman aspect and make it positively dangerous—what do I care for wife or child?—on the other hand, it makes it possible to recruit militant enthusiasm into the service of really ethical values. Without the concentrated dedication of militant enthusiasm neither art, nor science, nor indeed any of the great endeavours of humanity would ever have come into being. Whether enthusiasm is made to serve these endeavours, or whether man's most powerfully motivating instinct makes him go to war in some abjectly silly cause, depends almost entirely on the conditioning and/or imprinting he has undergone during certain susceptible periods of his life. There is reasonable hope that our moral responsibility may gain control over the primeval drive, but our only hope of it ever doing so rests on the humble recognition of the fact that militant enthusiasm is an instinctive response with a phylogenetically determined releasing mechanism and that the only point at which intelligent and responsible supervision can get control is in the conditioning of the response to an object which proves to be a genuine value under the scrutiny of the categorical question.

Like the triumph ceremony of the greylag goose, militant enthusiasm in man is a true autonomous instinct: it has its own appetitive behaviour, its own releasing mechanisms and, like the sexual urge or any other strong instinct, it engenders a specific feeling of intense satisfaction. The strength of its seductive lure explains why intelligent men may behave as irrationally and immorally in their political as in their sexual lives. Like the triumph ceremony it has an essential influence on the social structure of the species. Humanity is not enthusiastically combative because it is split into political parties, but it is divided into opposing camps because this is the adequate stimulus situation to arouse militant enthusiasm in a satisfying manner. "If ever a doctrine of universal salvation should gain ascendancy over the whole earth to the exclusion of all others," writes Erich von Holst, "It would at once fall into two strongly opposing factions (one's own true one and the other heretical one) and hostility and war would thrive as before, mankind being—unfortunately—what it is!"

The first prerequisite for rational control of an instinctive behaviour pattern is the knowledge of the stimulus situation which releases it. Militant enthusiasm can be elicited, with the predictability of a reflex, when the following environmental situations arise. First of all, a social unit with which the subject identifies himself must appear to be threatened by some danger from outside. That which is threatened may be a concrete group of people, the family, or a little community of close friends, or else it may be a larger social unit held together and symbolized by its own specific social norms and rites. As the latter assume the character of autonomous values they can, quite by themselves, represent the object in whose defence militant enthusiasm can be elicited. From all this it follows that this response can be brought into play in the service of extremely different objects, ranging from the sports club to the nation, or from the most obsolete mannerisms or ceremonials to the ideal of scientific truth or of the incorruptibility of justice.

A second key stimulus which contributes enormously to the releasing of intense militant enthusiasm is the presence of a hateful enemy from whom the threat to the above "values" emanates. This enemy, too, can be of a concrete or of an abstract nature. It can be "the" Jews, Huns, Boches, Tyrants, etc., or abstract concepts like world capitalism, bolshevism, fascism and any other kind of ism; it can be heresy, dogmatism, scientific fallacy or what not. Just as in the case of the object to be defended, the enemy against whom to defend it is extremely variable and demagogues are well versed in the dangerous art of producing supra-normal dummies to release a very dangerous form of militant enthusiasm.

A third factor contributing to the environmental situation eliciting the response is an inspiring leader figure. Even the most emphatically anti-fascistic ideologies apparently cannot do without it, as the giant pictures of leaders displayed by all kinds of political parties prove clearly enough. Again the unselectivity of the phylogenetically programmed response allows for a wide variation in the conditioning to a leader-figure. Napoleon, about whom so critical a man as Heinrich Heine became so enthusiastic, does not inspire me in the least: Charles Darwin does.

A fourth, and perhaps the most important prerequisite for the full eliciting of militant enthusiasm, is the presence of many other individuals all agitated by the same emotion. Their absolute number has a certain influence on the quality of the response. Smaller numbers at issue with a large majority tend to obstinate defence with the emotional value of "making a last stand," while very large numbers inspired by the same enthusiasm feel an urge to conquer the whole world in the name of their sacred cause.

Here the laws of mass enthusiasm are strictly analogous to those of flock formation; here, too, the excitation grows in proportion, perhaps even in geometrical progression, with the increasing number of individuals. This is exactly what makes militant mass enthusiasm so dangerous.

I have tried to describe, with as little emotional bias as possible, the human response of enthusiasm, its phylogenetic origin, its instinctive as well as its traditionally handed-down components and prerequisites. I hope I have made the reader realize, without actually saying so, what a jumble our philosophy of values is. What is a culture? A system of historically developed social norms and rites which are passed on from generation to generation because emotionally they are felt to be values. What is a value? Obviously, normal and healthy people are able to appreciate something as a high value for which to live and, if necessary, to die, for no other reason than that it was evolved in cultural ritualization and handed down to them by a revered elder. Is, then, a value only defined as the object on which our instinctive urge to preserve and defend traditional social norms has become fixated? Primarily and in the early stages of cultural development this undoubtedly was the case. The obvious advantages of loyal adherence to tradition must have exerted a considerable selection pressure. However, the greatest loyalty and obedience to culturally ritualized norms of behaviour must not be mistaken for responsible morality. Even at their best they are only functionally analogous to behaviour controlled by rational responsibility. In this respect they are no whit different from instinctive patterns of social behaviour. Also they are just as prone to miscarry under circumstances for which they have not been "programmed" by the great constructor, natural selection.

In other words, the need to control, by wise rational responsibility, all our emotional allegiances to cultural values is as great as, if not greater than, the necessity of keeping our other instincts in check. None of them can ever have such devastating effects as unbridled militant enthusiasm when it infects great masses and overrides all other considerations by its single-mindedness and its specious nobility. It is not enthusiasm in itself that is in any way noble, but humanity's great goals which it can be called upon to defend. That indeed is the Janus head of man: the only being capable of dedicating himself to the very highest moral and ethical values requires for this purpose a phylogenetically adapted mechanism of behaviour whose animal properties bring with them the danger that he will kill his brother, convinced that he is doing so in the interests of these very same high values. *Ecce homo!*

Noam Chomsky

The American linguist Noam Chomsky is famous for setting the study of language on a new course since the 1960s. In his technical works he has presented his theories of "transformational grammar," seeking to formulate general principles that underlie the complex variety of human languages. His review of Skinner's book *Verbal Behaviour* (in *Language,* Vol. 35, 1959) was regarded as a conclusive demolition of behaviorist accounts of language learning. He has defended a version of the rationalist tradition, arguing that a substantial element in what every normal human being implicitly knows—for instance, about the limits to the grammatical forms that human languages can take—is not learned from experience, but is innate in our species. Chomsky has always related his linguistic work to wider issues in psychology, anthropology, politics, and philosophy, and has been a staunch defender of universal human rights.

"Language and the Human Mind"

• • •

I think that there is some significance in the ease and willingness with which modern thinking about man and society accepts the designation "behavioral science." No sane person has ever doubted that behavior provides much of the evidence for this study—all of the evidence, if we interpret "behavior" in a sufficiently loose sense. But the term "behavioral science" suggests a not-so-subtle shift of emphasis toward the evidence itself and away from the deeper underlying principles and abstract mental structures that might be illuminated by the evidence of behavior. It is as if natural science were to be designated "the science of meter readings." What, in fact, would we expect of natural science in a culture that was satisfied to accept this designation for its activities?

Behavioral science has been much preoccupied with data and organization of data, and it has even seen itself as a kind of technology of control of behavior. Anti-mentalism in linguistics and in philosophy of language conforms to this shift of orientation. As I mentioned in my first lecture, I think that one major indirect contribution of modern structural linguistics results from its success in making explicit the assumptions of an anti-mentalistic, thoroughly operational and behaviorist approach to the phenomena of language. By extending this approach to its natural limits, it laid the groundwork for a fairly conclusive demonstration of the inadequacy of any such approach to the problems of mind.

More generally, I think that the long-range significance of the study of language lies in the fact that in this study it is possible to give a relatively sharp and clear formulation of some of the central questions of psychology and to bring a mass of evidence to bear on them. What is more, the study of language is, for the moment, unique in the combination it affords of richness of data and susceptibility to sharp formulation of basic issues.

It would, of course, be silly to try to predict the future of research, and it will be understood that I do not intend the subtitle of this lecture to be taken very seriously. Nevertheless, it is fair to suppose that the major contribution of the study of language will lie in the understanding it can provide as to the character of mental processes and the structures they form and manipulate. Therefore, instead of speculating on the likely course of

Excerpts from *Language and Mind* by Noam Chomsky, copyright © 1972 by Harcourt, Inc., reprinted by permission of the publisher.

research into the problems that are coming into focus today, I will concentrate here on some of the issues that arise when we try to develop the study of linguistic structure as a chapter of human psychology.

It is quite natural to expect that a concern for language will remain central to the study of human nature, as it has been in the past. Anyone concerned with the study of human nature and human capacities must somehow come to grips with the fact that all normal humans acquire language, whereas acquisition of even its barest rudiments is quite beyond the capacities of an otherwise intelligent ape—a fact that was emphasized, quite correctly, in Cartesian philosophy. It is widely thought that the extensive modern studies of animal communication challenge this classical view; and it is almost universally taken for granted that there exists a problem of explaining the "evolution" of human language from systems of animal communication. However, a careful look at recent studies of animal communication seems to me to provide little support for these assumptions. Rather, these studies simply bring out even more clearly the extent to which human language appears to be a unique phenomenon, without significant analogue in the animal world. If this is so, it is quite senseless to raise the problem of explaining the evolution of human language from more primitive systems of communication that appear at lower levels of intellectual capacity. The issue is important, and I would like to dwell on it for a moment.

The assumption that human language evolved from more primitive systems is developed in an interesting way by Karl Popper in his recently published Arthur Compton Lecture, "Clouds and Clocks." He tries to show how problems of freedom of will and Cartesian dualism can be solved by the analysis of this "evolution." I am not concerned now with the philosophical conclusions that he draws from this analysis, but with the basic assumption that there is an evolutionary development of language from simpler systems of the sort that one discovers in other organisms. Popper argues that the evolution of language passed through several stages, in particular a "lower stage" in which vocal gestures are used for expression of emotional state, for example, and a "higher stage" in which articulated sound is used for expression of thought—in Popper's terms, for description and critical argument. His discussion of stages of evolution of language suggests a kind of continuity, but in fact he establishes no relation between the lower and higher stages and does not suggest a mechanism whereby transition can take place from one stage to the next. In short, he gives no argument to show that the stages belong to a single evolutionary process. In fact, it is difficult to see what links these stages at all (except for the metaphorical use of the term "language"). There is no reason to suppose that the "gaps" are bridgeable. There is no more of a basis for assuming an evolutionary development of "higher" from "lower" stages, in this case, than there is for assuming an evolutionary development from breathing to walking; the stages have no significant analogy, it appears, and seem to involve entirely different processes and principles.

A more explicit discussion of the relation between human language and animal communication systems appears in a recent discussion by the comparative ethologist W. H. Thorpe. He points out that mammals other than man appear to lack the human ability to imitate sounds, and that one might therefore have expected birds (many of which have this ability to a remarkable extent) to be "the group which ought to have been able to evolve language in the true sense, and not the mammals." Thorpe does not suggest that human language "evolved" in any strict sense from simpler systems, but he does argue that the characteristic properties of human language can be found in animal communication systems, although "we cannot at the moment say definitely that they are all present in one particular animal." The characteristics shared by human and animal language are the properties of being "purposive," "syntactic," and "propositional." Language is purposive "in that there is nearly always in human speech a definite intention of getting something over to somebody else, altering his behavior, his thoughts, or his general attitude toward a situation." Human language is "syntactic" in that an utterance is a performance with an internal organization, with structure and coherence. It is "propositional" in that it transmits information. In this sense, then, both human language and animal communication are purposive, syntactic, and propositional.

All this may be true, but it establishes very little, since when we move to the level of abstraction at which human language and animal communication fall together, almost all other behavior is included as well. Consider walking: Clearly, walking is purposive behavior, in the most general sense of "purposive." Walking is also "syntactic" in the sense just defined, as, in fact, Karl Lashley pointed out a long time ago in his important discussion of serial order in behavior. . . . Furthermore, it can certainly be informative; for example, I can signal my interest in reaching a certain goal by the speed or intensity with which I walk.

It is, incidentally, precisely in this manner that the examples of animal communication that Thorpe presents are "propositional." He cites as an example the song of the European robin, in which the rate of alternation of high and low pitch signals the intention of the bird to defend its territory; the higher the rate of alternation, the greater the intention to defend the territory. The example is interesting, but it seems to me to show very clearly the hopelessness of the attempt to relate human language to animal communication. Every animal communication system that is known (if we disregard some science fiction about dolphins) uses one of two basic principles: Either it consists of a fixed, finite number of signals, each associated with a specific range of behavior or emotional state, as is illustrated in the extensive primate studies that have been carried out by Japanese scientists for the past several years; or it makes use of a fixed, finite number of linguistic dimensions, each of which is associated with a particular nonlinguistic dimension in such a way that selection of a point along the linguistic dimension determines and signals a certain point along the associated nonlinguistic dimension. The latter is the principle realized in Thorpe's bird-song example. Rate of alternation of high and low pitch is a linguistic dimension correlated with the non-linguistic dimension of intention to defend a territory. The bird signals its intention to defend a territory by selecting a correlated point along the linguistic dimension of pitch alternation—I use the word "select" loosely, of course. The linguistic dimension is abstract, but the principle is clear. A communication system of the second type has an indefinitely large range of potential signals, as does human language. The mechanism and principle, however, are entirely different from those employed by human language to express indefinitely many new thoughts, intentions, feelings, and so on. It is not correct to speak of a "deficiency" of the animal system, in terms of range of potential signals; rather the opposite, since the animal system admits in principle of continuous variation along the linguistic dimension (insofar as it makes sense to speak of "continuity" in such a case), whereas human language is discrete. Hence, the issue is not one of "more" or "less," but rather of an entirely different principle of organization. When I make some arbitrary statement in a human language—say, that "the rise of supranational corporations poses new dangers for human freedom"—I am not selecting a point along some linguistic dimension that signals a corresponding point along an associated nonlinguistic dimension, nor am I selecting a signal from a finite behavioral repertoire, innate or learned.

Furthermore, it is wrong to think of human use of language as characteristically informative, in fact or in intention. Human language can be used to inform or mislead, to clarify one's own thoughts or to display one's cleverness, or simply for play. If I speak with no concern for modifying your behavior or thoughts, I am not using language any less than if I say exactly the same things *with* such intention. If we hope to understand human language and the psychological capacities on which it rests, we must first ask what it is, not how or for what purposes it is used. When we ask what human language is, we find no striking similarity to animal communication systems. There is nothing useful to be said about behavior or thought at the level of abstraction at which animal and human communication fall together. The examples of animal communication that have been examined to date do share many of the properties of human gestural systems, and it might be reasonable to explore the possibility of direct connection in this case. But human language, it appears, is based on entirely different principles. This, I think, is an important point, often overlooked by those who approach human language as a natural, biological phenomenon; in particular, it seems rather pointless, for these reasons, to speculate about the evolution of human language from simpler systems—perhaps as absurd as it would be to speculate about the "evolution" of atoms from clouds of elementary particles.

As far as we know, possession of human language is associated with a specific type of mental organization, not simply a higher degree of intelligence. There seems to be no substance to the view that human language is simply a more complex instance of something to be found elsewhere in the animal world. This poses a problem for the biologist, since, if true, it is an example of true "emergence"—the appearance of a qualitatively different phenomenon at a specific stage of complexity of organization. Recognition of this fact, though formulated in entirely different terms, is what motivated much of the classical study of language by those whose primary concern was the nature of mind. And it seems to me that today there is no better or more promising way to explore the essential and distinctive properties of human intelligence than through the detailed investigation of the structure of this unique human possession. A reasonable guess, then, is that if empirically adequate generative grammars can be constructed and the universal principles that govern their structure and organization determined, then this will be an important contribution to human psychology, in ways to which I will turn directly, in detail.

In the course of these lectures I have mentioned some of the classical ideas regarding language structure and contemporary efforts to deepen and extend them. It seems clear that we must regard linguistic competence—knowledge of a language—as an abstract system underlying behavior, a system constituted by rules that interact to determine the form and intrinsic meaning of a potentially infinite number of sentences. Such a system—a generative grammar—provides an explication of the Humboldtian idea of "form of language," which in an obscure but suggestive remark in his great posthumous work, *Über die Verschiedenheit des Menschlichen Sprachbaues,* Humboldt defines as "that constant and unvarying system of processes underlying the mental act of raising articulated structurally organized signals to an expression of thought." Such a grammar defines a language in the Humboldtian sense, namely as "a recursively generated system, where the laws of generation are fixed and invariant, but the scope and the specific manner in which they are applied remain entirely unspecified."

In each such grammar there are particular, idiosyncratic elements, selection of which determines one specific human language; and there are general universal elements, conditions on the form and organization of any human language, that form the subject matter for the study of "universal grammar." Among the principles of universal grammar are those I discussed in the preceding lecture—for example, the principles that distinguish deep and surface structure and that constrain the class of transformational operations that relate them. Notice, incidentally, that the existence of definite principles of universal grammar makes possible the rise of the new field of mathematical linguistics, a field that submits to abstract study the class of generative systems meeting the conditions set forth in universal grammar. This inquiry aims to elaborate the formal properties of any possible human language. The field is in its infancy; it is only in the last decade that the possibility of such an enterprise has been envisioned. It has some promising initial results, and it suggests one possible direction for future research that might prove to be of great importance. Thus, mathematical linguistics seems for the moment to be in a uniquely favorable position, among mathematical approaches in the social and psychological sciences, to develop not simply as a theory of data, but as the study of highly abstract principles and structures that determine the character of human mental processes. In this case, the mental processes in question are those involved in the organization of one specific domain of human knowledge, namely knowledge of language.

The theory of generative grammar, both particular and universal, points to a conceptual lacuna in psychological theory that I believe is worth mentioning. Psychology conceived as "behavioral science" has been concerned with behavior and acquisition or control of behavior. It has no concept corresponding to "competence," in the sense in which competence is characterized by a generative grammar. The theory of learning has limited itself to a narrow and surely inadequate concept of what is learned—namely a system of stimulus-response connections, a network of associations, a repertoire of behavioral items, a habit hierarchy, or a system of dispositions to respond in a particular way under specifiable stimulus conditions. Insofar as behavioral psychology has been applied to education or therapy, it has correspondingly limited itself to this concept of "what is learned." But a generative grammar cannot be characterized in these terms. What is necessary, in addition to the concept of behavior and learning, is a concept of what is learned—a notion of competence—that lies beyond the conceptual limits of behaviorist psychological theory. Like much of modern linguistics and modern philosophy of language, behaviorist psychology has quite consciously accepted methodological restrictions that do not permit the study of systems of the necessary complexity and abstractness. One important future contribution of the study of language to general psychology may be to focus attention on this conceptual gap and to demonstrate how it may be filled by the elaboration of a system of underlying competence in one domain of human intelligence.

There is an obvious sense in which any aspect of psychology is based ultimately on the observation of behavior. But it is not at all obvious that the study of learning should proceed directly to the investigation of factors that control behavior or of conditions under which a "behavioral repertoire" is established. It is first necessary to determine the significant characteristics of this behavioral repertoire, the principles on which it is organized. A meaningful study of learning can proceed only after this preliminary task has been carried out and has led to a reasonably well-confirmed theory of underlying competence—in the case of language, to the formulation of the generative grammar that underlies the observed use of language. Such a study will concern itself with the relation between the data available to the organism and the competence that it acquires; only to the extent that the abstraction to competence has been successful—in the case of language, to the extent that the postulated grammar is "descriptively adequate"—can the investigation of learning hope to achieve meaningful results. If, in some domain, the organization of the behavioral repertoire is quite trivial and elementary, then there will be little harm in avoiding the intermediate stage of theory construction, in which we attempt to characterize accurately the competence that is acquired. But one cannot count on this being the case, and in the study of language it surely is not the case. With a richer and more adequate characterization of "what is learned"—of the underlying competence that constitutes the "final state" of the organism being studied—it may be possible to approach the task of constructing a theory of learning that will be much less restricted in scope than modern behavioral psychology has proved to be. Surely it is pointless to accept methodological strictures that preclude such an approach to problems of learning.

• • •

I think that if we contemplate the classical problem of psychology, that of accounting for human knowledge, we cannot avoid being struck by the enormous disparity between knowledge and experience—in the case of language, between the generative grammar that expresses the linguistic competence of the native speaker and the meager and degenerate data on the basis of which he has constructed this grammar for himself. In principle the theory of learning should deal with this problem; but in fact it bypasses the problem, because of the conceptual gap that I mentioned earlier. The problem cannot even be formulated in any sensible way until we develop the concept of competence, alongside the concepts of learning and behavior, and apply this concept in some domain. The fact is that this concept has so far been extensively developed and applied only in the study of human language. It is only in this domain that we have at least the first steps toward an account of competence, namely the fragmentary generative grammars that have been constructed for particular languages. As the study of language progresses, we can expect with some confidence that these grammars will be extended in scope and depth, although it will hardly come as a surprise if the first proposals are found to be mistaken in fundamental ways.

Insofar as we have a tentative first approximation to a generative grammar for some language, we can for the first time formulate in a useful way the problem of origin of knowledge. In other words, we can ask the question, What initial structure must be attributed to the mind that enables it to construct such a grammar from the data of sense? Some of the empirical conditions that must be met by any such assumption about innate structure are moderately clear. Thus, it appears to be a species-specific capacity that is essentially independent of intelligence, and we can make a fairly good estimate of the amount of data that is necessary for the task to be successfully accomplished. We know that the grammars that are in fact constructed vary only slightly among speakers of the same language, despite wide variations not only in intelligence but also in the conditions under which language is acquired. As participants in a certain culture, we are naturally aware of the great differences in ability to use language, in knowledge of vocabulary, and so on that result from differences in native ability and from differences in conditions of acquisition; we naturally pay much less attention to the similarities and to common knowledge, which we take for granted. But if we manage to establish the requisite psychic distance, if we actually compare the generative grammars that must be postulated for different speakers of the same language, we find that the similarities that we take for granted are quite marked and that the divergences are few and marginal. What is more, it seems that dialects that are superficially quite remote, even barely intelligible on first contact, share a vast central core of common rules and processes and differ very slightly in underlying structures, which seem to remain invariant through long historical eras. Furthermore, we discover a substantial system of principles that do not vary among languages that are, as far as we know, entirely unrelated.

The central problems in this domain are empirical ones that are, in principle at least, quite straightforward, difficult as they may be to solve in a satisfactory way. We must postulate an innate structure that is rich enough to account for the disparity between experience and knowledge, one that can account for the construction of the empirically justified generative grammars within the given limitations of time and access to data. At the same time, this postulated innate mental structure must not be so rich and restrictive as to exclude certain known languages. There is, in other words, an upper bound and a lower bound on the degree and exact character of the complexity that can be postulated as innate mental structure. The factual situation is obscure enough to leave room for much difference of opinion over the true nature of this innate mental structure that makes acquisition of language possible. However, there seems to me to be no doubt that this is an empirical issue, one that can be resolved by proceeding along the lines that I have just roughly outlined.

My own estimate of the situation is that the real problem for tomorrow is that of discovering an assumption regarding innate structure that is sufficiently rich, not that of finding one that is simple or elementary enough to be "plausible." There is, as far as I can see, no reasonable notion of "plausibility," no a priori insight into what innate structures are permissible, that can guide the search for a "sufficiently elementary assumption." It would be mere dogmatism to maintain without argument or evidence that the mind is simpler in its innate structure than other biological systems, just as it would be mere dogmatism to insist that the mind's organization must necessarily follow certain set principles, determined in advance of investigation and maintained in defiance of any empirical findings. I think that the study of problems of mind has been very definitely hampered by a kind of apriorism with which these problems are generally approached. In particular, the empiricist assumptions that have dominated the study of acquisition of knowledge for many years seem to me to have been adopted quite without warrant and to have no special status among the many possibilities that one might imagine as to how the mind functions.

• • •

To my knowledge, the only substantive proposal to deal with the problem of acquisition of knowledge of language is the rationalist conception that I have outlined. To repeat: Suppose that we assign to the mind, as an innate property, the general theory of language that we have called "universal grammar." This theory encompasses the principles that I discussed in the preceding lecture and many others of the same sort, and it specifies a certain subsystem of rules that provides a skeletal structure for any language and a variety of conditions, formal and substantive, that any further elaboration of the grammar must meet. The theory of universal grammar, then, provides a schema to which any particular grammar must conform. Suppose, furthermore, that we can make this schema sufficiently restrictive so that very few possible grammars conforming to the schema will be consistent with the meager and degenerate data actually available to the language learner. His task, then, is to search among the possible grammars and select one that is not definitely rejected by the data available to him. What faces the language learner, under these assumptions, is not the impossible task of inventing a highly abstract and intricately structured theory on the basis of degenerate data, but rather the much more manageable task of determining whether these data belong to one or another of a fairly restricted set of potential languages.

The tasks of the psychologist, then, divide into several subtasks. The first is to discover the innate schema that characterizes the class of potential languages—that defines the "essence" of human language. This subtask falls to that branch of human psychology known as linguistics; it is the problem of traditional universal grammar, of contemporary linguistic theory. The second subtask is the detailed study of the actual character of the stimulation and the organism-environment interaction that sets the innate cognitive mechanism into operation. This is a study now being undertaken by a few psychologists, and it is particularly active right here in Berkeley. It has already led to interesting and suggestive conclusions. One might hope that such study will reveal a succession of maturational stages leading finally to a full generative grammar.

A third task is that of determining just what it means for a hypothesis about the generative grammar of a language to be "consistent" with the

data of sense. Notice that it is a great oversimplification to suppose that a
child must discover a generative grammar that accounts for all the linguistic data that has been presented to him and that "projects" such data
to an infinite range of potential sound-meaning relations. In addition to
achieving this, he must also differentiate the data of sense into those utter-
ances that give direct evidence as to the character of the underlying grammar and those that must be rejected by the hypothesis he selects as ill-
formed, deviant, fragmentary, and so on. Clearly, everyone succeeds in
carrying out this task of differentiation—we all know, within tolerable
limits of consistency, which sentences are well formed and literally inter-
pretable, and which must be interpreted as metaphorical, fragmentary,
and deviant along many possible dimensions. I doubt that it has been fully
appreciated to what extent this complicates the problem of accounting for
language acquisition. Formally speaking, the learner must select a
hypothesis regarding the language to which he is exposed that rejects a
good part of the data on which this hypothesis must rest. Again, it is reasonable to suppose this is possible only if the range of tenable hypotheses
is quite limited—if the innate schema of universal grammar is highly
restrictive. The third subtask, then, is to study what we might think of as
the problem of "confirmation"—in this context, the problem of what relation must hold between a potential grammar and a set of data for this
grammar to be confirmed as the actual theory of the language in question.

I have been describing the problem of acquisition of knowledge of language in terms that are more familiar in an epistemological than a psychological context, but I think that this is quite appropriate. Formally
speaking, acquisition of "common-sense knowledge"—knowledge of a
language, for example—is not unlike theory construction of the most
abstract sort. Speculating about the future development of the subject, it
seems to me not unlikely, for the reasons I have mentioned, that learning
theory will progress by establishing the innately determined set of possible hypotheses, determining the conditions of interaction that lead the
mind to put forth hypotheses from this set, and fixing the conditions under
which such a hypothesis is confirmed—and, perhaps, under which much
of the data is rejected as irrelevant for one reason or another.

Such a way of describing the situation should not be too surprising to
those familiar with the history of psychology at Berkeley, where, after all,
Edward Tolman has given his name to the psychology building; but I want
to stress that the hypotheses I am discussing are qualitatively different in
complexity and intricacy from anything that was considered in the classical discussions of learning. As I have now emphasized several times,

there seems to be little useful analogy between the theory of grammar that a person has internalized and that provides the basis for his normal, creative use of language, and any other cognitive system that has so far been isolated and described; similarly, there is little useful analogy between the schema of universal grammar that we must, I believe, assign to the mind as an innate character, and any other known system of mental organization. It is quite possible that the lack of analogy testifies to our ignorance of other aspects of mental function, rather than to the absolute uniqueness of linguistic structure; but the fact is that we have, for the moment, no objective reason for supposing this to be true.

The way in which I have been describing acquisition of knowledge of language calls to mind a very interesting and rather neglected lecture given by Charles Sanders Pierce more than fifty years ago, in which he developed some rather similar notions about acquisition of knowledge in general. Pierce argued that the general limits of human intelligence are much more narrow than might be suggested by romantic assumptions about the limitless perfectibility of man (or, for that matter, than are suggested by his own "pragmaticist" conceptions of the course of scientific progress in his better-known philosophical studies). He held that innate limitations on admissible hypotheses are a precondition for successful theory construction, and that the "guessing instinct" that provides hypotheses makes use of inductive procedures only for "corrective action." Peirce maintained in this lecture that the history of early science shows that something approximating a correct theory was discovered with remarkable ease and rapidity, on the basis of highly inadequate data, as soon as certain problems were faced; he noted "how few were the guesses that men of surpassing genius had to make before they rightly guessed the laws of nature." And, he asked, "How was it that man was ever led to entertain that true theory? You cannot say that it happened by chance, because the chances are too overwhelmingly against the single true theory in the twenty or thirty thousand years during which man has been a thinking animal, ever having come into any man's head." A fortiori, the chances are even more overwhelmingly against the true theory of each language ever having come into the head of every four-year-old child. Continuing with Peirce: "Man's mind has a natural adaptation to imagining correct theories of some kinds. . . . If man had not the gift of a mind adapted to his requirements, he could not have acquired any knowledge." Correspondingly, in our present case, it seems that knowledge of a language—a grammar—can be acquired only by an organism that is "preset" with a severe restriction on the form of grammar. This innate restriction is a precondition, in the Kantian sense, for linguistic experience, and it appears to be the critical factor in determining the course and result of language learning. The child cannot know at birth which language he is to learn, but he must know that its grammar must be of a predetermined form that excludes many imaginable languages. Having selected a permissible hypothesis, he can use inductive evidence for corrective action, confirming or disconfirming his choice. Once the hypothesis is sufficiently well confirmed, the child knows the language defined by this hypothesis; consequently, his knowledge extends enormously beyond his experience and, in fact, leads him to characterize much of the data of experience as defective and deviant.

Peirce regarded inductive processes as rather marginal to the acquisition of knowledge; in his words, "Induction has no originality in it, but only tests a suggestion already made." To understand how knowledge is acquired, in the rationalist view that Peirce outlined, we must penetrate the mysteries of what he called "abduction," and we must discover that which "gives a rule to abduction and so puts a limit upon admissible hypotheses." Peirce maintained that the search for principles of abduction leads us to the study of innate ideas, which provide the instinctive structure of human intelligence. But Peirce was no dualist in the Cartesian sense; he argued (not very persuasively, in my opinion) that there is a significant analogy between human intelligence, with its abductive restrictions, and animal instinct. Thus, he maintained that man discovered certain true theories only because his "instincts must have involved from the beginning certain tendencies to think truly" about certain specific matters; similarly, "You cannot seriously think that every little chicken that is hatched, has to rummage through all possible theories until it lights upon the good idea of picking up something and eating it. On the contrary, you think that the chicken has an innate idea of doing this; that is to say, that it can think of this, but has no faculty of thinking anything else. . . . But if you are going to think every poor chicken endowed with an innate tendency towards a positive truth, why should you think to man alone this gift is denied?"

No one took up Peirce's challenge to develop a theory of abduction, to determine those principles that limit the admissible hypotheses or present them in a certain order. Even today, this remains a task for the future. It is a task that need not be undertaken if empiricist psychological doctrine can be substantiated; therefore, it is of great importance to subject this doctrine to rational analysis, as has been done, in part, in the study of language. I would like to repeat that it was the great merit of structural linguistics, as of Hullian learning theory in its early stages and of several other modern developments, to have given precise form to certain empiricist assumptions. Where this step has been taken, the inadequacy of the postulated mechanisms has been clearly demonstrated, and, in the case of language at least, we can even begin to see just why any methods of this sort must fail—for example, because they cannot, in principle, provide for the properties of deep structures and the abstract operations of formal grammar. Speculating about the future, I think it is not unlikely that the dogmatic character of the general empiricist framework and its inadequacy to human and animal intelligence will gradually become more evident as specific realizations, such as taxonomic linguistics, behaviorist learning theory, and the perception models, heuristic methods, and "general problem solvers" of the early enthusiasts of "artificial intelligence," are successively rejected on empirical grounds when they are made precise and on grounds of vacuity when they are left vague. And—assuming this projection to be accurate—it will then be possible to undertake a general study of the limits and capacities of human intelligence, to develop a Peircean logic of abduction.

Modern psychology is not devoid of such initiatives. The contemporary study of generative grammar and its universal substructure and governing principles is one such manifestation. Closely related is the study of the biological bases of human language, an investigation to which Eric Lanneberg has made substantial contributions. It is tempting to see a parallel development in the very important work of Piaget and others interested in "genetic epistemology," but I am not sure that this is accurate. It is not clear to me, for example, what Piaget takes to be the basis for the transition from one of the stages that he discusses to the next, higher stage. There is, furthermore, a possibility, suggested by recent work of Mehler and Bever, that the deservedly well-known results on conservation, in particular, may not demonstrate successive stages of intellectual development in the sense discussed by Piaget and his coworkers, but something rather different. If the preliminary results of Mehler and Bever are correct, then it would follow that the "final stage," in which conservation is properly understood, was already realized at a very early period of development. Later, the child develops a heuristic technique that is largely adequate but that fails under the conditions of the conservation experiment. Still later, he adjusts this technique successfully and once again makes the correct judgments in the conservation experiment. If this analysis is correct, then what we are observing is not a succession of stages of intellectual development, in Piaget's sense, but rather slow progress in bringing heuristic techniques into line with general concepts that have always been present. These are interesting alternatives; either way, the results may bear in important ways on the topics we are considering.

Still more clearly to the point, I think, are the developments in comparative ethology over the past thirty years, and certain current work in experimental and physiological psychology. One can cite many examples: for example, in the latter category, the work of Bower suggesting an innate basis for the perceptual constancies; studies in the Wisconsin primate laboratory on complex innate releasing mechanisms in rhesus monkeys; the work of Hubel, Barlow, and others on highly specific analyzing mechanisms in the lower cortical centers of mammals; and a number of comparable studies of lower organisms (for example, the beautiful work of Lettvin and his associates on frog vision). There is now good evidence from such investigations that perception of line, angle, motion, and other complex properties of the physical world is based on innate organization of the neural system.

In some cases at least, these built-in structures will degenerate unless appropriate stimulation takes place at an early stage in life, but although such experience is necessary to permit the innate mechanisms to function, there is no reason to believe that it has more than a marginal effect on determining *how* they function to organize experience. Furthermore, there is nothing to suggest that what has so far been discovered is anywhere near the limit of complexity of innate structures. The basic techniques for exploring the neural mechanisms are only a few years old, and it is impossible to predict what order of specificity and complexity will be demonstrated when they come to be extensively applied. For the present, it seems that most complex organisms have highly specific forms of sensory and perceptual organization that are associated with the *Umwelt* and the manner of life of the organism. There is little reason to doubt that what is true of lower organisms is true of humans as well. Particularly in the case of language, it is natural to expect a close relation between innate properties of the mind and features of linguistic structure; for language, after all, has no existence apart from its mental representation. Whatever properties it has must be those that are given to it by the innate mental processes of the organism that has invented it and that invents it anew with each succeeding generation, along with whatever properties are associated with the conditions of its use. Once again, it seems that language should be, for this reason, a most illuminating probe with which to explore the organization of mental processes.

Turning to comparative ethology, it is interesting to note that one of its earliest motivations was the hope that through the "investigation of the a priori, of the innate working hypotheses present in sub-human organisms," it would be possible to shed light on the a priori forms of human thought. This formulation of intent is quoted from an early and little-known paper by Konrad Lorenz. Lorenz goes on to express views very much like those Peirce had expressed a generation earlier. He maintains:

One familiar with the innate modes of reaction of subhuman organisms can readily hypothesize that the a priori is due to hereditary differentiations of the central nervous system which have become characteristic of the species, producing hereditary dispositions to think in certain forms. . . . Most certainly Hume was wrong when he wanted to derive all that is a priori from that which the senses supply to experience, just as wrong as Wundt or Helmholtz who simply explain it as an abstraction from preceding experience. Adaptation of the a priori to the real world has no more originated from "experience" than adaptation of the fin of the fish to the properties of water. Just as the form of the fin is given a priori, prior to any individual negotiation of the young fish with the water, and just as it is this form that makes possible this negotiation, so it is also the case with our forms of perception and categories in their relationship to our negotiation with the real external world through experience. In the case of animals, we find limitations specific to the forms of experience possible for them. We believe we can demonstrate the closest functional and probably genetic relationship between these animal a priori's and our human a priori. Contrary to Hume, we believe, just as did Kant, that a "pure" science of innate forms of human thought, independent of all experience, is possible.

Peirce, to my knowledge, is original and unique in stressing the problem of studying the rules that limit the class of possible theories. Of course, his concept of abduction, like Lorenz's biological a priori, has a strongly Kantian flavor, and all derive from the rationalist psychology that concerned itself with the forms, the limits, and the principles that provide "the sinews and connections" for human thought, that underlie "that infinite amount of knowledge of which we are not always conscious," of which Leibnitz spoke. It is therefore quite natural that we should link these developments to the revival of philosophical grammar, which grew from the same soil as an attempt, quite fruitful and legitimate, to explore one basic facet of human intelligence.

In recent discussion, models and observations derived from ethology have frequently been cited as providing biological support, or at least analogue, to new approaches to the study of human intelligence. I cite these comments of Lorenz's mainly in order to show that this reference does not distort the outlook of at least some of the founders of this domain of comparative psychology.

One word of caution is necessary in referring to Lorenz, now that he has been discovered by Robert Ardrey and Joseph Alsop and popularized as a prophet of doom. It seems to me that Lorenz's views on human aggression have been extended to near absurdity by some of his expositors. It is no doubt true that there are innate tendencies in the human psychic constitution that lead to aggressiveness under specific social and cultural conditions. But there is little reason to suppose that these tendencies are so dominant as to leave us forever tottering on the brink of a Hobbesian war of all against all—as, incidentally, Lorenz at least is fully aware, if I read him rightly. Skepticism is certainly in order when a doctrine of man's "inherent aggressiveness" comes to the surface in a society that glorifies competitiveness, in a civilization that has been distinguished by the brutality of the attack that it has mounted against less fortunate peoples. It is fair to ask to what extent the enthusiasm for this curious view of man's nature is attributable to fact and logic and to what extent it merely reflects the limited extent to which the general cultural level has advanced since the days when Clive and the Portuguese explorers taught the meaning of true savagery to the inferior races that stood in their way.

In any event, I would not want what I am saying to be confused with other, entirely different attempts to revive a theory of human instinct. What seems to me important in ethology is its attempt to explore the innate properties that determine how knowledge is acquired and the character of this knowledge. Returning to this theme, we must consider a further question: How did the human mind come to acquire the innate structure that we are led to attribute to it? Not too surprisingly, Lorenz takes the position that this is simply a matter of natural selection. Peirce offers a rather different speculation, arguing that "nature fecundates the mind of man with ideas which, when these ideas grow up, will resemble their father, Nature." Man is "provided with certain natural beliefs that are true" because "certain uniformities . . . prevail throughout the universe, and the reasoning mind is [it]self a product of this universe. These same laws are thus, by logical necessity, incorporated in his own being." Here, it seems clear that Peirce's argument is entirely without force and that it offers little improvement over the preestablished harmony that it was presumably intended to replace. The fact that the mind is a product of natural laws does not imply that it is equipped to understand these laws or to arrive at them by "abduction." There would be no difficulty in designing a device (say, programming a computer) that is a product of natural law, but that, given data, will arrive at any arbitrary absurd theory to "explain" these data.

In fact, the processes by which the human mind achieved its present stage of complexity and its particular form of innate organization are a total mystery, as much so as the analogous questions about the physical or mental organization of any other complex organism. It is perfectly safe to attribute this development to "natural selection," so long as we realize that there is no substance to this assertion, that it amounts to nothing more than a belief that there is some naturalistic explanation for these phenomena. The problem of accounting for evolutionary development is, in some ways, rather like that of explaining successful abduction. The laws that determine possible successful mutation and the nature of complex organisms are as unknown as the laws that determine the choice of hypotheses. With no knowledge of the laws that determine the organization and structure of complex biological systems, it is just as senseless to ask what the "probability" is for the human mind to have reached its present state as it is to inquire into the "probability" that a particular physical theory will be devised. And, as we have noted, it is idle to speculate about laws of learning until we have some indication of what kind of knowledge is attainable—in the case of language, some indication of the constraints on the set of potential grammars.

In studying the evolution of mind, we cannot guess to what extent there are physically possible alternatives to, say, transformational generative grammar, for an organism meeting certain other physical conditions characteristic of humans. Conceivably, there are none—or very few—in which case talk about evolution of the language capacity is beside the point. The vacuity of such speculation, however, has no bearing one way or another on those aspects of the problem of mind that can be sensibly pursued. It seems to me that these aspects are, for the moment, the problems illustrated in the case of language by the study of the nature, the use, and the acquisition of linguistic competence.

There is one final issue that deserves a word of comment. I have been using mentalistic terminology quite freely, but entirely without prejudice as to the question of what may be the physical realization of the abstract mechanisms postulated to account for the phenomena of behavior or the acquisition of knowledge. We are not constrained, as was Descartes, to postulate a second substance when we deal with phenomena that are not expressible in terms of matter in motion, in his sense. Nor is there much point in pursuing the question of psychophysical parallelism, in this connection. It is an interesting question whether the functioning and evolution of human mentality can be accommodated within the framework of physical explanation, as presently conceived, or whether there are new principles, now unknown, that must be invoked, perhaps principles that emerge only at higher levels of organization than can now be submitted to physical investigation. We can, however, be fairly sure that there will be a physical explanation for the phenomena in question, if they can be explained at all, for an uninteresting terminological reason, namely that the concept of "physical explanation" will no doubt be extended to incorporate whatever is discovered in this domain, exactly as it was extended to accommodate gravitational and electromagnetic force, massless particles, and numerous other entities and processes that would have offended the common sense of earlier generations. But it seems clear that this issue need not delay the study of the topics that are now open to investigation, and it seems futile to speculate about matters so remote from present understanding.

I have tried to suggest that the study of language may very well, as was traditionally supposed, provide a remarkably favorable perspective for the study of human mental processes. The creative aspect of language use, when investigated with care and respect for the facts, shows that current notions of habit and generalization, as determinants of behavior or knowledge, are quite inadequate. The abstractness of linguistic structure reinforces this conclusion, and it suggests further that in both perception and learning the mind plays an active role in determining the character of the acquired knowledge. The empirical study of linguistic universals has led to the formulation of highly restrictive and, I believe, quite plausible hypotheses concerning the possible variety of human languages, hypotheses that contribute to the attempt to develop a theory of acquisition of knowledge that gives due place to intrinsic mental activity. It seems to me, then, that the study of language should occupy a central place in general psychology. . . .

Henry M. Bracken

In this selection Henry M. Bracken (of Trinity College, Dublin, Ireland, at the time of its publication in 1973) diagnoses a long-standing racialist understanding of human nature in Western culture since the sixteenth century. He notes Aristotle's remark that some people are slaves by nature, so this story could be extended as far back as the Greeks and Romans, who made a sharp distinction between themselves and "barbarians."

Bracken draws our attention to defenses of slavery by Locke and Berkeley, and quotes an uninhibitedly racialist paragraph from Hume. He could also have quoted Kant—see Charles Mills, *The Racial Contract,* 1997, pages 69 to 72. This may shock those of us who have been brought up to revere these philosophers as cultural heroes, apostles of enlightenment, toleration, and human rights. But we have to recognize that for all their originality, and their opposition to some of the beliefs and practices of their day, they were in other ways men of their times. Their defense of human rights and freedoms, the respect for persons as ends in themselves, seem to have been applied primarily to white, middle-class, European men; only secondarily to women; and hardly at all to other "races."

Bracken argues that the empiricist conception of persons (represented in the selection from Hume above), though not entailing racial discrimination, made such discrimination easier to accept.

According to the rationalism of Descartes and Plato, the human essence consists in reason, and this was expressed metaphysically in the concept of a rational soul (see the selection from Descartes above). As an all-or-nothing distinction, it was difficult to deny the possession of a soul to all human beings (and many Christian thinkers accepted this, at least in theory). But Locke and Hume questioned the relevance, or even the coherence, of any such notion of incorporeal entity or substance. That made it easier to divide human beings into a number of "races," identified by a loose bundle of allegedly typical characteristics.

The scientific basis of racial differences is questioned by both sides in the modern debate about sociobiology (see the references in the introductions to Wilson and Rose et al. below).

"Essence, Accident and Race"

In this paper I assume that racism is endemic to our culture. I also assume that we wish to reduce its force and hence that as philosophers we are interested in some of the philosophical sources of racism. My concern is with one strand and one strand only within the complex development of our twentieth-century situation. I appreciate that the term "racism" is so widely and variedly used today that even for the purposes of a paper it is difficult to specify. However, I certainly mean to include the doctrine which a group may articulate in order to justify their oppressing another group by appealing to some putative flaw in the human essence, in recent times usually interpreted as the biological constitution, of the members of the oppressed group. Thus I mean to include within racism "congenital inferiority" by virtue of skin colour as well as by linguistic differences.

Philosophers are not the only people who have considered language to be a reflection of mind. Anthropologists have often provided linguistic data to show that the speaking of inferior languages is the mark of the inferior minds of inferior people. Just as university language programmes still consider only the superior cultures of superior peoples worthy of study. *Linguistic imperialism* is evident in the use of similar scientific or cultural-political claims concerning the several Celtic languages vis-à-vis

"Essence, Accident and Race," © *Hermathena: A Dublin University Review,* No. CXVI (Winter 1973).

English and French. In Canada the injunction "speak white" means speak English. Here is a statement of colour racism:

> I am apt to suspect the negroes and in general all the other species of men (for there are four or five different kinds) to be naturally inferior to the whites. There never was a civilized nation of any other complexion than white, nor even any individual eminent either in action or speculation. No ingenious manufactures amongst them, no arts, no sciences. On the other hand, the most rude and barbarous of the whites, such as the ancient GERMANS, the present TARTARS, have still something eminent about them, in their valour, form of government, or some other particular. Such a uniform and constant difference could not happen, in so many countries and ages, if nature had not made an original distinction betwixt these breeds of men. Not to mention our colonies, there are NEGROE slaves dispersed all over EUROPE, of which none ever discovered any symptoms of ingenuity; tho' low people, without education, will start up amongst us, and distinguish themselves in every profession. In JAMAICA indeed they talk of one negroe as a man of parts and learning; but 'tis likely he is admired for very slender accomplishments, like a parrot, who speaks a few words plainly. (From the essay "Of national characters'." Cf. Hume's *Essays: Moral, Political, and Literary,* eds T. H. Green and T. H. Grose, London, 1875, I, 252.)

The author of these lines was a one-time British Under-Secretary of State, in effect for Colonial Affairs, Mr. David Hume. It is an unhappy fact that many of the cultural heroes of the Enlightenment were anxious to establish that large numbers of the peoples of the world were somehow less than men. If we will reflect for a moment, we may recall that Hume was no lover of the Irish or of the Catholics either. R. H. Popkin has distinguished a number of rather different racist theories within the eighteenth and nineteenth centuries. For example: (1) non-whites are mentally deficient—a theory which is still advanced; (2) being non-white is a form of degeneracy based on environmental conditions (sun, food, etc.); (3) there are some beings that look human but which are really closer to the apes, a view which was given a "scientific" basis by Darwinians; (4) the thesis that there were separate creations of mankind, the Adamites and the pre-Adamites.

Thus, as in (2), sometimes a "cure" for the inferior elements could be provided through the right environment, assimilation, evolutionary upgrading, etc. More often, "alien" racial elements were to be driven out or exterminated—policies that were recommended in relation to the Irish and Jews in England in the nineteenth century. We have seen that Hume takes a hard line. So does Voltaire. He rejected the climate theory and opted for listing the negro as a member of a distinct species of man; specifically different because of lack of intelligence (cf. *La philosophie de l'histoire,* ch. ii.). Berkeley supported slavery but he rejected the specific difference thesis (*Works,* ed. A. A. Luce and T. E. Jessop, VII, 122). Darwin is interesting because of the importance he attributes to languages, because he would seek to defend treating separate races as separate species even if they were cross-fertile, and because one of his infrequent lapses from a lofty scientific style occurs when he includes some scurrilous quotations about the Irish (*Descent of Man,* 2 vols; London, 1871, I, 174).

Racism in the west appears to be a recent phenomenon. Judaism, Islam, and Christianity are universalistic. They sought and seek converts. It is apparently not until the Spanish Inquisition that one finds biological criteria taking precedence over religious conversion with the distinction of "new" vs. "old" Christians. "New" vs. "old" Protestant in eighteenth century Ireland represents a similar move. However, it was the discovery of the New World which gave real scope for racial theory. Despite the arguments of Las Casas, and Pope Paul III's bull *Sublimus Deus,* affirming the true manhood of Indians, the need to exploit two continents seems to have inclined men to prefer the guidance of Aristotle—some men are by nature slaves (although Aristotle was probably not providing an account of the human essence with that remark).

From our point of view, the most significant feature of the shifts in ideas between the sixteenth and nineteenth centuries is that racism not only runs counter to the three major religious traditions which have dominated the west, it runs counter to the doctrines of man still being articulated within the seventeenth century. Notice that if one is a Cartesian, a defender of mind/body dualism, it becomes impossible to state a racist position. Man's essential properties reside finally in his spirit. His colour, his language, his biology, even his sex—are in the strictest sense *accidental.* (From Plato to Descartes sexist doctrines have been more comfortably situated within the Aristotelian tradition than among the dualists.)

I cited a passage from Hume, but in many ways Locke seems to have been the more decisive influence. Recall Locke's views about substance and quality: he devotes considerable energy trying to determine how secondary qualities inhere in primary ones and how qualities generally inhere in substance. His tendency is to say that we do not know the "real Constitutions of Substances, on which each *secondary Quality* particularly depends," and that even if we did, "it would serve us only with experimental (not universal) Knowledge; and reach with Certainty no farther, than that bare Instance" (*Essay*, IV, vi, §7). The *even if* theme is constant, although the emphasis changes. At II, xxxi, paragraph 13, Locke writes that it is "very evident to the Mind . . . that whatever Collection of simple *Ideas* it makes of any substance that exists, it cannot be sure, that it exactly answers all that are in that Substance: Since not having tried all the Operations of all other substances upon it. . . . " Then Locke adds the *even if* clause: "And, after all, if we could have, and actually had, in our complex *Idea*, an exact Collection of all the secondary Qualities or Powers of any Substance, we should not yet thereby have an Idea of the Essence of that Thing. For since the Powers or Qualities, that are observable by us, are not the real Essence of that Substance, but depend on it, and flow from it, any Collection whatsoever of the Qualities, cannot be the real Essence of that Thing." In IV, vi, paragraph 9, he writes: "I would gladly meet with one general Affirmation, concerning any quality of *Gold*, that any one can certainly know is true." This is a remarkable claim because it indicates that Locke has no ground for excluding from the idea of the substance gold, pain—or *in*cluding malleableness *within* the idea of gold. Locke is prepared to grant (cf. IV, iii, §6) that matter might think.

Thus one side of Locke's discussion of substance constitutes an attack on the model of essential properties which had played a major role within Cartesianism and, for that matter, within Aristotelianism. It then becomes possible to treat any or no property as essential. Within the revised framework it becomes more difficult to distinguish men from the other animals. The older model had the advantage of trying to formulate what was essential to man. In so doing it provided a modest conceptual barrier to treating race, colour, religion, or sex as other than accidental.

Locke, of course, did *not* want to treat these things as accidental. His very considerable involvement in the Revolution of 1688 is still a matter of lively interest for historians. He has acquired a grand reputation as a man of religious tolerance. Yet he apparently had no difficulty in excluding Catholics from the body politic. I find it remarkable that Locke should have been canonized as the father of religious toleration. There were, after all, people around who had expressed genuinely tolerant sentiments. But one should not lose sight of the alteration in thinking about persons introduced by Locke together with his defences of the revolution. Are there connections between Locke's philosophical accounts of the substantial self or person and the ease with which he can treat Catholics as non-persons? Without answering that, one may consider another aspect of Locke's work. Peter Laslett has noted that Locke became a Commissioner of Appeals in 1689 and a founding member of the Board of Trade in 1696. "Locke himself played a large part in the creation of this second body, the architect of the old Colonial System." Locke indeed does write about slavery. According to Laslett, paragraphs 23, 24, and 85 of the *Two treatises* constitute "Locke's justification of slavery. It may seem unnecessary, and inconsistent with his principles, but it must be remembered that he writes as the administrator of slave-owning colonies in America. As Leslie Stephen pointed out, the *Fundamental constitutions of Carolina* provide that every freeman shall have absolute power and authority over his negro slaves . . . The Instructions to Governor Nicholson of Virginia, which Locke did much to draft in 1698, regard negro slaves as justifiably enslaved because they were captives taken in a just war, who had forfeited their lives 'by some Act that deserves Death'. . . . Locke seems satisfied that the forays of the Royal Africa Company were just wars of this sort, and that the negroes captured had committed such acts. . . ."

Just war enters because while Locke would not have countenanced slave-taking within the EEC of his day, he seems to have felt that *waste land* was fair game. Waste land was land not being put to proper economic use—i.e. land which was not the property of civilized, defined as money-exchanging, people. By a happy consequence of his universal principle, Africa and the Americas were waste land. If their residents resisted the take-over of these wastelands, they could properly be taken as captives in a just war and made perpetual slaves.

There is another side to Locke's discussion—the concept-acquisition model. The doctrine of substance and the consequent denial of thinking substance is supported by Locke's account of concept-formation. Locke's "way of ideas" was interpreted by many to provide something like what we might today call a "meaning criterion." And Locke found it unintelligible to say with Descartes that the soul always thinks, or that it has innate ideas. Although there are atomistic and corpuscular elements within Locke's theory of knowledge, his position often reads like a variation on the scholastic thesis that there is nothing in the intellect which is not first in the senses. Bishop Stillingfleet pressed Locke quite hard on the intelligibility of the "way of ideas" and argued that it created some awkward problems for the faithful. It meant that certain faith claims, e.g., that the soul is immortal, would be difficult to talk about since "soul" had been rendered meaningless on Locke's analysis. Locke appears to respond by holding that since the whole claim is a matter of faith anyway, there should be no difficulties.

For better or for worse, I submit that the issues in the innate idea arguments of Locke, Leibniz, Descartes, etc., are not narrowly or technically philosophical. What is a person? How does a person learn? These are the sorts of questions really being asked. Empiricism and rationalism offer rather different answers. It is my impression that we have observed in the process of time a continual increase in the techniques of manipulation, in the methods of control, and in the efficiency whereby people have been merchandised. I am not claiming that empiricism is responsible for that; or that a return to rationalism would herald a new age of human freedom. The connections between empiricism and the rise of manipulative models of man may be considered historical, not logical.

And yet the rationalists seem to have been more conscious that those features of man which get singled out as essential have a normative moral character. The empiricists understandably saw their accounts as descriptive. Value-free descriptions of certain peoples as essentially inferior, grounded in some "science," facilitate treating them as inferior. Which is not to say ingenious rationalists could not have articulated racist theories. That is why I hold that the relation between empiricism and racism is historical. But the lack of an "in principle" argument should not deter us from recognizing that empiricism has provided the methodology within which theories of political control were successfully advanced, and by means of which colour/brain-weight, IQ, etc., correlation studies have been pursued, and in terms of which the liberal ideology has been cast. Hence the role of empiricism has in fact been decisive within the English-speaking community.

If I urge that we look once again at the discarded Cartesian model it is in large measure because I claim it will help us to see more clearly where we stand and to appreciate how deeply rooted in ideological considerations some of our purest philosophical notions really are. We should also be reminded that the discarded model was not conceptually inadequate.

Perhaps because of Locke, we are inclined to think that the defenders of innate ideas were reactionaries to a man. Certainly John Yolton (in *John Locke and the way of ideas*) has produced incontrovertible evidence to show that there were dozens of people defending innate ideas in the very form Locke refutes. Generally, these were people who defended their pet prejudices simply by producing an innateness claim instead of an argument. But there is another side. Jean Calvin used innate ideas as part of his attempt to establish that a mere individual man was inherently capable of questioning a truth grounded in authority or tradition. And among the Cartesians, innate ideas were part of a general attack on any and all empirical accounts of concept-acquisition. For these purposes, an empiricist account is one which establishes that all knowledge is rooted in the senses by asserting that blind men do not know colour. Peter Geach remarked the difficulty about the appeal to the blind man in *Mental acts*. The empiricist point seems to be that if one closes off one sense channel then one cannot talk about things appropriate to that particular sense. In that form, of course, the claim will not stand up. There is ample evidence that blind people not only can learn the language of colour, they can use it in literary contexts in ways that make it impossible for us to identify the author as blind. On the other hand, if one means by blind-men-not-knowing-colour that they cannot, when handed a coloured object, identify its colour—that is a logical truth; it is not, says Geach, the sort of thing we should be citing in defence of an empirical claim about concept-acquisition.

Leibniz in discussing (in the *New essays*) the case cited in Locke's *Essay* of the blind man made to see by the removal of cataracts remarked that blind men could do geometry. A point the Cartesians had already noted. Indeed, the Cartesians had already decided that although we could talk about the same object as perceived through different senses, our actual cognition of the object could hardly be a function of any sort of resemblance holding between physical object and sensory data. Cartesians could not see how our ideas, how our concepts, could be derived from material things. Hence the introduction of innate ideas as a basis for guaranteeing the objectivity of human knowledge. But that is only part of the Cartesian account.

Descartes begins with a primitive awareness that human language is radically different from anything found elsewhere in the animal kingdom. Man's language skill reveals a unique capacity. In brief, man has a mind. And neither machines nor other animals do. A machine might be constructed which could talk, "But it never happens that it arranges its speech in various ways, in order to reply appropriately to everything that may be said in its presence, as even the lowest type of man can do. The second difference is, that although machines can perform certain things as well as or perhaps better than any of us can do, they infallibly fall short in others, by the which means we may discover that they did not act from knowledge, but only from the disposition of their organs." Or as it could be put today, human speech cannot be understood in stimulus-response terms. In fact, Descartes argues that our soul is entirely independent of our body. Which may in part be glossed as: we can think and talk about things which are not in front of our noses. In *Meditation* IV, Descartes again refers to man's creative capacity to spin out thoughts as a function of the freedom of the will.

A Cartesian like Louis de La Forge sees an empirical theory of linguistic meaning and of concept-acquisition as providing a foundation for a denial of human freedom. Our mental life is rooted in the mind's own activity, not in what may seem to be impressed via the sense channels. Man's linguistic creativity as a mark of the mental, in particular the non-imitative linguistic creativity of children, is also discussed by Bernard Lamy.

The Port-Royal wing of Cartesianism actually tried to provide a model of the human mind which would capture this radical freedom motif. They sought to produce a grammar which would do for mind what geometry did for matter. Noam Chomsky suggests that they failed because they did not have at their disposal mathematical models which would enable them to characterize the sorts of rules which might make intelligible our infinite capacity to generate sentences.

There is another dimension to the concept-acquisition discussion. The radical freedom thesis offends. The suggestion that people are autonomous is not attractive to those who want to have power over people—or who want to produce theories about how and why people behave in certain ways. In that context there is something reassuring about applying to humans methods of learning which have apparently been successful in animal experiments. The empirical model seems to reduce the possibility that the natives might get restless. Moreover, thinking of people as conditionable reserves a place for those who must do the conditioning. Which is to say that the empiricist model of man provides room for experts. Once in power they have a clear vested interest in the theories and categories they employ in talking about men and women. Those theories justify the experts' acceptance and use of power. Whereas people who do not behave in accordance with the theories threaten the adequacy of the theories and hence the original licence to power.

In brief, there are a number of reasons—having nothing to do with explanatory adequacy—why the dualist model was rejected in favour of the empiricist. While people spoke of the rights of man in ever grander terms from the eighteenth century onwards, more and more men were being enslaved. Very quickly the various sorts of racism described at the outset became widespread. When Patrick Henry of Virginia made his impassioned plea, "Give me liberty or give me death," he owned more than a dozen black slaves. There were, of course, occasional voices raised against slavery. But somehow it had become possible to say that there were different *species* of humans. Some were higher on the scale of personhood than others.

The racism of a Voltaire or a Hume became scientifically well-founded in the nineteenth century. The historical antecedent of colour/IQ correlations was the work of the craniologists. "In the human brain we find those characteristics which particularly distinguish man from the brute creation. The differences between the various races of men are fundamental differences in intellectual capacity, as well as in physical conformation." Prof. A. H. Keane of University College, London, writes as follows about the negro in the ninth edition (1884) of the *Encyclopaedia Britannica:*

> Nearly all observers admit that the Negro child is on the whole quite as intelligent as those of other human varieties, but that on arriving at puberty all further progress seems to be arrested. . . . "We must necessarily suppose that the development of the Negro and White proceeds on different lines. While with the latter the volume of the brain grows with the expansion of the brain-pan, in the former the growth of the brain is on the contrary arrested by the premature closing of the cranial sutures and lateral pressure of the frontal bone." [The citation is from Filippo Manetta, *La Razza Negra nel suo stato selvaggio* (Turin, 1864), p. 20.]

Keane comments on the negro's moral status: "It is more correct to say of the Negro that he is non-moral than immoral." An indication of negroes' inferior moral situation is that they engage in the slave trade, "where not checked by European Governments." Keane later held that the Chinese "seem in some respects to be almost as incapable of progress as the Negroes themselves, the only *essential* difference being that the arrest of mental development comes later in life for the yellow than for the black man." The discovery that neolithic and modern Europeans had the same brain capacity inclined him to place his emphasis on brain serratures being more complex "in the higher than in the lower races." He writes: "A better index [than cranial volume] between the mental capacity of the various human groups is afforded by the reasoning faculty, of which articulate speech is at once the measure and the outward expression" (p. 193). As to how languages were to be ranked, he had no doubts.

Nott and Gliddon, and Dr. Samuel Morton provided evidence on Celtic brain volumes as well as blacks. The data are included in J. B. Davis and J. Thurnam, *Crania Britannica* (London, 1865). The scientific evidence shows that English brains were best with 96 cubic inches and Germans were next with 95. But the "native Irish" were a mere 87 and the "native

African Family," 83.7. Dr. Robert Knox, *The races of man* (London, 1868), p. 12, writes, "There never was any Celtic literature, nor science, nor arts. . . ." He advises us that "the object of [his] work is to show that the European races, so called, differ from each other as widely as the . . . Esquimaux from the Basque" (p. 44). Since he speaks of "exterminating" (e.g. 229 f) various races, it is not surprising to read, "Sir Robert Peel's Encumbered Estate Bill aims simply at the quiet and gradual extinction of the Celtic race in Ireland: this is its sole aim, and it will prove successful. A similar bill is wanted for Caledonia . . ." (p. 27).

John Stuart Mill writes, *England and Ireland* (London, 1865), p. 35, that the Irish have "yet to prove their possession" of the "qualities which fit a people for self-government." Matthew Arnold notes, "Undoubtedly the native Irish have the faults which we commonly attribute to them," *Irish essays* (London, 1882), p. 12. The author of *Ireland from one or two neglected points of view* (London, 1888) asserts, "The cause [of Western Irish turbulence and lawlessness] is lowness of racial character. All the government conciliation in the world will not alter the moral character of a race of men. It is folly to talk of a governing race conciliating a lower one," (p. 43). A few pages later he asks, "How can the tricks of reading and writing alter the features of the Negro's face with the character that belongs to the features?" (p. 49). The same is presumably intended to hold for the Irish. L. Perry Curtis, Jr, *Apes and angels . . .* (Newton Abbot, 1971) shows how extensive was the effort to assimilate the Irish to the simian or the black—the black's inferior status already having been scientifically established.

Linguistic appeals have already been mentioned. They had been made in varying ways for several centuries. They had new force in the post-Darwinian world. A. Schleicher writes, "The development of language has accompanied, step by step, the development of the brain and of the organ of speech . . . the study of language conducts us unmistakably to the hypothesis of the gradual evolution of man from lower forms," cited by André Lefèvre, *Race and language* (London, 1894), p. 6. Darwinism not only gave added support to the polygenetic theories of man but also to polygenetic theories of language. Since the diversity of languages was taken to support diversity of man, ranking of men by species was paralleled by the ranking of languages; an end to Adam and Eve entails an end to a single pre-Babel language.

A chapter in de Gobineau's *Essai sur l'inégalité des races humaines,* second ed. 2 vols (Paris, 1884), is entitled: "Les langues, inégales entre elle, sont dans un rapport parfait avec le mérite relatif des races," (ch. xv). W. D. Whitney, in *Language and the study of language* (London, 1867), said, "It still remains true that, upon the whole, language is a tolerably sure indication of race" (pp. 373–4). Prof. A. H. Sayce entered a demur: "The spirit of vanity has invaded the science of language itself. We have come to think that not only is the race to which we belong superior to all others, but that the languages we speak are equally superior," *Introduction to the science of language* (London, 1880), II, 66. "Language," he said, "is no test of race, only of social contact" (I, 75). But the racial drive was more powerful. On the one hand Indian and African languages were inferior because they were mere extensions of animal noises, on the other hand they were inferior because they were lexically and syntactically too complex. Gaelic was of course also found to be inadequate.

As I mentioned at the outset neither racism nor linguistic racism had to wait for Darwin. The ground had been well prepared for several centuries. But anthropology succeeded in making racism scientifically respectable. It also thereby enhanced the political usefulness of the social sciences. The Canadian linguistic ethnologist, Horatio Hale, held that "speech alone, rightly studied, will indicate with sufficient clearness the circumstances of the [racial] mixture." He also wrote, "[Ethnology] is indispensable . . . to the politician who in any capacity aspires to direct [a nation's] future" (p. 351). The Irish and the negro questions came before the Anthropological Society of London on more than a few occasions. The following two passages suggest what a valuable contribution to the advancement of science anthropologists were making. One paper begins, "The object of this paper is to show that the peculiarities of the Irish character . . . are racial, hereditary, and ineradicable."Another says, "if only those in authority would but take the trouble to make themselves acquainted with certain race distinctions,—in fact, become anthropologists,—there would be fewer political mistakes than ruled at present; and less pandering to Negroes, the working classes, and the Celtic Irish. . . ."

From the eighteenth century to the present, social scientists have been striving to establish that people may be ranked racially. Hume or Voltaire or Jefferson did not have such elaborate studies at their disposal as later thinkers provided. Craniologists of the nineteenth century did for the cause what twentieth century IQ experts continue to do: produce, under the guise of science, correlations of colour or language with "intelligence." But as Chomsky has pointed out, there is no reason to think that there is any intellectual significance in correlating IQ and skin colour, height, etc. Nor would such studies entail any social consequences, "except in a racist society in which each individual is assigned to a racial category and dealt with not as an individual in his own right, but as a representative of this category."

In the eighteenth century one ranked people by race. One also finds parallel rankings of languages transparently in terms of their proximity to the pinnacles of civilization—the English, French, and Germans. Craniology provided hard, objective, value-free scientific data. Like philology it was related to man's intellectual activities. Yet taking the measure of a man in terms of his language or brain weight or head shape or IQ is not something which follows from defining man as a rational animal. As I have said, we apparently get into the ranking business in the first place because we want to justify, we want to make morally legitimate, our pushing people around.

The empiricist model of man did not produce the institution of racial slavery or the forms of racism which have been visited upon Ireland and the Americas. However, it made racism easier to justify by providing us with ways of counting colour, head shape, language, religion, or IQ as essential properties of the person. And it allowed us to think that colour/brain and similar correlations were legitimate scientific enquiries.

I began by citing David Hume's expression of racism. I then discussed John Locke's account of substance and essential properties. I advanced the thesis that racism is easily and readily stateable if one thinks of the person in accordance with empiricist teaching because the essence of the person may be deemed to be his colour, language, religion, etc., while the Cartesian dualist model provided what I called a modest conceptual brake to the articulation of racial degradation and slavery. *Secondly,* I have suggested that the empiricist blank tablet account of learning is a manipulative model and that Cartesians rejected the empiricist doctrine of concept-acquisition because they took it to entail a denial of the possibility of human freedom. In modern times the account of concept-acquisition and learning which they rejected has proved itself to be readily compatible with social conditioning and political control. *Thirdly,* I submit that this essence/accident strand within racism is important to us not only because it is rooted in English thought, but also because when taken together with empiricist learning theory and empiricism's fact/value distinction it has been crucial as an ideological bulwark behind which racially biased pseudo-science continues to flourish. . . .

Edward O. Wilson

The Harvard biologist Edward O. Wilson boldly claimed in his book *Sociobiology: The New Synthesis* (1975) to have formed a new scientific discipline by applying the rigorous methods of population biology to complex social systems in insects and many other animal species. In a provocative final chapter he sketched how his sociobiological approach could be applied to ourselves.

The controversy that ensued led Wilson to write *On Human Nature* (1978) in which he aimed to show how the evolutionary biology and genetics of human beings could be applied to the large issues of social theory and philosophy. The extracts here from chapters 1 and 2 show Wilson as an eloquent spokesman for the view that "the only way forward is to study human nature as part of the natural sciences." (But where does that leave philosophy, religion, politics, and literature, one wonders?) The whole book is eminently readable and worth thinking about critically (the chapters cover heredity, development, emergence, aggression, sex, altruism, religion, and hope—so there should be something there for everybody).

Of particular relevance to feminist issues is Wilson's section on differences between the sexes in humans (pp. 125ff)—where he says "the evidence for a genetic difference in behaviour is varied and substantial" (p. 129). But just how much is genetic, and how much is cultural, remains very controversial. Wilson also discusses alleged racial differences (pp. 47ff), concluding that "mankind viewed over many generations shares a single human nature within which relatively minor hereditary influences recycle through ever changing patterns, between the sexes and across families and entire populations" (p. 50).

On Human Nature

These are the central questions that the great philosopher David Hume said are of unspeakable importance: How does the mind work, and beyond that why does it work in such a way and not another, and from these two considerations together, what is man's ultimate nature?

We keep returning to the subject with a sense of hesitancy and even dread. For if the brain is a machine of ten billion nerve cells and the mind can somehow be explained as the summed activity of a finite number of chemical and electrical reactions, boundaries limit the human prospect— we are biological and our souls cannot fly free. If humankind evolved by Darwinian natural selection, genetic chance and environmental necessity, not God, made the species. Deity can still be sought in the origin of the ultimate units of matter, in quarks and electron shells (Hans Küng was right to ask atheists why there is something instead of nothing) but not in the origin of species. However much we embellish that stark conclusion with metaphor and imagery, it remains the philosophical legacy of the last century of scientific research.

No way appears around this admittedly unappealing proposition. It is the essential first hypothesis for any serious consideration of the human condition. Without it the humanities and social sciences are the limited descriptors of surface phenomena, like astronomy without physics, biology without chemistry, and mathematics without algebra. With it, human nature can be laid open as an object of fully empirical research, biology can be put to the service of liberal education, and our self-conception can be enormously and truthfully enriched.

But to the extent that the new naturalism is true, its pursuit seems cer-

Reprinted by permission of the publisher from *On Human Nature* by Edward O. Wilson, Cambridge, Mass.: Harvard University Press, Copyright © 1978 by the President and Fellows of Harvard College.

tain to generate two great spiritual dilemmas. The first is that no species, ours included, possesses a purpose beyond the imperatives created by its genetic history. Species may have vast potential for material and mental progress but they lack any immanent purpose or guidance from agents beyond their immediate environment or even an evolutionary goal toward which their molecular architecture automatically steers them. I believe that the human mind is constructed in a way that locks it inside this fundamental constraint and forces it to make choices with a purely biological instrument. If the brain evolved by natural selection, even the capacities to select particular esthetic judgments and religious beliefs must have arisen by the same mechanistic process. They are either direct adaptations to past environments in which the ancestral human populations evolved or at most constructions thrown up secondarily by deeper, less visible activities that were once adaptive in this stricter, biological sense.

The essence of the argument, then, is that the brain exists because it promotes the survival and multiplication of the genes that direct its assembly. The human mind is a device for survival and reproduction, and reason is just one of its various techniques. Steven Weinberg has pointed out that physical reality remains so mysterious even to physicists because of the extreme improbability that it was constructed to be understood by the human mind. We can reverse that insight to note with still greater force that the intellect was not constructed to understand atoms or even to understand itself but to promote the survival of human genes. The reflective person knows that his life is in some incomprehensible manner guided through a biological ontogeny, a more or less fixed order of life stages. He senses that with all the drive, wit, love, pride, anger, hope, and anxiety that characterize the species he will in the end be sure only of helping to perpetuate the same cycle. Poets have defined this truth as tragedy. Yeats called it the coming of wisdom:

> Though leaves are many, the root is one;
> Through all the lying days of my youth
> I swayed my leaves and flowers in the sun;
> Now I may wither into the truth.

The first dilemma, in a word, is that we have no particular place to go. The species lacks any goal external to its own biological nature. It could be that in the next hundred years humankind will thread the needles of technology and politics, solve the energy and materials crises, avert nuclear war, and control reproduction. The world can at least hope for a stable ecosystem and a well-nourished population. But what then? Educated people everywhere like to believe that beyond material needs lie fulfillment and the realization of individual potential. But what is fulfillment, and to what ends may potential be realized? Traditional religious beliefs have been eroded, not so much by humiliating disproofs of their mythologies as by the growing awareness that beliefs are really enabling mechanisms for survival. Religions, like other human institutions, evolve so as to enhance the persistence and influence of their practitioners. Marxism and other secular religions offer little more than promises of material welfare and a legislated escape from the consequences of human nature. They, too, are energized by the goal of collective self-aggrandizement. The French political observer Alain Peyrefitte once said admiringly of Mao Tse-tung that "the Chinese knew the narcissistic joy of loving themselves in him. It is only natural that he should have loved himself through them." Thus does ideology bow to its hidden masters the genes, and the highest impulses seem upon closer examination to be metamorphosed into biological activity.

The more somber social interpreters of our time, such as Robert Heilbroner, Robert Nisbet, and L. S. Stavrianos, perceive Western civilization and ultimately mankind as a whole to be in immediate danger of decline. Their reasoning leads easily to a vision of post-ideological societies whose members will regress steadily toward self-indulgence. "The will to power will not have vanished entirely," Gunther Stent writes in *The Coming of the Golden Age,*

> but the distribution of its intensity will have been drastically altered. At one end of this distribution will be the minority of the people whose work will keep intact the technology that sustains the multitude at a high standard of living. In the middle of the distribution will be found a type, largely unemployed, for whom the distinction between the real and the illusory will still be meaningful. . . . He will retain interest in the world and seek satisfaction from sensual pleasures. At the other end of the spectrum will be a type largely unemployable, for whom the boundary of the real and the imagined will have been largely dissolved, at least to the extent compatible with his physical survival.

Thus the danger implicit in the first dilemma is the rapid dissolution of transcendental goals toward which societies can organize their energies. Those goals, the true moral equivalents of war, have faded; they went one by one, like mirages, as we drew closer. In order to search for a new morality based upon a more truthful definition of man, it is necessary to look inward, to dissect the machinery of the mind and to retrace its evolutionary history. But that effort, I predict, will uncover the second dilemma, which is the choice that must be made among the ethical premises inherent in man's biological nature.

At this point let me state in briefest terms the basis of the second dilemma, while I defer its supporting argument to the next chapter: innate censors and motivators exist in the brain that deeply and unconsciously affect our ethical premises; from these roots, morality evolved as instinct. If that perception is correct, science may soon be in a position to investigate the very origin and meaning of human values, from which all ethical pronouncements and much of political practice flow.

Philosophers themselves, most of whom lack an evolutionary perspective, have not devoted much time to the problem. They examine the precepts of ethical systems with reference to their consequences and not their origins. Thus John Rawls opens his influential *A Theory of Justice* (1971) with a proposition he regards as beyond dispute: "In a just society the liberties of equal citizenship are taken as settled; the rights secured by justice are not subject to political bargaining or to the calculus of social interests." Robert Nozick begins *Anarchy, State, and Utopia* (1974) with an equally firm proposition: "Individuals have rights, and there are things no person or group may do to them (without violating their rights). So strong and far-reaching are these rights they raise the question of what, if anything, the state and its officials may do." These two premises are somewhat different in content, and they lead to radically different prescriptions. Rawls would allow rigid social control to secure as close an approach as possible to the equal distribution of society's rewards. Nozick sees the ideal society as one governed by a minimal state, empowered only to protect its citizens from force and fraud, and with unequal distribution of rewards wholly permissible. Rawls rejects the meritocracy; Nozick accepts it as desirable except in those cases where local communities voluntarily decide to experiment with egalitarianism. Like everyone else, philosophers measure their personal emotional responses to various alternatives as though consulting a hidden oracle.

That oracle resides in the deep emotional centers of the brain, most probably within the limbic system, a complex array of neurons and hormone-secreting cells located just beneath the "thinking" portion of the cerebral cortex. Human emotional responses and the more general ethical practices based on them have been programmed to a substantial degree by natural selection over thousands of generations. The challenge to science is to measure the tightness of the constraints caused by the programming, to find their source in the brain, and to decode their significance through the reconstruction of the evolutionary history of the mind. This enterprise will be the logical complement of the continued study of cultural evolution.

Success will generate the second dilemma, which can be stated as follows: Which of the censors and motivators should be obeyed and which ones might better be curtailed or sublimated? These guides are the very core of our humanity. They and not the belief in spiritual apartness distinguish us from electronic computers. At some time in the future we will have to decide how human we wish to remain—in this ultimate, biological sense—because we must consciously choose among the alternative emotional guides we have inherited. To chart our destiny means that we must shift from automatic control based on our biological properties to precise steering based on biological knowledge.

Because the guides of human nature must be examined with a complicated arrangement of mirrors, they are a deceptive subject, always the philosopher's deadfall. The only way forward is to study human nature as part of the natural sciences, in an attempt to integrate the natural sciences with the social sciences and humanities. I can conceive of no ideological or formalistic shortcut. Neurobiology cannot be learned at the feet of a guru. The consequences of genetic history cannot be chosen by legislatures. Above all, for our own physical well-being if nothing else, ethical philosophy must not be left in the hands of the merely wise. Although human progress can be achieved by intuition and force of will, only hardwon empirical knowledge of our biological nature will allow us to make optimum choices among the competing criteria of progress.

• • •

Reduction is the traditional instrument of scientific analysis, but it is feared and resented. If human behavior can be reduced and determined to any considerable degree by the laws of biology, then mankind might appear to be less than unique and to that extent de-humanized. Few social scientists and scholars in the humanities are prepared to enter such a conspiracy, let alone surrender any of their territory. But this perception, which equates the method of reduction with the philosophy of diminution, is entirely in error. The laws of a subject are necessary to the discipline above it, they challenge and force a mentally more efficient restructuring, but they are not sufficient for the purposes of the discipline. Biology is the key to human nature, and social scientists cannot afford to ignore its rapidly tightening principles. But the social sciences are potentially far richer in content. Eventually they will absorb the relevant ideas of biology and go on to beggar them. The proper study of man is, for reasons that now transcend anthropocentrism, man.

Heredity

We live on a planet of staggering organic diversity. Since Carolus Linnaeus began the process of formal classification in 1758, zoologists have catalogued about one million species of animals and given each a scientific name, a few paragraphs in a technical journal, and a small space on the shelves of one museum or another around the world. Yet despite this prodigious effort, the process of discovery has hardly begun. In 1976 a specimen of an unknown form of giant shark, fourteen feet long and weighing sixteen hundred pounds, was captured when it tried to swallow the stabilizing anchor of a United States Naval vessel near Hawaii. About the same time entomologists found an entirely new category of parasitic flies that resemble large reddish spiders and live exclusively in the nests of the native bats of New Zealand. Each year museum curators sort out thousands of new kinds of insects, copepods, wireworms, echinoderms, priapulids, pauropods, hypermastigotes, and other creatures collected on expeditions around the world. Projections based on intensive surveys of selected habitats indicate that the total number of animal species is between three and ten million. Biology, as the naturalist Howard Evans expressed it in the title of a recent book, is the study of life "on a little known planet."

Thousands of these species are highly social. The most advanced among them constitute what I have called the three pinnacles of social evolution in animals: the corals, bryozoans, and other colony-forming invertebrates; the social insects, including ants, wasps, bees, and termites; and the social fish, birds, and mammals. The communal beings of the three pinnacles are among the principal objects of the new discipline of sociobiology, defined as the systematic study of the biological basis of all forms of social behavior, in all kinds of organisms, including man. The enterprise has old roots. Much of its basic information and some of its most vital ideas have come from ethology, the study of whole patterns of behavior of organisms under natural conditions. Ethology was pioneered by Julian Huxley, Karl von Frisch, Konrad Lorenz, Nikolaas Tinbergen, and a few others and is now being pursued by a large new generation of innovative and productive investigators. It has remained most concerned with the particularity of the behavior patterns shown by each species, the ways these patterns adapt animals to the special challenges of their environments, and the steps by which one pattern gives rise to another as the species themselves undergo genetic evolution. Increasingly, modern ethology is being linked to studies of the nervous system and the effects of hormones on behavior. Its investigators have become deeply involved with developmental processes and even learning, formerly the nearly exclusive domain of psychology, and they have begun to include man among the species most closely scrutinized. The emphasis of ethology remains on the individual organism and the physiology of organisms.

Sociobiology, in contrast, is a more explicitly hybrid discipline that incorporates knowledge from ethology (the naturalistic study of whole patterns of behavior), ecology (the study of the relationships of organisms to their environment), and genetics in order to derive general principles concerning the biological properties of entire societies. What is truly new about sociobiology is the way it has extracted the most important facts about social organization from their traditional matrix of ethology and psychology and reassembled them on a foundation of ecology and genetics studied at the population level in order to show how social groups adapt to the environment by evolution. Only within the past few years have ecology and genetics themselves become sophisticated and strong enough to provide such a foundation.

Sociobiology is a subject based largely on comparisons of social species. Each living form can be viewed as an evolutionary experiment, a product of millions of years of interaction between genes and environment. By examining many such experiments closely, we have begun to construct and test the first general principles of genetic social evolution. It is now within our reach to apply this broad knowledge to the study of human beings.

Sociobiologists consider man as though seen through the front end of a telescope, at a greater than usual distance and temporarily diminished in size, in order to view him simultaneously with an array of other social experiments. They attempt to place humankind in its proper place in a catalog of the social species on Earth. They agree with Rousseau that "One needs to look near at hand in order to study men, but to study man one must look from afar."

This macroscopic view has certain advantages over the traditional anthropocentrism of the social sciences. In fact, no intellectual vice is more crippling than defiantly self-indulgent anthropocentrism. I am reminded of the clever way Robert Nozick makes this point when he constructs an argument in favor of vegetarianism. Human beings, he notes, justify the eating of meat on the grounds that the animals we kill are too far below us in sensitivity and intelligence to bear comparison. It follows that if representatives of a truly superior extraterrestrial species were to visit Earth and apply the same criterion, they could proceed to eat us in good conscience. By the same token, scientists among these aliens might find human beings uninteresting, our intelligence weak, our passions unsurprising, our social organization of a kind already frequently encountered on other planets. To our chagrin they might then focus on the ants, because these little creatures, with their haplodiploid form of sex determination and bizarre female caste systems, are the truly novel productions of the Earth with reference to the Galaxy. We can imagine the log declaring, "A scientific breakthrough has occurred; we have finally discovered haplodiploid social organisms in the one- to ten-millimeter range." Then the visitors might inflict the ultimate indignity: in order to be sure they had not underestimated us, they would simulate human beings in the laboratory. Like chemists testing the structural characterization of a problematic organic compound by assembling it from simpler components, the alien biologists would need to synthesize a hominoid or two.

This scenario from science fiction has implications for the definition of man. The impressive recent advances by computer scientists in the design of artificial intelligence suggests the following test of humanity: that which behaves like man *is* man. Human behavior is something that can be defined with fair precision, because the evolutionary pathways open to it have not all been equally negotiable. Evolution has not made culture all-powerful. It is a misconception among many of the more traditional Marxists, some learning theorists, and a still surprising proportion of anthropologists and sociologists that social behavior can be shaped into virtually any form. Ultra-environmentalists start with the premise that man is the creation of his own culture: "culture makes man," the formula might go, "makes culture makes man." Theirs is only a half truth. Each person is molded by an interaction of his environment, especially his cultural environment, with the genes that affect social behavior. Although the hundreds of the world's cultures seem enormously variable to those of us who stand in their midst, all versions of human social behavior together form only a tiny fraction of the realized organizations of social species on this planet and a still smaller fraction of those that can be readily imagined with the aid of sociobiological theory.

The question of interest is no longer whether human social behavior is genetically determined; it is to what extent. The accumulated evidence for a large hereditary component is more detailed and compelling than most persons, including even geneticists, realize. I will go further: it already is decisive.

That being said, let me provide an exact definition of a genetically determined trait. It is a trait that differs from other traits at least in part as a result of the presence of one or more distinctive genes. The important point is that the objective estimate of genetic influence requires comparison of two or more states of the same feature. To say that blue eyes are inherited is not meaningful without further qualification, because blue eyes are the product of an interaction between genes and the largely physiological environment that brought final coloration to the irises. But to say that the *difference* between blue and brown eyes is based wholly or partly on differences in genes is a meaningful statement because it can be tested and translated into the laws of genetics. Additional information is then sought: What are the eye colors of the parents, siblings, children, and more distant relatives? These data are compared to the very simplest model of Mendelian heredity, which, based on our understanding of cell multiplication and sexual reproduction, entails the action of only two genes. If the data fit, the differences are interpreted as being based on two genes. If not, increasingly complicated schemes are applied. Progressively larger numbers of genes and more complicated modes of interaction are assumed until a reasonably close fit can be made. In the example just cited, the main differences between blue and brown eyes are in fact based on two genes, although complicated modifications exist that make them less than an ideal textbook example. In the case of the most complex traits, hundreds of genes are sometimes involved, and their degree of influence can ordinarily be measured only crudely and with the aid of sophisticated mathematical techniques. Nevertheless, when the analysis is properly performed it leaves little doubt as to the presence and approximate magnitude of the genetic influence.

Human social behavior can be evaluated in essentially the same way, first by comparison with the behavior of other species and then, with far greater difficulty and ambiguity, by studies of variation among and within human populations. The picture of genetic determinism emerges most sharply when we compare selected major categories of animals with the human species. Certain general human traits are shared with a majority of the great apes and monkeys of Africa and Asia, which on grounds of anatomy and biochemistry are our closest living evolutionary relatives:

- Our intimate social groupings contain on the order of ten to one hundred adults, never just two, as in most birds and marmosets, or up to thousands, as in many kinds of fishes and insects.

- Males are larger than females. This is a characteristic of considerable significance within the Old World monkeys and apes and many other kinds of mammals. The average number of females consorting with successful males closely corresponds to the size gap between males and females when many species are considered together. The rule makes sense: the greater the competition among males for females, the greater the advantage of large size and the less influential are any disadvantages accruing to bigness. Men are not very much larger than women; we are similar to chimpanzees in this regard. When the sexual size difference in human beings is plotted on the curve based on other kinds of mammals, the predicted average number of females per successful male turns out to be greater than one but less than three. The prediction is close to reality; we know we are a mildly polygynous species.

- The young are molded by a long period of social training, first by closest associations with the mother, then to an increasing degree with other children of the same age and sex.

- Social play is a strongly developed activity featuring role practice, mock aggression, sex practice, and exploration.

These and other properties together identify the taxonomic group consisting of Old World monkeys, the great apes, and human beings. It is inconceivable that human beings could be socialized into the radically different repertories of other groups such as fishes, birds, antelopes, or rodents. Human beings might self-consciously *imitate* such arrangements, but it would be a fiction played out on a stage, would run counter to deep emotional responses and have no chance of persisting through as much as a single generation. To adopt with serious intent, even in broad outline, the social system of a nonprimate species would be insanity in the literal sense. Personalities would quickly dissolve, relationships disintegrate, and reproduction cease.

At the next, finer level of classification, our species is distinct from the Old World monkeys and apes in ways that can be explained only as a result of a unique set of human genes. Of course, that is a point quickly conceded by even the most ardent environmentalists. They are willing to agree with the great geneticist Theodosius Dobzhansky that "in a sense, human genes have surrendered their primacy in human evolution to an entirely new, nonbiological or superorganic agent, culture. However, it should not be forgotten that this agent is entirely dependent on the human genotype." But the matter is much deeper and more interesting than that. There are social traits occurring through all cultures which upon close examination are as diagnostic of mankind as are distinguishing characteristics of other animal species—as true to the human type, say, as wing tessellation is to a fritillary butterfly or a complicated spring melody to a wood thrush. In 1945 the American anthropologist George P. Murdock listed the following characteristics that have been recorded in every culture known to history and ethnography:

Age-grading, athletic sports, bodily adornment, calendar, cleanliness training, community organization, cooking, cooperative labor, cosmology, courtship, dancing, decorative art, divination, division of labor, dream interpretation, education, eschatology, ethics, ethnobotany, etiquette, faith healing, family feasting, fire making, folklore, food taboos, funeral rites, games, gestures, gift giving, government, greetings, hair styles, hospitality, housing, hygiene, incest taboos, inheritance rules, joking, kin groups, kinship nomenclature, language, law, luck superstitions, magic, marriage, mealtimes, medicine, obstetrics, penal sanctions, personal names, population policy, postnatal care, pregnancy usages, property rights, propitiation of supernatural beings, puberty customs, religious ritual, residence rules, sexual restrictions, soul concepts, status differentiation, surgery, tool making, trade, visiting, weaving, and weather control.

Few of these unifying properties can be interpreted as the inevitable outcome of either advanced social life or high intelligence. It is easy to imagine nonhuman societies whose members are even more intelligent and complexly organized than ourselves, yet lack a majority of the qualities just listed. Consider the possibilities inherent in the insect societies. The sterile workers are already more cooperative and altruistic than people and they have a more pronounced tendency toward caste systems and division of labor. If ants were to be endowed in addition with rationalizing brains equal to our own, they could be our peers. Their societies would display the following peculiarities:

Age-grading, antennal rites, body licking, calendar, cannibalism, caste determination, caste laws, colony-foundation rules, colony organization, cleanliness training, communal nurseries, cooperative labor, cosmology, courtship, division of labor, drone control, education, eschatology, ethics, etiquette, euthanasia, fire making, food taboos, gift giving, government, greetings, grooming rituals, hospitality, housing, hygiene, incest taboos, language, larval care, law, medicine, metamorphosis rites, mutual regurgitation, nursing castes, nuptial flights, nutrient eggs, population policy, queen obeisance, residence rules, sex determination, soldier castes, sisterhoods, status differentiation, sterile workers, surgery, symbiont care, tool making, trade, visiting, weather control,

and still other activities so alien as to make mere description by our language difficult. If in addition they were programmed to eliminate strife between colonies and to conserve the natural environment they would have greater staying power than people, and in a broad sense theirs would be the higher morality.

Civilization is not intrinsically limited to hominoids. Only by accident was it linked to the anatomy of bare-skinned, bipedal mammals and the peculiar qualities of human nature.

Freud said that God has been guilty of a shoddy and uneven piece of work. That is true to a degree greater than he intended: human nature is just one hodgepodge out of many conceivable. Yet if even a small fraction of the diagnostic human traits were stripped away, the result would probably be a disabling chaos. Human beings could not bear to simulate the behavior of even our closest relatives among the Old World primates. If by perverse mutual agreement a human group attempted to imitate in detail the distinctive social arrangements of chimpanzees or gorillas, their effort would soon collapse and they would revert to fully human behavior.

It is also interesting to speculate that if people were somehow raised from birth in an environment devoid of most cultural influence, they would construct basic elements of human social life *ab initio*. In short time new elements of language would be invented and their culture enriched. Robin Fox, an anthropologist and pioneer in human sociobiology, has expressed this hypothesis in its strongest possible terms. Suppose, he conjectured, that we performed the cruel experiment linked in legend to the Pharaoh Psammetichus and King James IV of Scotland, who were said to have reared children by remote control, in total social isolation from their elders. Would the children learn to speak to one another?

I do not doubt that they could speak and that, theoretically, given time, they or their offspring would invent and develop a language despite their never having been taught one. Furthermore, this language, although totally different from any known to us, would be analyzable to linguists on the same basis as other languages and translatable into all known languages.

But I would push this further. If our new Adam and Eve could survive and breed—still in total isolation from any cultural influences—then eventually they would produce a society which would have laws about property, rules about incest and marriage, customs of taboo and avoidance, methods of settling disputes with a minimum of bloodshed, beliefs about the supernatural and practices relating to it, a system of social status and methods of indicating it, initiation ceremonies for young men, courtship practices including the adornment of females, systems of symbolic body adornment generally, certain activities and associations set aside for men from which women were excluded, gambling of some kind, a tool- and weapon-making industry, myths and legends, dancing, adultery, and various doses of homicide, suicide, homosexuality, schizophrenia, psychosis and neuroses, and various practitioners to take advantage of or cure these, depending on how they are viewed.

Not only are the basic features of human social behavior stubbornly idiosyncratic, but to the limited extent that they can be compared with those of animals they resemble most of all the repertories of other mammals and especially other primates. A few of the signals used to organize the behavior can be logically derived from the ancestral modes still shown by the Old World monkeys and great apes. The grimace of fear, the smile, and even laughter have parallels in the facial expressions of chimpanzees. This broad similarity is precisely the pattern to be expected if the human species descended from Old World primate ancestors, a demonstrable fact, and if the development of human social behavior retains even a small degree of genetic constraint, the broader hypothesis now under consideration.

The status of the chimpanzee deserves especially close attention. Our growing knowledge of these most intelligent apes has come to erode to a large extent the venerable dogma of the uniqueness of man. Chimpanzees are first of all remarkably similar to human beings in anatomical and physiological details. It also turns out that they are very close at the molecular level. The biochemists Mary-Claire King and Allan C. Wilson have compared the proteins encoded by genes at forty-four loci. They found the summed differences between the two species to be equivalent to the genetic distance separating nearly indistinguishable species of fruit flies, and only twenty-five to sixty times greater than that between Caucasian, Black African, and Japanese populations. The chimpanzee and human lines might have split as recently as twenty million years ago, a relatively short span in evolutionary time. . . .

This account of the life of the chimpanzee is meant to establish what I regard as a fundamental point about the human condition: that by conventional evolutionary measures and the principal criteria of psychology we are not alone, we have a little-brother species. The points of similarity between human and chimpanzee social behavior, when joined with the compelling anatomical and biochemical traces of relatively recent genetic divergence, form a body of evidence too strong to be dismissed as coincidence. I now believe that they are based at least in part on the possession of identical genes. If this proposition contains any truth, it makes even more urgent the conservation and closer future study of these and the other great apes, as well as the Old World monkeys and the lower primates. A more thorough knowledge of these animal species might well provide us with a clearer picture of the step-by-step genetic changes that led to the level of evolution uniquely occupied by human beings.

To summarize the argument to this point: the general traits of human nature appear limited and idiosyncratic when placed against the great backdrop of all other living species. Additional evidence suggests that the more stereotyped forms of human behavior are mammalian and even more specifically primate in character, as predicted on the basis of general evolutionary theory. Chimpanzees are close enough to ourselves in the details of their social life and mental properties to rank as nearly human in certain domains where it was once considered inappropriate to make comparisons at all. These facts are in accord with the hypothesis that human social behavior rests on a genetic foundation—that human behavior is, to be more precise, organized by some genes that are shared with closely related species and others that are unique to the human species. The same facts are unfavorable for the competing hypothesis which has dominated the social sciences for generations, that mankind has escaped its own genes to the extent of being entirely culture-bound.

Let us pursue this matter systematically. The heart of the genetic hypothesis is the proposition, derived in a straight line from neo-Darwinian evolutionary theory, that the traits of human nature were adaptive during the time that the human species evolved and that genes consequently spread through the population that predisposed their carriers to develop those traits. Adaptiveness means simply that if an individual displayed the traits he stood a greater chance of having his genes represented in the next generation than if he did not display the traits. The differential advantage among individuals in this strictest sense is called genetic fitness. There are three basic components of genetic fitness: increased personal survival, increased personal reproduction, and the enhanced survival and reproduction of close relatives who share the same genes by common descent. An improvement in any one of the factors or in any combination of them results in greater genetic fitness. The process, which Darwin called natural selection, describes a tight circle of causation. If the possession of certain genes predisposes individuals toward a particular trait, say a certain kind of social response, and the trait in turn conveys superior fitness, the genes will gain an increased representation in the next generation. If natural selection is continued over many generations, the favored genes will spread throughout the population, and the trait will become characteristic of the species. In this way human nature is postulated by many sociobiologists, anthropologists, and others to have been shaped by natural selection.

It is nevertheless a curious fact, which enlarges the difficulty of the analysis, that sociobiological theory can be obeyed by purely cultural behavior as well as by genetically constrained behavior. An almost purely cultural sociobiology is possible. If human beings were endowed with nothing but the most elementary drives to survive and to reproduce, together with a capacity for culture, they would still learn many forms of social behavior that increase their biological fitness. But as I will show, there is a limit to the amount of this cultural mimicry, and methods exist by which it can be distinguished from the more structured forms of biological adaptation. The analysis will require the careful use of techniques in biology, anthropology, and psychology. Our focus will be on the closeness of fit of human social behavior to sociobiological theory, and on the evidences of genetic constraint seen in the strength and automatic nature of the predispositions human beings display while developing this behavior.

Let me now rephrase the central proposition in a somewhat stronger and more interesting form: if the genetic components of human nature did not originate by natural selection, fundamental evolutionary theory is in trouble. At the very least the theory of evolution would have to be altered to account for a new and as yet unimagined form of genetic change in populations. Consequently, an auxiliary goal of human sociobiology is to learn whether the evolution of human nature conforms to conventional evolutionary theory. The possibility that the effort will fail conveys to more adventurous biologists a not unpleasant whiff of grapeshot, a crackle of thin ice.

We can be fairly certain that most of the genetic evolution of human social behavior occurred over the five million years prior to civilization, when the species consisted of sparse, relatively immobile populations of hunter-gatherers. On the other hand, by far the greater part of cultural evolution has occurred since the origin of agriculture and cities approximately 10,000 years ago. Although genetic evolution of some kind continued during this latter, historical sprint, it cannot have fashioned more than a tiny fraction of the traits of human nature. Otherwise surviving hunter-gatherer people would differ genetically to a significant degree from people in advanced industrial nations, but this is demonstrably not the case. It follows that human sociobiology can be most directly tested in studies of hunter-gatherer societies and the most persistent preliterate herding and agricultural societies. As a result, anthropology rather than sociology or economics is the social science closest to sociobiology. It is in anthropology that the genetic theory of human nature can be most directly pursued.

The power of a scientific theory is measured by its ability to transform a small number of axiomatic ideas into detailed predictions of observable phenomena; thus the Bohr atom made modern chemistry possible, and modern chemistry recreated cell biology. Further, the validity of a theory is measured by the extent to which its predictions successfully compete with other theories in accounting for the phenomena; the solar system of Copernicus won over that of Ptolemy, after a brief struggle. Finally, a theory waxes in influence and esteem among scientists as it assembles an ever larger body of facts into readily remembered and usable explanatory schemes, and as newly discovered facts conform to its demands: the round earth is more plausible than a flat one. Facts crucial to the advancement of science can be obtained either by experiments designed for the purpose of acquiring them or from the inspired observation of undisturbed natural phenomena. Science has always progressed in approximately this opportunistic, zig-zagging manner.

In the case of the theory of the genetic evolution of human nature, if it is ever to be made part of real science, we should be able to select some of the best principles from ecology and genetics, which are themselves based on the theory, and adapt them in detail to human social organization. The theory must not only account for many of the known facts in a more convincing manner than traditional explanations, but must also identify the need for new kinds of information previously unimagined by the social sciences. The behavior thus explained should be the most general and least rational of the human repertoire, the part furthest removed from the influence of day-to-day reflection and the distracting vicissitudes of culture. In other words, they should implicate innate, biological phenomena that are the least susceptible to mimicry by culture.

These are stern requirements to impose on the infant discipline of human sociobiology, but they can be adequately justified. Sociobiology intrudes into the social sciences with credentials from the natural sciences and, initially, an unfair psychological advantage. If the ideas and analytical methods of "hard" science can be made to work in a congenial and enduring manner, the division between the two cultures of science and the humanities will close. But if our conception of human nature is to be altered, it must be by means of truths conforming to the canons of scientific evidence and not a new dogma however devoutly wished for.

Nancy Holmstrom

In this selection Nancy Holmstrom (of Rutgers University at the time of publication in 1982) makes some valuable methodological points about the concept "nature" in general, and its application to human nature and women's alleged nature in particular.

On the basis of her conceptual arguments, and a survey of the empirical evidence at the time of writing, Holmstrom concurs with J. S. Mill's judgment (see above) and concludes that "psychological differences between the sexes are most probably overwhelmingly social in origin." She thus takes issue with the view, asserted by E. O. Wilson, that psychological differences between men and women are mainly genetic. Holmstrom finds support in Marx for a concept of "natures" or "social roles" as socially created and therefore changeable. (For an interesting proposal to emend Marxist theory to take account of feminism, see Alison Jaggar, *Feminist Politics and Human Nature* (Totowa: Rowman & Littlefield, 1983), Chapter 4.) This debate will run and run: new evidence, new arguments, new social analyses keep emerging.

"Do Women Have a Distinct Nature?"

Feminists have good reason to be suspicious of any talk of a distinct women's nature. The very phrase contains a sexist bias in that men are implicitly taken as the norm and women as "the other," to use de Beauvoir's term. Despite some pious talk of complementarity, the different characteristics attributed to men and women have always been evaluated differently, and for thousands of years theories of a distinct women's nature have been used to justify the subordination of women to men. The theories are taken to imply that these natures cannot change and also that one ought not even try to change them. Most theories of *human* nature have served a similar function. Either women have been explicitly taken to lack the traits designated by the theories as essentially human, e.g., rationality, or else traits historically more true of men than women, such as participating in politics, have been designated as essentially human. Most of these theories have been exposed by feminists as pseudo-scientific rationalizations of cultural prejudices. Not only has a distinct women's nature not been established, feminists argue, but even if it had no normative implications would follow automatically.

The question can, however, be posed in unbiased terms: are there sex-differentiated natures? In this sense, if women have a distinct nature then it is equally true that men have a distinct nature. This question refuses to be disposed of—in part because of the tremendous social importance the answer is presumed to have and also because of the enormous variety and complexity of the issues involved. First of all there are conceptual, methodological and ontological issues: what exactly is a nature or essence? When are similarities between things sufficient to constitute a common nature and when do differences constitute different natures? To help elucidate a methodology, I will turn to biology which has the most developed and precise system of classifications of things in nature. I will argue that a nature or essence should be understood as an underlying structure that generates laws and that natures in this sense often play a crucial explanatory role. There are also, of course, empirical questions to be answered regarding differences between men and women that might determine their respective social roles. Examining the research on psychological sex differences, I conclude that there probably are significant

"Do Women Have a Distinct Nature?," © *The Philosophical Forum,* Vol. XIV No. 1 (Fall 1982).

differences between the sexes. However I also conclude that the most important determinants of these differences are social. The usual inference would be that men and women do not have different natures, and in the traditional sense of "natures," this is correct. However, the traditional conception depends upon a contrast between nature and society that, I argue, is mistaken, particularly in the case of human beings. Natures can also be socially constituted. Whether men and women have different natures depends, I contend, on certain theoretical considerations. As an illustration of what I mean by this claim, I discuss Marx's theory of human nature. In conclusion I discuss what would follow if men and women do have distinct natures in this sense.

Although biology has the most precise system of classifications in nature and involves few, if any, social and political factors, nevertheless, even in biology there is considerable disagreement as to the criteria for differentiating species, behind which lie different philosophies of science. The essentialist, or typological approach, coming from Aristotle, holds that species are differentiated by sets of individually necessary and jointly sufficient characteristics which constitute the nature or essence of that species. Since these essences were supposed to be unchanging, this approach became less dominant after the discovery of evolution. Another contemporary school of taxonomists (called pheneticists) rejects essences and argues that the only proper scientific basis for classification is the overall similarity of things. Taxonomists who emphasize evolution correctly reply that there is no such thing as overall similarity. Every individual is similar to and different from every other individual in a variety of ways. Hence there are always many possible orderings. However, this does not make all classifications arbitrary and all generalizations accidental. What similarities and differences are most important can only be decided in terms of theoretical considerations. Classifications and generalizations backed up by a theory are neither accidental nor arbitrary. Evolutionary and gene theory do not define species in terms of similarity. There can be greater variations of certain kinds within a species, e.g., between a Chihuahua and a St. Bernard, among dogs, than between two species, e.g., dogs and wolves. This is because some differences are more important than others for biological theory. Taxonomists who emphasize evolution conceive of a species as, roughly speaking, a class of individual organisms which (either do or could) consistently interbreed with fertile offspring. The actual distribution of properties among organisms is such that, contrary to the Aristotelian view, most taxa names can only be defined disjunctively. Any of the disjuncts is sufficient and the few properties that are necessary are far from sufficient. Thus most concepts of so-called natural kinds are cluster concepts. These classes of organisms change over time to such an extent that individuals in the later generations are no longer classified as belonging to the same species as those of earlier generations.

Although it is superior to the alternatives discussed, I would agree with those philosophers called realists who argue that the evolutionary approach is still not adequate. Suppose we ask why things that fit that sort of disjunctive definition should figure in evolutionary theory? Why should such a group have the requisite stability? Why is it that they can interbreed? Realists argue that it is necessary to posit some underlying structure common to the things so defined which generates this set of properties and causes the variations in different individuals. In the case of a species, this underlying structure would be the gene pool. The disjunctive definition is sufficient to define the species, if it is, only because it is reflective of the underlying structure. The theories, which back up some generalizations and not others, should provide some account of the mechanisms generative of the regularities. In traditional terminology, the set of properties which justifies the use of the common term is called the nominal essence; the internal constitution which generates these manifest properties in accordance with laws is called the real essence. I am arguing, then, that the notion of a nature or essence—stripped of the metaphysical assumptions found in Plato and Aristotle's use of the concept—often plays an important explanatory function. Whether it is applicable to men and women depends on the facts about the sexes and the theories which explain the facts. However, it should be clear that the concept as I have explained it carries no evaluative implications. If a group has a distinct nature, nothing follows automatically about how its members ought or ought not to behave.

Since the concept of distinct male and female natures has been used to explain and justify distinct social roles for the sexes, the sexual differences we are concerned with are those which would be explanatory of those social roles. Some of the physical differences between the sexes are true by definition—which makes tautological talk of sex-differentiated natures based on these differences. To explain sexual/social roles from distinct natures in this sense would be an empty exercise. Therefore we are only concerned with physical differences between men and women if it can be shown that they determine or dispose men and women to their respective social roles. Now why should biological differences per se have such systematic social implications? The linkage is usually made through psychology. Those who emphasize the biological differences between the sexes as critical to their social roles and their natures usually maintain (or simply assume) that the biological differences cause psychological differences and these in turn determine their respective social roles. So what we need to find out, first of all, is whether there are psychological differences between men and women, in terms of cognitive abilities and styles and other personality characteristics, that suit them to their respective social roles, for example, that women are more nurturant than men, and therefore are the primary caretakers of their own and other peoples' children. The second question would be the source of such differences.

As we have seen, the properties that constitute the nature of a group need not be unique nor common to all its members. What we should look for as a beginning, then, are statistically significant differences between the sexes. Social scientists approach the question in this way but unfortunately they rarely go further. One problem with *only* looking for statistically significant differences is that even minute differences are statistically significant given a large enough sample. Furthermore it is a measure that is very manipulable. We also need to consider the magnitude of the differences between the sexes and the degree to which they overlap. Even more crucial, as we saw, is that the differences must be of a kind that is theoretically important. We need therefore to look for a theoretical framework in which to evaluate the data. As our discussion of taxonomy revealed, it is often impossible to tell what differences are important without a theory. A new theory can even change our minds about what needs to be explained. Newtonian theory, for example, showed that certain kinds of unaccelerated motion, such as a passenger in a car continuing to move when the car stops suddenly, do not need an explanation, as had previously been supposed. This is one of the reasons that after determining what if any psychological differences there are between the sexes, we then need to determine their source.

The literature in the field of psychological sex differences is actually quite confusing because the experts disagree. However, if we examine the literature we can arrive at conclusions that are fairly reliable. One of the most recent and authoritative books in the field, often cited by feminists, is *The Psychology of Sex Differences* by Eleanor Maccoby and Carol Jacklin, which attempts an exhaustive analysis of the research in the field, with an emphasis on the developmental literature. According to their results, there are fewer psychological differences between men and women than commonly believed (and fewer still that appear to be biologically based). Among the beliefs about sex differences that they conclude to be unfounded are: that girls are more "social" and more "suggestible"

than boys, that girls have lower self-esteem and lack achievement motivation, that girls are better at rote learning while boys are more analytic
and better at tasks requiring higher cognitive processing. The areas of
alleged psychological sex differences that they judge to be, at present,
open questions, either because of insufficient evidence or unclear results,
are the following: (1) tactile sensitivity, (2) fear, timidity, anxiety, (3)
activity level, (4) competitiveness, (5) dominance, (6) compliance, (7)
nurturance and "maternal" behavior. The alleged sex differences that they
find to be fairly well established are that girls have greater verbal ability
while boys have greater visual/spatial and also mathematical ability
(though this did not show up until age 12–13) and that males are more
"prepared for" aggression. Except for this greater "preparedness" for
aggression in boys, their findings simply show that with respect to a few
traits more men than women have the trait to a higher degree than most
people do (or vice versa). This allows that some women have as much or
more of it than any man, and even that a majority of the group may lack
the trait found more frequently among their group.

Feminists might feel vindicated by these results, but they should be
somewhat surprised too. It would be naive and idealistic to think that the
differences in opportunities, expectations, socialization, and, in general,
the social environment in which boys and girls and men and women live
and function would have so little effect. And in fact there seem to be very
good reasons for being skeptical about Maccoby and Jacklin's conclusions. Another expert in the field, Jeanne Block, points out that their conclusions conflict with other surveys of the research in the field and raises
very serious questions about their methodology and the evidential support for their conclusions.

One of the most interesting problems that Block points out is that Maccoby and Jacklin concentrate on sex differences in the performance of
various tasks and ignore the interrelationships between intellectual performance and personality characteristics. These interrelationships are
critical in understanding motivation, and there is much evidence that the
differences in how the traits are linked together in the sexes are more
important than the differences in average scores on various tests.
Achievement motivation in girls brings out the importance of this point.
Females appear to have greater needs to be close to people than males.
Conflict between these needs and achievement needs cuts into achievement, and since this conflict will occur more frequently in girls, this will
reduce their achievement. Girls would rather "lose the game than lose the
man." However, level of achievement is not the only factor to consider

because even when, at younger ages, achievement is the same or higher in girls, "it appears that female achievement behavior . . . is motivated by a desire for love rather than mastery."

Most crucial for the concerns of this paper is the criticism that Maccoby and Jacklin's results are based predominantly on pre-adolescent children. Breaking down their results into different age groups, one finds that the percentage of studies in which there are clear and significant sex differences increases significantly with older age groups, especially beginning with adolescence, and this accords with other studies that show personality differences between the sexes increasing with age. All in all, then, it seems that there probably are greater personality differences between the sexes than Maccoby and Jacklin conclude, particularly among the age groups most relevant to our examination of the social roles of men and women.

The next question to consider is the source of the psychological differences between men and women. Hoffman's research suggests that many have their origins in differences in childrearing practices. However, she and others who want to argue that the psychological differences between men and women are due to differences in their socialization and in the social contexts in which they find themselves have insufficient research to appeal to. This neglect of social context is not only an obstacle to discovering the aetiology of psychological sex differences but may also lead to incorrect assessment of the facts. Studies of males and females in artificial contexts (like most of Maccoby and Jacklin's data), may yield results that are not predictive of their feelings and behavior in ordinary life where they find themselves in very different social contexts. Studies of men and women in actual social contexts would likely show greater differences between the sexes. (One reason why there are so many inconsistent findings in this area might be the different contexts in which the studies were done.)

Actually it is not only the social approach to aetiology which suffers from inadequate research. As indicated earlier, there is a prevailing hostility within academic research psychology to any theoretical explanatory framework. Research psychologists do not try to determine cause and effect; they only look for statistical relationships. Longitudinal studies, more relevant to establishing cause and effect, are also more costly and more speculative. This empiricist bias obviously makes it very difficult to determine an explanation for relationships they discover.

Given this state of the research, any position on the aetiology of psychological sex differences is necessarily somewhat speculative. Although serious questions have been raised as to the likelihood that any specific and variable human behavioral traits are under genetic control, I will ignore this general question about sociobiology. With respect to psychological sex differences in particular, there are a number of findings and arguments which strongly suggest that social factors are far more important determinants than biological ones: (1) Black males and white females, different biologically but with similar social handicaps, are similar in: patterns of achievement scores, fear of success, and conformity and perceptual judgment; (2) Protestant, Jewish and Catholic women (who do not differ biologically) nevertheless experience significant differences in menstrual discomfort. (3) The same physiological state can yield very different emotional states and behavior depending on the social situation. Adrenalin produces a physiological state very much like that present in extreme fear, yet subjects injected with it became euphoric when around another person who acted euphoric and very angry when around another person who acted very angry. Thus even if sex hormonal differences between men and women affect brain functioning, as some psychologists contend, it would not follow that there necessarily would be consistent emotional and behavioral differences between men and women. (4) Different behavioral propensities, thought by many to be biologically based, disappear given certain social conditions. In one study, both sexes were rewarded for aggressive behavior, and the sex differences disappeared. (5) Studies of hermaphrodites show that the crucial variable determining their gender identity is neither chromosomal sex nor hormones administered pre- or postnatally but "the consistency of the experiences of being reared as feminine, especially in the early years." (6) The studies of psychological sex differences are based overwhelmingly on white middle class Americans living in college towns. The generalizability of these findings cannot be assumed, as evidenced by the differences between whites and blacks discussed above. Moreover, anthropology reveals significant differences in sex roles in different cultures. Although rigorous cross-cultural psychological research has not been done, it appears that the personality differences between the sexes also show some cross-cultural differences. If there is any connection between sex roles and psychological traits (whatever the direction of the causation), then one would expect further research to reveal that psychological sex differences vary cross-culturally. In the absence of a biological explanation, a variation according to culture strongly suggests that there is a social explanation.

The above points seem to offer dramatic evidence in favor of environmental factors as the *primary* determinants of psychological differences. There certainly does not seem to be any direct link between biological and psychological factors. In addition, there is a general methodological argument in favor of taking environmental factors as decisive. It can be summed up as follows: "Although future research may uncover important biological factors, the present data give more than sufficient evidence that environmental shaping of sex differentiated behavior does exist. At this time it seems evident that the environment in which all American children mature clearly projects sex role stereotypes. These stereotypic expectations and the differential responses they elicit are sufficiently clear and unambiguous to account for the cognitive and personality differences in children that ultimately lead to the different roles that they fulfill." Much the same argument, using the principle of methodological simplicity, is made by J. S. Mill in *The Subjection of Women,* where he argues that there is no basis for talking about the nature of men and women so long as they have only been in the present relations to each other. I would concur with this opinion and thus conclude that the most reasonable position at present is that psychological differences between the sexes are most probably overwhelmingly social in origin.

By "social" I simply mean "not biological." Such factors could include family structure, organization of the economy, and innumerable more specific factors. It is important to note that if psychological differences between the sexes do owe much to family structure, that is, to the fact that women are the primary child rearers, it does not follow that the biological (reproductive) differences between the sexes are the real cause of the psychological differences. Women's ability to bear children does not automatically determine that they are the primary rearers of children. The reproductive differences between the sexes, just because they are universal, cannot explain the social and historical variations in the personalities and roles of men and women. The *significance* of the biological differences depends on social, historical facts, and, moreover, is maintained in every society by complicated social practices.

Consider this analogous example. Suppose that the division of slaves into house and field workers was based entirely on the slaves' size and strength, bigger and stronger slaves becoming field workers, smaller and weaker ones becoming house workers. It is well known that there were differences in attitudes and, to some extent, personality between house and field slaves (so-called "house niggers" and "field niggers"). What was the cause of these differences? Most writers point to the differences in work, working conditions and social relations of house and field slaves.

If different social conditions would have produced different psychological results, then it would be mistaken to point to the physical differences as the cause—even though they were the basis of their being in their respective social conditions.

It seems then that there probably are not differences in male and female natures—so long as natures are understood as biologically based and immutable. However, this inference depends on certain equations and contrasts that are usually presupposed in this discussion. The natural is contrasted with the social and the former is taken to be biological in origin. What's biological/natural is taken to be inevitable and what's social in origin is taken to be alterable. These assumptions are found in both popular and academic discussions of the issue, e.g., in traditional philosophical theories of essence which exclude socially variant properties as essential.

These assumptions cannot go unquestioned. Our discussion of taxonomy shows how mistaken is the assumption that the biological is unchangeable. In rejecting static essentialism and trying to fit classifications into evolutionary theory, taxonomists have rejected the equation of the natural with the unchangeable. That things change is built into nature, although, of course, until recently the big changes have been quite slow. Not only do biological facts undergo slow change on their own, but they can be changed or their results affected by social conditions and by deliberate human action. For example: the disadvantages of people with Pku deficiency can be removed by human action. We have just discussed other examples of this. So even if the differences between men and women were based more in biology than they seem to be, it would not make those differences inevitable. They could still be outweighed by deliberate human action and by social conditions, e.g., by altering childrearing practices. Therefore whether the differences between men and women are primarily biological or social in origin need not have the momentous importance it is usually assumed to have by people on both sides of the question.

If there is not in fact such a sharp contrast between what is biologically based and what is socially based then there is less reason to maintain a sharp conceptual contrast between what is natural and what is social in origin. Nor should it be assumed that what is natural is inevitable and immutable. This is not true of biological facts, as we have just seen, and if species can be understood as evolving sorts of things, there seems no reason to assume that natures must be unchanging. More precisely, if the classes of organisms classified as a particular species can change to the point where they should be classified as belonging to another species, then why should it be understood as having a different nature? If the underlying genetic basis of the classification into species can change, why can't natures themselves change? In other words, even if natures are taken to be biological in origin there seems little basis for the assumption that natures are unchanging.

Moreover there seems no reason to assume that natures must be exclusively biological. I argued earlier that natures should be understood as underlying structures that explain a range of behavior. What kinds of structures these are depends on the behavior and the organism we are seeking to explain. While human beings are undeniably biological beings they are also social beings with a history. Their biological characteristics have evolved somewhat but their social and cultural characteristics have evolved more rapidly and to a much greater extent. If we are concerned with human beings as distinct from other biological beings, then their natures are biological. But if we are concerned with humans as social beings, then their natures, i.e., the underlying structures that explain their behavior—must be understood as socially constituted and historically evolving. Hence social changes could cause changes in natures even if they had no biological effect. This brings out the point that there are many levels of generating structures, many levels of explanation appropriate to human beings. If one accepts the view that freedom and determinism are not necessarily incompatible, then this account does not deny human freedom; it simply makes clear the constraints within which human agency functions. To what extent people are free depends on the extent to which they can be said to be self-determining. And this depends on the kinds of explanations, the kinds of determining structures of their behavior.

A similar distinction to that just made for human beings can be made for men and women. The distinction between males and females is a biological one. Hence the nature of a woman, *qua* female, is biological. However, the categories men and women are also social categories— what is called gender. Hence men and women, *qua* social beings, might have distinct natures which would be explanatory of the sex related differences in behavior. As we saw, natures in the biological sense cannot by themselves explain sexual/social roles. If the sex differences in personality and cognitive traits discussed earlier are primarily social in origin the natures which generate and explain them would be primarily social in origin. However, this is all hypothetical. As we saw earlier, in the absence of a theoretical framework it is impossible to determine whether the psychological differences between men and women are sufficiently important to constitute differences in natures.

To clarify how a theoretical framework could be applied to help resolve this question I will discuss the example of the Marxist theory of historical materialism which accords fairly well with the methodology set out earlier in the paper. Marx argued vehemently against theories of a fixed, trans-historical human nature, offering instead a social and historical account. There are few transhistorical features of human beings, he maintained, and those there are—basic needs and capacities—are transformed throughout history and hence are in part socially constituted. "Hunger is hunger but the hunger gratified by cooked meat eaten with a knife and fork is a different hunger from that which bolts down raw meat with the aid of hand, nail and tooth." These human needs are expressed, shaped, and even created through the activity of satisfying needs, that is, through labor. Because the labor of society is institutionalized into sets of social practices and social relations, Marx says that by their labor people are thereby producing their whole life. Although biological structures make possible the forms of human labor, they do not determine a particular form as the biology of other animals does. Given that on Marx's theory labor is the key to an explanation of social life and social change—which was his concern—he emphasized the characteristic form of labor rather than the biology. The differing forms of human labor (and the resultant social practices and institutions) change the mental and physical capacities of human beings. Although there will be some transhistorical features of human beings, there will also then be certain characteristic differences in the psycho-physical structures of people who do very different sorts of labor in different modes of production. These structures would generate and explain a wide range of human behavior within that mode of production which the transhistorical features would not do. These psycho-physical structures would constitute the nature of humans *qua* social beings. Although there would be certain common features, these structures as a whole vary from one mode of production to another. Hence there is no transhistorical human nature. However there would be historically specific forms of human nature, that is, human nature specific to feudalism, to capitalism, to socialism, and so on.

This approach can be applied to particular social groups, such as women, as well as to human beings. If particular social groups do labor that is sufficiently different as to generate distinct social relations, practices and institutions associated with that labor, then they probably have distinct natures as well. There will probably be generalizations subsumable under a theory that would explain much of the group's behavior. Women appear to fit this condition. There are several levels of generalizations (sociological, psychological . . .) distinctive of women which are relevant—both as cause and as effect—to their distinct social roles. Using a Marxist theoretical framework in which to evaluate the sexual differences, we would look to see whether they are connected to the different sorts of labor women do in society and the different social relations this puts them in. Although much more investigation needs to be done, particularly cross-cultural research, there is a lot of evidence that this is so. Despite the variations, there is and has always been a sexual division of labor in which women have primary responsibility for childcare and most of the everyday household work, whatever else they do as well. In a society with a significantly different sexual division of labor, this theory implies that other differing generalizations would be true of men and women and where there was no sexual division of labor, there would likely be few or no non-accidental generalizations true of women and not men—other than biological ones, of course, and fewer perhaps of these. The generalizations true of women and not men describe behavioral dispositions reflective of specific cognitive/affective structures found more often among women which generate the different sets of traits found under different conditions. These structures would constitute the distinctive natures of women as social beings.

Much more work is necessary before we can determine whether men and women have distinct social natures. We would need to establish the validity of a particular theoretical framework and do the research dictated by that framework. In the Marxist case we would need to establish both that the sexual differences are due to the sexual division of labor and that this theoretical framework is a valid one. The point of the excursion into Marxist theory was simply to illustrate how a theoretical framework could lead to the conclusion that there are sex-differentiated natures which are social in origin. This question should be pursued with other theories as well.

Suppose men and women do have distinct natures in this social sense— whatever the theoretical grounding. What follows? Well, first of all it is important to see that many of the implications usually thought to follow do not follow when natures are understood in the sense I have explained. This nature is not fixed and inevitable; natures can change. The crucial determinants are social, not biological. That there is a distinct women's nature in this sense would not entail that every woman has this nature. If we recall that most species names only admit of disjunctive definitions we see that there need not be any one trait that is universally more common to women than to men. There could be a common core of psychological traits found more among women than men around the world, but women of different cultures or subcultures have different subsets of this common core of traits. This would make the concept of women's (social) nature a cluster concept, as are most "natural kinds" concepts. Although probably very few women would have none of the traits generated by the distinctive cognitive/affective structures, some might have them to only a minimal degree. Individual men could have more of this women's nature than do some women. Thus some one might be biologically female but not share the gender of other females. This is because one is a biological category, the other a social category. Even women who have this nature fully do not necessarily have more in common with other such women than with any man. This women's nature is only one aspect of her individual human nature and is not necessarily more determinant than all the other factors, individually much less collectively. Furthermore, and perhaps most important, the statement that women have a distinct nature in this sense has no evaluative implications. Nothing follows about how they ought or ought not to live or how society ought to be structured. This does not logically follow from the traditional view of natures either, but it is a more plausible conclusion to draw, given that if natures are immutable, they certainly set severe constraints on possible social arrangements. Moreover, if women live and become a different way, they will not be violating their nature; their nature will simply have changed. In fact we could predict that new social conditions would redefine women's nature. Less oppressive conditions would develop potentialities presently unrealized. It is quite likely that under some social conditions there would be no sex-differentiated natures.

Given all these disclaimers, given all the ways in which my sense of a women's nature differs from the usual meaning, a reasonable objection might be that I should not call this a nature; in fact, given the sexist associations of most such talk, it is positively dangerous to do so. I agree that the term could be misleading and even dangerous in certain contexts, but "nature" is also a technical, theory-laden term that is useful in summing up certain relationships. To summarize the conditions under which I think it would be useful to employ the term about women (and men): (1) there is a cluster of traits that women tend to have more than men which are systematically related to one another and which are important in explaining a wide range of their behavior; (thus not every factor explanatory of women's behavior would be part of a women's nature); (2) it seems probable that there are certain psychic structures distinctive of the sexes which generate these traits; and (3) these sexual differences can in turn be explained within a broader theoretical framework which can also explain where women differ from one another as well as where they are similar. If these conditions are met, then talk of women's (and men's) natures is a way of bringing out the importance that a person's sex, thus far in history, has tended to have for their personality and behavior. Although the term itself is not important, this fact is important and is given its due prominence if the term is used. If "nature" is understood as a theory-laden term, then talk of women's nature carries the implications of that theory. I would argue that if the theory were adequate, the concept of a woman's nature would refer to something dynamic rather than static, primarily social/historical in origin rather than innate, and so on. If understood correctly, then, the concept does have a function and need not be misleading or dangerous.

Steven Rose,
Richard Lewontin,
and Leon J. Kamin

The emergence in the 1970s of a new wave of evolutionary thinking about human nature, especially in the sociobiological theorizing of E. O. Wilson, stimulated a heated controversy that was as
much political as scientific.

In 1984 Steven Rose, Richard Lewontin, and Leon J. Kamin—
professors respectively at the Open University in England, at Harvard, and at Princeton—jointly authored a book entitled *Not in
Our Genes: Biology, Ideology and Human Nature*. In this they
made a systematic assault on what they saw as the pernicious doctrines of reductionism and biological determinism. Included
below is the programmatic opening chapter of their book. As open
supporters of left-wing political views, they argued that much of
what was being presented as neutral, objective biological science
was really right-wing ideology.

The reader should try to decide for himself or herself how far
this charge applies to Wilson's sociobiological approach, or to
more recent evolutionary theorizing (exemplified by the reading
from Ridley that follows). The issues here are tricky. What exactly
is the status of the seven propositions—listed under bullet heads in
the reading below—which Rose and colleagues set out to rebut?
Are they empirical claims about contingent facts, to be confirmed
or disconfirmed by the methods of science? It is not clear that they

are. What sort of claims are being made, then? And what counts for or against them? Tricky questions in the philosophy of science arise here.

Also to be recommended from *Not in Our Genes* is the survey of evidence about supposed racial differences from Chapter 5 ("Human 'racial' differentiation is, indeed, only skin deep. Any use of racial categories must take its justification from some other source than biology" [p. 127]); the more extended treatment of alleged differences between the sexes and diagnosis of "patriarchal science" in Chapter 6; and the critical analysis of E. O. Wilson's sociobiological approach in Chapter 9.

Not in Our Genes: Biology, Ideology and Human Nature

The authors of *Not in Our Genes* are respectively an evolutionary geneticist, a neurobiologist, and a psychologist. Over the past decade and a half we have watched with concern the rising tide of biological determinist writing, with its increasingly grandiose claims to be able to locate the causes of the inequalities of status, wealth, and power between classes, genders, and races in Western society in a reductionist theory of human nature. Each of us has been engaged for much of this time in research, writing, speaking, teaching, and public political activity in opposition to the oppressive forms in which determinist ideology manifests itself. We share a commitment to the prospect of the creation of a more socially just—a socialist—society. And we recognize that a critical science is an integral part of the struggle to create that society, just as we also believe that the social function of much of today's science is to hinder the creation of that society by acting to preserve the interests of the dominant class, gender, and race. This belief—in the possibility of a critical and liberatory science—is why we have each in our separate ways and to varying degrees been involved in the development of what has become known over the 1970s and 1980s, in the United States and Britain, as the radical science movement.

The need was, we felt, for a systematic exploration of the scientific and

From *Not in Our Genes: Biology, Ideology and Human Nature,* Steven Rose, Richard Lewontin, and Leon J. Kamin, © Pantheon 1984, Penguin 1984.

social roots of biological determinism, an analysis of its present-day social functions, and an exposure of its scientific pretensions. More than that, though, it was also necessary to offer a perspective on what biology and psychology can offer as an alternative, a liberatory, view of the "nature of human nature." Hence, *Not in Our Genes.*

The New Right and the Old Biological Determinism

The start of the decade of the 1980s was symbolized, in Britain and the United States, by the coming to power of new conservative governments; and the conservatism of Margaret Thatcher and Ronald Reagan marks in many ways a decisive break in the political consensus of liberal conservatism that has characterized governments in both countries for the previous twenty years or more. It represents the expression of a newly coherent and explicit conservative ideology* often described as the New Right.

New Right ideology has developed in Europe and North America in response to the gathering social and economic crises of the past decade. Abroad, in Africa, Asia, and Latin America, there have been struggles against nationalist forces determined to throw off the yoke of political and economic exploitation and colonialism. At home, there has been increasing unemployment, relative economic decline, and the rise of new and turbulent social movements. During the sixties and early seventies, Europe and North America experienced an upsurge of new movements, some of which were quite revolutionary: struggles of shop-floor workers against meritocratic ruling elites, blacks against white racism, women against patriarchy, students against educational authoritarianism, welfare clients against the welfare bureaucrats. The New Right criticizes the liberal response to these challenges of the previous decades, the steady increase in state intervention, and the growth of large institutions, result-

---

*We should make it clear that we use the term *ideology* here and throughout this book with a precise meaning. Ideologies are the ruling ideas of a particular society at a particular time. They are ideas that express the "naturalness" of any existing social order and help maintain it:

> The ideas of the ruling class are in every epoch the ruling ideas; i.e. the class which is the ruling material force of society is at the same time its ruling intellectual force. The class which has the means of material production at its disposal has control at the same time over the means of mental production, so that thereby, generally speaking, the ideas of those who lack the means of mental production are subject to it. The ruling ideas are nothing more than the ideal expression of the dominant material relationships. [Marx].

ing in individuals losing control over their own lives, and hence an erosion of the traditional values of self-reliance which the New Right regards as characterizing the Victorian laissez-faire economy. This movement has been strengthened, in the later seventies and eighties, by the fact that liberalism has fallen into a self-confessed disarray, leaving the ideological battlefield relatively open to the New Right.

The response of the liberal consensus to challenges to its institutions has always been the same: an increase in interventive programs of social amelioration; of projects in education, housing, and inner-city renewal. By contrast, the New Right diagnoses the liberal medicine as merely adding to the ills by progressively eroding the "natural" values that had characterized an earlier phase of capitalist industrial society. In the words of the conservative theoretician Robert Nisbet, it is a reaction against the present-day "erosion of traditional authority in kinship, locality, culture, language, school, and other elements of the social fabric."

But New Right ideology goes further than mere conservatism and makes a decisive break with the concept of an organic society whose members have reciprocal responsibilities. Underlying its *cri de coeur* about the growth in state power and the decline in authority—underlying even the monetarism of Milton Friedman—is a philosophical tradition of individualism, with its emphasis on the priority of the individual over the collective. That priority is seen as having both a moral aspect, in which the rights of individuals have absolute priority over the rights of the collectivity—as, for example, the right to destroy forests by clear-cutting in order to maximize immediate profit—and an ontological aspect, where the collectivity is nothing more than the sum of the individuals that make it up. And the roots of this methodological individualism lie in a view of human nature which it is the main purpose of this book to challenge.

Philosophically this view of human nature is very old; it goes back to the emergence of bourgeois society in the seventeenth century and to Hobbes's view of human existence as a *bellum omnium contra omnes,* a war of all against all, leading to a state of human relations manifesting competitiveness, mutual fear, and the desire for glory. For Hobbes, it followed that the purpose of social organization was merely to regulate these inevitable features of the human condition. And Hobbes's view of the human condition derived from his understanding of human biology; it was biological inevitability that made humans what they were. Such a belief encapsulates the twin philosophical stances with which this book is concerned, and to which, in the pages that follow, we will return again and again.

The first is *reductionism*—the name given to a set of general methods and modes of explanation both of the world of physical objects and of human societies. Broadly, reductionists try to explain the properties of complex wholes—molecules, say, or societies—in terms of the units of which those molecules or societies are composed. They would argue, for example, that the properties of a protein molecule could be uniquely determined and predicted in terms of the properties of the electrons, protons, etc., of which its atoms are composed. And they would also argue that the properties of a human society are similarly no more than the sums of the individual behaviors and tendencies of the individual humans of which that society is composed. Societies are "aggressive" because the individuals who compose them are "aggressive," for instance. In formal language, reductionism is the claim that the compositional units of a whole are ontologically prior to the whole that the units comprise. That is, the units and their properties exist *before* the whole, and there is a chain of causation that runs from the units to the whole.

The second stance is related to the first; indeed, it is in some senses a special case of reductionism. It is that of *biological determinism.* Biological determinists ask, in essence, Why are individuals as they are? Why do they do what they do? And they answer that human lives and actions are inevitable consequences of the biochemical properties of the cells that make up the individual; and these characteristics are in turn uniquely determined by the constituents of the genes possessed by each individual. Ultimately, all human behavior—hence all human society—is governed by a chain of determinants that runs from the gene to the individual to the sum of the behaviors of all individuals. The determinists would have it, then, that human nature is fixed by our genes. The good society is either one in accord with a human nature to whose fundamental characteristics of inequality and competitiveness the ideology claims privileged access, or else it is an unattainable utopia because human nature is in unbreakable contradiction with an arbitrary notion of the good derived without reference to the facts of physical nature. The causes of social phenomena are thus located in the biology of the individual actors in a social scene, as when we are informed that the cause of the youth riots in many British cities in 1981 must be sought in "a poverty of aspiration and of expectation created by family, school, environment, and genetic inheritance."

What is more, biology, or "genetic inheritance," is always invoked as an expression of inevitability: What is biological is given by nature and proved by science. There can be no argument with biology, for it is unchangeable, a position neatly exemplified in a television interview given by British Minister for Social Services Patrick Jenkin in 1980 on working mothers:

> Quite frankly, I don't think mothers have the same right to work as fathers. If the Lord had intended us to have equal rights to go to work, he wouldn't have created men and women. These are biological facts, young children do depend on their mothers.

The use of the double legitimation of science and god is a bizarre but not uncommon feature of New Right ideology: the claim to a hotline to the deepest sources of authority about human nature.

The reductionist and biological determinist propositions that we shall examine and criticize in the pages of this book are:

- Social phenomena are the sums of the behaviors of *individuals.*
- These behaviors can be treated as objects, that is, *reified* into properties located in the brain of particular individuals.
- The reified properties can be measured on some sort of scale so that individuals can be ranked according to the amounts they possess.
- Population norms for the properties can be established: Deviations from the norm for any individual are *ab*normalities that may reflect medical problems for which the individual must be treated.
- The reified and medicalized properties are *caused* by events in the brains of individuals—events that can be given anatomical localizations and are associated with changed quantities of particular biochemical substances.
- The changed concentrations of these biochemicals may be partitioned between genetic and environmental causes; hence the "degree of inheritance" or *heritability* of differences may be measured.
- Treatment for abnormal amounts of the reified properties may be either to eliminate undesirable genes (eugenics, genetic engineering, etc.); or to find specific drugs ("magic bullets") to rectify the biochemical abnormalities or to excise or stimulate particular brain regions so as to eliminate the site of the undesirable behavior. Some lip service may be paid to supplementary environmental intervention, but the primary prescription is "biologized."

Working scientists may believe, or conduct experiments, based on one or more of these propositions without feeling themselves to be full-fledged determinists in the sense that we use the term; nonetheless, adherence to this general analytical approach characterizes determinist methodology.

Biological determinism *(biologism)* has been a powerful mode of explaining the observed inequalities of status, wealth, and power in contemporary industrial capitalist societies, and of defining human "universals" of behavior as natural characteristics of these societies. As such, it has been gratefully seized upon as a political legitimator by the New Right, which finds its social nostrums so neatly mirrored in nature; for if these inequalities are biologically determined, they are therefore inevitable and immutable. What is more, attempts to remedy them by social means, as in the prescriptions of liberals, reformists, and revolutionaries, "go against nature." Racism, Britain's National Front tells us, is a product of our "selfish genes." Nor are such political dicta confined to the ideologues: Time and again, despite their professed belief that their science is "above mere human politics" (to quote Oxford sociobiologist Richard Dawkins), biological determinists deliver themselves of social and political judgments. One example must suffice for now: Dawkins himself, in his book *The Selfish Gene,* which is supposed to be a work on the genetic basis of evolution and which is used as a textbook in American university courses on the evolution of behavior, criticizes the "unnatural" welfare state where

> we have abolished the family as a unit of economic self-sufficiency and substituted the state. But the privilege of guaranteed support for children should not be abused. . . . Individual humans who have more children than they are capable of raising are probably too ignorant in most cases to be accused of conscious malevolent exploitation. Powerful institutions and leaders who deliberately encourage them to do so seem to me less free from suspicion.

The point is not merely that biological determinists are often somewhat naive political and social philosophers. One of the issues with which we must come to grips is that, despite its frequent claim to be neutral and objective, science is not and cannot be above "mere" human politics. The complex interaction between the evolution of scientific theory and the evolution of social order means that very often the ways in which scientific research asks its questions of the human and natural worlds it proposes to explain are deeply colored by social, cultural, and political biases.

Our book has a two fold task: we are concerned first with an explanation of the origins and social functions of biological determinism in general—the task of the next two chapters—and second with a systematic examination and exposure of the emptiness of its claims vis-à-vis the nature and limits of human society with respect to equality, class, race, sex, and "mental disorder." We shall illustrate this through a study of specific themes: IQ theory, the assumed basis of differences in "ability" between sexes and races, the medicalization of political protest, and, finally, the overall conceptual strategy of evolutionary and adaptationist explanation offered by sociobiology in its modern forms. Above all, this means an examination of the claims of biological determinism regarding the "nature of human nature."

In examining these claims and in exposing the pseudoscientific, ideological, and often just simply methodologically inadequate findings of biological determinism, it is important for us, and for our readers, to be clear about the position we ourselves take.

Critics of biological determinism have frequently drawn attention to the ideological role played by apparently scientific conclusions about the human condition that seem to flow from biological determinism. That, despite their pretensions, biological determinists are engaged in making political and moral statements about human society, and that their writings are seized upon as ideological legitimators, says nothing, in itself, about the scientific merits of their claims. Critics of biological determinism are often accused of merely disliking its political conclusions. We have no hesitation in agreeing that we do dislike these conclusions; we believe that it is possible to create a better society than the one we live in at present; that inequalities of wealth, power, and status are not "natural" but socially imposed obstructions to the building of a society in which the creative potential of all its citizens is employed for the benefit of all.

We view the links between values and knowledge as an integral part of doing science in this society at all, whereas determinists tend to deny that such links exist—or claim that if they do exist they are exceptional pathologies to be eliminated. To us such an assertion of the separation of fact from value, of practice from theory, "science" from "society" is itself part of the fragmentation of knowledge that reductionist thinking sustains and which has been part of the mythology of the last century of "scientific advance" (see Chapters 3 and 4). However, the least of our tasks here is that of criticizing the social implications of biological determinism, as if the broad claims of biological determinism could be upheld. Rather, our major goal is to show that the world is not to be understood as biological determinism would have it be, and that, as a way of explaining the world, biological determinism is fundamentally flawed.

Note that we say "the world," for another misconception is that the criticism of biological determinism applied only to its conclusions about human societies, while what it says about nonhuman animals is more or less valid. Such a view is often expressed—for instance about E. O. Wilson's book *Sociobiology: The New Synthesis,* which we discuss at length in Chapter 9. Its liberal critics claim that the problem with *Sociobiology* lies only in the first and last chapters, where the author discusses human sociobiology; what's in between is true. Not so, in our view: what biological determinism has to say about human society is more wrong than what it says about other aspects of biology because its simplifications and misstatements are the more gross. But this is not because it has developed a theory applicable only to nonhuman animals; the method and theory are fundamentally flawed whether applied to the United States or Britain today, or to a population of savanna-dwelling baboons or Siamese fighting fish.

There is no mystical and unbridgeable gulf between the forces that shape human society and those that shape the societies of other organisms; biology is indeed relevant to the human condition, although the form and extent of its relevance is far less obvious than the pretensions of biological determinism imply. The antithesis often presented as an opposition to biological determinism is that biology stops at birth, and from then on culture supervenes. This antithesis is a type of cultural determinism we would reject, for the cultural determinists identify narrow (and exclusive) causal chains in society which are in their own way reductionist as well. Humanity cannot be cut adrift from its own biology, but neither is it enchained by it.

Indeed, one may see in some of the appeal of biological determinist and New Right writing a reassertion of the "obvious" against the very denial of biology that has characterized some of the utopian writings and hopes of the revolutionary movements of the past decade. The post-1968 New Left in Britain and the United States has shown a tendency to see human nature as almost infinitely plastic, to deny biology and acknowledge only social construction. The helplessness of childhood, the existential pain of madness, the frailties of old age were all transmuted to mere labels reflecting disparities in power. But this denial of biology is so contrary to actual lived experience that it has rendered people the more ideologically vulnerable to the "commonsense" appeal of reemerging biological determinism. Indeed, we argue in Chapter 3 that such cultural determinism can be as oppressive in obfuscating real knowledge about the complexity of the world we live in as is biological determinism. We do not offer in this book a blueprint or a catalogue of certainties; our task, as we see it, is to point the way toward an integrated understanding of the relationship between the biological and the social.

We describe such an understanding as dialectical, in contrast to reductionist. Reductionist explanation attempts to derive the properties of wholes from intrinsic properties of parts, properties that exist apart from and before the parts are assembled into complex structures. It is characteristic of reductionism that it assigns relative weights to different partial causes and attempts to assess the importance of each cause by holding all others constant while varying a single factor. Dialectical explanations, on the contrary, do not abstract properties of parts in isolation from their associations in wholes but see the properties of parts as arising out of their associations. That is, according to the dialectical view, the properties of parts and wholes codetermine each other. The properties of individual human beings do not exist in isolation but arise as a consequence of social life, yet the nature of that social life is a consequence of our being human and not, say, plants. It follows, then, that dialectical explanation contrasts with cultural or dualistic modes of explanation that separate the world into different types of phenomena—culture and biology, mind and body—which are to be explained in quite different and nonoverlapping ways.

Dialectical explanations attempt to provide a coherent, unitary, but nonreductionist account of the material universe. For dialectics the universe is unitary but always in change; the phenomena we can see at any instant are parts of processes, processes with histories and futures whose paths are not uniquely determined by their constituent units. Wholes are composed of units whose properties may be described, but the interaction of these units in the construction of the wholes generates complexities that result in products qualitatively different from the component parts. Think, for example, of the baking of a cake: the taste of the product is the result of a complex interaction of components—such as butter, sugar, and flour—exposed for various periods to elevated temperatures; it is not dissociable into such-or-such a percent of flour, such-or-such of butter, etc., although each and every component (and their development over time at a raised temperature) has its contribution to make to the final product. In a world in which such complex developmental interactions are always occurring, history becomes of paramount importance. Where and how an organism is now is not merely dependent upon its composition at this time but upon a past that imposes contingencies on the present and future interaction of its components.

Such a world view abolishes the antitheses of reductionism and dualism; of nature/nurture or of heredity/environment; of a world in stasis whose components interact in fixed and limited ways, indeed in which change is possible only along fixed and previously definable pathways. In the chapters that follow, the explication of this position will appear in the course of the development of our opposition to biological determinism—in our analysis, for instance, of the relationship of genotype and phenotype (in Chapter 5), and of mind and brain.

Let us take just one example here, that of the relationship of the organism to its environment. Biological determinism sees organisms, human or nonhuman, as adapted by evolutionary processes to their environment, that is, fitted by the processes of genetic reshuffling, mutation, and natural selection to maximize their reproductive success in the environment in which they are born and develop; further, it sees the undoubted plasticity of organisms—especially humans—as they develop as a series of modifications imposed upon an essentially passive, recipient object by the buffeting of "the environment" to which it is exposed and to which it must adapt or perish. Against this we counterpose a view not of organism and environment insulated from one another or unidirectionally affected, but of a constant and active interpenetration of the organism with its environment. Organisms do not merely receive a given environment but actively seek alternatives or change what they find.

Put a drop of sugar solution onto a dish containing bacteria and they will actively move toward the sugar till they arrive at the site of optimum concentration, thus changing a low-sugar for a high-sugar environment. They will then actively work on the sugar molecules, changing them into other constituents, some of which they absorb, others of which they put out into the environment, thereby modifying it, often in such a way that it becomes, for example, more acid. When this happens, the bacteria move away from the highly acid region to regions of lower acidity. Here, in miniature, we see the case of an organism "choosing" a preferred environment, actively working on it and so changing it, and then "choosing" an alternative.

Or consider a bird building a nest. Straw is not part of the bird's environment unless it actively seeks it out so as to construct its nest; in doing so it changes its environment, and indeed the environment of other organisms as well. The "environment" itself is under constant modification by the activity of all the organisms within it. And to any organism, all others form part of its "environment"—predators, prey, and those that merely change the landscape it resides in.

Even for nonhumans, then, the interaction of organism and environment is far from the simplistic models offered by biological determinism. And this is much more the case for our own species. All organisms bequeath to their successors when they die a slightly changed environment; humans above all are constantly and profoundly making over their environment in such a way that each generation is presented with quite novel sets of problems to explain and choices to make; we make our own history, though in circumstances not of our own choosing.

It is precisely because of this that there are such profound difficulties with the concept of "human nature." To the biological determinists the old credo "You can't change human nature" is the alpha and omega of the explanation of the human condition. We are not concerned to deny that there *is* a "human nature," which is simultaneously biologically and socially constructed, though we find it an extraordinarily elusive concept to pin down; in our discussion on sociobiology in Chapter 9 we analyze the best list of human "universals" that protagonists of sociobiology have been able to present.

Of course there *are* human universals that are in no sense trivial: humans are bipedal; they have hands that seem to be unique among animals in their capacity for sensitive manipulation and construction of objects; they are capable of speech. The fact that human adults are almost all greater than one meter and less than two meters in height has a profound effect on how they perceive and interact with their environment. If humans were the size of ants, we would have an entirely different set of relations with the objects that constitute our world; similarly, if we had eyes that were sensitive, like those of some insects, to ultraviolet wavelengths, or if, like some fishes, we had organs sensitive to electrical fields, the range of our interactions with each other and with other organisms would doubtless be very different. If we had wings, like birds, we would construct a very different world.

In this sense, the environments that human organisms seek and those they create are in accord with their nature. But just what does this mean? The human chromosomes may not contain the genes that, in the development of the phenotype, are associated with ultraviolet vision, or sensitivity to electrical fields, or wings. Indeed, in the last case there are structural reasons quite independent of genetic ones why organisms of the weight of humans cannot develop wings large or powerful enough to enable them to fly. And indeed, for a considerable proportion of human history it has gone against human nature to be able to do any of these things. However, as is apparent to all of us, in our present society we can do all of these things: see in the ultraviolet; detect electrical fields; fly by machine, wind, or even pedal power. It is, clearly, "in" human nature to so modify our environment that all these activities come well within our range (and hence within the range of our genotype).

Even where the acts we perform on our environment appear to be biologically equivalent, they are not necessarily socially equivalent. Hunger is hunger (the anthropologist Lévi-Strauss has made this given the basis of a complex human structural typology); yet hunger satisfied by eating raw meat with hands and fingers is quite different from that satisfied by eating cooked meat with a knife and fork. All humans are born, most procreate, all die; yet the social meanings invested in any of these acts vary profoundly from culture to culture and from context to context within a culture.

This is why about the only sensible thing to say about human nature is that it is "in" that nature to construct its own history. The consequence of the construction of that history is that one generation's limits to the nature of human nature become irrelevant to the next. Take the concept of intelligence. To an earlier generation, the capacity to perform complex long multiplication or division was laboriously acquired by children fortunate enough to go to school. Many never achieved it; they grew up lacking, for whatever reason, the ability to perform the calculations. Today, with no more than minimal training, such calculating power and considerably more are at the disposal of any five-year-old who can manipulate the buttons on a calculator. The products of one human generation's intelligence and creativity have been placed at the disposal of a subsequent generation, and the horizons of human achievement have been thereby extended. The intelligence of a school-child today, in any reasonable understanding of the term, is quite different from and in many ways much greater than that of his or her Victorian counterpart, or that of a feudal lord or of a Greek slaveowner. Its measure is itself historically contingent.

Because it is in human nature so to construct our own history, and because the construction of our history is made as much with ideas and words as with artifacts, the advocacy of biological determinist ideas, and the argument against them, are themselves part of that history. Alfred Binet, the founder of IQ testing, once protested against "the brutal pessimism" that regards a child's IQ score as a fixed measure of his or her ability, rightly seeing that to regard the child as thus fixed was to help ensure that he or she remained so. Biological determinist ideas are part of the attempt to preserve the inequalities of our society and to shape human nature in their own image. The exposure of the fallacies and political content of those ideas is part of the struggle to eliminate those inequalities and to transform our society. In that struggle we transform our own nature.

Matt Ridley

Matt Ridley did research in zoology at Oxford University, and then became a science writer and journalist. He is the author of *Warts and All,* about U.S. presidential politics, and *The Red Queen,* about the evolution of sex.

In *The Origins of Virtue* (1996) Ridley very readably and stylishly discusses human nature in the light of recent biological theory and older economic theory. The new biology of the 1960s and 70s—associated with such names as G. C. Williams, W. D. Hamilton, J. Maynard Smith, and R. Dawkins—involved the application of the mathematical theory of games to animal behavior and genetic evolution. Ridley does an excellent job of interpreting these technical topics for the nonexpert. He covers topics such as genes, division of labor, prisoner's dilemmas, altruism and reciprocity, food sharing, emotions and moral sentiments, cooperation and competition, group prejudice and war, trade, ecology, and property rights. There is perhaps some danger of misrepresenting Ridley in reprinting this final chapter without his preceding argument, which carefully analyzed both the human social instincts and the attendant dangers of genocidal tribalism. But perhaps this excerpt will tempt readers to study the rest of his book.

This selection consists of Chapter 13 of *The Origins of Virtue,* entitled "Trust: In which the author suddenly and rashly draws political lessons." Here Ridley ranges very widely (it is remarkable how many of the thinkers represented in this anthology get referred to!), and he reveals some sympathy with a certain kind of new conservatism in politics. This contrast to the left-wing sympathies of Rose, Lewontin, and Kamin reminds us—if any reminder is needed—just how controversial any supposedly scientific theorizing about human nature is likely to be. It is always difficult to be objective about ourselves, either individually or collectively.

I hope that this anthology as a whole will encourage deeper thought about how human nature has evolved in the past, and how best we can cope with our human future in the light not just of that biological knowledge, but of all other sources of wisdom.

The Origins of Virtue

Our minds have been built by selfish genes, but they have been built to be social, trustworthy and cooperative. That is the paradox this book has tried to explain. Human beings have social instincts. They come into the world equipped with predispositions to learn how to cooperate, to discriminate the trustworthy from the treacherous, to commit themselves to be trustworthy, to earn good reputations, to exchange goods and information, and to divide labour. In this we are on our own. No other species has been so far down this evolutionary path before us, for no species has built a truly integrated society except among the inbred relatives of a large family such as an ant colony. We owe our success as a species to our social instincts; they have enabled us to reap undreamt benefits from the division of labour for our masters—the genes. They are responsible for the rapid expansion of our brains in the past two million years and thence for our inventiveness. Our societies and our minds evolved together, each reinforcing trends in the other. Far from being a universal feature of animal life, as Kropotkin believed, this instinctive cooperativeness is the very hallmark of humanity and what sets us apart from other animals.

The evolutionary perspective is a long one. This book has in passing tried to nail some myths about when we adopted our cultured habits. I have argued that there was morality before the Church; trade before the state;

"Trust," from *The Origins of Virtue* by Matt Ridley. Copyright © 1996 by Matt Ridley. Used by permission of Viking Penguin, a division of Penguin Putnam, Inc.

exchange before money; social contracts before Hobbes; welfare before the rights of man; culture before Babylon; society before Greece; self-interest before Adam Smith; and greed before capitalism. These things have been expressions of human nature since deep in the hunter-gatherer Pleistocene. Some of them have roots in the missing links with other primates. Only our supreme self-importance has obscured this so far.

But self-congratulation is premature. We have as many darker as lighter instincts. The tendency of human societies to fragment into competing groups has left us with minds all too ready to adopt prejudices and pursue genocidal feuds. Also, though we may have within our heads the capacity to form a functioning society, we patently fail to use it properly. Our societies are torn by war, violence, theft, dissension and inequality. We struggle to understand why, variously apportioning blame to nature, nurture, government, greed or gods. The dawning self-awareness that this book has chronicled ought—indeed must—have some practical use. Knowing how evolution arrived at the human capacity for social trust, we can surely find out how to cure its lack. Which human institutions generate trust and which ones dissipate it?

Trust is as vital a form of social capital as money is a form of actual capital. Some economists have long recognized this. "Virtually every commercial transaction has within itself an element of trust," says the economist Kenneth Arrow. Lord Vinson, a successful British entrepreneur, cites as one of his ten commandments for success in business: "Trust everyone unless you have a reason not to." Trust, like money, can be lent ("I trust you because I trust the person who told me he trusts you"), and can be risked, hoarded or squandered. It pays dividends in the currency of more trust.

Trust and distrust feed upon each other. As Robert Putnam has argued, soccer clubs and merchant guilds have long reinforced trust in the successful north of Italy and fallen apart because of lack of trust in the more backward and hierarchical south. That is why two such similar peoples as the north Italians and the south Italians, equipped with much the same mixtures of genes, have diverged so radically simply because of a historical accident: the south had strong monarchies and godfathers; the north, strong merchant communities.

Indeed, larger parallels spring to mind. Putnam argues that the North Americans developed a successful civic-minded society because they inherited a horizontally bonded version from the particular Britons who founded their cities, while the South Americans, stuck with the nepotism, authoritarianism and clientelism of medieval Spain, fell behind. You can take this too far. Francis Fukuyama argues unconvincingly that there is a broad difference between successful economies such as America and Japan and unsuccessful ones such as France and China because of the latter's addiction to hierarchical power structures. None the less, Putnam is indisputably on to something. Social contracts between equals, generalized reciprocity between individuals and between groups—these are at the heart of the most vital of all human achievements: the creation of society.

The War of All Against All

Much of this book has been a modern rediscovery—with added genetics and mathematics—of an age-old philosophical debate, a debate known by the name "the perfectibility of man." In various guises and at various times philosophers have argued that man is basically nice if he is not corrupted, or basically nasty if he is not tamed. Most famously, the debate pits Thomas Hobbes, on the side of nastiness, against Jean-Jacques Rousseau on the side of niceness.

Hobbes, though, was not the first to argue that man is a beast whose savage nature must be tamed by social contracts. Machiavelli said much the same two centuries before ("it must needs be taken for granted that all men are wicked," he wrote). The Christian doctrine of original sin, refined by St Augustine, expressed a similar point: goodness comes as a gift from God. The Sophist philosophers of ancient Greece thought people inherently hedonistic and selfish. But it was Hobbes who made the argument political.

Hobbes's intention, writing *Leviathan* in the 1650s in the wake of a century of religious and political civil war in Europe, was to argue that strong sovereign authority was required to prevent a state of perpetual fratricidal struggle. This was an unfashionable notion, for most seventeenth-century philosophers hewed to the ideal of a bucolic state of nature, typified in the supposedly peaceful and plentiful lives of American Indians, to justify their own search for a perfectly ordered society. Hobbes turned this on its head, arguing that the state of nature was one of war, not peace.

Thomas Hobbes was Charles Darwin's direct intellectual ancestor. Hobbes (1651) begat David Hume (1739), who begat Adam Smith (1776), who begat Thomas Robert Malthus (1798), who begat Charles Darwin (1859). It was after reading Malthus that Darwin shifted from thinking about competition between groups to thinking about competition between individuals, a shift Smith had achieved in the century before. The Hobbesian diagnosis—though not the prescription—still lies at the heart of both economics and modern evolutionary biology (Smith begat Friedman; Darwin begat Dawkins). At the root of both disciplines lies the notion that, if the balance of nature was not designed from above but emerged from below, then there is no reason to think it will prove to be a harmonious whole. John Maynard Keynes would later describe *The Origin of Species* as "simply Ricardian economics couched in scientific language," and Stephen Jay Gould has said that natural selection "was essentially Adam Smith's economics read into nature." Karl Marx made much the same point: "It is remarkable," he wrote to Friedrich Engels in June 1862, "how Darwin recognises among beasts and plants his own English society with its division of labour, competition, opening up of new markets, "inventions," and the Malthusian struggle for existence. It is Hobbes' *bellum omnium contra omnes.*"

Darwin's disciple, Thomas Henry Huxley, chose exactly the same quotation from Hobbes to illustrate his argument that life is a pitiless struggle. For primitive man, he said, "life was a continual free fight, and beyond the limited and temporary relations of the family, the Hobbesian war of each against all was the normal state of existence. The human species, like others, plashed and floundered amid the general stream of evolution, keeping its head above the water as it best might, and thinking neither of whence nor whither." It was this essay that provoked Kropotkin to write *Mutual Aid.*

The argument between Huxley and Kropotkin had a personal edge. Huxley was a self-made man; Kropotkin an aristocratic revolutionary. Huxley was a meritocratic success with little time for dreamy outcast princes born in privilege; their falls from grace proved, to Huxley, their unfitness as surely as Huxley's own rise proved his fitness. "It is open to us to try our fortune; and if we avoid impending fate, there will be a certain ground for believing that we are the right people to escape. *Securus judicat orbis.*"

It was a short step from Huxley's meritocracy to the cruelty of eugenics. Evolution worked by sorting the strong from the weak, and it could be given a helping hand. Predestined not by their god but by their genes, the Edwardians came enthusiastically to the logical conclusion and began to sort the wheat from the chaff. Their successors in America and Germany committed the naturalistic fallacy, and sterilized and murdered millions of people in the belief they were thus improving the species or race. Although this project reached obscene depths under Hitler, it was widely supported, especially in the United States, by those on the left of the political spectrum, too. Indeed, Hitler was merely carrying out a genocidal policy against "inferior" incurable or reactionary tribes that Karl Marx and Friedrich Engels had advocated in 1849 and that Lenin had begun to practise as early as 1918. It is even possible that Hitler got his eugenics not from Darwin or Spencer but from Marx, whom he read carefully when in Munich in 1913 and echoed closely on the topic. Many socialists were enthusiastic about eugenics, notably H. G. Wells who said, about "black, and brown, and dirty-white, and yellow people who do not come into the new needs of efficiency" that they "will have to go."

The Hobbesian search for a perfect society ended, therefore, in the gas chambers of Auschwitz, expressing not the human instinct for cooperation but the human instinct for genocidal tribalism, the Faustian bargain that comes, as we have seen, with groupishness.

The Noble Savage

Hobbesian views prevailed in the century between 1845 and 1945. In the century before and the half century after, kinder and more Utopian views of human nature dominated political philosophy. They, too, failed but not because they exploited the darker instincts of human beings. Instead, they mistakenly exaggerated the better instincts. And in a strange way, twice these Utopian ideals foundered in the South Pacific.

Of all the eighteenth-century Utopians, Jean-Jacques Rousseau was by far the most fanciful and by far the most influential. In his *Discourse on Inequality*, published in 1755, Rousseau painted a picture of humankind as a basically virtuous creature corrupted by civilization. Rousseau's idea of the noble savage, living in a harmonious state of nature until the invention of the evils of social life and property, was part daydream (Rousseau was awkward in grand society and resented it) and part polemic. For whereas Hobbes had wanted to justify authority after a period of anarchy, Rousseau wanted to undermine a corrupt, extravagant and potent monarchy that presided over, and taxed, a miserable populace. Until the invention of property and government, he argued, people had lived lives of freedom and equality. Modern society was a natural product of history, but it was decadent and ill. (Rousseau would have been at home in the modern environmental movement.)

> Do not forget that society is natural to mankind as decrepitude is to man; that arts, laws, and governments are necessary to races as crutches are to the old; and the state of society being the extreme term at which men can arrive either sooner or later, it is not useless to show them the danger of

going too quickly, and the miseries of a condition which they mistake for perfection.

In 1768, when Rousseau's idea of the noble savage was at the height of its influence, Louis-Antoine de Bougainville discovered the island of Tahiti, named it New Cythera after the Peleponnesian isle where Aphrodite had first emerged from the sea, and compared it to the Garden of Eden. Despite Bougainville's own caution, his companions' description of the natives—beautiful, amorous, scantily clad, peaceable and wanting for nothing—caught the imagination of Paris, and of Rousseau's friend Denis Diderot in particular. Diderot wrote a fanciful supplement to Bougainville's account of his voyage in which a Tahitian sage expounds the virtues of their existence ("We are innocent; we are happy: and thou canst not but spoil our happiness. We follow the pure instinct of nature: thou hast sought to efface its character from our souls.") and a Christian chaplain is embarrassed by the generous sexual hospitality offered by Tahitian women.

James Cook visited Tahiti the next year and brought back similar reports of the plentiful, easy and strife-free life led by the islanders. They did not know shame, or hard work, or cold, or hunger. John Hawkesworth, commissioned to write up Cook's journal, laid it on thick, emphasizing especially the charms of the young ladies of Tahiti. Briefly, the South Seas were all the rage in art, in pantomime and poetry. The scorn of satirists like Samuel Johnson and Horace Walpole was ignored. The noble savage had been found in an eighteenth-century sexual fantasy.

Reaction was inevitable. On Cook's second voyage, the darker side of Tahitian life emerged: the human sacrifices, the regular practice of infanticide by a priestly caste, the vicious internecine quarrels, the rigid class hierarchy, the strict taboos on women eating in the presence of men, the incessant thievery practised by the natives upon the European's possessions, the venereal disease—probably introduced by Bougainville's men. Jean François de Galaup, Comte de La Pérouse, who explored the Pacific and vanished in 1788, was especially hurt by his own disillusionment. Before he disappeared, he wrote bitterly: "The most daring rascals of all Europe are less hypocritical than the natives of these islands. All their caresses were false." As the eighteenth century ended, with a French dictator waging war on the world and Parson Malthus persuading William Pitt that the poor laws only encouraged breeding and eventual famine, it was little wonder that the party was over in the South Pacific. Missionaries began to mobilize, intent on civilizing, or at least endowing with guilt, savages who now seemed more Hobbesian than Rousseauian.

Paradise Refound

History was to repeat itself in the South Seas. The twenty-three-year-old Margaret Mead went to Samoa in 1925 and returned, as Bougainville and Cook had returned from Tahiti nearly two hundred years before, with tales of a natural paradise free of the sins of the Western world, in which young men and young women lived easy, graceful, promiscuous lives largely free of the want, jealousy and violence that corrupted Western adolescence. Mead was a disciple of the anthropologist Franz Boas, who had reacted against an undue emphasis on eugenics in his native Germany. Boas, his face scarred from innumerable youthful duels, was not one to do things by halves. Instead of arguing that human behaviour was the product of both nature and nurture, he went to the other extreme, cultural determinism, and denied that anything but culture affected behaviour. To prove his point he needed to show the totipotency of human nature, the blank slate of John Locke. Given the right culture, he argued, we could create a society without jealousy, without love, without marriage, without hierarchy. Therefore humankind was infinitely malleable, and any Utopia was possible. To believe otherwise was irredeemably fatalist.

Mead was hailed for proving this to be more than wishful thinking. She brought back from Samoa apparently hard evidence of a society in which a different culture had produced a very different human nature. A culture of uninhibited free love among the Samoan youth prevented any adolescent angst, she argued. For fifty years Mead's Samoans stood as definitive proof of the perfectibility of man.

But like Bougainville's Tahitian mirage, Mead's vanished on closer inspection. Whereas she had spent only five months in Manu'a, where her fieldwork was carried out, and only about twelve weeks of that on the research project Boas had required her to undertake, Derek Freeman spent over six years there in the 1940s and 1960s, and he discovered that Mead had been duped by her own wishful thinking and a mischievous streak in her informants. Observed without rose-tinted spectacles by Freeman, the Samoans could be like the Tahitians Cook came to distrust on later visits, every bit as jealous, vicious and duplicitous as the rest of us. Virginity among unmarried adolescent girls was not a lightly held Christian novelty for free-loving Samoan women, but an ancient, respected cult whose violation had been punishable by death in pre-Christian days. Rape, far from being unknown, was so common that Samoa had one of the highest rates of rape in the world. Mead had let her Rousseauian preconceptions guide her, and she had missed the Hobbesian side.

Indeed, in 1987 one of Mead's chief informants came forward and admitted that she and her friend had as a prank hoaxed Mead with their accounts of their own supposedly flagrant promiscuity. As Freeman put it, "Never can giggly fibs have had such far-reaching consequences" (although there was a precedent: the French traveller Labillardière was fooled in the eighteenth century by Tongans into reciting before the Academy of Sciences in Paris a string of phrases that he thought were Tongan numerals, but were actually obscenities).

The reaction of anthropologists to Freeman's revelation was itself the perfect refutation of Mead's creed. They reacted like a tribe whose cult had been attacked and shrine desecrated, vilifying Freeman in every conceivable way except by refuting him. If even cultural anthropologists, supposedly devoted to empirical truth and cultural relativism, act like a typical tribe, then there must be a universal human nature after all. They hold that there is no such thing as human nature independent of culture. They demonstrated that there is no such thing as culture independent of human nature. The slate is not blank after all.

Margaret Mead committed, and many modern sociologists, anthropologists and psychologists continue to commit, a sort of reverse naturalistic fallacy. The naturalistic fallacy, identified by Hume and named by G. E. Moore, is to argue that what is natural is moral: deducing an "ought" from an "is." Almost all biologists who speculate about the behaviour of bipedal apes are accused by the humanitarian establishment of committing this fallacy, even if they do not (many do). But the same establishment shows no embarrassment in continually and enthusiastically committing the reverse naturalistic fallacy: arguing from ought to is. Because something ought to be, then it must be. This logic is known today as political correctness, but it was shown in the drive launched by Boas, Benedict and Mead to argue that human nature must be infinitely malleable by culture because (they thought, wrongly) the alternative is fatalism, which is unacceptable.

Mead's creed spilled over into biology. Behaviourism held that animals' brains were black boxes which relied upon pure association to learn any task with equal ease. Its prophet, B. F. Skinner, wrote a science-fiction fantasy, *Walden Two,* about a world run by people like himself. "We have no truck," says Frazier, the founder of Walden Two, "with philosophies of innate goodness—or evil either for that matter. But we do have faith in our power to change human nature."

Thus spake Lenin. The 1920s and 1930s, often seen as a time of lunatic obsession with genetic determinism, was also a time of lunatic obsession with environmental determinism: the belief that man could be remade entirely into new man just by education, propaganda and force. Under Stalin this Lockean faith in changing nature was even applied to wheat. Trofim Lysenko argued, and those who gainsaid him were shot, that wheat could be made more frost-hardy not by selection but by experience. Millions died hungry to prove him wrong. The inheritance of acquired characteristics remained an official doctrine of Soviet biology until 1964. Unlike the genetic determinism of Hitler, Stalin's environmental variety went on to infect other peoples.

In her extraordinary autobiographical account of the Chinese revolution, *Wild Swans,* Jung Chang gives the perfect example of why Communism failed because it failed to change human nature. In 1949 her mother married a young Communist official, who repeatedly refused to use his position to help her or other members of his family. He would not let her share his car on a long journey which she undertook on foot, lest it seem like favouritism; he refused to pardon a convicted counter-revolutionary guerrilla who had saved her life, because, he argued, the man had tipped her off precisely in the hope of currying favour with her husband; he demoted her by two grades in the party hierarchy just to forestall any suggestion that she had been given a higher rank than was justified; he intervened to veto his own elder brother's promotion in a tea-marketing business; again and again he refused to show a normal preference for his family, because he put the revolution first and believed that to be nice to your relatives was to discriminate against your non-relatives. He was right. Communism would have worked if there were more such men, though it would have been a bleak kind of success in which people could not be nice to their relatives. But most people are not like Wang Shou-yu. Indeed, given their immunity from criticism, Communist officials have consistently proved more corruptible and more nepotistic than democratic ones. Universal benevolence evaporates on the stove of human nature.

As Herbert Simon has put it, "In our century we have watched two great nations, the People's Republic of China and the Soviet Union, strive to create a 'new man,' only to end up by acknowledging that the 'old man'—perhaps we should say the 'old person'—self-interested and concerned with his or her economic welfare, or the welfare of the family, clan, ethnic group, or province, was still alive and well."

Fortunately, there proved to be, in Lionel Trilling's words, "a residue of human quality beyond cultural control." Otherwise, Russians would now be irredeemably corrupted people, which they plainly are not. Karl Marx designed a social system that would only have worked if we were angels; it failed because we were beasts. Human nature had not been changed at all. "I would rather hope [that man has some innate nature] than be stuck with a human tabula rasa on which any tyrants or do-gooders can write their (always benign) messages at will. And I think man has such a nature, that it is intensely social, and that it gives the lie to all sanctimonious manipulators from Mill through Stalin," said Robin Fox.

Who Stole the Community?

If the refashioning of society by competitive struggle led to the gas chambers, and the refashioning of society by cultural dogma led to the horrors of Mao's Cultural Revolution, then would it not be safer to abandon all ideas of importing science into politics altogether? Perhaps so. Certainly, I am not going to fall into the trap of pretending that our dim and misty understanding of the human social instinct can be instantly translated into a political philosophy. For a start, it teaches us that Utopia is impossible, because society is an uneasy compromise between individuals with conflicting ambitions, rather than something designed directly by natural selection itself.

None the less, the new "gene-tilitarian" understanding of human instincts that this book has explored leads to a few simple precepts for avoiding mistakes. Human beings have some instincts that foster the greater good and others that foster self-interested and anti-social behaviour. We must design a society that encourages the former and discourages the latter.

Consider, for example, a glaring paradox of free enterprise. If we declare that Smith, Malthus, Ricardo, Friedrich Hayek and Milton Friedman are right, and that man is basically motivated by self-interest, do we not by that very declaration encourage people to be more selfish? By recognizing the inevitability of greed and self-interest, we seem to approve it.

The essayist William Hazlitt certainly believed so, fulminating in his "Reply to Malthus" that:

> It is neither generous nor just to come in the aid of the narrow prejudices and hard-heartedness of mankind, with metaphysical distinctions and the cobwebs of philosophy. The balance inclines too much on that side already, without the addition of false weights.

In other words, the reason we must not say that people are nasty is that it is true. More than 150 years later, Robert Frank discovered that economics students, after being taught that people were essentially self-interested, grew more so themselves: they defected in prisoner's dilemma games more than other students. The real Ivan Boesky and the fictitious Gordon Gecko (in the film *Wall Street*) both notoriously eulogized greed. "Greed is all right, by the way," said Boesky in his commencement address at the University of California at Berkeley, in May 1986. "I want you to know that. I think greed is healthy. You can be greedy and still feel good about yourself." Spontaneous applause broke out.

It has become almost axiomatic that injunctions such as this are responsible for the breakdown of community spirit of recent years. Taught in the 1980s, against our better natures, to be selfish and greedy we have dropped our civic responsibilities and caused our societies to descend into amorality. This is the standard, soft-left explanation for rising crime and insecurity.

So the first thing we should do to create a good society is to conceal the truth about humankind's propensity for self-interest, the better to delude our fellows into thinking that they are noble savages inside. It is a distasteful idea for those of us who think the truth is more interesting than lies, however white. But the distaste need not worry us for long, because the white-lying is already happening. As we have repeatedly encountered in this book, propagandists always exaggerate the niceness of people, partly to flatter them and partly because the message is more palatable. People wish to believe in noble savages. As Robert Wright has argued:

> The new [selfish gene] paradigm strips self-absorption of its noble raiment. Selfishness, remember, seldom presents itself to us in naked form. Belonging as we do to a species (*the* species) whose members justify their actions morally, we are designed to think of ourselves as good and our behaviour as defensible, even when these propositions are objectively dubious.

Only those politicians who enjoy saying unpopular things will rock this particular boat. Said Margaret Thatcher, notoriously and scandalously: "There's no such thing as society. There are individual men and women, and there are families."

Of course, Thatcher had a serious point. At the core of her philosophy was the idea that if you fail to recognize the basic opportunism of human beings, then you fail to notice how government is composed of self-interested individuals rather than saints who only work for the greater good. Government is then just a tool for interest groups and budget-max-imizing bureaucrats to bid up each other's power and reward at the expense of the rest of us. It is not a neutral, motiveless machine for deliv-ering social benefits. She was against government's inherent corruption, rather than its ideals.

And yet Thatcher and her allies were articulating what is, in some ways, the most Rousseauian argument—that government does not impose virtue on inherently evil people, but corrupts the original virtue of the market place. Her mentor, Friedrich Hayek, appealed to a golden age when the noble savage was free of all regulation: without regulation from the state there would not be chaos but prosperity.

Time magazine, profiling Newt Gingrich as its man of the year in December 1995, made the point succinctly:

> Here's the way the world used to work: Liberals believed human beings, if not perfectible, were at least subject to improvement. . . . Conservatives believed human beings were fundamentally flawed. . . . Here's the way the world works today: conservatives believe . . . human beings aren't evil; the government is. Liberals, on the other hand, believe conservatives are dan-gerous romantics. . . . They are ready to believe some souls are inherently evil and beyond redemption.

If my argument in this book is right, then the conservatives are not such dangerous romantics, because the human mind contains numerous instincts for building social cooperation and seeking a reputation for niceness. We are not so nasty that we need to be tamed by intrusive gov-ernment, nor so nice that too much government does not bring out the worst in us, both as its employees and as its clients.

So let us examine the individualists' case: that government is the prob-lem, not the solution. The collapse of community spirit in the last few decades, and the erosion of civic virtue, is caused in this analysis not by the spread and encouragement of greed but by the dead hand of Leviathan. The state makes no bargain with the citizen to take joint responsibility for civic order, engenders in him no obligation, duty or pride, and imposes obedience instead. Little wonder that, treated like a naughty child, he behaves like one.

As Putnam's Italian example shows, where authority replaces reciproc-ity, the sense of community fades. In Britain, the welfare state and the mixed-economy "corpocracy" replaced thousands of effective commu-nity institutions—friendly societies, mutuals, hospital trusts and more, all based on reciprocity and gradually nurtured virtuous circles of trust—

with giant, centralized Leviathans like the National Health Service, nationalized industries and government quangos, all based on condescension. Because more money was made available through higher taxes, something was gained at first. But soon the destruction wrought to Britain's sense of community was palpable. Because of its mandatory nature the welfare state encouraged in its donors a reluctance and resentment, and in its clients not gratitude but apathy, anger or an entrepreneurial drive to exploit the system. Heavy government makes people more selfish, not less.

I hold to no foggy nostalgia that the past was any better. Most of the past was a time of authority, too—the hierarchical authority of a feudal, aristocratic or industrial system. (It was also, of course, a time of less material prosperity, but that is down to inferior technology, not inferior government.) The medieval vassal and the factory worker had no freedom to build trust and reciprocity between equals either. I am not contrasting the present with the past. But I do believe that there have been glimpses of a better way, of a society built upon voluntary exchange of goods, information, fortune and power between free individuals in small enough communities for trust to be built. I believe such a society could be more equitable, as well as more prosperous, than one built upon bureaucratic statism.

I live close to one of the great old cities of Britain, Newcastle upon Tyne. In two centuries it has been transformed from a hive of enterprise and local pride, based on locally generated and controlled capital and local mutual institutions of community, into the satrapy of an all-powerful state, its industries controlled from London or abroad (thanks to the collectivization of people's savings through tax relief for pension funds), and its government an impersonal series of agencies staffed by rotating officials from elsewhere whose main job is to secure grants from London. Such local democracy as remains is itself based entirely on power, not trust. In two centuries the great traditions of trust, mutuality and reciprocity on which such cities were based have been all but destroyed—by governments of both stripes. They took centuries to build. The Literary and Philosophical Society of Newcastle, in whose magnificent library I researched some of this book, is but a reminder of the days when the great inventors and thinkers of the region, almost all of them self-made men, were its ambitious luminaries. The city is now notorious for shattered, impersonal neighbourhoods where violence and robbery are so commonplace that enterprise is impossible. Materially, everybody in the city is better off than a century ago, but that is the result of new technology, not government. Socially, the deterioration is marked. Hobbes lives, and I blame too much government, not too little.

If we are to recover social harmony and virtue, if we are to build back into society the virtues that made it work for us, it is vital that we reduce the power and scope of the state. That does not mean a vicious war of all against all. It means devolution: devolution of power over people's lives to parishes, computer networks, clubs, teams, self-help groups, small businesses—everything small and local. It means a massive disassembling of the public bureaucracy. Let national and international governments wither into their minimal function of national defence and redistribution of wealth (directly—without an intervening and greedy bureaucracy). Let Kropotkin's vision of a world of free individuals return. Let everybody rise and fall by their reputation. I am not so naïve as to think this can happen overnight, or that some form of government is not necessary. But I do question the necessity of a government that dictates the minutest details of life and squats like a giant flea upon the back of the nation.

For St Augustine the source of social order lay in the teachings of Christ. For Hobbes it lay in the sovereign. For Rousseau it lay in solitude. For Lenin it lay in the party. They were all wrong. The roots of social order are in our heads, where we possess the instinctive capacities for creating not a perfectly harmonious and virtuous society, but a better one than we have at present. We must build our institutions in such a way that they draw out those instincts. Pre-eminently this means the encouragement of exchange between equals. Just as trade between countries is the best recipe for friendship between them, so exchange between enfranchised and empowered individuals is the best recipe for cooperation. We must encourage social and material exchange between equals for that is the raw material of trust, and trust is the foundation of virtue.